A Casebook of
Family Interventions
for Psychosis

A Casebook of
Family Interventions
for Psychosis

Edited by

Fiona Lobban and Christine Barrowclough

A John Wiley & Sons, Ltd, Publication

This edition first published 2009
© 2009 John Wiley & Sons Ltd.

Wiley-Blackwell is an imprint of John Wiley & Sons, formed by the merger of Wiley's global Scientific, Technical, and Medical business with Blackwell Publishing.

Registered Office
John Wiley & Sons Ltd, The Atrium, Southern Gate, Chichester, West Sussex, PO19 8SQ, UK

Editorial Offices
The Atrium, Southern Gate, Chichester, West Sussex, PO19 8SQ, UK
9600 Garsington Road, Oxford, OX4 2DQ, UK
350 Main Street, Malden, MA 02148-5020, USA

For details of our global editorial offices, for customer services, and for information about how to apply for permission to reuse the copyright material in this book please see our website at www.wiley.com/wiley-blackwell.

Library of Congress Cataloging-in-Publication Data

A casebook of family interventions for psychosis / edited by Fiona Lobban and
Christine Barrowclough.
    p. ; cm.
  Includes bibliographical references and index.
  ISBN 978-0-470-02707-3 – ISBN 978-0-470-02708-0
  1. Psychoses.   2. Psychoses–Patients–Family relationships.   3. Family psychotherapy.
I. Lobban, Fiona.   II. Barrowclough, Christine.
  [DNLM: 1. Psychotic Disorders–therapy.   2. Family Therapy–methods.
WM 200 C3373 2009]
  RC512.C368   2009
  616.89′156–dc22   2008052788

A catalogue record for this book is available from the British Library.

Set in 10.5/13pt Minion by Aptara Inc., New Delhi, India
Printed in the United Kingdom by TJ International Ltd, Padstow, Cornwall

1   2009

Contents

About the Editors

Dr Fiona Lobban (BA Hons (Oxon), D. Clin. Psy., PhD)
Fiona is a Senior Lecturer in Clinical Psychology at the Spectrum Centre for Mental Health Research at Lancaster University in the North West of England. She also works as a Consultant Clinical Psychologist supporting family work in the Early Intervention Service for Psychosis in Lancashirecare NHS Trust. Fiona is an active researcher in the areas of psychosis, bipolar disorder and family work. She has published 17 peer reviewed papers and two book chapters in these areas.

Professor Christine Barrowclough (BA, MSc Clin. Psy., PhD)
Christine is Professor of Clinical Psychology in the School of Psychological Sciences, University of Manchester, UK. She contributed to one of the first family intervention studies in the 1980s and is co-author of a book (Barrowclough & Tarrier) detailing cognitive behavioural family intervention for people with psychosis. Christine has been actively engaged in research around families and psychosis for over 20 years and has published widely in this area.

Contributors

Professor Jean Addington (PhD)
Director PRIME Clinic, Centre for Addiction and Mental Health, Department of Psychiatry, University of Toronto, Toronto, Canada.

Sabrina Baker
First Episode Psychosis Programme, Centre for Addiction and Mental Health, Toronto, Canada.

Professor Christine Barrowclough
Division of Clinical Psychology, School of Psychological Sciences, University of Manchester, Manchester, UK.

Claudia Benzies
Cool Recovery Ltd, The Cool House, Torquay, UK.

Dr Samantha E. Bowe
Clinical Psychologist, Greater Manchester West Mental Health NHS Foundation Trust, Greater Manchester, UK.

Frank Burbach
Consultant Clinical Psychologist, Somerset Partnership NHS and Social Care Trust, Somerset, UK.

Gwen Butcher
Cool Recovery Ltd, The Cool House, Torquay, UK.

April Collins
Deputy Administrative Director, Schizophrenia Programme, Centre for Addiction and Mental Health, Toronto, Canada.

Kingsley Crisp
Outpatient Case Manager/Family Worker, ORYGEN Youth Health, Melbourne, Australia.

Dr Gráinne Fadden
Director of the Meriden West Midlands Family Programme, Birmingham and Solihull Mental Health NHS Trust, Birmingham, UK.

Associate Professor John Gleeson
Department of Psychology, University of Melbourne and North Western Mental Health, Melbourne, Australia.

David Glentworth
Lead Practitioner for Psychosocial Interventions, Greater Manchester West Mental Health Foundation NHS Trust, Greater Manchester, UK.

Martin Gregory
Father

René Keet
GGZ Noord Holland Noord, Wijkteam Centrum, Alkmaar, The Netherlands.

Elizabeth Kuipers
Professor of Clinical Psychology, Chartered Clinical Psychologist, King's College London, Institute of Psychiatry, London, UK.

Tom Kuipers
Psychiatrist, Medical Director of GGz Nijmegen, Mental Health Centre, Nijmegen, The Netherlands.

Virginia Lafond
Schizophrenia Programme, Royal Ottawa Mental Health Centre, Ottawa, Canada.

Don Linszen
Professor of Psychiatry, Academic Medical Centre, University of Amsterdam, Amsterdam, The Netherlands.

Tom Linton
Cool Recovery Ltd, The Cool House, Torquay, UK.

Dr Fiona Lobban
Senior Lecturer in Clinical Psychology, Spectrum Centre for Mental Health Research, University of Lancaster, Lancashire, UK; Consultant Clinical Psychologist, Early Intervention Service, Lancashire Care NHS Trust, Lancashire, UK.

Dr Ian Lowens
Consultant Clinical Psychologist, Greater Manchester West Mental Health NHS Foundation Trust, Greater Manchester, UK.

Mr Chris Mansell
The Meriden West Midlands Family Programme, Birmingham and Solihull Mental Health Trust, Birmingham, UK.

Amanda McCleery
Department of Psychology, Kent State University, Kent, OH, USA.

Dr Julianna Onwumere
Research Clinical Psychologist, Institute of Psychiatry, London, UK.

Michelle O'Shea
Clinical Psychologist, University of Birmingham and Sandwell Mental Health and Social Care Trust, Birmingham, UK.

Maarten Smeerdijk
Department of Psychiatry, Academic Medical Centre, Amsterdam, The Netherlands.

Dr Ben Smith
Clinical Psychology, University College London and North East London Mental Health Trust, London, UK.

Dr Jo Smith
Consultant Clinical Psychologist and Worcestershire Early Intervention Lead, Worcestershire Mental Health Partnership NHS Trust, Worcestershire, UK.

Roger Stanbridge
Consultant Family Therapist, Somerset Partnership NHS and Social Care Trust, Somerset, UK.

Preface

The aim of this book is to provide a range of examples of clinical work currently being done with families in which an individual has experienced psychosis. Working with families can be very challenging and many clinicians do not feel confident to offer this kind of intervention. We hope that in reading detailed accounts of family work offered by other professionals, more people will feel inspired to work in this way. It is sometimes difficult for clinicians to envisage how the specific needs of families might be accommodated in family interventions. By sampling a range of different ways of working in varied contexts and with individuals presenting different challenges and needs, we hope to allow people to see how family work can be developed and adapted to suit virtually any circumstances. The case studies also document the current status of clinical work in this area and provide a baseline from which we can continue to develop more effective approaches to supporting families.

The book will be of interest to anyone who has experienced psychosis, is a close friend/family member of someone with psychosis, clinicians working with people with psychosis, or researchers trying to understand this area. The cases are described by clinicians from a range of professional backgrounds including psychiatry, psychology, nursing, social work and family therapy, and by relatives who have taken part in family interventions. They share in common the recognition of the importance of the interpersonal climate within the family in aiding recovery, and the needs of family members in trying to deal with these experiences.

There is evidence that family interventions for psychosis are effective at reducing relapse rates and improving outcome for people with psychosis (Pfammatter et al, 2006; Pharoah et al, 2006). Consequently, services are being set up internationally with a remit to offer these interventions. In

Britain the National Institute for Clinical Excellence Guidelines (2003) for services for people with psychosis states that family interventions should be offered to 100% of families of individuals with schizophrenia who have experienced a recent relapse, are considered to be at risk of relapsing, or who have persisting symptoms, and are living with or in close contact with their family. There are currently a number of manuals describing the theoretical background to working with families, which give guidelines on how to carry out specific interventions (e.g. Kuipers *et al.*, 2002; Falloon, 1993, Barrowclough & Tarrier, 1992). Some courses on psychosocial interventions for psychosis also offer a family intervention component (e.g. COPE, University of Manchester, UK). However, it is our experience that there are a lot of clinicians with skills in supporting individuals with psychosis, who are asked to offer a service to family members, who have read the available manuals, but who have little first hand experience of how these interventions can be applied. They generally lack confidence in their ability to offer family interventions. Consequently many families do not get the quality of service that they deserve (Fadden, 2006).

This book differs from the manuals listed above in that rather than describing what to do 'in theory', this gives detailed accounts of what actually happens 'in practice', including managing situations that may arise unexpectedly. Each chapter describes a clinical case in detail. Some details have been changed to protect the confidentiality of the individuals involved, but the details of the process have been maintained. The aim is to provide a 'real world' view of family interventions and cases and therefore to include aspects of the intervention that were not successful as well as those that were, with reflection on the reasons for this. The aim was not to describe how a perfect clinical intervention should look, but to show what happens in reality and what can be learnt from this process.

Each chapter begins with an overview and gives some context to the case including the theoretical background of the clinician, a description of the wider clinical service, and relevant details about the therapist(s). A detailed account is then given of the process from referral into the service, assessment, formulation, intervention, critical reflection and reformulation. Finally, the authors highlight the main conclusions from each case.

The first chapter is written by the father of a young man who experiences psychosis. This chapter highlights the difficulties that families face in coming to understand what has happened. It describes how the family became involved in a family intervention, and why it is so important that family orientated services are made more widely available. The next 3 chapters all focus on the importance of offering support to families as soon as they need it. This is generally at the very onset of the first episode and aims to minimise the impact of the psychosis on the family. Helping families to understand psychosis and to find effective ways to manage it can reduce the development of unhelpful beliefs and coping strategies and consequently reduce conflict within the family. Chapter 4 shows how family members can also become important agents in preventing relapse by learning to recognise early warning signs of further episodes.

Chapters 5 and 6 both describe interventions explicitly designed to address issues associated with psychosis and drug use. Many of the cases throughout the book refer to drug use as a possible factor in the development or maintenance of psychosis, but these two chapters describe motivational approaches to target this as the main focus of the intervention. Chapter 5 combines the techniques of MI and CBT to help a family faced with very challenging problems around the use of crack cocaine. Chapter 6 describes a group intervention for relatives of people experiencing psychosis who use cannabis. The group aims to facilitate family members to learn how their own behaviour can influence both the drug use of the person with psychosis and their own levels of distress.

Chapters 7 to 10 describe single family cases that highlight the variety of issues that clinicians are likely to face when offering a family intervention service. Chapter 7 describes how cognitive behavioural interventions can be used to modify the key attributions thought to underlie common problems in day to day family interaction. Grief is also a common experience for family members when they recognise the loss that can be associated with the impact of psychosis. Chapter 8 highlights the importance of working with family members to acknowledge and validate this loss which can often go unrecognised. In chapter 9, Jo Smith and colleagues make an excellent case for the importance of including siblings in our work with families. Siblings are often given a very low profile in this area of work (and interestingly do not appear in many of the cases described in this book). Many service users will have younger siblings but often clinicians working in adult mental health do not feel they have the skills or confidence to work with this age group. This chapter highlights why it is so important to include siblings and describes ways in which this can be done. Given the evidence to suggest that people from ethnic minority groups are more likely to experience psychosis (see chapter 10), it is important that clinicians develop confidence in working with families from ethnic and cultural backgrounds that may be different to their own. Chapter 10 describes an intervention in the UK with a black and minority ethnic family and shows how the process of engagement, psycho education, and communication can all be adapted to take account of ethnic and cultural differences.

As well as demonstrating the variation in the kinds of challenges arising within the families referred to family intervention services, the book chapters illustrate the variation in the context in which the interventions are offered. Chapter 11 describes how services can harness the support relatives offer to each other using multiple family groups which focus on providing important information, but also benefit from the many advantages of group interventions including normalisation, social support and peer group learning. Chapter 12 describes the advantages and challenges of offering family interventions when someone is currently an inpatient. This chapter highlights many of the organisational barriers that can prevent family interventions being offered. However, the case example describes how these can be managed and worked around.

Organisational issues are addressed more directly and in more detail in the penultimate section of the book in which 2 chapters describe the experience of setting up family interventions services in the National Health Service of the UK. The chapters are inspirational in their demonstration of the perseverance required and the gains that can be made, and provide excellent guidance for individuals who are considering embarking on this journey.

The final chapter allows us to give the last word back to the relatives. This chapter describes how the recent lack of effective support for families has led to a strong motivation for relatives to help themselves and each other. In the face of being unsupported and often excluded by services, relatives in the UK formed an independent charity which offers a range of services to relatives. The chapter describes how some of these relatives have experienced their own journeys of recovery.

We feel privileged to have had the opportunity of sharing the experiences of so many expert clinicians and relatives and service users from across the world. We have very much enjoyed reading the chapters and we are confident that you will find them as informative and inspiring as we have. We also hope that the book will stimulate debate about the nature of family interventions for psychosis. If reading the book also leads to an increase in interventions offered to support families of people with psychosis, then this will be a very welcome bonus.

Acknowledgements

We would like to acknowledge all of the service users and relatives who took part in the interventions described in this book. Thank you.

References

Barrowclough, C. and Tarrier, N. (1992) *Families of schizophrenic patients: cognitive behavioural intervention.* Chapman & Hall, London.

Fadden, G. (2006) Training and disseminating family interventions for schizophrenia: developing family intervention skills with multi-disciplinary groups. *Journal of Family Therapy*, **28**, 23–38.

Falloon, I. (1993) *Managing Stress in Families: Cognitive and Behavioural Strategies for Enhancing Coping Skills (strategies for mental health).* Routledge.

Kuipers, E., Leff, J. and Lam, D. (2002) *Family Work for schizophrenia – a practical guide.* 2nd edn. Gaskell, London.

NICE guidelines for Schizophrenia (2003) National Institute for Clinical Excellence.

Pfammatter, M., Junghan, U. M. and Drenner, H. D. (2006) Efficacy of Psychological Therapy in Schizophrenia: conclusions from meta-analyses. Schizophrenia Bulletin, 32, S64–S80.

Pharoah, F., Mari, J., Rathbone, J. and Wong, W. (2006) Family intervention for schizophrenia. *Cochrane Database of Systematic Reviews*, Issue 4

I

Introduction

1

Why Are Family Interventions Important? A Family Member Perspective

Martin Gregory

Introduction

I have written this chapter as the father of a son who has suffered from schizophrenia. Our family unit benefited very considerably from participating in behavioural family therapy (BFT), and I will describe our experiences since our son first developed difficulties. After painting the picture of the family background, I will describe our family's story under the following headings:

- The roller coaster that comes about from mental health problems.
- Getting started on family therapy.
- The process and its structure.
- How the family benefited.
- Family meetings.
- How family therapy has helped with our son's social rehabilitation.
- The longer term outcomes of the family intervention.

The chapter includes a section written by my wife, who talks about how she felt during the family therapy sessions and the pressures it put on her emotions.

There is a section on the perspectives of our son, and the thoughts of the two key therapists involved are also given.

The chapter concludes with some final messages and my reflections on the whole experience.

A Casebook of Family Interventions for Psychosis   Edited by Fiona Lobban and Christine Barrowclough
© 2009 John Wiley & Sons, Ltd

The Background to the Family

This story and its messages relate to a family from England and to the developments within the family during the 1990s. I worked in a managerial capacity within the corporate world of industry and my wife worked in a sales development and logistics capacity within a Swiss owned engineering business. In the early 1990s, our daughter was proceeding through secondary and further education whilst our son (who was 5 years younger) was at secondary school.

Simon was a nice boy. He was well presented and well balanced and seemed to be taking life and education in his stride. Although never strong academically, he coped well enough and, like many boys, seemed to have a fairly laid-back approach. It was in sport that he really excelled and represented his school at rugby, cricket and badminton (the county too in this sport). Outside of school he soon became a very competent squash player and played for both club and county. However, it was on the hockey field that he really shone and from an early age his blond hair and skilful play ensured that he stood out when playing for school and county. He played for the County U14 team when only 12 and went on to get to the final stage of an England trial. It was a significant disappointment to all in the family when he failed to gain selection for the County U16 squad, but by this time he was beginning to get established in senior club hockey.

In addition to all this he was in the choir of a prominent local church, and with other typical boy's activities such as cubs and scouts, he had a busy and active life. With his laid-back and cheerful approach, it was always difficult to gauge what his potential in life really was, or if he was capable of achieving more in any of these activities or in education.

His life seemed to be evolving quite straightforwardly, and with his 6 GCSEs he went off at 16 to a local college to do a BTEC course with a view to going on to further education like his sister. Typically, he did just enough to be accepted on a degree course in Transport and Logistics, this being a course of his own choice, although his grades were such that he had only two colleges to choose from.

So in September 1993, Simon went off to Wales to start his degree course with us as his parents having no hint of any problems or difficulties in his life. Being at college as opposed to a university, no student accommodation was available and so he found a bedsit in 'downtown' Swansea and seemed to settle in quite quickly. On the hockey front, he quickly established a regular first team place with the local HC, one of the top two sides in Wales, and was selected for the Welsh Universities squad.

It was only in his second term that there was any hint of a problem and it was during this period that we discovered that he was a regular user of cannabis (subsequently it was established that he had started taking cannabis several years earlier). It transpired that he was not attending college courses and spent much of his time shut in his own room. Then the phone calls home started late at night and during the night with the regular use of expletives (not previously a feature of his dialogue) and with him shouting and yelling accusations at both of us and indeed all and sundry who had any involvement in his life. Appointments were made for him to either go to a doctor or for a doctor to go to him, but neither came to fruition. The extent of the problem became clearer when eventually I was able get access to the bedsit and was told by Simon that he had just seen on TV that he was to become the next King of England.

It proved extremely difficult for us to ascertain what to do next because while it was possible to get very general information from libraries and the family GP (general practitioner), nobody actually offered advice on what to do. This was brought to a head when the landlord of the bedsit wanted Simon evicted due to a potential threat of violence to others living in the house.

We did not know where to go for real help: people such as our GP showed sympathy but were unable to offer practical advice on what actions we should take. Eventually I spoke to my MD at work, who had some experience of mental health services and he arranged for us to meet the Manager of a local Day Centre who explained to us that we were entitled to request a mental health assessment. With this new information we were able to access a social worker who was the first person to offer practical help. In due course, he facilitated an assessment with police in attendance involving a really helpful psychiatrist and a GP, as well as the social worker himself. Thanks to the great skills of the psychiatrist, Simon was admitted to the psychiatric unit in Swansea as a voluntary patient.

The Roller Coaster

In April 1994 Simon started his first period of hospitalisation in Wales, but immediately ceased to recognise us as his parents and blamed us for his problems. Communication with him became virtually impossible and although we travelled down each weekend to see him, he would never talk to us. Whilst we were given an indication that he may be suffering from schizophrenia, at no stage was this confirmed and neither was he informed of this. After a few months he was transferred to supported accommodation locally, and at this stage he became slightly more communicative and was showing signs of recovery. This progress continued and after a few more months he transferred back to his home locality and returned to live in the family home.

Everything seemed to be moving forward for him; he resumed college, he got a job relevant to his career ambitions, and his hockey went well – indeed he represented the county at senior level. But then the roller coaster started, which was probably attributable to his own denial of the illness. He stopped taking his medication and returned to cannabis for comfort.

The next few years were a nightmare for all of us with difficult periods living at home, attempts to live in his own accommodation which highlighted his own fears, and several periods of hospitalisation. He blamed us for his problems, would not communicate with us rationally, and yet it was still us he turned to when in difficulty. He could not live with us but he could not live without us.

During this period, support from the community health team was spasmodic and ineffective and the fact that Simon kept disappearing and was non-compliant contributed significantly to this. Eventually, yet another major crisis arose whilst he was living at home, but this time his behaviour led to him being sectioned, which was the first time that his problems could be addressed on a compulsory basis. The behavioural circumstances leading to this included Simon locking himself in his room and seldom coming out. When he did come out, he was threatening and aggressive, particularly to his mother. In addition, a neighbour complained that Simon was trespassing on their property and spending time in a shed they had in an adjacent field. The social worker (supported by the psychiatrist) considered that sectioning was the only way forward. A change in personnel also facilitated a different type of approach to his care and treatment, and also to the way in which we were treated and involved as his carers.

Getting Started on Family Therapy

The new community psychiatric nurse (CPN) had recently completed a BFT training course, following the model originally developed by Falloon,

Boyd and McGill (1984) and the social worker was also due to attend the same course. As a result, they suggested one day, when Simon was slightly improved, that perhaps BFT might be helpful to us as a family. They were keen to try their new intervention and considered that our family might benefit from BFT, particularly due to the communication problems we experienced. In their work with us, the approach they used was described in a detailed manual (Falloon *et al.*, 2004).

As his carers, we had received very little support and were still ignorant about the illness and its treatments, and so when we were offered help as a family, we saw this as a potential lifeline – what could we lose? Could this programme really help us to understand things better and would we have an opportunity to talk through some of the problems that we as his carers faced? Although we were by no means certain of the answers to these questions, it did seem that the model of family work that was offered to us (BFT) could not make things worse so we accepted the offer.

We were given an outline of what BFT consisted of and what the potential outcomes and benefits might be, but we really needed very little persuasion. The therapists felt that it would be a good idea for our family and that it was possible that BFT would give us some of the information and support that we were looking for. In particular, we were told that the communications aspects of BFT might help the day-to-day relationship within the family. It was explained that we would need to meet every 2–3 weeks or so for maybe an hour at a time, and that there would be some practical work to help improve our skills.

Simon's sister did not take part in the sessions. It was impractical for her as by now she was living about an hour away from home and worked even further away. Apart from that, she had become a little nervous and reluctant to get too involved as Simon had seen her new home as a 'bolt hole', and when he had turned up there she became a little frightened. She was also building a new long-term relationship and was wary of this being disrupted. In any event, she came to the family home infrequently.

Getting Simon to buy in was a different matter. He was still in hospital at the time of the offer although he was allowed home on leave one evening a week. He was ambivalent about getting involved in the programme himself but, very fortunately, did not put any barriers in the way for his Mum and me to get started. Although this was not ideal within the BFT model, the support team now engaged with our family had the foresight to agree to proceed on the basis that Simon might join in later.

So after a preparatory meeting talking about goal setting, we started the programme with sessions being held in the family home on the evening of Simon's home leave. We left the lounge door open so that we were not talking behind closed doors, and for the first session or two Simon showed no interest in our discussions. However, it was not long before he started to pop in for a few minutes and gradually he became involved in discussions. This soon led to the agreement that home leave night was BFT night and this, linked to a Chinese take away (always a favourite of his!), made the whole package quite acceptable – indeed it became an evening that he looked forward to.

The Process and Its Structure

As with much of Simon's care in recent years, we have been very fortunate with the calibre of staff in his support team. This includes the psychiatrists, social workers, CPN, the members of assertive outreach and the support team for the supported house in which he now lives. This certainly applied with the therapists delivering BFT who were his social worker (who has been involved for many years) and his CPN. We will always be grateful for the way they handled our BFT programme, which was done sympathetically but in a very supportive way to each of us. The same two people remained with the programme for most of the modules so providing continuity, but importantly, this enabled them to gain a detailed understanding of the make-up of the family and the problems faced by each family member. It also was important to us that they were members of Simon's support team so that they did not walk away from the case at the end of each BFT session.

As previously explained, our BFT programme started without Simon, so immediately on commencement we were able to talk about ourselves, our attitudes, and address the objectives of the programme and the goals for mother and father individually. This was done by separate one-to-one meetings, and then sharing the goals of each of us and discussing these openly. For both of us, it was key that we found our own time and space both individually and together, and maybe have a holiday that we could enjoy without undue worry and stress. This in particular was something that we were able to revisit throughout the programme and see just how far we were moving on in achieving this.

It was very soon after this that Simon joined in the sessions, albeit initially for very short periods. At the beginning of each meeting, he would agree how long a period he thought he would be comfortable to stay, be it 10 or 15 minutes, and as soon as that period was up he would leave. Much later he felt able to stay for longer periods extending to 30 and then 45 minutes.

Over many months we addressed each of the modules within the model including positive and negative communication, making requests, expressing feelings, active listening and sharing information. While clinicians would probably find it helpful to know how long we spent on each topic and over what time frame, as a family member I did not experience or think of the therapy in that way. Neither can I remember at this stage how long we spent on each topic.

We also spent some time learning more about the illness, positive and negative symptoms and most importantly the types of medication. This was the first occasion in Simon's illness that we had been given the opportunity to talk freely about these things and without feeling the pressure of a time factor (as applies in clinical appointments). If we did not have time to deal with a particular query, we always addressed it next time round.

The really practical outcomes that we talked and learned about were family meetings (which I will come back to later in the chapter) and problem solving. We did not realise when we did the problem-solving work just how often we would use this simple technique (or at least our version of it) in the future.

The session on early warning signs proved the most problematical due to Simon's vulnerability to so many of these signs. This particular session was very upsetting to him (and consequently to us) and we had to keep 'parking' it until eventually, when he was so much better, it was completed partly outside of the meetings, and indeed it then resulted in the agreement of an advance directive to give guidance to each of us on our actions should there be signs of a relapse. An advance directive or advance statement is a document which mental health service users can complete when they are well. It allows them to say how they would like to be cared for during times of mental health crisis, loss of capacity and/or admission to acute psychiatric care. It can cover medical care and treatment and domestic arrangements.

Most of the sessions took place in the lounge at the family home, but we were always mindful of who sat where and we tried to rotate the seating positions. This was particularly important in the early stages when it was not possible for Simon and his mother to sit opposite each other. This was linked with one of Simon's ideas that his mother could control him through her eyes.

There was a period during BFT when it was inappropriate for Simon to leave hospital and so there were two occasions when the sessions took place in a room in the hospital. This worked quite well and it was also good that ward staff could see that it was possible for BFT to be handled within an acute care environment.

How We Have Benefited

This is arguably the easiest section in this chapter for me to write primarily because the benefits are there for us all to see and secondly because I talk very frequently about these benefits in a variety of forums as well as privately. In essence, BFT has helped all family members to get their life back and to cope with a variety of different situations and problems, and I list below some of the ways it has achieved this although it should be made clear that these are not listed in any significant order:

- It has enabled my wife and me to become fully involved in the care and recovery programme because we are better equipped to understand the part we can play and how to become involved.
- BFT has enabled us all to gain a greater understanding of mental illness and its treatments and increased our knowledge very significantly.
- The communications modules such as talking positively and negatively have improved our skills in being able to handle difficult situations, address issues and generally improve relationships within the family.
- It is the treatment that best uses the unique knowledge and experiences of each of us in the family so that we have all felt able to contribute to the process as equal members of the team.
- The fact that our sessions have been held regularly (with a date fixed for the next session on each occasion) meant that we were able to meet with knowledgeable and supportive professionals on a frequent basis. We all welcomed the opportunity for regular dialogue with, in our case, those who were key members of the support team.
- The fact that one or two sessions were conducted in an acute care setting helped considerably because it meant that when we visited him in hospital, the awkward and uncomfortable silences were replaced by

a purposeful and sometimes productive BFT session which gave a lot more meaning to a hospital visit.

- Hopefully, it can be seen that from all these benefits we were able to reduce stress levels significantly and develop coping mechanisms. When a problem loomed, we were able to say to ourselves, 'That's something we can discuss at our next BFT session.'
- In the early stages of the family intervention, the BFT sessions were the only occasions when Simon communicated with us so they became very valuable to us both emotionally and practically.

Maintaining Progress: The Family Meeting

As part of our help from the therapists, we discussed whether or not a regular family meeting would be helpful to us all. This would be a meeting that we could run as a family without either of the therapists being present. In the end, we concluded that it was worth a try and so on alternate Sundays (Simon came to the parental home most Sundays when well enough) we had a short family meeting in the kitchen at home. We found that in the early stages of these meetings the real benefit was sitting around a table and talking to each other albeit in a semi-structured way and for only 4–5 minutes at first, later increasing to 10–15 minutes and this was a major breakthrough.

The agenda concentrated on fairly practical things like any travel arrangements needed during the week ahead, homework for the next BFT session, possible sporting activities for Simon and other domestic or leisure matters – we tended to avoid topics that might have been difficult at least in the early stages. One of us would take a few notes whilst another would chair the meeting – Simon performed both these tasks at various times. Gradually, we settled into a routine for these meetings and found them really helpful in opening up a dialogue that might not otherwise have been possible.

By having family meetings before Sunday lunch, we were able to deal with many issues in the meeting leaving the lunch itself as 'protected' time. This avoided difficult dialogues over the lunch table so resulting in a much pleasanter family occasion. As our relationships began to improve, we found less need to have the meetings on such a regular basis and just brought them into play as and when a specific need arose, but the mechanism of the family meeting was always there for us to access when needed.

In more recent times, we have used the family meeting approach to facilitate discussions regarding activities relevant to Simon's social rehabilitation.

The Contribution of Family Therapy
to Social Rehabilitation

I hope I have painted a picture which has reflected the very difficult times we all had in Simon's early years of experiencing mental health problems. At the time of writing, it is just so great to be able to say how well Simon is now doing and to reflect on the progress he has made that we would never have dreamed was possible several years ago.

We still meet regularly, albeit at Simon's request only around every 3 months, for a session called BFT (one therapist has remained throughout and the other is Simon's current key worker), but in truth these are more care programme reviews or, to be more specific, they are meetings at which we discuss Simon's social rehabilitation. However, we have continued to use the description BFT because it is a term that we are all comfortable with and we all use the meeting framework we have developed and the skills we have learned to move Simon's activities forward.

I really believe that this framework helps significantly in the planning and implementation of the social rehabilitation agenda for a whole raft of reasons which include the following:

- Each of us has been able to input his/her own perspectives into actions.
- We all feel involved in the care and recovery programme.
- Individual actions are discussed and agreed.
- We all share successes.
- Through these meetings we have been able to discuss freely and agree (sometimes using the problem-solving model) actions and outcomes such as
  - assessing suitable and realistic activities;
  - planning a short break/holiday;
  - addressing day-to-day issues;
  - reviewing achievements and agreeing targets.

As an example, the problem-solving model was very helpful when we planned a short break and we addressed this in a family meeting type setting.

Simon had not had a holiday for around 6 years, the last being when he had a major relapse in Corfu and spent several months in hospital there. As a result, there were lots of considerations in reaching our decision, not least the importance of being in a location that Simon would feel comfortable in. So we talked through the pros and cons of each of these destinations covering travel arrangements, where we would stay and the potential activities at each. Then Simon scored each out of 5, this being a simple technique that had been used before and in the end he chose Skegness probably because he knew it from when he was a child and he had a feeling that he would feel secure there. So the three of us duly went to Skegness and had a really good time there which proved to be a really big stepping stone in Simon's rehabilitation.

We have used this format on several occasions including reviewing potential leisure type activities and each time it has worked really well.

The Longer Term Outcomes of the Family Intervention

As I write this, Simon's progress has been such that we all have a comfortable and relatively stress-free life totally compatible with the objectives we set when we started BFT many years ago.

He still lives in excellent supported accommodation but the time is fast approaching when he will move into his own flat or house with outreach type support. He has a part-time job in a local garage which he thoroughly enjoys and which has been key to him feeling able to lead a normal life again. The people he works with are very helpful to him and he does not appear to encounter any stresses in this work environment. He plays hockey every Saturday in the winter months and is keen to progress his golf maybe by joining a local club. He has recently bought himself a car and this too has given him a big boost.

All this progress is attributable to several things not least of which are the efforts Simon has made himself to move his life forward. He has continued to receive great support and help from psychiatrists, assertive outreach staff and the visiting support team in his accommodation. However, there is no doubt in my mind that the BFT programme has also played a significant part in his treatment and development, particularly in the development of his interpersonal skills and levels of activity. BFT in this case has been a really good example of how psychological treatments can interface with medications and an efficient care programme to give a holistic approach to his treatment with a very satisfactory outcome to date.

Within the family communication, discussion on any topic is now so much easier and more effective than hitherto, and whilst much of this is clearly to do with Simon's improvement, there is no doubt that the skills we all learned and often use have also enabled this to happen. We continue to use the problem-solving method, and recently used it to very good effect in helping Simon to deal with his anxiety about visiting the dentist to begin to have his teeth looked after.

Simon's relationship with his sister has improved quite substantially and they are probably as close now as they ever have been. He occasionally visits her on his own, which has never really happened before, and he is absolutely devoted to her two little boys, his nephews. He is really proud of the family unit and gives it very high priority at all times.

For my own part, since retiring, I have become an active and involved carer with a part-time role in promoting and facilitating carer involvement and a full portfolio of speaking and training engagements on a variety of mental health topics, and I feel that I contribute more to society than ever before. This would certainly never have happened without BFT.

Simon's improvement in recent times has helped us to forget the many difficult times of the past, but we have to remember that our aspirations for him in life have changed dramatically since he was a schoolboy of potential. Also the knowledge of mental health that we have developed through BFT means that we have to remind ourselves from time to time that relapse is not impossible. However, it is now so easy to say that we are so pleased for him that he is able to get a quality of life that we never thought possible a few years ago. We are also proud of him in what he has achieved and coped with.

My Feelings about BFT – As Written by Mum

When BFT was first suggested to me, I was both nervous and happy to join the programme, mainly because I was desperate for someone to talk to who had professional knowledge of my son's illness. Even so, I worried about being in a situation of discussing mental illness and treatments whilst my son was present as I did not want him to be upset or annoyed with us for discussing him or an illness which he did not believe he had.

As the time approached for our BFT programme to start, my anxiety increased, worrying about his reactions; however, it became necessary for him to be sectioned, and we were told that we would be able to start without him and as soon as he was well enough he would be able to join us.

So we started without him, covering the modules concerning the different medications and treatments available. I found these discussions very helpful and interesting and could take part quite calmly, but often, unaccountably, I would find it very difficult to keep my emotions under control. I would squeeze my fingernails into my palms to stop myself from crying. I wanted to appear 'grown-up' and civilised about our discussions, but the effect of having lived with Simon and his illness for years, coping with him and his behaviour, making allowances for him and being careful not to let him see me looking at him, bubbled to the surface in the company of our caring and supportive team. I had firmly avoided crying, as I thought that it was a luxury I could not afford; I felt that if I once started I would never be able to stop. As a result, I had chosen not to discuss my son's illness outside the family and indeed my work colleagues were not aware of the way in which my husband and I were living. We slept in turns at night, as this was always Simon's worst time. He could not sleep and wandered the landing talking and discussing scenarios we would have been better not to have heard. Talking all this through during our BFT sessions was difficult, but our team handled it in a very patient way and guided us back to practical issues giving us coping strategies. I felt that with knowledge came acceptance, and with acceptance came the power to cope.

Simon first agreed to join us in our meetings, only because he liked the idea of an evening out of the hospital, and also the promise of a Chinese take away. He would stay in the meeting for a very short period of time, just long enough to qualify for the 'take away', and during this time, it was important that he and I were positioned so that he did not have to look at me. (Simon thought that my eyes had a power over him, and this made him uncomfortable.) We believe that he did listen to our discussions, but he rarely joined in, and when he had enough he would get up and leave the room. However, little by little he began to join in, and when he did, what he had to say was always a revelation to us all. We had our setbacks of course, but we continued with the meetings, as they were tailored to suit Simon's progress and ours. It has been a very long journey, fraught with emotion at times, but when the day came when we realised that he had regained cognitive thought, and he began to be able to speak with clarity and intelligence, which was such a joy to all of us.

I looked forward to our BFT meetings and knew that I had a very supporting team with whom I could discuss each new problem and with their help find a way of handling it. Indeed my husband and I feel very strongly that we would not have the life we have if it were not for our BFT team.

Simon's Perspectives

When I talked to Simon about BFT and asked him to reflect on what he thought about BFT, it was perhaps not surprising that he only really wanted to recall the more recent meetings when we have spent a lot of time talking about his activities and generally moving his life forward.

He was reluctant to give his perspectives on whether he had found it helpful during the more difficult periods of his illness although he acknowledged that we (Mum and Dad) had found it helpful and he did not have any problem with that. At no stage did he have any negative feelings about BFT but he chose not to recognise any benefits he had gained in terms of communications skills and other parts of the course.

These are some of the phrases he used:

- BFT was OK.
- You [Mum and Dad] seemed to like it and that was OK with me.
- I liked reviewing what I had been doing over the past weeks.
- BFT seemed to make things happen.
- The problem solving was good in looking at my sport and leisure activities.
- Helped me to arrange things for myself.
- The Chinese meal was good!

The Perspectives of the Therapists

The first two therapists that we had were Simon's social worker and community nurse and they remained with the programme as a pair for around 3 years, which was the really critical period. These are some of the phrases they used to describe our BFT programme:

- Simon was one of the most disabled patients either of us had encountered.

- We learned so much about Simon and the family from the BFT sessions which helped us considerably in assessing how we could best help each member of the family.
- For both of us, you were our first family and so we went through the journey together.
- We had to adapt the model and be very flexible in the way we delivered it in order to encourage Simon to join in.
- Although both Mum and Dad were receptive, Mum found it easier to engage because she really needed the support that this programme gave.
- Dad was more difficult because he thought it was theoretical, but once he realised the communications aspects were helpful to him at work he engaged much more easily – he liked the practical benefits.
- The training gave me the tools – the family taught me how to adapt the equipment.
- My initial perceptions of Simon were so wrong once he started to communicate with us.
- We were able to collaborate with Mum and Dad in helping Simon together.
- It was amazing how Simon would suddenly start to talk lucidly within the BFT sessions, whilst outside of these meetings he was reluctant to talk to parents or his care teams.

Final Messages

I hope that from this chapter it can be seen how much we as a family have benefited and continue to benefit from the family intervention that we were fortunate enough to undertake. As I go around the world of mental health, it has been a constant disappointment to me to discover how relatively few families have been offered BFT or similar type family intervention. I am very aware of all the obstacles that there are to implementation with families, but I do sometimes wonder whether the efforts to overcome these obstacles have been determined enough.

My hope is that readers who have got this far in reading my chapter are likely to be committed therapists and not just professionals who are looking to able to include the term 'Trained Family Therapist' on their CV.

Finally, please remember that family member carers are, in the main, lifetime project managers and want to help and be involved in the care of their loved one – BFT can help to achieve this.

Reflections for readers implementing family work:

- The need to be flexible when the service user does not wish to become involved at the outset – the therapists handled this.
- The issue of family workers also being case managers. Some clinicians feel that this is not appropriate, but it was really helpful in our situation and provided continuity.
- The importance of flexibility and negotiation throughout, for example agreeing how long Simon was able to stay in meetings.
- Simon as service user was able to chair family meetings and take notes when he was given the opportunity to do so.
- The importance of family meetings.

References

Falloon, I.R.H., Boyd, J.L. and McGill, C.W. (1984) *Family Care of Schizophrenia*, Guilford Press, New York.

Falloon, I.R.H., Fadden, G., Mueser, K. *et al.* (2004) *Family Work Manual*, Meriden Family Programme, Birmingham.

Resources

Aldridge, J. and Becker, S. (2003) *Children Caring for Parents with Mental Illness*, Policy Press, Bristol.

Alexander, K. (1991) *Understanding and Coping with Schizophrenia – 14 Principles for the Relatives*, Wilkinson Books, Melbourne.

Atkinson, J.M. (1985) *Schizophrenia : A Guide for Sufferers and Their Families*, Turnstone Press, Wellingborough.

Atkinson, J.M. (1986) *Schizophrenia at Home: A Guide to Helping the Family*, Croom Helm, Kent.

Fuller Torrey, E. (1983) *Surviving Schizophrenia: A Family Manual*, Harper & Row, New York.

Kuipers, E. and Bebbington, P. (1987) *Living with Mental Illness: A Book for Relatives and Friends*, Souvenir Press, London.

Mueser, K.T. and Gingerich, S. (2006) *The Complete Family Guide to Schizophrenia*, Guilford Press, New York.

Ramsay, R., Gerada, C., Mars, S. and Szmukler, G. (2001) *Mental Illness: A Handbook for Carers*, Jessica Kingsley, London.

Rethink (2003) *Caring and Coping: A Rethink Guide for People Caring for Someone with Severe Mental Illness*, Rethink, Surrey.

Wilkinson, G. and Kendrick, T. (1996) *A Carer's Guide to Schizophrenia*, Royal Society of Medicine Press, London.

Video

Living with Schizophrenia: The Carers' Story, Pavillion Press, Brighton.

Web sites

www.rethink.org – contains a useful document called *Reach out to help someone cope with severe mental illness – a guide for carers* (accessed 5 January 2009).

www.scbnetwork.org – Supporting Carers Better Network (accessed 5 January 2009).

www.makingspace.co.uk (accessed 5 January 2009).

www.world-schizophrenia.org (accessed 5 January 2009).

www.carers.org – Princess Royal Trust for Carers (accessed 5 January 2009).

www.grippers.org.uk – a web site created by carers of people with early psychosis in Gloucestershire (accessed 5 January 2009).

www.partnersincare.co.uk – Royal College of Psychiatrists web site on the Partners in Care Campaign (accessed 5 January 2009).

www.meridenfamilyprogramme.com – contains a range of information on family issues (accessed 5 January 2009).

II

First Episode Psychosis

2

Family Work in Early Psychosis

Gráinne Fadden and Jo Smith

Overview

The rationale for working with families in early psychosis is very clear. Because of the age of onset of psychosis, many young people are still living with or in close contact with their parents, grandparents and family of origin (Addington and Burnett, 2004). Many have young brothers or sisters who are affected by their sibling's difficulties (Fisher, Bordass and Steele, 2004). Others are already in relationships and are parents of young children. It is difficult therefore to see how appropriate mental healthcare can be provided in early intervention services without family work playing a key role, and this is recognised in guidelines and policy relating to early intervention services (Department of Health, 2001; IRIS Guidelines, 2000). The current case study will illustrate the issues that are common when working with young people with psychosis and their families.

Working with the family and others who are important in the young person's social network ensures that their difficulties are understood in a social context. It facilitates the establishment of effective collaborative working relationships between the individual, family and healthcare services. Offering help at this early stage supports the family's understanding, the way in which they relate to each other, and their adjustment to the major changes they face in their lives. It also helps to minimise the risk of problems developing for individuals and for the family as a whole.

In spite of this clear rationale, many early intervention services struggle to offer appropriate support and care to families. This is a result of the

A Casebook of Family Interventions for Psychosis   Edited by Fiona Lobban and Christine Barrowclough
© 2009 John Wiley & Sons, Ltd

interplay between reactions of the family and the skills, experiences and confidence of staff. These will be explained in the following section.

Context

Specific issues for families of those with early psychosis

The development of mental health difficulties in a young member of the family is clearly a traumatic event for all involved. The available literature on this area highlights how common family distress is (Martens and Addington, 2001), and even in early studies, it was clear that higher levels of distress are common and more profound in newer caregivers compared with those who have been caring over time (Gibbons *et al.*, 1984; Gopinath and Chaturvedi, 1992). This distress is evident whether or not the young person is living at home. The literature on expressed emotion (EE) in early psychosis is consistent with studies of more general measures of distress. High EE is reported as present in over 50% of families, and the evidence for its predictive value is equivocal, with the weight of evidence suggesting that high EE during the first 2 years is probably not predictive of relapse (Bachmann *et al.*, 2002; Heikkila *et al.*, 2002; Huguelet *et al.*, 1995; Patterson, Birchwood and Cochrane, 2000). High levels of emotion and distress therefore are common in families of those with early psychosis, and are not indicative of particular difficulties in the family.

In terms of what the distress is linked with, the EE literature referred to suggests that 'illness' factors such as symptom-type and severity, age of onset, diagnosis or length of illness are not associated with EE (Heikkila *et al.*, 2002). On the other hand, distress has been found to be associated with functional difficulties such as disorganisation, impaired interpersonal functioning, difficult behaviour and social withdrawal (Tennakoon *et al.*, 2000). Other studies have emphasised the family's perceptions of behaviour and their psychological appraisal of the impact of the mental health difficulties on them as being the most significant predictor of distress and poor psychological well-being (Addington *et al.*, 2003; Addington, McCleery and Addington, 2005b; Raune, Kuipers and Bebbington, 2004). For some families, the trauma and shock is so great that initially they are in denial (Slade, Holloway and Kuipers, 2004). Other themes that emerge from the literature include the family coping with grief and loss, adjustment to the major changes that have occurred in the family, and coping with issues of uncertainty related to understanding what the problem is and what the chances of recovery are (Gleeson *et al.*, 1999).

There can be many reasons why a family may be reluctant to engage with mental health services. Many parents believe their children are going through a phase and find it difficult to distinguish between pre-psychotic/psychotic and normal adolescent behaviour. Some are afraid of what they might hear and are concerned about the stigma associated with mental health difficulties. A key factor is their unfamiliarity with a complex healthcare system. It may be difficult to access secondary mental health services through primary care, and others may fall in the divide that often exists between Child and Adolescent Services and Adult Mental Health Services. It is not surprising therefore that families identify finding a way through the 'service maze' as one of their primary needs early on (White, 2002).

All of the well-established early intervention services such as those in Melbourne, Australia (EPPIC, 1997; Gleeson *et al.*, 1999); Calgary, Canada (Addington and Burnett, 2004) and Birmingham, United Kingdom (Fadden *et al.*, 2004) identify family work as a core component of what should be delivered in order to maximise family functioning and to minimise risks of long-term difficulties. However, evidence from developing early intervention services in the United Kingdom suggests that while staff offer a minimum level of support and advice to families, they often feel ill-equipped to offer more structured types of help and quote issues such as lack of materials and resources and lack of confidence in dealing with children (Slade, Holloway and Kuipers, 2004).

Theoretical influences on family work in early psychosis

While the literature on family work in early psychosis is not as extensive as it is in relation to longer term psychotic difficulties, there are sufficient studies indicating that psychoeducational-style family approaches are beneficial. One of the earliest much-quoted studies of psychoeducational family intervention, that of Goldstein *et al.* (1978) focused on early psychosis, and demonstrated that a brief family intervention consisting of stress management, problem solving, the provision of information and relapse prevention strategies had highly beneficial outcomes. While the quality of research studies in this area varies, those that use psychoeducational approaches demonstrate significantly better outcomes or changes from high to low EE (Rund *et al.*, 1995; Zhang *et al.*, 1994). Lehtinen (1993) using a systemic family therapy and crisis approach found that the intervention group had lower readmission rates after 1 year. Results from the Calgary Early Psychosis Programme have consistently shown positive effects for family members in terms of improvements in psychological well-being and reductions in levels of distress and negative aspects of caring (Addington *et al.*, 2002; Addington *et al.*, 2005a).

One study, that of Linszen *et al.* (1996) found that family work was no more effective than individual work. It should be noted, however, that relapse rates were very low in both groups in this study, and the control group received a very detailed package of care. The research that is emerging in relation to family work in early psychosis in particular, makes it clear that there is much variation among families, and that brief, targeted individualised interventions are most helpful (White, 2002). There is sufficient evidence to date therefore that family work is a central part of effective early intervention services, and recent reviews of psychological treatments in first-episode psychosis attest to this (Haddock and Lewis, 2005; Penn *et al.*, 2005).

Those who are interested in reading about what family work should consist of can read detailed accounts from services that have been established for some time (Addington and Burnett, 2004; Gleeson *et al.*, 1999). Gleeson *et al.* (1999) describe a stage model of working with families, with different types of help being offered at different phases of psychosis. Given the awareness of the wide variation in family reactions when faced with psychosis, however, caution should be exerted in relation to any models suggesting fixed stages. An individualised approach based on a detailed assessment of each family is likely to be most profitable.

Therapist attributes, training and service issues

What then are the issues relating to family work for staff working in the early intervention services? This workforce is likely to be drawn from existing services, and there is ample evidence about the difficulties in implementing family work in adult mental health services in general (Fadden, 1997; Fadden *et al.*, 2004). Staff are often uncomfortable about issues such as diagnostic uncertainty, or concerned about confidentiality conflicts. Dealing with acute psychosis can prove difficult for clinicians who have not worked for some time in acute settings, and for adult mental health staff, there is often a lack of confidence in dealing with young children or adolescents. For many, anxiety

Table 2.1 Overview of the Process of Family Work

Those new to this approach often enquire about the order in which the various components are introduced to the family. Because this is a behavioural approach, it is not possible to be rigid about the sequence in which the different skills are introduced to families. Behavioural approaches by nature are responsive to the particular needs of the individual or family and characterised by a thorough assessment which determines the content of the intervention. There are some general principles: assessment usually takes place before intervention begins; information about the relevant disorder is provided early on in meetings with the family; simple skills are introduced before complex skills; skills with a positive focus are taught before those where the focus is more difficult.

The general pattern of Behavioural Family Therapy is as follows:

1. Meeting with the family to discuss the benefits of the approach
2. Agreeing with the family that they are willing to try the approach
3. Assessment of individual family members
4. Assessment of family communications and problem solving
5. Formulation by the family worker of family resources, problems and goals; this is done in collaboration with the family
6. Meeting with a family to discuss/plan how to proceed and establishment of family meetings without the family worker
7. Sharing of information about the disorder and its impact
8. Communication skills training
   a. Active listening
   b. Expressing positive feelings
   c. Making positive requests
   d. Expressing unpleasant feelings
9. Problem solving
10. Booster sessions
11. Disengagement from family if appropriate

It is important to remember these are general guidelines, and there are times when the sequence will be different because of the needs of the particular family. For example, the family may be in the middle of a crisis when the first contact with them is made, and the family worker may have to introduce problem solving before the different assessments can take place. Another situation is where the family members are already proficient in a particular skill, for example making requests of each other. In this case, the family worker would not need to spend time on the 'Making Positive Requests' module.

The main points for the family worker to remember are that the approach is structured though not rigid in nature, is flexible and most of all is responsive to the needs of the family and the individual family members.

---

and discomfort in dealing with raw and intense emotions is common, as is a fear of 'opening up' something that they will not be able to manage.

Working with families in early psychosis brings with it the need for adequate training in a range of areas. Clinicians need a good grounding in one of the psychoeducational models of family work – the approach taken in the case study below is based on a Behavioural Family Therapy approach where a detailed training manual is available (Falloon *et al.*, 2004). A summary of the process of therapy within this model is provided in Table 2.1. There are areas that clinicians may be less familiar with where they may benefit from training, such as how to cope with grief, loss and fielding questions to which there are no answers. A number of texts are helpful in this area (Burns and Schulz, 2001; Lafond, 2002; Miller, 1996). Helping families to 'grieve' while holding positive hope for recovery can be challenging. Equally, specific training in dealing with the complexity of confidentiality issues may also be necessary.

Adult mental health staff may need to refresh their knowledge of 'normal' adolescence, while Child and Adolescent Mental Health Services staff may need to update their knowledge of psychosis. For all staff dealing with strong emotional reactions and conflicting or diverse needs, adequate supervision and support is crucial. If this is not in place, it is unlikely that positive working alliances will be established with families.

The following case study illustrates some of the issues that can arise when working with families. While all families differ, many of the issues that have been referred to from the literature such as a desire for information and understanding, the intense emotions experienced and their relationship with the health service will be apparent.

Case Example

Context and referral

The family was referred by a Community Mental Health Team to a service which specialised in family work. The reason for the referral was that it was felt there were very complex issues in the family, and in the words of the consultant psychiatrist, the parents were 'quite dysfunctional, colluding with their son in his delusional beliefs and failing to set any boundaries on his unreasonable behaviour'.

The client (Tom) is a 19-year-old man who had previously been admitted to a general adult ward following a suicide attempt. There were no specialist early intervention services in the area. While the family recognised that some of the staff on the ward were helpful and were trying to do their best, they were appalled by the physical conditions and surroundings on the ward. They were particularly shocked by the presence of very disturbed people, violent incidents that occurred during visits and the fact that Tom had told them that he had been offered street drugs by other residents on the ward.

They removed him from the ward and admitted him to a private hospital where he spent 8 weeks. However, this was proving to be a drain on their finances, and they were also unhappy with the treatment he received. They felt he was becoming 'zombie-like' and that the only treatment was medication, which they felt was too strong for him, resulting in him being 'doped up and uncommunicative'. They felt they had no choice but to try to manage him at home again with the support of a community mental health team. One of their key concerns was in relation to what would happen if he needed to be hospitalised again.

The family

Mother. Patricia (Patty) (52) is a health visitor working in primary care. She had been married previously and has a son Adam (26) from her first marriage. At the time of referral she was feeling very stressed, and had been prescribed sleeping tablets by her GP as she had been lying awake at night worrying about Tom. She also sees a counsellor at the surgery, which her husband is aware of, but she does not want the children to know.

Father. Dan (56) is a successful businessman in a senior position in an insurance firm. He is used to coping and being in charge of his life. He finds the contrast between his work life and dealing with his son's health issues, where everything seems uncertain and unpredictable, difficult to cope with. He is worried about having to take so much time away from his work, as the company has offered early retirement to other people of his age. He feels he has always been committed to his family, and regards Adam as his child as well as he has known him since he was 4 – he and Patty were married when Adam was 6.

Adam (26). He lives away from home. He always did very well in his studies, went to university and is working in a successful business. He has a girlfriend (Karen), they are saving to buy a house and plan to marry within a couple of years. He is concerned about Tom, tries to be supportive of his parents and visits for a weekend a month.

Tom (19). He began to experience difficulties when aged 14 while studying for his GCSE examinations. He found it difficult to concentrate and study. He was irritated by his younger sister, and missed his older brother who had left home to attend university. He passed his GCSE examinations, felt more relaxed for a while, then began to feel anxious again in the second year of his 'A Level' course. He began to be troubled by voices telling him to kill himself and had persistent ideas that his parents were evil and were trying to harm him. He attempted suicide (overdose) 6 months before he was due to take his 'A Level' examinations, and did not return to school. He has a girlfriend who is at university, and he would like to move to be with her and find a job there.

Becky (15). She feels that her brother's issues have taken over the life of the family. She is confused because she is concerned about her brother, but resents the fact that he gets so much of their parents' attention. She is seeing a school counsellor, but does not want her brothers to know this.

Engagement with the family

The family was offered an appointment for the therapist to meet them in their home. Both parents took time off work to attend the first appointment, and they had taken Becky out of school which she was not very happy about.

At the first meeting, there was a lot of anger from the parents towards the mental health system. They felt it was not adequate to meet Tom's needs as a young person, and that they had been blamed and labelled simply because they were assertive. In spite of this, they were willing to see somebody new, and ensure that all the family (except Adam) was present because they were very concerned about Tom. Becky made it clear that she was fed up having to do things for her brother, and Tom said that he just wanted to get on with his life – to 'move out and move on'.

This was the scenario facing the therapist against the backdrop of a message from the system to 'tread carefully' because this family had already previously made a complaint. It is important to be aware of this context, and to consider the various pressures a therapist can experience when entering the engagement process.

It is interesting in reflecting on the engagement process, to note the key factors that emerge as important in establishing a positive initial connection. The skills of successful engagement are very much about the human, Rogerian-type skills that are not as easy to quantify as the more concrete communication and problem-solving skills that will also be referred to later in the chapter. With this family, what seemed important were the following:

- *Humanity*. 'Hang on – give me a chance, this is the first time I'm hearing all of this' factor. There has to be a human-to-human connection where the therapist is recognised as a person and not just a representative of the system. This requires confidence on the part of the therapist, but is important when faced with anger and criticism as was the case in this first meeting.
- *Genuine concern*. It is important for the therapist to convey their concern for what the family has been going through. In this case, the family had to face what must be one of the most difficult things for any family – the risk of death of one of their family members through suicide. Therapists should consistently remind themselves of how they would feel if this was happening in their own family. It is easy for clinicians to become inured to what are very traumatic events through constant exposure to them in the healthcare system. For the family, especially in early psychosis, it is often their first time to have exposure to mental distress of this intensity, and also to a confusing healthcare system. In this articulate family, apart from the client, two other family members were receiving support or counselling in order to help them cope with the situation.
- *Listening to their story*. It is difficult not to be influenced by the views of other clinicians and information in case notes. When meeting with a family, it is good to try to 'start afresh' without preconceptions, and to let them know that is what you are trying to do. The therapist must convey a clear message that this is what their intention is, and that there will be time to do this.
- *Therapist's relationship with the healthcare system*. The therapist needs to be able to be of the system, yet willing to reflect critically on the system and acknowledge what aspects may be unsatisfactory. In this case, it was clear that the acute ward was not an appropriate environment for a young person, and that residential care facilities for adolescents were

not adequately developed in the area. It is more challenging to manage differing philosophical viewpoints among colleagues – in this instance the family having been told that they were 'dysfunctional' by a member of the community team. It is best to try to keep the focus on what you are offering now, and help the family to move forward.

- *Reassurance, lack of blame and normalising.* Usually the family's confidence will be knocked by what they have been through. The parents in this situation needed reassurance that they were trying to do the best for their son; that people find it difficult to separate what is normal adolescence and what constitutes mental health problems; that it is difficult to set boundaries when you are concerned about the possibility of suicide.
- *Flexibility.* Being willing to negotiate times and venues for appointments helps with the establishment of a relationship. Arranging meetings in their home, or at the beginning or end of the day for those who work or study make it much more likely that they will attend.

Family assessments

The therapist was working broadly in a Behavioural Family Therapy Framework. Within this model, following the engagement session(s) with the family, each member of the family is seen individually to get their views on what has been happening, how they perceive the issues and what they personally want to change or achieve. This is followed by an assessment of the family as a unit.

This section will provide relevant details about the family members obtained during the individual interviews, and information on what each family member was hoping to achieve:

1. *Mother.* Patty wondered if she was to blame for Tom's difficulties. In reflecting on how she had acted towards her children, she felt that Tom had been compared to Adam both by herself and her husband, and that he had been expected to 'live up to' Adam, even though he had always found schoolwork more difficult. She felt that she gave in to him too much, but didn't know what to do when he threatened to commit suicide by crashing the car. One of her concerns was that everyone expected her to know what to do because she was working in healthcare, but she had little experience of mental health. Apart from wanting a normal family life back, in terms of individual goals she

wanted to come off sleeping tablets, to manage her stress better and to be able to spend some quality time with her husband.

2. *Father.* Dan said he felt quite bewildered by what had happened, and could not make sense of it. He was not used to feeling this way and it unsettled him. He thought that sometimes Tom's behaviour was linked with his mental health difficulties, but that at other times he was 'trying it on'. The problem was, he couldn't discriminate which was which. He felt angry with Tom, and thought that at times he was too hard on him. He wanted to be able to get on with his life, and also to be able to get back to focusing on his work. He wanted to take Patty away for a break on their own as he felt she deserved it, and that recent events had impacted on their relationship.

3. *Tom.* He felt the others in the family didn't understand what he had gone through and how much he had suffered. He also thought that his parents did not trust him, and treated him like a child sometimes, for example refusing to give him the car. He felt that he had got over his problems and wanted to concentrate on the future. His relationship with his girlfriend was very important to him because he felt she understood him. He was worried that she might meet somebody else as she had moved away to college. He therefore wanted to move to be with her, to get a job and work for a year or so, and maybe do a course later when he had got some money together.

4. *Becky.* She felt that her parents were more concerned about her brother than about her. In fact, at times, she thought that they valued Adam and Tom's girlfriends more than her. Before Tom developed problems, she used to spend time with her mum, but this no longer happened. It seemed that all of her parents' time was taken up with Tom – when he was there, they were talking with him and when he was out, they were also talking about him. She found it very helpful talking to the school counsellor who helped her to 'sort things in her head'. She would like to spend more time on her own with her mum, and wanted some space in the house where she could bring her friends in.

Assessment of the family as a unit

Following the individual assessments, the family were seen together in order to assess how they generally addressed issues, and discussed difficulties which they faced currently. They reported that in recent times, attempts to discuss issues that led to disagreements generally ended up in heated arguments with all of them shouting at each other. As a consequence, they tended to avoid discussions, and were not communicating openly with each other. It was sometimes better when Adam was at home at a weekend as he was good at keeping the peace.

The therapist asked them to discuss an issue that was current in the family. They chose the disagreements between Tom and Becky about the use of the family room which had a computer and music system. Becky felt that she could not use it at weekends because Tom and his girlfriend Rachel were always in the room. Becky and Tom quickly started shouting at each other, with Tom arguing that as he only saw Rachel at weekends, he should be able to use it then and that Becky could see her friends during the week. The parents tried to intervene, pointing out that Tom had not been well, and that his relationship with Rachel was helping him to get better. The discussion ended without resolution, with Becky stating that Tom always got his own way, and that maybe she should start hearing voices too.

Formulation

The purpose of the next meeting was to reach a shared understanding of what the issues were. The therapist began by acknowledging again how stressful it had been for all of them, and the difficult situations they had faced, such as Tom's attempted suicide. It was clear that their previously calm family life had been overturned. Much time was spent on complimenting them on how they had tried to deal with all the difficulties they faced, how they had supported each other and clearly were very concerned about each other. The parents talked about how difficult it was to deal with totally unfamiliar situations such as Tom talking to imaginary people, and that sometimes they had gone along with what he said because it seemed to make him calmer. There was discussion about boundary setting and limits, and an acknowledgement that all families had to deal with these issues, particularly as their adolescent children became increasingly independent. Becky and Tom seemed quite comfortable with this, and gave various examples of the experiences their friends had with their parents.

The fact that they all shared a common desire to move on and get back to normal was highlighted. Individual goals were shared. Some of this was quite emotional, for example when Becky talked about wanting more time with her mother, and Patty felt upset that she had neglected her daughter.

They agreed that they would like some help as a family in how to deal with situations in which there were disagreements, and on how to get back to talking more calmly to each other. They also wanted help in knowing how to respond when Tom experienced voices or threatened suicide. They wondered about Adam attending some meetings, but felt this would be impractical except occasionally. Meetings were agreed for the end of the day at 5 p.m. when Becky would be home from school, and Dan and Patty could finish work early. They did not want to commit to a number of sessions but wanted to see how family work progressed.

Intervention

When formal family intervention started, the therapist had already met with the family members (individually and collectively) for 6 weeks and by now, knew them all quite well.

Session 1: developing a shared understanding. This first session focused on experiences linked with Tom's psychosis, and in helping all family members to understand each other's perspectives on this. Tom found it difficult to reflect on a time when he was very distressed, but was willing to share how frightened he had been, and how alone he had felt. The worst thing for him had been the idea that his parents were trying to harm him, as he then felt his security was gone and he had no one to turn to. This had contributed to him wanting to die, although none of the family wanted to talk about suicide during this meeting. The therapist discussed Tom's psychosis in terms of a stress–vulnerability model (Zubin and Spring, 1977) which made sense to all the family. Tom was able to identify a range of stressors at various points in time including those linked with school, and his brother leaving home.

All of the family discussed how to respond when Tom was hearing voices or experiencing unusual ideas, and Tom identified those he found most helpful. This session was very positive with the family commenting at the end on how helpful they had found it.

Session 2: addressing the issue of suicide risk. At the beginning of each session, the therapist checked how the family members were progressing towards the goals they had identified at the initial individual interviews, and that they were working on alongside the family sessions.

In this second session, the family wanted to discuss Tom's attempted suicide and threats of suicide. This was very emotional for all of them, but they clearly felt that they needed to discuss it. Tom described how he sometimes felt so frightened by what was happening that he felt he could not cope anymore. He was not sure if he wanted to die or get some relief from distressing experiences. While his Dad accepted that Tom had been very unwell when he made his suicide attempt, he sometimes felt now that he threatened suicide in order to get his own way. He therefore did not take him very seriously when he talked about it. Becky was angry with Tom for upsetting everyone in the family by trying to kill himself, and began to talk about poverty in the developing world and people who had no choice about dying. It was important to keep a focus in the session on what was painful for all of them to talk about. Patty was particularly upset thinking about the possibility that Tom might take his own life.

In the second half of the session, the therapist talked with the family about the importance of taking Tom seriously when he discussed suicide, and about the risk of suicide in early psychosis. This was hard for all of them, but they found it easier when considering how they would handle this situation should it arise again. They found it helpful to have contact names for staff in the community team and assurances from Tom that he would talk with them if he felt like this again.

The idea of a relapse prevention plan was discussed, and it was agreed to pursue this further at the next meeting.

Session 3: addressing problem situations. When the therapist arrived, Tom was in his room and had told his parents that he did not want to attend the meeting that day. He had found the previous meeting upsetting because he felt it was all about him, and he did not want to spend another meeting talking about difficult experiences from the past. Dan persuaded him to come to the meeting, at least to say what concerned him.

The therapist thanked him for coming, and talked with the whole family about the rationale for having a relapse prevention or 'staying well' plan; that the purpose is positive and aimed at avoiding a recurrence of difficulties experienced previously. Tom was adamant that he did not want to talk anymore about what had happened previously. The only contribution from Becky (who sat reading a book on Bob Geldof) was to say 'Where's the point?' and the parents also felt they would prefer to put all that had happened previously behind them and move on. It was agreed that if they wanted to come back to this at any point they could do so, but that the meeting would be spent discussing more current issues.

The therapist suggested using the meeting to look at the problem-solving method (Falloon *et al.*, 2004), which had been mentioned in initial meetings, and suggested discussing the issue of the use of the room with the TV and music system that Tom and Becky often argued about, and which affected all of them, as the parents were usually drawn in to arbitrate between them. Becky became very interested and put her book down. The family were able to identify the issue, and came up with a range of solutions based around rotas and turn-taking. Becky wanted to know that she could use the room on particular nights so that she could have her friends around. Tom was unhappy with all of the suggestions that were being made, saying that he and his girlfriend never knew until the particular night whether or not they would be going out. He wanted it agreed that the room was his to use at weekends, but that if he and Rachel went out, Becky could have it. She pointed out that this meant she could not plan anything with her friends.

The parents began to insist on turn-taking, stating that Becky has as much right to use the room as Tom had. Tom became very angry saying that he was the one who had been unwell, and that everyone should be trying to help him to get better. Once again, both parents were quite firm pointing out to Tom that he could not on one hand say everything was in the past, and on the other use what had happened in the past to get his own way. The therapist thought that Tom was going to leave the room, but he stayed, complaining that nobody cared about what he had been through, and that only his girlfriend understood him. It was agreed that the next session should focus on something positive as the last two sessions had been difficult.

Comment. This was a very significant session in that it was the first time that Dan and Patty had challenged Tom and set boundaries around what were acceptable and unacceptable demands.

Up to this session, the meetings had been weekly, but the family asked if they could be two-weekly instead as they had found it all quite intensive. They also felt it would give them more time to practice skills such as problem solving between meetings.

Session 4: communication skills. At the beginning of this session, the family reported that there had been some issues between them since the last session. On one occasion, the parents had refused to give Tom the car, as he would not say what time he would bring it back. He had gone to stay at his girlfriend's home for the weekend, but they had a constructive discussion about this during the week.

This session focused on communication skills, in particular on the topic of how to say pleasant things to each other. This was a much lighter session than the previous two, and the family thought it was fun. They said that they were going to practice on Adam and his girlfriend who were coming to stay for the weekend. Both Dan and Patty commented that they knew some people in both their workplaces who would benefit from learning some of these skills.

Session 5: individual meeting with father. During the following week, Dan phoned and asked to see the therapist on his own, as he wanted to discuss some personal issues which he did not want to discuss in front of everyone. All family members were aware that within this model of family work, it was possible to have individual meetings as well as family meetings.

Dan began by talking about the fact that he no longer felt in control of his work, that he was always used to coping, and that it was difficult for him to feel like this. He felt that everything that had happened at home was taking its toll on work. He then talked about the anger he felt towards Tom, and that sometimes it got so intense he worried he was going to hit him. He then got really upset, crying and sobbing and talking about how sorry he was that Tom had gone through such difficult experiences at a young age. He talked about the times he felt disappointed in Tom because of not doing well at school, and for having no sense of direction in life. One of the issues he found hard to admit to himself was that he felt a sense of rivalry with Patty because his son Tom was not doing very well, while her son, Adam, was the 'golden boy'. He hated thinking in this way as he considered Adam to be his son too, though in a different way, but he could not help it.

He said he felt relieved to have been able to talk about his feelings, and that he had tried to keep them bottled up for a long time. The therapist talked about the range of emotions that family members experience when someone in the family had the kind of difficulties Tom had gone through, and reassured him that he was coping, even if at times he felt he was not. Dan declined any offers of ongoing individual help, and said he had just needed to 'get things off his chest'. At the end of the session, he said he felt drained and a bit embarrassed, but that talking had been helpful.

This was the only meeting that was held in a health setting rather than the family home.

Session 6: communication skills. At the beginning of this session, Dan talked about why he had asked for an individual meeting with the therapist, and the fact that he had felt everything had been getting on top of him. All of the other family members were very supportive of him, while Becky shared in front of her brother for the first time that she had talked to the school counsellor. While Patty did not talk about receiving specific help, she said that because of where she worked, she always had people she could talk to. The therapist discussed again the differing impacts on all family members, when one of the family experiences mental health difficulties, and complimented the family on how well they had all coped with very trying experiences.

The family agreed that the focus of this session would continue to be on how they communicated together, with a particular emphasis on how they asked each other for things. They all identified the relevance of this: Becky felt that she was not good at asking, for example for special time with her mother, because she was conscious of her brother's needs; Tom said that he had been thinking, and felt he sometimes acted like a 'stroppy teenager', and that he needed to grow up a bit. Both parents said that they sometimes did not ask the children to do things in the best way, especially when they were tired or stressed.

The session went very well, with all four family members practicing asking for things in a more reasonable manner. They agreed to try to put this into practice routinely.

Note. There was a 3-week break between this and the next session because of holidays. Tom wanted to be with his girlfriend, and the parents had decided to take a long weekend away together.

Session 7: endings. The family talked about how well everything had been going for them: the parents had enjoyed their break, and Becky and her mum had spent time together while Becky was off school. Tom and Rachel had spent time where she was at university looking around for potential jobs, and he had decided to go and live there for a while to see how things would go. Dan and Patty talked about their anxieties around this, and whether Tom should go back to study at some point. They all decided together that it was a bit soon to think about this, and maybe it was better to leave this for a year or so.

The family also said at this meeting that they did not feel they needed to meet any more with the therapist. In one way, this came as a surprise in that ending the meetings had not been discussed. On the other hand, it was obvious that things were going well for them, and as they had said at the beginning, they all wanted to move on and put the past behind them.

The therapist talked about options of having one further meeting to plan what to do if Tom began to experience difficulties again. However, none of them wanted to do this, and Tom was adamant that talking about a very difficult time in his past did not help him. Another offer from the therapist was to have a follow-up meeting a couple of months later, but the family felt they would prefer to arrange this if they needed it. The clear underlying message from them was 'Don't call us, we'll call you!' The therapist made it very clear that they were welcome to contact at any time, either to arrange a meeting or simply to talk things through. The family said that it gave them a lot of reassurance to know that someone would be available if they needed it.

It seemed appropriate to spend the rest of the session reflecting on what had been helpful, and discussing if anything needed to be done before finishing. They mentioned some specific things that had been helpful such as understanding what Tom had been going through, and finding ways of discussing difficult issues together. Tom commented that the meetings had helped him see other people's perspectives. He realised that he had got very caught up in himself, and was unaware in the past of the impact his difficulties were having on others in the family.

What the family had valued most was being listened to, having time to go through everything, and meeting a professional who treated them as an ordinary family. The parents commented that in some ways the meetings made it feel safe for them to challenge Tom about some of his behaviour. Dan commented that he had found the individual session helpful because everything had been building up for a long time, and he had needed an outlet for his feelings.

In terms of tying up loose ends, the family said that they found the formulation meeting helpful and thought it would be good if the community team understood them in that way. It was agreed that a letter would be written by the therapist, and the family wanted a message in it that they were just an ordinary family and not dysfunctional! After a discussion about who the letter should be sent to, it was agreed that the letter would be sent to them summarising the issues, and the shared understanding of what had happened, and that this would be copied to the team.

There was a telephone call from Dan two months later to thank the therapist again, and to say that everything was going well. Tom had found a job and they did not see much of him, and Becky was very happy that she could have her friends around. He said he would make contact if they needed to.

Reflection

The reader will no doubt have taken various points to reflect on from this account of family work. The following may be helpful to think about:

- *Who participates in family meetings?* In this family, the older brother who lived away from home did not attend meetings as this was not practical.
- *When does assessment end, and intervention begin?* There were seven sessions comprising engagement, assessment and formulation and seven intervention sessions. However, the early assessment and formulation sessions were a crucial part of the therapeutic intervention.
- *Flexibility.* Having an intervention framework and therapeutic 'tools' that are applied flexibly to the particular needs of the family is important. Similarly, the capacity within this model to have family meetings and individual meetings is very beneficial, although some clinicians have difficulty with the same therapist doing both. This often results in a number of mental health staff being involved with the family. How are decisions made about this issue?
- *Turning points in therapy.* The points at which the parents challenged Tom, and the individual meeting with the father seemed important.
- *Endings happen in different ways.* In this situation, the therapist had to recognise their own anxiety about the suddenness of the ending, and the fact that the family had not been willing to discuss the possibility of future difficulties. Ultimately however, the control should rest with the family.
- *Relationship with the mental health system.* This was an issue with this family, and therapists need to reflect on how this is managed, facilitated and supported.

Conclusion

What then should family interventions in early psychosis consist of? It is possible to draw up a list based on existing knowledge from the literature:

- Reaching a shared understanding about what has happened.
- How to access/understand/negotiate services.
- Information sharing.
- Relapse prevention strategies.

- Stress management.
- Problem solving about everyday issues.
- Counselling about grief loss, and adjustment to changed expectations.
- Different types of family input at different points in time.
- Attention to individual differences and needs.

This is an evolving area which is challenging but manageable for staff with adequate training. Hopefully, the current text will go some way to assisting clinicians to develop the necessary skills.

References

Addington, J. and Burnett, P. (2004) Working with families in the early stages of psychosis, in *Psychological Interventions in Early Psychosis: A Practical Treatment Handbook* (eds P. McGorry and J. Gleeson), John Wiley & Sons, Ltd, Chichester.

Addington, J., Coldham, E.L., Jones, B. *et al.* (2002) Family work in an early psychosis programme: a longitudinal study. *Acta Psychiatrica Scandinavica*, **106** (Suppl. 413), 101.

Addington, J., Coldham, E.L., Jones, B. *et al.* (2003) The first episode of psychosis: the experience of relatives. *Acta Psychiatrica Scandinavica*, **108**, 285–9.

Addington, J., Collins, A., McCleery, A. and Addington, D. (2005a) The role of family work in early psychosis. *Schizophrenia Research*, **79**, 77–83.

Addington, J., McCleery, A. and Addington, D. (2005b) Three-year outcome of family work in an early psychosis program. *Schizophrenia Research*, **79**, 107–16.

Bachmann, S., Bottmer, C., Jacob, S. *et al.* (2002) Expressed emotion in relatives of first-episode and chronic patients with schizophrenia and major depressive disorder – a comparison. *Psychiatry Research*, **112**, 239–50.

Burns, E.J. and Schulz, C.L. (2001) *Nonfinite Grief and Loss. A Psychoeducational Approach*, PH Brookes Publishing Company, Baltimore.

Department of Health (2001) *The Mental Health Policy Implementation Guide*, HMSO, London.

Early Psychosis Prevention and Intervention Centre (EPPIC) (1997) *Working with Families in Early Psychosis*, No. 2 in a Series of Early Psychosis manuals. Psychiatric Services Branch, Human Services, Victoria, Australia.

Fadden, G. (1997) Implementation of family interventions in routine clinical practice following staff training programs: a major cause for concern. *Journal of Mental Health*, **6** (6), 599–612.

Fadden, G., Birchwood, M., Jackson, C. and Barton, K. (2004) Psychological therapies: implementation in early intervention services, in *Psychological*

Interventions in Early Psychosis: A Practical Treatment Handbook (eds P. Mc-Gorry and Jo Gleeson), John Wiley & Sons, Ltd, Chichester.

Falloon, I.R.H., Fadden, G., Mueser, K. *et al.* (2004) *Family Work Manual*, Meriden Family Programme, Birmingham.

Fisher, H., Bordass, E. and Steele, H. (2004) Siblings' experience of having a brother or sister with first-episode psychosis. *Schizophrenia Research*, 70 (Suppl. 1), 88.

Gibbons, J.S., Horn, S.H., Powell, J.M. and Gibbons, J.L. (1984) Schizophrenic patients and their families: a survey in a psychiatric service based on a DGH unit. *British Journal of Psychiatry*, 144, 70–7.

Gleeson, J., Jackson, H.J., Staveley, H. and Burnett, P. (1999) Family intervention in early psychosis, in *The Recognition and Management of Early Psychosis* (eds P.D. McGorry, and H.J. Jackson), Cambridge University Press, Cambridge.

Goldstein, M.J., Rodnick, E.H., Evans, J.R. *et al.* (1978) Drug and family therapy in the aftercare of acute schizophrenics. *Archives of General Psychiatry*, 35 (10), 1169–77.

Gopinath, P.S. and Chaturvedi, S.K. (1992) Distressing behaviour of schizophrenics at home. *Acta Psychiatrica Scandinavica*, 86 (3), 185–8.

Haddock, G. and Lewis, S. (2005) Psychological interventions in early psychosis. *Schizophrenia Bulletin*, 31, 697–704.

Heikkila, J., Kartsson, H., Taminien, T. *et al.* (2002) Expressed emotion is not associated with disorder severity in first episode mental disorder. *Psychiatry Research*, 111, 155–65.

Huguelet, P., Favre, S., Binyet, S. *et al.* (1995) The use of the Expressed Emotion Index as a predictor of outcome in first admitted psychiatric patients in a French speaking area of Switzerland. *Acta Psychiatrica Scandinavica*, 92, 447–52.

Initiative to Reduce the Impact of Schizophrenia (IRIS) (2000) *Early Intervention in Psychosis: Clinical Guidelines and Service Frameworks*, West Midlands IRIS (Initiative to Reduce the Impact of Schizophrenia), West Midlands Partnership for Mental Health, Birmingham.

Lafond, V. (2002) *Grieving Mental Illness: A Guide for Patients and Their Caregivers*, University of Toronto Press Inc., Toronto.

Lehtinen, K. (1993) Need-adapted treatment of schizophrenia: a five-year follow-up study from the Turku project. *Acta Psychiatrica Scandinavica*, 87, 96–101.

Linszen, D., Dingemans, P., Van Der Does, J.W. *et al.* (1996) Treatment, expressed emotion and relapse in recent onset schizophrenic disorders. *Psychological Medicine*, 26, 333–42.

Martens, L. and Addington, J. (2001) Psychological well-being of family members with schizophrenia. *Social Psychiatry and Psychiatric Epidemiology*, 36, 128–33.

Miller, F. (1996) Grief therapy for relatives of persons with serious mental illness. *Psychiatric Services*, 47, 633–7.

Patterson, P., Birchwood, M. and Cochrane, R. (2000) Preventing the entrenchment of high expressed emotion in first episode psychosis: early developmental attachments pathways. *Australian and New Zealand Journal of Psychiatry,* **34,** S191–7.

Penn, D.L., Waldheter, E.J., Perkins, D.O. *et al.* (2005) Psychosocial treatment for first-episode psychosis: a research update. *American Journal of Psychiatry,* **162,** 2220–32.

Raune, D., Kuipers, E. and Bebbington, P.E. (2004) Expressed emotion at first-episode psychosis: investigating a carer appraisal model. *British Journal of Psychiatry,* **184,** 321–6.

Rund, B.R., Aeie, M., Borchgrevink, T.S. and Fjell, A. (1995) Expressed emotion, communication deviance and schizophrenia. *Psychopathology,* **28,** 220–8.

Slade, M., Holloway, F. and Kuipers, E. (2004) Skills development and family interventions in an early psychosis service. *Journal of Mental Health,* **12** (4), 405–15.

Tennakoon, L., Fannon, D., Doku, V. *et al.* (2000) Experience of care-giving: relatives of people experiencing a first episode of psychosis. *British Journal of Psychiatry,* **177,** 529–33.

White, A. (2002) *Working with Families: Evaluation of an Integrated Positive Approach to Recent Onset Psychosis.* Presentation at the BABCP 30th Anniversary Annual Conference, University of Warwick, UK.

Zhang, M., Wang, M., Li, J. and Phillips, M.R. (1994) Randomised-control trial of family intervention for 78 first-episode male schizophrenic patients. *British Journal of Psychiatry,* **165** (24), 96–102.

Zubin, J. and Spring, B. (1977) Vulnerability – a new view of schizophrenia. *Journal of Abnormal Psychology,* **86,** 103–26.

Resources

To get *help* as a young person or carer, you could initially talk to a relative, youth worker, teacher or school/college nurse or counsellor. For more information or advice about psychosis contact:

- your local doctor;
- your local early intervention service;
- web sites.

www.youngminds.org.uk (accessed 1 October 2008) – Youth mental health site targeted at 16–25 year olds providing useful information and support for understanding and coping with mental health issues.

www.bcss.org (accessed 1 October 2008) – British Columbia web site with lots of downloadable helpful information.

www.iris-initiative.org.uk (accessed 1 October 2008) – UK site promoting good practice in early intervention services for psychosis.

www.rethink.org (accessed 1 October 2008) – UK Rethink site which has user friendly mental health information and loads of helpful links.

www.readthesigns.org (accessed 1 October 2008) – Colourful interactive youth site promoting understanding and open mindedness about mental health in Britain.

www.psychosissucks.ca (accessed 1 October 2008) – Informative Canadian site with youth appeal and helpful explanations of psychosis.

www.getontop.org (accessed 1 October 2008) – Australian site aimed at helping young people cope with and manage mental health issues.

www.eppic.org.au (accessed 1 October 2008) – Web site of influential Australian service for people with first-episode psychosis with comprehensive downloadable information sheets for young people and families.

Further Reading

Addington, J., Addington, D., Jones, B. and Ko, T. (2001) Family intervention in an early psychosis program. *Psychiatric Rehabilitation Skills*, **5** (2), 272–86.

Kuipers, E. and Raune, D. (2000) EE and burden in first onset psychosis, in *Psychosis: Psychological Approaches and Their Effectiveness* (eds M. Birchwood, D. Fowler and C. Jackson), Gaskell Press, London.

Newstead, L. and Kelly, M. (2003) Early intervention in psychosis: who wins, who loses, who pays the price? *Journal of Psychiatric and Mental Health Nursing*, **10**, 83–8.

Wolthaus, J.E.D., Dingemans, P.M.A.J., Schene, A.H. *et al.* (2002) Caregiver burden in recent onset schizophrenia and spectrum disorders: the influence of symptoms and personality traits. *Journal of Nervous and Mental Disease*, **190**, 241–7.

Yang, L.H., Phillips, M.R., Licht, D.M. and Healey, J.M. (2004) Causal attributions about schizophrenia in families in China: expressed emotion and patient relapse. *Journal of Abnormal Psychology*, **113** (4), 592–602.

3

A Model of Family Work in First-Episode Psychosis: Managing Self-Harm

Jean Addington, April Collins, Amanda McCleery and Sabrina Baker

Using a recovery-based framework, this chapter will describe an intervention approach that is specifically designed for families affected by early psychosis. Described initially in Addington *et al.* (2005), this recovery framework was developed in the Calgary Early Psychosis Programme (EPP) (Addington and Addington, 2001) and has since been expanded for use in the Toronto First Episode of Psychosis Programme (FEPP). Given that self-harm is a common risk for young people in the first few years following the onset of illness, we have incorporated a case study which addresses this issue in the context of our work with families.

Introduction

Distress, and even psychiatric morbidity, has been reported in the relatives of families at the First Episode of Psychosis (Addington *et al.*, 2003; Addington, McCleery and Addington, 2005; Kuipers and Raune, 2000; Tennakoon *et al.*, 2000). At this juncture, there is compelling evidence that demonstrates (i) that psychosis has an impact on families, (ii) that families can influence the course and outcome of illness (Smith, Berthelsen and O'Connor, 1997) and (iii) that informal family caregivers provide the vast majority of care for those in the early phases of a psychotic illness. Thus, the development of family programmes has to be an integral part of any comprehensive First-Episode Programme. The specific needs of the family have to be acknowledged not only because the family has a significant impact on the person's experience

---

A Casebook of Family Interventions for Psychosis   Edited by Fiona Lobban and Christine Barrowclough
© 2009 John Wiley & Sons, Ltd

and recovery but also because the family needs support through what is undoubtedly a bewildering and distressing period.

The problem of psychosis and self-harm

A real and potentially devastating problem in schizophrenia is self-harm. For those suffering from schizophrenia the lifetime risk of suicide is high, ranging from 10% to 13% (Tsuang, 1978) and the rates of parasuicide are higher, ranging from 25% to 50% (Meltzer, 2001). The most commonly reported risk factors for suicide in schizophrenia are young age, male gender, high premorbid functioning and early stages of the illness, having multiple relapses, depression and previous suicide attempts (Birchwood, Todd and Jackson, 1998; Young *et al.*, 1998). The first year of a psychotic illness is a particularly high-risk period (Addington, Addington and Patten, 1998; Mortensen and Juel, 1993). Clinicians need to be aware that suicidal behaviour may be triggered by feelings of hopelessness, distress due to psychotic symptoms, and occasionally can be attributed to command hallucinations or is secondary to delusional content (Addington *et al.*, 2004).

Specific issues associated with nature of specific client group

When working with families at the first episode, the aim is to maximise adaptive functioning of the family, minimise disruption to family life and the risk of long-term grief, stress and burden and reduce the risk of negative outcomes for the patient. The family must be collaborators in this process (Addington and Burnett, 2004). Although first-episode families face many of the same difficulties endured by families of patients with a more chronic course of illness, some issues are unique to the first episode (Goldstein, 1996; Linzen, 1993). Specifically, first-episode families have no prior experience with psychosis and the acuteness of the first psychotic episode can be mystifying. Often there is diagnostic ambiguity during the first episode, and psychoeducation is less specific than it would be for those with a more chronic course of illness (Addington and Burnett, 2004).

The clinical service

The goals of first-episode programmes such as the Calgary EPP and the Toronto FEPP are early identification of the psychotic illness, reduction in the delays in initial treatment, treatment of the primary symptoms of psychosis, reduction of secondary morbidity, reduction of the frequency and severity of relapse, promotion of normal psychosocial development and reduction of the burden for families. These programmes are specifically designed to meet the needs of individuals diagnosed with a first episode of psychosis. In addition to using a family approach, these programmes offer optimal pharmacotherapy, case management, cognitive behavioural therapy and group treatment.

Theoretical influences on approach used

Developing a model was first based on the notion that a stressful family environment can have an impact on outcome (Kavanagh, 1992; Kuipers and Raune, 2000; Nuechterlein, Snyder and Mintz, 1992; Stirling *et al.*, 1991). Secondly, interventions were then developed from psychoeducational and cognitive behavioural models of working with families that include education, coping strategies and communication and problem-solving training (Falloon *et al.*, 1982; Leff *et al.*, 1982; McFarlane *et al.*, 1995; Mueser and Glynn, 1999; Penn and Mueser, 1996; Tarrier, Barrowclough and Porceddu, 1988) in the context of the specific needs of first-episode patients and their families (Addington and Burnett, 2004).

Our 3-year follow-up of a large sample of first-episode families from the Calgary EPP demonstrated several clinically relevant results (Addington *et al.*, 2003; Addington, McCleery and Addington, 2005). First-episode families have high levels of distress and are experiencing many difficulties. Notably, the level of distress was increased if the ill family member was young or had an early age of onset. Secondly, distress improved significantly after 1 year but those with more severe distress often took 2 years to recover. Finally, it was the families' appraisals of the impact and consequences of the illness that was most associated with their psychological well-being not the severity of the illness. More than 80% of available families participated and of those participating 50% were still available after 3 years. These results are encouraging because they indicate that family interventions are acceptable, can be effective in real clinical situations, and that it is advantageous to engage with families at the first episode. In addition, although our programme was available to families for over 3 years, the average number of sessions each year was relatively low (i.e. an average of 12 sessions over 3 years). This suggests that family intervention that is long term (i.e. 1–3 years) does not necessarily need to be intensive.

Style and structure of the intervention: the recovery stage model

The recovery stage model for families is based upon the course of recovery for a person experiencing their first psychotic episode. Described initially in Addington *et al.* (2005), the recovery model was developed in the Calgary EPP and has since been expanded for use in the Toronto FEPP. The model has four stages: (1) managing the crisis, (2) initial stabilisation and facilitating recovery, (3) consolidating the gains and (4) prolonged recovery; where each stage has specific interventions and clearly defined goals.

Therapists: training, role and attributes

In the Calgary EPP, the family worker works exclusively with the family and does not serve other roles such as case manager. As such, the family worker is a highly trained professional and an integral member of the treatment team; he or she works closely with the psychiatrist and case manager as well as other team members. EPP has two masters-level clinicians from different disciplines (social work and nursing) who have special training in family work at the graduate level. These clinicians are dedicated to working specifically with families. This underscores the importance of the family work both within the programme and to the family itself. It also allows for family work to continue should a conflictual situation arise between the patient and the family.

What follows is an in-depth description of the recovery stage model and the interventions associated with each stage. Within this framework, we will present a case study which describes how family programmes can offer a broad menu of services including individual and group family work, education, coping strategies, communication and problem-solving training that are sensitive to the stage and phase of the illness and recovery trajectory of the young person with the psychotic illness. Although based on issues and concerns that do occur in early psychosis, this case study is not based on a true case that is recognisable.

The Clinical Case

Background/referral information

Peter, an only child, is 19 years old and lives at home with his parents. He was referred to the First-Episode Psychosis Programme for an assessment because he had become suspicious and was isolating himself. The previously straight A student was falling behind in his assignments and had failed a number of tests. Peter's parents were concerned about the change in his behaviour, his apparent decline in school and overall functioning. He was more irritable than usual and had threatened, 'to kill the person who was making his life a misery'. Peter's previous medical and psychiatric history was unremarkable. However, there was a family history of schizophrenia in a paternal aunt.

Stage 1: Managing the Crisis

Briefly, at the first stage of treatment the primary goal is crisis management, engaging the family and developing a good working relationship. Individual families are provided with support and education about psychosis. The second stage focuses on stabilising the patient and family and facilitating recovery. Families are offered both individual and group treatment at this stage. In stage three, the family worker helps the family integrate the information and skills learned in the previous stages into their daily life. In the final stage of treatment, families are prepared for transition into appropriate long-term treatment programmes. Note that at each phase of treatment, families identified as high risk for difficulty are offered additional interventions and support. Length of the stages varies with the needs of the family and the rate of recovery for the individual. Typically, the crisis stage may last a few months, followed by a 3–12 month recovery stage and a 12-month consolidation stage. The number of sessions can vary at each stage as reported above.

Patients can be part of the family sessions and are encouraged to attend. We find that patients usually attend half of the time.

At the clinic

Peter's parents were invited to attend the initial appointment. At the first meeting with the family, the staff psychiatrist met with Peter while a case manager gathered collateral information from his parents. Alex and Marina reported that they had noticed a change in Peter's behaviour approximately 18 months ago. At that time, Peter, a relatively mild mannered adolescent, became increasingly irritable with his parents and his grades started dropping at school. He stopped going out socially and spent hours in his room, alone on the computer, playing *Dungeons and Dragons*. Over time, Peter became increasingly vigilant. He appeared concerned about the safety of his family. As a result he started sleeping with a baseball bat in his room to fend off potential attackers.

During the interview with the psychiatrist, Peter was vague about when his difficulties started but went on to describe an elaborate belief system that involved a conspiracy against him and his parents. He endorsed hearing voices that were calling him names and threatening to kill him. When questioned, Peter said that he would take his life and the lives of his parents if he were unable to stop the perpetrator of these threats. Of particular concern was that Peter could not be dissuaded from his ideas. He grew increasingly agitated and lost in his thoughts as the interview went on. Given the severity of his symptoms, the psychiatrist was unable to obtain a comprehensive history. The collateral information obtained at the first assessment interview is always important, but in this situation, it became a crucial part of the assessment process.

The parents: Alex and Marina

The case manager asked Alex and Marina about their respective ideas about Peter's current difficulties. Both parents reported that initially they thought that Peter was going through a 'phase' and was 'rebelling against his family'. On closer probing, Alex reported that Peter had been 'hanging around with a bad crowd in the last year and using cannabis on a regular basis'. He believed that 'these bad influences' had contributed to his son's current difficulties.

After getting a sense of the initial problem and how the parents were reacting, the case manager began to complete a more detailed collateral history. She established that the family had come from an Eastern European country. Alex was an engineer by training and Marina was a qualified teacher. The couple had lived with Marina's parents until the time they had decided to immigrate to Canada. The grandparents were largely responsible for raising Peter. Alex, Marina and Peter immigrated to Canada for economic reasons

Table 3.1 Stage 1: Managing the Crisis

Goals are to	Individual family treatment
Engage with the family	Frequent contact
Develop a good working relationship	High support
Collect a detailed collateral history and needs assessment	Practical and emotional support to minimise impact of trauma
Help manage the crisis	Repeated and clear messages about psychosis and its treatment
Offer an initial explanatory model of psychosis	Education about the role of the family in treatment
Identify high-risk families	

Source: From Addington *et al.* (2005). Copyright 2005 by Elsevier. Reprinted with permission.

and to give Peter a 'good education and a better life than he could have had in Eastern Europe'. Peter was 11 years old when they moved. However, life was not as easy as they had imagined. The family had no support system in Canada and their professional qualifications were not recognised. As such, Alex had ended up driving a taxi, often 16 hours a day and Marina worked as a teaching assistant.

Table 3.2 Stage 2: Initial Stabilisation and Facilitating Recovery

Goals are to	Individual family treatment
Assess family functioning	Support and education
Develop a therapeutic alliance	Family coping with a focus on staying well
Increase family's knowledge of psychosis	Problem solving and coping strategies for dealing with psychosis
Help family understand the recovery process and to be able to identify early warning signs	Intensive work for high-risk families
Identify those at high risk and those with sustained patterns of interaction likely to interfere with patient outcome	Family group treatment
	Short term
	Psychosis Education Group
	Family coping group with focus on staying well

Source: From Addington *et al.* (2005). Copyright 2005 by Elsevier. Reprinted with permission.

Peter had always been an A student and remained studious, maintaining his grades until the age of 15. According to the couple, Peter started to smoke cannabis regularly at this age and started to mix with the 'wrong crowd'. It became evident over the course of the interview that Peter's parents had different beliefs about child rearing and discipline. Each parent blamed the other for Peter's 'bad' behaviour and described giving in to him rather than 'rocking the boat'.

Alex and Marina described 'reaching a breaking point when Peter started to isolate himself and started expressing paranoid and threatening ideas'. According to his parents, Peter had not made specific threats about hurting himself or others, but rather he made general comments about feeling hopeless and helpless about the situation in general. From the information gathered from the initial assessment and collateral history, the team, consisting of the psychiatrist and case manager made the decision that Peter was suffering from a first episode of psychosis, with a preliminary diagnosis of psychosis not otherwise specified. Based on his level of agitation, perceived suicide risk and his parents' concern that Peter was a potential risk to harm others, the decision was made to offer a voluntary admission to the in-patient unit of the First-Episode Programme (EPU) to Peter. The psychiatrist was prepared to admit him involuntarily had Peter refused to come into hospital willingly. The team offered an explanatory model of psychosis to Peter and his family and introduced the idea about treatment and recovery and recommended that Peter come into hospital immediately.

The hospital admission

Arrangements were made to admit Peter from the outpatient clinic that same day and put on continuous observation for the first 48 hours while his risk was being assessed. Peter and his family were given clear messages about our concern regarding Peter's risk for self-harm and the need to take this issue seriously. Like most parents, Alex and Marina were distressed to think of their son being hospitalised, wondered what was happening and fluctuated between believing Peter was talking about suicide to get attention and worried that he might actually kill himself. We believe that connecting with families early on is critical because alliance is the vehicle within which therapeutic gain is facilitated. The goal always is to develop a good working relationship with families and help them develop some sense of control over the situation. The team needed to prove to Alex and Marina that they were trustworthy and genuinely concerned about the health and well-being of their son. After all, handing the care of a loved one over to strangers is not something that comes easily for anyone. Over the course of the first week of the admission, the team regularly met with Peter to assess his level of risk and his parents to gather information about how he was doing from their perspective. By the end of the week, we were relatively confident that Peter did not have an active plan to harm himself but continued to have passive suicidal ideation. The doctor and primary nurse worked closely with Peter to develop a plan to manage his suicidal ideation. His parents were involved in the planning process and role-playing and rehearsal strategies were used to help incorporate the information. In addition to careful planning around issues related to risk, the inpatient social worker provided the family with ongoing support and education throughout the admission and facilitated discussions which focused on issues related to diagnosis and treatment. The couple needed help to manage this crisis in their lives, and required time to work through their own feelings of anticipatory loss and grief, which were precipitated by Peter's deterioration and recent hospitalisation. The social worker talked about recovery and prevention of relapse and reminded Alex and Marina that it was important to take recovery 1 day at a time and stay present focused. Approximately 3 weeks later, Peter was ready for discharge from the inpatient unit and referred to the First-Episode Psychosis Outpatient Clinic for follow-up.

High-risk families

The assessment of families must be distinguished from the process of gathering a collateral history related to the presenting problems of the young person. In our First-Episode Psychosis Services, a number of issues are explored and assist with our formulation of the issues to be addressed. Key details include: the family's immediate concerns about the psychosis, their knowledge about the illness and treatments, their beliefs about the illness and treatments, the impact of the illness upon individuals in the family, the family's current coping resources, their appraisal of their coping resources, their history of coping with stress and their patterns of communication and problem solving. In this situation, the team was mindful that Alex and Marina were identified as 'high risk' and in need of additional support from the specialised family worker in the First-Episode Psychosis Programme to help them better equip themselves to integrate their son back into the family

Table 3.3 Family Groups

1. Psychosis Education Group	2. Taking Care of the Caregiver Group
Educates about	Helps family members
• What psychosis is	• To promote and maintain overall good physical and emotional health
• Symptoms and diagnoses	
• Causes, theories and models of psychosis	• To understand the impact of stress on general functioning
• Individual explanatory models	• To become aware of different techniques of coping with stress
• The stress–vulnerability model	
• Impact of substance use	• To improve coping and competence
• Use of medications	• To increase social interaction and interpersonal relationships
• Identification of warning signs	
• Relapse prevention	• To universalise issues and offer mutual support to family members
• Available psychosocial treatments	
Offers	
• Increased social interaction and interpersonal relationships	
• Improved coping and competence	
• Support from other families	

home and promote his continued recovery. Based on the initial social work assessment and the results of the meetings the couple had with the specialised family worker prior to discharge, it appeared that both parents had difficulty establishing boundaries between family members. They used avoidant coping strategies, such as blocking out or avoiding confrontation to deal with Peter's deteriorating behaviour and emotional state. Additionally, there appeared to be marital discord between the couple. However, the family worker was unclear whether this was a long-standing issue for them or whether the conflict was a result of their different styles in coping with this current crisis.

In order to gain a better understanding of Alex and Marina as a couple and as parents, they were invited to tell their story. Each was given equal time to explain their different perspectives on Peter's difficulties and their expertise and experience with their son was acknowledged. During these sessions, it is important to work collaboratively with the family and let them set the pace for the sessions. This is especially crucial early on and is a powerful engagement strategy.

During the first meeting with the family worker, Marina and Alex expressed their confusion about what 'had happened to Peter' describing him as 'a completely different person from what he had been before'. They vented their feelings of grief and loss, lamenting that their son had always been a bright boy with a 'brilliant future ahead of him'. They were fearful now that 'he would amount to nothing'. Their different explanatory models were explored and expressed. The family worker acknowledged that many families had difficulty accepting that their relative has a chemical imbalance of the brain and that part of the work that they had to do was to present possible explanatory models about psychosis that would make sense for the family. The family worker talked about the stress–vulnerability model and continued with the effort to teach them about psychosis so that they could better help their son in his recovery.

Stage 2: Initial Stabilisation and Facilitating Recovery

In this second stage, the family recovery model is geared towards stabilising the client and family and facilitating recovery. Here, families need information both about the disorder and about their own reactions to stress, as well as practical and emotional support to prevent longer term problems. The goals of this stage are to continue to assess family functioning after the initial crisis has waned, continue to solidify the therapeutic alliance and increase the family's knowledge of psychosis. Specifically, we want to help the family understand the recovery process (including their role in it) and raise their awareness of early warning signs of relapse. Another goal at this stage is to ensure that those families who are at high risk are engaged in specialised family care targeting the specific challenges that exist within the family. At this stage, the focus of the family intervention is largely concentrated on support, education, discussion about coping strategies and problem-solving skills around dealing with the psychosis and the impact on the young person with the illness and the family.

Back home

The family worker arranged to meet with the couple on a weekly basis to help them cope with having Peter home again. During the first few sessions, the family worker was able to assess the family's functioning and, continued to witness the friction and open conflict that existed within their marriage. They tended to blame one another for their son's illness, and were inconsistent and divided in their parenting approach. The family worker talked about treatment and recovery and stressed the importance of reducing the level of stress in the household. She encouraged them to work together as a parenting system to promote better outcomes for their son. The family worker acknowledged the couple's marital problems and contracted with them to shelve these issues for the time being until Peter was stabilised. They remained concerned that although Peter seemed to be having a positive response to his medication, he seemed listless, sad and hopeless about the future.

After a month had passed, the couple became more comfortable with the family worker and had settled into a better routine at home. Over time, it became apparent that the crisis precipitated by Peter's hospitalisation had brought other unresolved losses to the fore. These included Alex's loss of his father in a car accident when he was 10 years old and feeling 'abandoned', the losses involved in immigrating to Canada, the loss of intimacy in their marriage and the anticipated loss of the hopes, dreams and expectations that they had for their only child. The family worker facilitated these discussions and taught the couple how to communicate with one another in a more assertive way and explored their different parenting strategies. Connecting with the family in this way allowed them to better 'hear' and integrate the information that they were getting regarding First-Episode Psychosis and recovery. It also allowed them to better participate in discussions about early warning signs and being ready to deal with a potential relapse or crisis in a timely fashion.

After the foundation was set, the couple was ready to attend the Family Psychosis Education Group. This decision was made because the couple was less stressed and anxious, were well allied with the team, had made some excellent gains vis-à-vis their efforts at home with Peter and were able to focus on more than Peter's illness.

Alex and Marina attended both the 'Family Psychosis Group' and the 'Taking Care of Caregiver Group'. The groups provided Alex and Marina with ongoing emotional, educational and practical support. The Taking Care of the Caregiver Group encourages family members to find a balance between supporting their recovering relative and finding time to take care of themselves. Following the groups, the couple and family worker contracted to meet every 2–3 weeks with the understanding that should the family's need for family support change, that this contract would be amended.

Stage 3: Consolidating the Gains

Work at stage three focuses on helping the family incorporate the information they have received into their day-to-day lives. Families work on readjusting their expectations and maintaining psychological well-being. Individual treatment at this stage involves booster sessions that are focused on early warning signs of relapse, treatment adherence and targeted problem solving. The individual treatment component aims to promote for the family increased independence and individuation from the mental health system. Families identified as high risk or high need continue to receive more intensive family work from an expert family therapist, which focuses on their unique needs and challenges. Finally, at this stage families are prepared for termination from the programme.

Consolidating recovery

Over the course of several weeks, Alex and Marina tried to provide more structure for Peter and to schedule time for themselves individually and as

Table 3.4 Stage 3: Consolidating the Gains

Goals are to help family	Individual family treatment
Incorporate knowledge into day-to-day practices	Booster sessions
Actively involve the patient in a programme focused on recovery of skills	Focus on early warning signs, treatment adherence and targeted problem solving
Manage relapse risk	Promote increased independence and individuation from the system
Readjust expectations	More intensive family work from expert family therapist for high-risk and high-need families
Maintain personal psychological well-being	Termination

Source: From Addington *et al.* (2005). Copyright 2005 by Elsevier. Reprinted with permission.

Table 3.5 Stage 4: Prolonged Recovery

Goals focus on	Individual family treatment
Changing expectations	Work in this stage is individual and
Adapting to less than a full recovery	may focus on grief and loss
Transition to longer term services	
Developing a consensus regarding	
longer term prognosis	

Source: From Addington *et al.* (2005). Copyright 2005 by Elsevier. Reprinted with permission.

a couple. The family worker worked with them to increase their repertoire of parenting skills through discussion and role-playing. They enjoyed some success in their new approach and started to feel more confident in their role as parents. The family worker started to introduce the idea of termination and referral to another service for ongoing care. Peter concentrated on returning to school and was actively working with his case manager, and was making use of some of the psychosocial groups available through the First-Episode Programme. He remained socially withdrawn and reticent in these groups but was making modest gains.

Moving between stages

Families do move through the stages of recovery but this is not always smooth. Unfortunately, marital conflict between the couple re-emerged as Peter started to stabilise and returned to school. Marina arrived at one session alone and in tears. She reported that there was a lot of 'screaming and shouting going on in the family' and that Peter had been drawn into his parents' conflict. Alex and Marina had rallied together and worked as a parenting team to support their son in the early days of Peter's recovery but had now reverted to their old patterns. In hindsight, it appears that both the return to school and the conflict at home between his parents may have contributed to Peter's decision to stop his medication. Over the course of a couple of months he began to decompensate and became increasingly isolated, irritable and suspicious. His behaviour grew increasingly bizarre and Peter refused to meet with his psychiatrist and case manager. The outpatient team decided to enlist the help of the first-episode mobile team to assist with the management of this situation. Daily visits were organised so that Peter's mental status could be regularly assessed. Notably, despite the fact that Peter had become floridly psychotic, he consistently denied any suicidal or homicidal ideation. The family worker met with Alex and Marina regularly. Strategies for dealing with emergencies were discussed and rehearsed.

Despite the intense support and supervision for Peter, Marina came home one day and discovered that he had attempted to kill himself by cutting his wrists. Peter was rushed to the emergency department at his local hospital, was medically stabilised and transferred back to EPU for ongoing psychiatric treatment. It was only after the suicide attempt that Peter's father agreed to be reinvolved in the care of his son. Not unexpectedly, there was much blaming going on and the couple expressed anger about what had occurred. The solid relationship that the team had developed with this family was also on shaky ground. Specifically, the couple took an angry and blaming stance towards one another and the treatment team. It took considerable effort to reconnect with the couple following Peter's suicide attempt. Alex and Marina were understandably shaken by Peter's actions and benefited from prompt family intervention.

Alex and Marina were united in their fear and uncertainty for their son's future. Several sessions were devoted towards reminding them of the information that they had received on early warning signs of relapse, treatment and recovery which they had received in the Psychosis Education Group and in individual booster sessions with the family worker. When Peter had stabilised, he too was enlisted in discussions about the circumstances that led up to him feeling so bad that he wanted to take his life and to problem solve around identifying and responding to suicidal feelings if they emerged again. Only after absolving themselves and the team of blame could the couple come together to work on the conflict that they were experiencing. The family worker provided the couple with marital therapy during this vulnerable time and also bolstered them as a parenting unit.

Stage 4: Prolonged Recovery

The final stage of the recovery model prepares the family for transition back to either a primary care practitioner when recovery has been substantive and the ongoing services of a specialist are no longer required, or into a programme of longer term care. The focus of this stage is often centred on changing the expectations of the family, adapting to less than a full recovery and to develop a consensus regarding longer term prognosis for the patient. In these cases, treatment for the family focuses mainly on grief and loss.

Moving on

The team worked with Peter and his family for almost 2.5 years. Peter had made some gains and managed to pass his high school equivalency test. The medication was working well for Peter and he was able to achieve a good remission from psychotic symptoms. Peter had made modest gains but remained socially isolated and continued to display negative symptoms. Alex and Marina were relieved that Peter was more stable and no longer appeared to be a suicide risk, but it remained difficult for them to accept that he had a remitting and relapsing illness that may necessitate him being on medication for the rest of his life. Initially, the couple was devastated that Peter would not become an engineer or doctor as they hoped. However, as they noticed their son's steady gains, they became relieved that he was alive and could formulate new goals for himself.

During the family sessions, the family worker continued to encourage Alex and Marina to resume their lives and urged them to take care of themselves through this whole period of recovery. The family worker and the treatment team negotiated a discharge from the programme after 3 years. They worked closely with Alex, Marina and Peter to ensure that the termination and transition to the next team went as smoothly as possible.

Conclusion

We have described in detail a family intervention component embedded within a comprehensive treatment programme for individuals experiencing their first episode of psychosis. Our family component is based on a recovery of the patient framework. Our case is complicated but serves to illustrate the various interventions that can be offered along the way on the path to recovery. The issue of suicide remains a very real risk for young people and their families facing a first episode of psychosis. One that must be assessed for regularly, openly discussed with patients and their families and managed in a way that reduces or ideally eliminates the likelihood of acting on suicidal ideation.

References

Addington, J. and Addington, D. (2001) Early intervention for psychosis: the Calgary early psychosis treatment and prevention program. *The Canadian Psychiatric Association Bulletin*, **33**, 11–6.

Addington, D., Addington, J. and Patten, S.B. (1998) Depression in people with first-episode schizophrenia. *British Journal of Psychiatry*, **172** (Suppl. 33), 90–2.

Addington, J. and Burnett, P. (2004) Working with families in the early stages of psychosis, in *Psychological Interventions for Early Psychosis* (eds J.F.M. Gleeson and P.D. McGorry), John Wiley & Sons, Ltd, Chichester, pp. 99–116.

Addington, J., Coldham, E., Jones, B. *et al.* (2003) The first episode of psychosis: the experience of relatives. *Acta Psychiatrica Scandinavica*, **108**, 285–9.

Addington, J., Collins, A., McCleery, A. and Addington, D. (2005) The role of family work in early psychosis. *Schizophrenia Research*, **79**, 77–83.

Addington, J., McCleery, A. and Addington, D. (2005) Three year outcome of family work in an early psychosis program. *Schizophrenia Research*, **79**, 107–16.

Addington, J., Williams, J., Young, J. and Addington, D. (2004) Suicidal behaviour in early psychosis. *Acta Psychiatrica Scandinavica*, **109**, 116–20.

Birchwood, M., Todd, P. and Jackson, C. (1998) Early intervention in psychosis: the critical-period hypothesis. *International Clinical Psychopharmacology*, **13** (Suppl. 1), 31–40.

Falloon, I., Boyd, J.L., McGill, C.W. *et al.* (1982) Family management in the prevention of exacerbations of schizophrenia. *New England Journal of Medicine*, **306**, 1437–44.

Goldstein, M.J. (1996) Psychoeducation and family treatment related to the phase of a psychotic disorder. *International Journal of Clinical Psychopharmacology*, **11** (Suppl. 2), 77–83.

Kavanagh, D.J. (1992) Recent developments in expressed emotion and schizophrenia. *British Journal of Psychiatry*, **160**, 601–20.

Kuipers, E. and Raune, D. (2000) The early development of expressed emotion and burden in the families of first-onset psychosis, in *Early Intervention in Psychosis* (eds M. Birchwood, D. Fowler and C. Jackson), John Wiley & Sons, Ltd, Chichester, pp. 128–40.

Leff, J.P., Kuipers, L., Berkowitz, R. *et al.* (1982) A controlled trial of social intervention in the families of schizophrenic patients. *British Journal Psychiatry*, **141**, 121–34.

Linzen, D. (1993) Recent onset schizophrenic disorders: outcome prognosis and treatment. Unpublished doctoral dissertation, University of Amsterdam, Netherlands.

McFarlane, W.R., Lukens, E., Link, B. *et al.* (1995) Multiple-family groups and psychoeducation in the treatment of schizophrenia. *Archives of General Psychiatry*, **52**, 679–87.

Meltzer, H.Y. (2001) Treatment of suicidality in schizophrenia, in *The Clinical Science of Suicide Prevention. Annals of the New York Academy of Science*, Vol **932** (eds H. Hendi and J.J. Mann), pp. 44–60.

Mortensen, P.B. and Juel, K. (1993) Mortality and the causes of death in first admitted schizophrenic patients. *British Journal of Psychiatry*, **163**, 183–9.

Mueser, K.T. and Glynn, S.M. (eds) (1999) *Behavioral Family Therapy for Psychiatric Disorders*, 2nd edn, New Harbinger Publications, Inc., Oakland, CA.

Nuechterlein, K.H., Snyder, K.S. and Mintz, J. (1992) Paths to relapse: possible transactional processes connecting patient illness onset, expressed emotion and psychotic relapse. *British Journal of Psychiatry*, **161** (Suppl. 18), 88–96.

Penn, D. and Mueser, K. (1996) Research update on the psychosocial treatment of schizophenia. *American Journal of Psychiary*, **153**, 607–17.

Smith, J., Berthelsen, D. and O'Connor, I. (1997) Child adjustment in high conflict families. *Child Care and Health Development*, **23**, 113–33.

Stirling, J., Tantam, D., Thomas, P. *et al.* (1991) Expressed emotion and early onset schizophrenia: a one-year follow-up. *Psychological Medicine*, **21**, 675–85.

Tarrier, N., Barrowclough, C. and Porceddu, K. (1988) The community management of schizophrenia: a controlled trial of behavioural intervention with families to reduce relapse. *British Journal of Psychiatry*, **153**, 532–42.

Tennakoon, L., Fannon, D., Doku, V. *et al.* (2000) Experience of caregiving: relatives of people experiencing a first episode of psychosis. *British Journal of Psychiatry*, **177**, 529–33.

Tsuang, M.T. (1978) Suicide in schizophrenics, manics, depressives, and surgical controls. *Archives of General Psychiatry*, **35**, 153–5.

Young, A.S., Nuechterlein, K.H., Mintz, J. *et al.* (1998). Suicidal ideation and suicide attempts in recent-onset schizophrenia. *Schizophrenia Bulletin*, **24**, 629–34.

Resources

1. The Centre for Suicide Prevention – Youth at Risk of Suicide, http://www.suicideinfo.ca/youthatrisk/index.htm (accessed 5 January 2009).

    Operated by the Centre for Suicide Prevention in Calgary Canada, this website provides useful information about suicide to young people, their families and mental health workers.

2. Schizophrenia Society of Canada (SSOC), www.schizophrenia.ca (accessed 5 January 2009).

    The SSOC web page contains useful links for support and education available to family members including web-based pamphlets, a toll-free support line and a discussion board. Also available on this site is the .pdf version of *Rays of Hope*, the SSOC's reference manual for families, http://www.schizophrenia.ca/RaysofHope.pdf (accessed 5 January 2009).

3. Baklar, P. (1995) At risk: suicide and schizophrenia, in *The Family Face of Schizophrenia: True Stories of Mental Illness with Practical Counsel from America's Leading Experts*, Putnam, New York, pp. 201–23.

    This chapter opens with a case example of a mother's struggle with her son's psychotic illness and eventual suicide attempt, followed by a commentary by J.L. Geller, M.D.

4

Working with Families to Prevent Relapse in First-Episode Psychosis

Kingsley Crisp and John Gleeson

Outline of the Chapter

This chapter provides an overview of a family intervention for the prevention of relapse in First-Episode Psychosis (FEP). The research context for the intervention is described, the theoretical basis and structure of the therapy is outlined and a detailed case example is provided.

Context for the Intervention

The intervention was developed at the Early Psychosis Prevention and Intervention Centre (EPPIC) (McGorry *et al.*, 1996). Within the EPPIC outpatient programme, family work developed as an integral component of case management, supplemented by an introductory group-based psychoeducational programme for families, specialist individual family work and a family peer support programme (Gleeson *et al.*, 1999). The principles of family work at EPPIC are:

- Family work needs to be developed within a collaborative framework.
- Family work should empower the family to cope and adjust to the crisis of the psychotic illness.
- The overall goals of intervention are to minimise the disruption to the life of the family and to maximise the adaptive functioning of the family after the acute episode (Gleeson *et al.*, 1999).

A Casebook of Family Interventions for Psychosis   Edited by Fiona Lobban and Christine Barrowclough
© 2009 John Wiley & Sons, Ltd

- The specific needs of the family should be acknowledged because the family environment may impact on the young person's experience and recovery but also because the family needs support through a distressing period (Addington and Burnett, 2004).
- The approach to pre-existing problems within the family should be guided by general crisis intervention principles.

Alongside the evolution of the clinical programme, a significant programme of clinically focused research has occurred at EPPIC, including a tradition of psychosocial studies (Edwards *et al.*, 2003; Edwards *et al.*, 2002; Jackson *et al.*, 2001). An initial naturalistic follow-up study undertaken in the mid and late 1990s by the second author (JG) examined the predictive validity of psychological variables in relapse in FEP clients who had reached remission on psychotic symptoms (Gleeson *et al.*, 2005; Gleeson *et al.*, 2006). This work formed the basis for a collaboration that initiated a relapse prevention trial at EPPIC (Gleeson, 2005).

The next step was to develop an intervention that could be evaluated within a randomised controlled trial, which was entitled EPISODE II (Gleeson, 2005). The study, funded by Eli Lilly via the Lilly Melbourne Academic Consortium (Singh *et al.*, 2004), aimed to prevent the rate of relapse and the time to relapse in FEP clients who responded to treatment.

The rationale for the study was based on findings from naturalistic follow-up studies that, despite the high rate of remission following the commencement of treatment after diagnosis in FEP, relapse rates are in the range 50–80% over the 2-year follow-up period (Gitlin *et al.*, 2001; Robinson *et al.*, 1999). The longer term prevention of a second episode remains an avowed (but largely unrealised) aim for many clients of specialist FEP programmes (Edwards and McGorry, 2002).

The design of EPISODE II consisted of an effectiveness trial with standard EPPIC follow-up treatment used as the control 'treatment-as-usual' intervention for a specific relapse-prevention treatment (RPT) that combined individual and family components.

In the process of consenting to treatment, clients were asked to provide consent for a family member to be approached for participation in baseline and follow-up family measures, and if randomised to RPT, separate individual family sessions.

Recruitment to the study was completed in May 2005, with 82 participants recruited to the study and randomised, with 127 clients refusing participation. To be eligible clients needed to score at a mild or lower range for at least 4 weeks on the psychotic items of the Brief Psychiatric Rating Scale (Ventura *et al.*, 1993). A total of 66 consented to their family being involved, with 25 families eventually participating within the RPT condition. All families were engaged as soon as possible after remission was reached. Many families had already received introductory psychoeducation, and had been offered peer support.

Collection of follow-up data is expected to be completed by December 2007. Treatment manuals have been developed for both the individual and family-based components and are available on request from the second author (JG).

Theoretical influences on the approach used

The research team was strongly influenced by behavioural family therapy tradition in schizophrenia and FEP (Falloon, 1988), but were also mindful that these interventions were most effective in high expressed emotion family contexts. The present intervention was designed to be applicable to all families with a relative who had responded to treatment. The scope of the interventions was therefore deliberately broadened beyond communications skills and problem solving to educate and enlist the family as critical agents in activating relapse prevention strategies when required, and to address the emotional needs of the family.

The CBT (cognitive behavioural therapy) framework informed the assessment and individualised formulation of potentially problematic coping responses and communication patterns within the family. For example, the family worker paid specific attention to the assessment of beliefs and attributions regarding the psychosis and responses of the family to their relative (Barrowclough and Hooley, 2003), and the therapist adopted an active style in intervening to assist families to revise problematic patterns. For the purposes of this intervention, these techniques were targeted towards family-specific issues, beliefs and cognitions, particularly those associated with

- inappropriate self-blame and profound anxiety;
- misattributions regarding problems (controllability, illness/non-illness differentiation);
- unrealistic expectations (regarding client functioning, of family members themselves, aspects of treatment or the role of clinicians);
- inaccurate information (regarding any aspect of disorder/treatment).

Specific issues associated with working with first-episode families

Specific issues and challenges were explored in weekly supervision sessions, which consisted of both individual sessions for the family worker and group supervision sessions, which were also attended by the individual therapists. Many of these challenges were familiar to the family worker and the research team from prior clinical experience.

Engagement and motivation. The motivation of family members to attend family meetings is often high in the early stages of treatment and recovery (Addington *et al.*, 2003). The level of involvement of families in the treatment process and supportive programmes can wane in later phases, particularly if a good symptomatic remission is achieved and there is an absence of comorbid difficulties. Some ambivalence regarding family member participation in the intervention was expected, as it has been found to be difficult to engage families in relapse prevention focused interventions during remission or periods of relative stability (Miklowitz and Goldstein, 1997).

Explanatory models of psychosis. Forming an explanation for what has happened to their relative is often a difficulty for FEP families. During the aftermath of the initial episode, the family may not yet have a shared explanation of psychosis. Competing or conflicting explanations may affect perceptions of behaviour, beliefs about the future and fuel conflict within the family. For some family members, ideas regarding vulnerability to relapse may be incongruent with their explanation.

Illness/non-illness differentiation. The onset of psychosis typically occurs in late adolescence or early adulthood, which is a period of intense change and development. It may be difficult to differentiate between the product of an illness process and other developmental issues, increasing the potential for conflicting interpretations of behaviour.

The challenge of balancing anxiety and optimism. Striking a balance between remaining optimistic, by emphasising positive and realistic outcomes for the client on the one hand, and equipping the family for potential challenges ahead is a significant challenge. The research team was mindful of avoiding 'over sensitising' family members which could lead to unnecessary levels of vigilance or anxiety, perhaps placing pressure on relationships and increasing a sense of burden.

Detecting early warning signs (EWS). Research on relapse prevention within psychosis has focused on multi-episode schizophrenia and bipolar disorder (Birchwood and Spencer, 2001; Herz *et al.*, 2000). 'Relapse signatures' have typically been identified by reviewing EWS within relapse prodromes (Birchwood *et al.*, 1989). However, in FEP, the EWS and degree of vulnerability to relapse are difficult to predict. Despite these limitations, the current intervention placed strong emphasis on the value of EWS detection as one important approach to the prevention of relapse.

Information needs. In FEP, families often have little or no prior knowledge of the disorder. Confusion is often further compounded by the prevalence of several DSM-IV (APA, 1994) Axis I and Axis II comorbid disorders (Strakowski *et al.*, 1993). In addition to receiving information, family members also need an opportunity to come to terms with the emotional impact of psychosis and process their own reactions.

Style and structure of the intervention

The intervention was comprised of the following phases:

- Phase I – Engagement and assessment, including a review of the family's experience of their relative's psychosis, burden and coping.
- Phase II – Information sharing – consisting of psychoeducation regarding psychosis and relapse.
- Phase III – EWS recognition and management, including documentation of a relapse prevention plan.
- Phase IV – Role of family in recovery – including the assessment of communication skills and problem solving.
- Phase V – Addressing problems and achieving goals; a needs-based phase which included additional cognitive behavioural interventions for specific problems.
- Phase VI – Review and completion.

Interventions typically included psychoeducation regarding psychosis with a specific emphasis upon relapse, behavioural experimentation, circular and Socratic questioning, communication skills enhancement and formal problem solving. All families were actively engaged in a process of constructing likely lists of EWS and planning for their occurrence.

The individual family work dovetailed with the individual therapy in a joint session during the development of the relapse prevention plan.

Therapist Training and Experience

The first author (KC) was the sole family therapist in the EPISODE II intervention. He had 8 years experience as the outpatient Family Worker at EPPIC. He was formally trained in systemic family therapy and cognitive behavioural family approaches.

The Clinical Service

The EPPIC is a comprehensive mental health service for young people aged 15–25 years residing in the Western Metropolitan Region of Melbourne who are experiencing the onset of a first episode of a psychotic disorder (McGorry *et al.*, 1996). The core components of the clinical service include: a triage and assessment team, a home treatment team, an acute inpatient unit, an outpatient case management programme, a group programme and an intensive outreach programme.

Constraints on the Intervention

The constraints of the research study required that the family intervention be provided within a 7-month period, including up to 15 sessions, usually 1–1.5 hours in duration. The young person's formal consent was required in order to invite the families to participate.

Case Example

Background

Ruben is an 18-year-old unemployed male residing at home with his parents, Juan and Ana, and his 12-year-old brother, Elias. Ruben was initially referred to ORYGEN Youth Health by his school welfare coordinator in

December 2003, with a 2-month history of deterioration in mental state characterised by depressed mood associated with suicidal thoughts, poor sleep and appetite, weight loss and increased alcohol consumption. In addition, he reported a 6-week history of mood-congruent auditory hallucinations, persecutory beliefs and ideas of reference.

Juan and Ana began to be concerned about Ruben when he started spending more time with peers involved in gangs and less time at school, where he was in his final year of secondary education. They also noticed that he had become withdrawn as well as verbally aggressive and threatening towards them, particularly his father. Attempts to have Ruben assessed by their family General Practitioner and counselled by their priest were rejected by Rubin.

Possible precipitants included the breakdown of Ruben's relationship with his girlfriend of 2 years and the stabbing murder of a friend 3 months prior to his admission.

Juan, Ana and Ruben were born in El Salvador and moved to Australia to escape the civil war when Ruben was 6 months old. Some of Juan's family members had subsequently joined them, while the majority of Ana's family remained in El Salvador. While they all had some difficulties adjusting to their new home and language, they reported settling in well, with Rubin doing well at school and both Juan and Ana finding work. They described the family as 'very close' and there was no known family history of mental illness.

Ruben was commenced on anti-depressant and anti-psychotic medications during an admission to the ORYGEN Inpatient Unit and was readmitted in early February 2004, in the context of being intoxicated with alcohol and threatening to harm himself and others. This led to his father physically restraining him until the arrival of the assessment team. Once discharged, Ruben remained well engaged and cooperative with treatment, achieving remission of all positive symptoms in May 2004.

Prior to involvement with EPISODE II, Juan and Ana were involved in psychosocial interventions including a four-session psychoeducation group, monthly attendance at a support group and regular meetings with treating team members.

Referral to EPISODE II

Having reached remission, Ruben was referred to the EPISODE II trial by his case manager in June 2004. Although he had previously declined to be involved in family work, he was happy for his parents to meet regularly with a family worker, who was not directly involved in his care. Once Rubin was randomised to the therapy group, Ana was contacted by the Research Assistant who introduced her to the project and gave an outline of the aims of the intervention. The family worker then arranged a time to meet with Ana and Juan, who were keen to be involved.

Engagement methods/issues

The first two sessions of the intervention were conceptualised as the engagement and assessment phase.

Engagement was facilitated by outlining the goals of the sessions with an emphasis on the preventative nature of the work, along with the likely benefits of participation.

The following points were made to 'set the scene' and convey a non-blaming attitude:

- Families do not cause psychosis but can play an important role in helping their relative to recover and stay well.
- The purpose of the meetings is to help support the family, not to judge or blame.
- Families have important information that will assist in helping their relative.
- Relapse rates are high and we do not have an accurate or reliable way of predicting who will or will not relapse.
- The sessions help prepare a plan of action in case early signs reappear.
- Having families, clients and clinicians involved and 'pulling' together is important and can be strengthened by involvement in the sessions.

Already highly motivated to engage in the work, the first meeting progressed into a debriefing or reflecting session in which Juan and Ana recapped the 'story so far'.

Assessment methods

The needs of the family were assessed by reviewing their experience of the treatment system, the impact of the psychosis on the family and the identification of immediate concerns, social support needs and strengths.

The second session focused on the assessment of their knowledge and understanding of psychosis, including beliefs about the possibility of relapse, current expectations of Ruben and how they were relating with him.

A formulation was developed, facilitated by individual and group supervision sessions. The latter included Ruben's individual therapist who was able to report on his perspective of the situation at home.

Formal assessment of communication and problem-solving skills was undertaken in phase IV. The rationale for the teaching of these skills and their assessment has been described elsewhere in detail (Falloon, 1988; Mueser and Glynn, 1999).

Formulation (shared understanding of problems)

It was clear that Juan and Ana were very caring and supportive parents, had remarkably similar views and concerns and were highly anxious about Ruben's future and their need to 'do more' to support him. Their experiences of the war appeared to have contributed to their belief formation that the world is an unsafe place, which led to extreme anxiety about Ruben's safety, even in response to developmentally appropriate behaviour. Their fears seemed to be confirmed by the recent stabbing death of one of Ruben's friends and the emergence of the psychotic episode.

In the prodromal phase, they initially attributed Ruben's behaviour change to 'teenage bad behaviour' and sometimes angrily confronted him. After increased aggression from Ruben, they soon took a 'hands-off' parenting approach until it became clear that he was unwell. They now felt guilty about this and had since become wary of making any demands on him for fear of causing more conflict and 'stressing him out'.

The profound emotional impact of the episode was described as a 'nightmare' that shocked and frightened them. The confusing and traumatic nature of the episode was reflected in Ana's statement, 'People took our child away and we didn't know why.'

In terms of their understanding of the episode, they were able to identify the positive psychotic symptoms Ruben had experienced but continued to be puzzled as to whether behaviour changes were illness related.

Their causal explanation for the episode was 'external' and 'unstable' – that is, they attributed changes to outside stressors and influences (bad 'gang' friends, conflict with girlfriend, listening to 'depressing/angry music') that would resolve once removed. This led them to perceive their role as primarily one of protecting him from stress, which they were attempting to do by

- restricting his late-night phone use to ensure he had enough sleep;
- vetting phone calls from 'gang' members;
- checking on him by phoning him multiple times when he was out, or driving over to his new girlfriend's house to see if he was there, rather than with 'gang' members;
- restricting his use of the family car;
- attempting to shield him from 'depressing' television shows and music;
- monitoring his medication compliance;
- taking responsibility for Ruben's attendance at outpatient appointments.

Their determination to be more involved in this way appeared to be fuelled by feelings of guilt and regret regarding a sense of having failed to 'protect' him, as well as a perception, not shared by the treating team members, that Ruben was suffering from an enduring illness that needed continuous close monitoring. However, they were aware that their attempts to shield him from stress were perceived as invasive and resulted in conflict or avoidance. This in turn, increased their levels of anxiety and vigilance, making it difficult to 'step back'.

Although they had both returned to work after a period of absence during the acute phase, they had not returned to their usual routines regarding recreational and social activities and they were both having occasional sleeping difficulties. They felt their son's illness reflected badly on them as parents and talked about feeling 'like a failure as parents' and that they 'must have done something wrong'.

They were obviously burdened with an enormous sense of responsibility for Ruben's well-being, placing them at high risk of 'burnout' and escalating conflict. After sharing the formulation with them, the following goals were developed:

- Increase understanding of psychosis (including relapse risks and realistic expectations).
- Develop an EWS action plan (including strategies for reducing the risk of relapse).
- Reduce conflict with Ruben (including establishing household rules).

They agreed with the suggestion that additional areas to focus on would be to

- manage their own anxiety and stress;
- resume usual roles and routines;
- increase supports available to the family (including Elias)
- identify the strengths of the family.

Intervention

Phase II information sharing (two sessions at weekly intervals). Sessions 3 and 4 were offered as an opportunity to 'fill in the gaps' of knowledge using EPPIC fact sheets and other written materials to facilitate discussion. Information regarding psychosis was shared from a bio-psychosocial perspective using a vulnerability–stress model (Zubin and Spring, 1977). Particular reference was made to the symptoms exhibited by Ruben to maximise the relevancy of the information and it was suggested that Juan and Ana keep handouts from this and future meetings in a folder that they could bring to subsequent sessions.

Ana and Juan were encouraged to read information again between sessions and to bring any questions they had to the next meeting. They returned the following week with a lengthy list, which underlined a tendency to blame themselves for not having acted to circumvent the episode, regret at not noticing prodromal symptoms (despite evidence to the contrary), and uncertainty as to how best to support Ruben.

Specific coping skills that facilitate recovery and reduce the families' sense of burden were then reviewed with emphasis on the many positive ways in which they were supporting Ruben, including providing a stable living situation, offering warmth and support, learning more about psychosis and seeking support for themselves. Finally, factors associated with an increased risk of relapse were discussed and it was noted that Ruben and the family were doing all the 'right' things in this regard.

The difficulty of predicting a client's vulnerability to relapse in the first episode formed the basis for 'realistic optimism', while focusing attention on preventative opportunities and acknowledging that there will be factors that remain outside of the control of the family.

Phase III – development of an early warning signs action plan (three sessions at weekly intervals). The fifth session began by providing the rationale for

EWS identification and a brief discussion regarding some common EWS. Given their level of anxiety regarding their son's future, heavy emphasis was placed on the positive connotation of the word 'warning' as something that 'gives notice' and allows time to prepare and act. A thorough review of Juan and Ana's experience of the prodrome was used as the basis for identifying possible EWS and to construct a prevention and action plan. The aims of this process were to

- provide further opportunity to discuss and process an array of emotional reactions associated with the chaos of the emerging illness;
- gather the experience and knowledge gained by the family during the initial episode and incorporate it into future planning;
- further differentiate between possible early symptoms and 'problem' behaviour;
- decrease the likelihood of 'false positives';
- further identify and explore beliefs that might influence how family members are likely to act in the future;
- emphasise and maximise Ruben's role in relapse prevention;
- clarify the limitations of their role – hopefully reducing their sense of responsibility for monitoring.

Additional signs noted in the medical records assessment were discussed and added to the list they had generated (see Table 4.1 for final list).

This was a difficult process, particularly for Ana, who became teary when recalling the incidents preceding the second admission. These feelings were acknowledged and normalised in the context of an emerging illness they could not have predicted. Concerns that they did not act quickly enough persisted, despite contrary evidence that they had arranged two appointments with their General Practitioner.

It was emphasised that early signs were likely to involve a number of changes occurring over a few days, as it became clear that Ana and Juan believed a single stressful event would lead to a full relapse.

At the start of the sixth session, Juan and Ana reported that Ruben had instigated a discussion regarding prodromal symptoms during the week, a task he had agreed to undertake as part of his individual relapse prevention therapy running in parallel with the family work. They were very pleased with this, as it was the first time he had talked to them about what had happened and, in the course of the discussion, they recalled additional early behavioural changes, which were added to the list.

Table 4.1 Early Warning Signs Action Plan

	Early warning signs	What Ruben can do	What family can do
Early (more than one sign for more than a few days)	Confused/puzzled Not feeling like eating[1] Decreased concentration Spending more money than usual Thinking or feeling I'm being laughed at or talked about[1] (neighbour) Withdrawn[1] Non-communicative[1] Having a lot of showers[2]	Talk about problems with family members Mention to Mum and Dad that I'm having a hard time Use Uncle Andre and Godmother as extra supports Remember it is important to get help early to prevent relapse Contact Case Manager or Doctor Try strategies to help to reduce tension–exercise. Listen to music, write poems about how I'm feeling, drink chamomile tea	Speak to Ruben and each other about any changes that have been noticed Understand that Ruben may need some 'space' Talk clearly without 'nagging' Encourage him to contact doctor Encourage Ruben to use his strategies to reduce tension
Middle	Sleep becoming restless or unsettled[1] Feeling aggressive or pushy[1] Becoming more rebellious and arrogant, speaking my mind[1] Being preoccupied with one or two things Feeling quiet or withdrawn[1] Thoughts racing Feeling tired, having less energy[1]		

(*Continued*)

Table 4.1 (*Continued*)

	Early warning signs	What Ruben can do	What family can do
Middle	Feeling useless/helpless Having migraines Needing very little sleep Behaving odd or differently Feeling depressed/low[1] Feeling stubborn/refusing simple tasks Feeling dissatisfied with myself Hearing things others cannot hear	Make sure I've called ORYGEN, get an appointment to see them Take time out Keep up social contacts and supports Avoid alcohol Try to get back on medication if I have stopped it, talk to doctor about options for increasing or changing medication and if this will help	Speak to Ruben about calling Doctor/Case manager for advice Allow space Try to reduce our own stress Use our supports Speak to our Priest
Late	Feeling like I'm going crazy Losing my temper[1] Being irritable and quick tempered[1] Feeling violent (violent drawings)[2] Being more aware of my surroundings Increased anxiety/panic attacks Suicidal ideas[2]	Talk to Case Manager and Doctor about things to help manage anger Think about going to inpatient unit for a short stay to get things back on track and to protect the family	Tell Ruben we will contact Doctor/Case Manager

[1] Indicates signs identified by Ruben and parents.
[2] Indicates signs identified by parents only.

They also brought in a letter Ana had written which summarised the main points of the discussion, while indicating they had continuing regrets. The letter read, in part:

> When our son was starting to get this illness we didn't know that this (sic) were the symptoms ... we thought that those things (preoccupation, being tense, tired, afraid, not wanting to eat, always in his room listening to music very loud) were teenage behaviours ... he also had thoughts of harming himself because he thought that not (sic) body did care about him. But he was wrong because he knows now that his family cares and loves him very much.

This led to further normalising of emotional reactions and a discussion regarding the difficulty of early detection. It was highlighted that they took swift action in seeking help even though the exact nature of their concerns was unclear.

Having identified several signs, the information was organised in chronological order using a timeline exercise on a white board. The symptoms were then sorted into phases (early, middle, late) (Smith, 2001). Stressful events that may have triggered the symptoms were then identified before further discussion of how they sought help, their emotional reactions and associated key thoughts and beliefs.

When asked what they would do differently if they had their time again, they replied that they would speak to Ruben earlier, as he was thought to be too angry and unwell by the time they initially raised concerns. They could not think of other ways in which they might have acted differently and this was emphasised in an attempt to allay persistent guilt.

The session ended with a brief discussion of the aims of the next session, a joint one that would include Ruben and his individual therapist.

During a group supervision session prior to this session, the family worker and individual therapist met to compare the EWS lists generated by Ruben and his parents and they were found to have many common elements. It was clear from Ruben's strategy list that he interpreted many of his parents' current actions as intrusive and unwanted and this was a motivating factor for his involvement in the next meeting.

A clear agenda was set for the joint meeting to keep the focus on the task of developing the EWS action plan and to establish a 'client-as-expert' approach. The meeting was used to share information regarding EWS, stress management strategies and to discuss roles regarding monitoring, emphasising the potential benefits of working on this together such as

- offering the family an opportunity to learn more about Ruben's experience and have a clear agreed plan of action;
- clarifying how Ruben would like to be supported;
- helping Ana and Juan not to 'panic' or 'jump the gun';
- assisting in developing a shared language with which to discuss mental health concerns and differentiate them from other issues (e.g. parental authority regarding household rules, disagreements regarding limits).

Ruben shared a copy of his EWS list and coping strategies and he agreed to add additional signs his parents had noticed, before discussing the coping strategies he had identified in working with his individual therapist.

In discussing Ruben's request for 'space', his intention to protect his parents from worry became apparent, leading to a cycle of avoidance and non-communicativeness sparking greater parental anxiety and increased monitoring and questioning.

They were all encouraged to appraise the advantages and disadvantages of communicating concerns and attempting to circumvent the cycle, which led to the following exchange:

ANA: We would worry less if you can say what is happening, it would help us to know why things are different.

JUAN: Yes it would help us to be able to give you space.

RUBEN: I hope so. I got frustrated because you panicked last time and got stressed, and that made me more stressed. That's why I lashed out so much.

Other elements of the plan were discussed involving the anticipation of any difficulties regarding how it might be implemented. Still not quite convinced of his parents' ability not to 'panic', Ruben suggested that he might contact his uncle to discuss problems as a first step and that he should also have a copy of the plan. Finally, the opportunity was taken to highlight their positive efforts in supporting each other and the extent of Ruben's recovery was emphasised.

At the next session, Ana and Juan reported that their anxiety regarding the likelihood of relapse was unchanged, but they felt better equipped should it occur.

Phase IV role of the family in managing stress

Sessions 8 and 9 (fortnightly intervals). This phase of the intervention began with a review of the many positive ways in which Ana and Juan had helped to create a positive emotional environment to support Ruben during his recovery. These included managing conflict with him, modifying their expectations of him during the acute and early recovery stages and communicating love, warmth and support.

This led to a further discussion of the importance of attending to factors the family can realistically hope to influence, such as allowing Juan 'space' at times, and the recovery of the family (looking after themselves, managing their own stress and resuming usual family life). The meeting then segued into the major focus of this phase, the introduction and assessment of the core skills involved in communicating clearly and the use of a six-step problem-solving model.

Both Juan and Ana were able to demonstrate sound communication skills in practice role-play, as they had done throughout the previous meetings. It was also clear they possessed good problem-solving skills and were proficient in using the six-step model.

Phase V – solving problems and achieving goals

Sessions 10–14 (fortnightly intervals). At the start of the next session, time was taken to reflect on the progress towards the goals and to re-establish an agenda for the remaining sessions. Ana and Juan felt they had a clearer understanding of psychosis and were now better prepared to know when and how to seek help if early signs reappeared. This helped lessen their concern that Ruben would relapse suddenly.

However, at each session they continued to present with concerns relating to their perceived failure to restrict Ruben's socialising and hence, reduce his stress. It was noted that, as Ruben's recovery continued, the focus of their anxiety centred on his general safety when not at home.

A revised agenda was set with the following goals:

- Establish rules regarding Ruben's use of the family car.
- Resume previous activities (Juan to play soccer/Ana to visit friends and family).
- Explore ways of reducing monitoring of Ruben.

- Develop strategies to reduce Ana and Juan's anxiety.
- Explore strategies to reduce conflict between Elias and Ruben (explain illness and modified expectations to Elias and spend more time with him).
- Update and finalise the EWS action plan.

In establishing the agenda, it was clear that the problem regarding the continuing conflict associated with the use of the family car was their top priority.

A cognitive behavioural assessment of the problem was undertaken, which revealed the extent of their worry and the impact of their attempts to set limits and cope. This included the following:

- Ringing Ruben every $\frac{1}{2}$ hour while he was out.
- Taking the car keys from him when he returned home (to ensure he did not go out again).
- Inability to sleep until he returned home (particularly Ana).
- Having relatives phone to check on him when he was home alone.
- Ongoing conflict with Ruben.

They were well aware that their anxiety was excessive and had negative consequences, which were clarified by bringing the absent Ruben 'into the room', as illustrated by the following exchange:

FAMILY WORKER:	If he was sitting here and we asked him, 'How do you want your parents to support you, what would you like them to do and not do?' What would he say?
ANA:	I know we have to protect him, but sometimes we are so protective, I don't think it is right.
JUAN:	Maybe we are over reacting.
FAMILY WORKER:	Is that what Ruben would say?
JUAN:	Yes, that we were worrying for nothing.
FAMILY WORKER:	What else would he say?
ANA:	You should trust me; you should not tell me who I can see.
JUAN:	Yes but how, if he doesn't always tell us the truth about where he is going?
FAMILY WORKER:	Why is that do you think?
JUAN:	He doesn't want us to know who he is with.
FAMILY WORKER:	And why is that?
JUAN:	He doesn't want us to worry.

Further, exploration of the content of their worry elicited several catastrophic thoughts relating to Ruben being harmed in some way, including gang violence and motor vehicle accidents. The importance of the impact of the psychotic episode was discussed, with Ana stating, 'Before he was sick, I never thought like this. I remember saying to my sister, "My children are too good to be true." Two months later Ruben got sick and now I think, "What else will go wrong?" ' This led to a discussion of the perceived benefits of the protective power of anxiety and remaining 'on guard', with Juan adding another possible advantage with a story from his past. When he was Ruben's age, his father had not set limits on him, but had allowed him to do 'anything I wanted'. Juan had interpreted this as his father 'not caring', and he was determined not to convey that message to his son.

Traditional cognitive behavioural methods were used to address catastrophic thoughts associated with Ruben being home later than expected. A thought record was used to identify the event, thoughts, feelings (with rating of intensity) and behavioural responses, before exploring the evidence for and against the thoughts. Alternative thoughts were easily generated by both Juan and Ana, who were then encouraged to test the effects of new behaviour as illustrated below:

FAMILY WORKER: It's hard for you to see him going out late at night at the moment. It sounds like what you are trying to do is to show you support him and want to protect him from stress.

ANA: Yes, but I don't want to nag him and fight about it.

FAMILY WORKER: Are there other things you could say or do that would better fit in with your intention to support him and the alternative, realistic thoughts you have identified?

ANA: I'm not sure.

FAMILY WORKER: What if we wrote down the realistic thoughts you identified so you could refer to them the next time he is out late at night, would that help?

ANA: I guess I could remind myself that he's most likely ok. I'm not sure if it will help though.

FAMILY WORKER: I'm not either. I guess it will be an experiment to see if it does help.

ANA: Ok, I'll try it this week.

FAMILY WORKER: Ok, is there anything else you could do that might lessen your worry at these times?

JUAN: Stop trying to ring him. He won't answer anyway and you just worry more.

FAMILY WORKER: What might you do instead of ring?
ANA: I could try writing to my cousin who lives in El Salvador.
                              That might take my mind off worrying.

Both agreed that they would need to explain to Ruben that they would be 'backing off' and their reasons for this, with statements being generated and rehearsed during the session.

At the start of session 14, Ana reported that Ruben had attended an outpatient appointment with his case manager during the week, even though she and Juan had forgotten about this and had not reminded or woken him as they usually would. This opened the door to finding other ways of 'stepping back' and giving more responsibility to Ruben that would also convey greater trust.

Attention then turned to the recent conflict between Elias and Ruben. This was thought to be driven by resentment regarding the amount of time Juan and Ana had been spending with Ruben since his psychotic episode. The commonality of this issue was discussed prior to setting goals aimed at increasing time with Elias. Finally, homework regarding the resumption of social and recreational activities was set.

Phase VI (review and completion)

Session 15 (3 weeks later). The last session was spent reviewing and reinforcing the positive work they had done throughout the intervention. Both reported a reduction in anxiety and improved sleep, although Ana had made partial progress on her goals relating to resuming social activities.

The EWS plan was revisited and updated with relevant contact numbers. Hints for communicating with professionals in the event of EWS were reviewed, prior to emphasising 'take-home' messages, such as

- several days/weeks of warning are most likely;
- They are both knowledgeable regarding what signs are likely to give warning and how to support Ruben;
- They know how to seek help if needed.

The importance of continuing to focus on further reducing their stress levels was captured when Juan said, 'We need to look after our own stress, because that is what might make us have bad judgement.'

The final word went to Ana: 'I am less stressed than before, but still worried about doing the wrong thing.'

Critical reflection

All members of the family seem to have been aware of their emotions and that their attempts to cope with them provided some relief but also entrenched problems. The family work aimed to provide a space to reflect on these emotions and the communication patterns they gave rise to. It seemed important to focus on strengths and communicate a non-blaming attitude to provide enough safety for the family to acknowledge the benefits of stepping out of their usual patterns of relating with Ruben. Although the focus of the work was on current problems and patterns, the assessment of the background themes of trauma and feeling cared for, seemed helpful in building a meaningful therapeutic alliance. In addition, it was important to collaboratively re-examine these issues in order to help enable the family to use another framework to experiment with alternative ways of using their sound problem-solving skills.

Ruben's involvement in this process also seems to have helped to create some space for him to more directly negotiate his needs. Booster sessions would have been helpful to consolidate gains but this was not possible due to time constraints.

Comments from the family

Eighteen months after completion of the intervention, Juan, Ana and Ruben (not their real names) were contacted to seek their permission to write the case study and to include their comments. They granted permission on the proviso that their names be changed.

Looking back, Ana reported the most helpful aspect for her was the focus on her thinking and ways of reducing stress. Juan thought the development of the EWS action plan and the opportunity to hear about Ruben's experiences was most valuable and helped to clarify expectations of each other. Both would have liked the opportunity to have more meetings involving Ruben. Although not keen on this, Ruben thought the meetings had helped to reduce tension at home.

Since completion of the family work, Ana and Juan's anxiety levels have risen on a few occasions, most notably when Ruben ceased medication shortly after being discharged from EPPIC to the care of a private psychiatrist. Juan and Ana reported to have used the EWS plan twice to facilitate discussion with Ruben regarding behaviour changes. At the time of writing, Ruben remained symptom free.

Conclusion

The case example presented here is representative of a subgroup of families who participated in the EPISODE II intervention and highlights the often-overwhelming emotional impact of FEP.

The tendency for some families to blame themselves for their relative's condition was evident here, and this can be difficult to address with information and reassurance alone.

Like many FEP families, they prioritised the well-being of their relative above their own and it was necessary to be assertive regarding focusing on their own goals and stress.

This case illustrates an attempt to integrate a cognitive behavioural approach within a systemic perspective and provides a family-based parallel with the recent emphasis in the individual CBT literature upon the role of emotional processes in maintaining psychosis and the place for CBT in ameliorating them (Birchwood, 2003).

References

Addington, J. and Burnett, P. (2004) Working with families in the early stages of psychosis, in *The First Psychotic Relapse: Understanding the Risks and the Opportunities for Prevention* (eds J.F. Gleeson and P.D. McGorry), John Wiley & Sons, Ltd, Chichester.

Addington, J., Coldham, E.L., Jones, B. *et al.* (2003) The first episode of psychosis: the experience of relatives. *Acta Psychiatrica Scandinavica*, **108**, 285–9.

American Psychiatric Association (1994) *Diagnostic and Statistical Manual of Mental Disorders*, 4th edn, American Psychiatric Association, Washington, DC.

Barrowclough, C. and Hooley, J.M. (2003) Attributions and expressed emotion: a review. *Clinical Psychology Review*, **23**, 849–80.

Birchwood, M. (2003) Pathways to emotional dysfunction in first-episode psychosis. *British Journal of Psychiatry*, **182**, 373–5.

Birchwood, M., Smith, J., Macmillan, F. *et al.* (1989) Predicting relapse in schizophrenia: the development of an early signs monitoring system using patients and families as observers, a preliminary investigation. *Psychological Medicine*, **19**, 649–56.

Birchwood, M. and Spencer, E. (2001) Early intervention in psychotic relapse. *Clinical Psychology Review. Special Issue: Psychosis*, **21**, 1211–26.

Edwards, J., Hinton, M., Elkins, K. and Athanasopolous, O. (2003) Cannabis abuse and first-episode psychosis, in (eds H.L. Graham, A. Copello, M. Birchwood and K.T. Mueser), *Substance Misuse in Psychosis: Approaches to Treatment and Service Delivery*, John Wiley & Sons, Ltd, Chichester.

Edwards, J., Maude, D., Herrmann-Doig, T. *et al.* (2002) A service response to prolonged recovery in early psychosis. *Psychiatric Services*, 53, 1067–9.

Edwards, J. and McGorry, P.D. (2002) *Implementing Early Intervention in Psychosis: A Guide to Establishing Early Psychosis Services*, Martin Dunitz, London.

Falloon, I.R.H. (1988) *Handbook of Behavioral Family Therapy*, Guildford Press, New York.

Gitlin, M., Nuechterlein, K., Subotnik, K.L. *et al.* (2001) Clinical outcome following neuroleptic discontinuation in patients with remitted recent-onset schizophrenia. *American Journal of Psychiatry*, 158, 1835–42.

Gleeson, J.F. (2005) Preventing EPISODE II: relapse prevention in first-episode psychosis. *Australasian Psychiatry*, 13, 384–7.

Gleeson, J.F., Jackson, H.J., Stavely, H. and Burnett, P. (1999) Family intervention in early psychosis, in *The Recognition and Management of Early Psychosis: A Preventive Approach* (eds P.D. McGorry and H.J. Jackson), Cambridge University Press, New York, NY, pp. 376–406.

Gleeson, J.F., Rawlings, D., Jackson, H.J. and McGorry, P.D. (2005) Agreeableness and neuroticism as predictors of relapse after first-episode psychosis: a prospective follow-up study. *Journal of Nervous and Mental Disease*, 193, 160–9.

Gleeson, J.F., Rawlings, D., Jackson, H.J. and McGorry, P.D. (2006) Early warning signs of relapse following a first episode of psychosis. *Schizophrenia Research*, 180, 107–11.

Herz, M.I., Lamberti, J.S., Mintz, J. *et al.* (2000) A program for relapse prevention in schizophrenia. *Archives of General Psychiatry*, 57, 277–83.

Jackson, H., McGorry, P., Henry, L. *et al.* (2001) Cognitively oriented psychotherapy for early psychosis (COPE): a 1-year follow-up. *British Journal of Clinical Psychology*, 40, 57–70.

McGorry, P.D., Edwards, J., Mihalopoulos, C. *et al.* (1996) EPPIC: an evolving system of early detection and optimal management. *Schizophrenia Bulletin*, 22 (2), 305–26.

Miklowitz, D.J. and Goldstein, M.J. (1997) *Bipolar Disorder: A Family-Focused Treatment Approach*, Guilford Press, New York.

Mueser, K.T. and Glynn, S.M. (1999) *Behavioral Family Therapy for Psychiatric Disorders*, 2nd edn, New Harbinger, Oakland, CA.

Robinson, D.G., Woerner, M.G., Alvir, J. *et al.* (1999) Predictors of relapse following response from a first episode of schizophrenia or schizoaffective disorder. *Archives of General Psychiatry*, 56, 241–7.

Singh, B., Copolov, D., Grainger, D. and Goh, J. (2004) Partnerships between academic psychiatry and the pharmaceutical industry: the Lilly MAP Initiative. *Australasian Psychiatry*, 12, 220–6.

Smith, J. (2001) *Early Signs Self Management Training Manual for Individuals with Psychosis,* Worcestershire Community and Mental Health NHS Trust, Worcester.

Strakowski, S.M., Tohen, M., Stoll, A.L. *et al.* (1993) Comorbidity in psychosis at first hospitalization. *American Journal of Psychiatry,* **150,** 752–7.

Ventura, J., Green, M.F., Shaner, A. and Liberman, R.P. (1993) Training and quality assurance with the Brief Psychiatric Rating Scale: 'The Drift Busters'. *International Journal of Methods in Psychiatric Research,* **3,** 221–44.

Zubin, J. and Spring, B. (1977) Vulnerability – a new view of schizophrenia. *Journal of Abnormal Psychology,* **86,** 103–26.

Resources

Episode II Family Work Manual

Mueser, K.T. and Glynn, S.M. (1999) *Behavioral Family Therapy for Psychiatric Disorders,* 2nd edn, New Harbinger, Oakland, CA.

Addington, J. and Burnett, P. (2004) Working with families in the early stages of psychosis, in *The First Psychotic Relapse: Understanding the Risks and the Opportunities for Prevention* (eds J.F. Gleeson and P.D. McGorry), John Wiley & Sons, Ltd, Chichester.

III

Interventions Focusing on Drug Use

5

Family Intervention for Complex Cases: Substance Use and Psychosis

Ian Lowens, Samantha E. Bowe and Christine Barrowclough

Focus of the Chapter

When a family member has a psychosis complicated by problems associated with persistent and heavy substance use, it inevitably increases the complexity of difficulties encountered. Despite this being a common occurrence, there have been relatively few reports of working with families where concerns and problems associated with substance use dominate the intervention. This chapter will describe working with such a family. We feel that the work illustrates a number of issues inherent in family intervention for complex cases, such as the need for an ongoing awareness of engagement issues, the development of a formulation that captures the complex interactive family dynamics and flexibility to ensure that interventions address changes in the family's needs.

We would like to thank the members of the family we worked with for the courage they regularly demonstrated during our work together and for allowing us to write up the work. In order to maintain anonymity pseudonyms have been used throughout.

Contextual Issues

The small amount of published research available indicates that stress has a high prevalence in households where a member has a psychosis and an associated substance use problem (Barrowclough, 2003). This is hardly

A Casebook of Family Interventions for Psychosis   Edited by Fiona Lobban and Christine Barrowclough
© 2009 John Wiley & Sons, Ltd

surprising given that the dual problems are known to be associated with many adverse outcomes for the service user including an increased probability of symptom exacerbation and subsequent relapse, along with increasingly severe family arguments, potential homelessness and subsequent vulnerability to harm from others during periods of significant vulnerability. In this context, service users can have multiple and persistent problems and it is often difficult for relatives to understand fluctuations in their relative's well-being and to know how best to help them. Family reactions can be complex, with many conflicting emotions. For example, there may be criticism and anger associated with beliefs that the service users are to some extent to blame for their problems (Barrowclough *et al.*, 2005). These attitudes are hardly surprising given that dominant societal attitudes in Western culture tend to blame substance users for their behaviour (Turner, 1998). On the other hand, relatives may at the same time be fearful and anxious for the service user's well-being (Mueser and Gingervich, 1994): concerns that are often very realistic given the many adverse problems associated with the dual nature of the problems.

How can we best assist family members in this context? The limited evidence base available for how best to help families of people with psychosis and substance use suggests that a cognitive behavioural therapy (CBT) approach, complemented by principles from Motivational Interviewing (MI) and the stages of change (SOC) model is likely to be beneficial (e.g. Barrowclough *et al.*, 2001). Briefly, the SOC model describes how change is likely to involve a number of states or stages of readiness, ranging from pre-contemplation (not seeing a problem or feeling the need to change), contemplation (both considering change and continued use), preparation/action (building motivation to make change) and either maintenance (taking steps to keep up the change) or lapse (a return to an earlier stage). Although the scientific basis of the SOC framework has been questioned (e.g. West, 2005), it remains, in our view, a clinically useful heuristic in helping families to understand motivational issues. MI is a style of interviewing designed to provide an interpersonal context maximising the probability of exploration, and subsequent facilitation of increased motivation for change. Key MI concepts include that ambivalence is normal; that resolving ambivalence is the key to change; that responsibility for problems associated with substance use and their consequences is best left with the client (aimed to increase the client's awareness of the disadvantages of substances); that help is most effective when it matches the client's state of readiness for change and trying to persuade the client to change through arguments or other means will be counter productive.

A key assumption of our family intervention (FI) approach was that the family environment would influence the service user's motivational state for change. Consequently, we sought to promote a family response consistent with MI values/strategies. Hence, for people who are at best 'contemplative', FI might be directed at helping relatives to appreciate that attempts to try to make people change their substance use, or to buffer the consequences of their use would be counterproductive. Rather, the family might be better to set limits and boundaries increasing the probability that the consequences of the use impinge on the client rather than on themselves. For example, not rescuing clients by bailing them out financially or covering up for periods of intoxication, and establishing collaborative (i.e. arrived at through discussion with the family member using substances), reasonable and clearly communicated house rules about acceptability of behaviour.

The general approach to the cognitive behavioural intervention used in the case study has been documented (Barrowclough and Tarrier, 1992) with discussion of adaptations for working with families where there is a substance use problem (Barrowclough, 2003). The formulation also drew on the illness perception literature in relation to mental health (Lobban, Barrowclough and Jones, 2003) and in particular the work of Leventhal and colleagues is evident in Figure 5.2, later in this chapter (see e.g. Leventhal, Nerenz and Steele, 1984). Assessments were carried out with all key members of the family involving both standard measures, and a cognitive behavioural style assessment aiming to identify the relatives key problem areas, and their key intervention needs. The intervention also drew on Compassionate Mind Focused Therapy (Gilbert, 2005; Gilbert and Leahy, 2007), providing a framework to help the parents to have a more compassionate approach towards their own and each other's difficulties in dealing with the challenges their son's behaviour posed.

The therapists (IL and SB) had extensive experience in working with people with psychosis using both CBT and MI approaches. Both were Clinical Psychologists who had also completed postgraduate Cognitive Therapy Diplomas. IL was also a registered MINT trainer (i.e. the Motivational Interviewing Network of Trainers). CB provided supervision on the work in regular meetings.

The clinical service

At the time this work was carried out IL and SB were working in a small team of therapists (the IMPACT (investigating the merits of psychoeduation and cognitive therapy) service) in Salford that provided Cognitive Therapy and FI for people who are between the ages of 14 and 35 years, who were within their first year of experiencing their first episode of psychosis or the first year of an episode being recognised by services. The team of therapists linked to local community health teams for care co-ordination and psychiatry input. More recently, the team has now moved into an early intervention team with dedicated care co-ordinators (the Salford Early Intervention Service).

The Clinical Case

Mike's experience of psychosis

Mike experienced his first episode of psychosis at the end of his first year of university following a prolonged period of crack cocaine use, which he used alongside other street drugs and alcohol. During his psychotic episode, Mike experienced himself to be on a specific mission, which led to him feeling energised and special, but also threatened, as he felt that others were out to harm him. Mike was unable to concentrate, his sleep deteriorated significantly and he frequently experienced his thoughts racing. Due to these experiences, he left university, returned home and soon after this contacted his local GP. He was then referred to his local Community Mental Health Team (CMHT) for assessment, who then referred him to the IMPACT team for psychological work.

Mike's family

His family included his mother, Jane, father, Paul and older siblings Kevin and Elaine. Kevin declined to participate in the family sessions and this in part appeared to be due to a long history of tension between the two brothers.

Overall aim of the intervention

As Mike's recovery from his episode of psychosis was complicated by the physiological, psychological and social consequences of his ongoing polysubstance use, we aimed to reduce the distress experienced by the family members; maximise the support that could be provided to Mike in his longer term recovery and increase the probability that Mike would have informed choice over his drug use.

Engagement and assessment sessions and tentative formulation of family issues

Jane and Paul had previously attended the 'multiple friends and family group' in the service, but had felt that the complexity of their difficulties required a more in-depth intervention. The rationale of working together in the family sessions to gain the 'bigger picture' was acceptable to all (i.e. gaining a shared understanding consisting of everyone's views, which would then be used as a basis on which to collaboratively and systematically develop family-wide solutions). Following initial 'scene-setting sessions', each family member was interviewed separately, with the aim of gathering a range of information, including general background information; each family member's explanation for the occurrence of Mike's psychotic episode; their predicted consequences of Mike's experience of psychosis; likely length of time for recovery; how the family members were trying to help; their experience of the care provided by the CMHT and the issues that family members wished to place on their joint problem list. Prior to these sessions, it was agreed that all information discussed would be shared in the subsequent family session. The information gathered from the initial assessments is shown in the formulation (Figure 5.1) indicating relationship strengths and the main themes of problems.

Mike's assessment. A structured assessment based upon the Positive and Negative Symptom Scale (Kay, Opler, and Lindermayer, 1989) revealed that Mike was experiencing paranoid thoughts that, at times, caused him considerable distress. No other positive symptoms of psychosis or other mental health issues were disclosed at this stage.

Drug use was seen as a normal and pleasurable part of everyday life for Mike and he frequently used substances in the family home, despite his awareness of the strong objections of others. He predominantly used crack cocaine, but also amphetamine, cannabis and alcohol. Feelings of euphoria, increased confidence and the avoidance of low mood were the main reasons reported for use. Mike described considerable tension between himself and

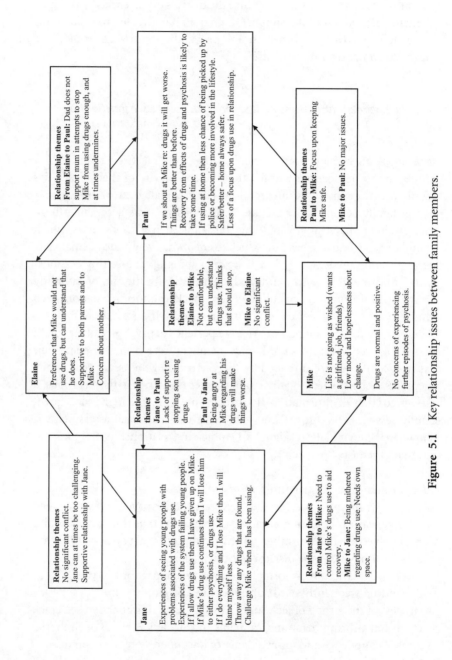

Figure 5.1 Key relationship issues between family members.

his mother, stating that she did not respect his space, and that she was continually 'getting on his case'. Mike understood his episode of psychosis as being an amplified version of his many transient 'psychotic-like' experiences brought on by drug use, and therefore did not see it as threatening or holding significance for him. Mike appeared to be demonstrating a 'sealing pattern' (e.g. McGlashan, 1987), contributing to a lack of integration of information regarding psychosis in general, and substance use and psychosis in particular. Understandably, Mike found the idea of attending FI sessions in which attention would be focused upon his recovery uncomfortable. However, he agreed to try them out.

Jane. In her work as a health professional, Jane had seen many young people struggling with mental health problems. These experiences heightened her concerns regarding the potential implications of her son's episode of psychosis. Jane was determined to do everything in her power to increase the probability of him making a full and speedy recovery, and her rule of 'going the extra mile' for Mike epitomised her approach. At assessment, Jane predicted that if she were to continually do all she could, her son would make a successful recovery in approximately a year from his first episode.

Jane viewed Mike's continued drug use with great fear, dreading the possibility that it would trigger a further episode of psychosis, which would alter him to such an extent that he would no longer be recognisable as the son she had known. She was aware that she was highly stressed, but felt that the demands that she placed upon herself needed to continue if her son were to be able to recover quickly.

In summary, Jane viewed Mike's experience of psychosis as being a potentially catastrophic event, her timeline for Mike's recovery was brief, and Jane strongly believed that Mike could control his recovery if he would only stop taking drugs.

Paul. While also being very concerned about Mike's recovery, Paul did not experience Jane's intensity of threat. He gained comfort from the fact that his son's general situation was greatly improved. (Mike had previously become involved with the local drug's gang, becoming considerably in debt to a local dealer, which had caused Paul considerable concern for his son's safety.) Paul also predicated that Mike's recovery would be a lengthy process, allowing him to limit his immediate expectations and slow the pace at which he attempted to help his son. Although 'loathing drug use', Paul was less distressed by Mike's use of drugs in the house, as he thought there was less chance that Mike would become further involved with the drug culture or run into difficulties with the police. Being aware of Jane's concerns, Paul encouraged Mike to hide his drugs from his mother (something that caused considerable friction in the family) as he reasoned that once thrown away, Mike would again place himself in a relatively high-risk situation when visiting the local dealers. Paul was very worried about the affect the situation was having on Jane.

In summary, Paul was very concerned about Mike's recovery, but viewed Mike's episode as being less threatening. His timeline for Mike's recovery was longer, but as with Jane, he believed that Mike could have some control over his situation (i.e. if he were able to stop his drug use), but this belief was held with significantly less conviction when compared with Jane's beliefs.

Elaine. Although Elaine expressed considerable dislike of drugs, she indicated that she was able to understand why Mike would be motivated to use (i.e. to gain feelings of pleasure that would otherwise be presently unavailable to him). Her sense of threat to her brother connected to his experience of psychosis was less than her mother's, and her timeline for Mike's recovery fluctuated somewhat, moving between a brief and lengthier expected recovery. A considerable source of distress to Elaine was her awareness of how much her mother was struggling, and her view that her father ought to be supporting her mother in her efforts to stop Mike from using drugs. Elaine also believed that Mike could do more to help his recovery, but again not to the same extent as Jane.

The initial sessions

The key area that all family members, other than Mike, identified they wished to discuss was Mike's ongoing use of drugs. The sessions therefore began to focus upon this area very slowly and with considerable care since emotions were running high. Although Mike did attend the family meetings, problems soon emerged. Hearing others discussing their concerns was too much for him and early on in the second session Mike experienced a rapid increase in anger, which we were unable to de-escalate, which resulted in the session being cut short. We learnt that Mike's anger had continued after the session when the family had returned home, culminating in him threatening Jane, and punching a wall in front of her. Following this, and being mindful of the need to discuss difficult topics with the family as a whole while maintaining the safety of all involved, it was agreed that separate sessions would be held for Jane, Paul and Elaine (provided by IL and SB), which would run alongside individual sessions for Mike (provided by SB). Later, some separate sessions were also provided to Jane (by IL).

We were able to use Mike's individual sessions to provide feedback on the family's concerns and discussions, and then to request his feedback, which was then discussed at the next family meeting. Pacing was individually tailored to Mike's needs, maximising the possibility of de-escalating difficult situations. This arrangement was acceptable to Mike and he attended his individual appointments regularly.

Reactions to drug use in the house

Jane's need to protect her son from the negative aspects of drug use led her to repeatedly search Mike's bedroom when he was out. Various types of substances, pipes and tin foil and other drug-taking equipment were regularly found and immediately thrown away. This led to a subsequent mix of emotions: relief in the short term; anger that Mike continued to do something that threatened his well-being; and anxiety about the ongoing threat to her son. Jane was aware that Mike would, as soon as possible, go out and buy more drugs. When in the house Mike had a clear pattern of behaviour associated with his drug use (e.g. playing a particular type of music loudly). Jane was well aware of these cues. Mike also demonstrated clear signs of use (e.g. appearing with white powder around his nose; becoming suddenly far more energised, animated and difficult to follow in conversations). At times, when this happened, Jane would feel unable to hold back her anger and anxiety for his welfare and serious arguments would develop extremely quickly. For example, on one occasion Jane burst into Mike's room and confronted him about the potential consequences of his behaviour. Within this type of situation, Mike would tend to become extremely angry with Jane for not respecting his privacy and serious arguments would escalate. See Figure 5.2 for a review of the various factors contributing to Jane's attempts to control Mike's behaviour, and the subsequent difficulties between Jane and Mike.

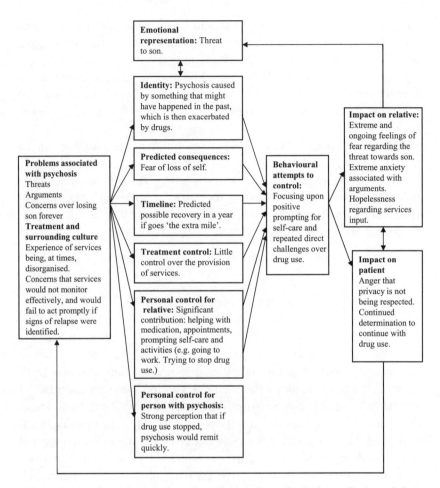

Figure 5.2 A formulation of Jane's understanding of Mike's psychosis and drug use.

Views on the best ways to help with Mike's recovery

Considerable disagreement existed in the family as to the best way to assist Mike in his recovery from psychosis, and naturally his drug use was a central concern. In comparison to Jane, Paul would generally tend to take a 'gentle' non-confrontational approach to this. Both Jane and Mike were also experiencing continued high levels of tension in the house, and they would frequently argue, further increasing the overall stress in the family home.

Early Family Intervention Strategies

Introducing a more compassionate approach

Jane and Mike appeared to have lost sense of the degree of difficulty they were facing as parents caring for their son. In order to facilitate the development of a more compassionate approach (i.e. how they responded to their own, and each other's distress), Jane and Mike were guided to consider the extraordinarily difficult nature of their situation. Normalising feelings of overwhelm was important, and difficulties with coping and problems with communication and support were similarly emphasised as being a natural part of this process. In this way, we hoped that Paul and Jane could begin to weaken the vicious circle they had become locked into (i.e. criticising each other's attempts to cope, and progressively distancing themselves from each other, becoming less sensitive to each others distress and working with the situation in isolation without support), and begin to communicate more freely.

Separate sessions with Jane

In separate sessions from the family work, Jane explored the background issues to her approach. She disclosed that she thought that Mike's psychosis meant that she had failed as a mother. Jane also disclosed that she repeatedly and severely criticised herself for having failed to identify early signs of developing psychosis and therefore missing her chance to stop its progress. When analysing the function of Jane's repeated self-attacking, we noted that it motivated her to increase her vigilance of any further problems for Mike. However, this ongoing self-attacking had significant unintended side effects (e.g. feeling extremely low). We collaboratively reviewed in detail whether any specific action or inaction on her part might have contributed to the emergence of psychosis. Despite considerable efforts we were unable to identify any specific events. For example, Jane was concerned that she might not have provided Mike with enough attention when he was young as he was a middle child, but she had been far from negligent in the way that she had cared for her son. Jane was then guided to consider an alternative possibility that Mike's psychosis may have been far more likely to have been caused by his prolonged use of multiple street drugs, which could have interacted with a pre-existing vulnerability (consisting of a combination of psychological, social and potentially biological factors), and that his chronic use of drugs would have made it extremely difficult to identify the emergence of psychosis. Jane later disclosed that part of her powerful motivation to try her best for her son stemmed from the idea that if she had done everything possible, and Mike was 'lost' to psychosis or drug use, she would be less likely to punish herself afterwards (i.e. would be more able to live with herself). Jane was able to recognise that her efforts to enhance her son's recovery were, in part, an attempt to protect herself from her own potential accusations. This discovery appeared to somewhat free Jane in terms of thinking about the costs and advantages of her present way of coping.

Jane's experience of loss

When Jane's self-attacking began to reduce somewhat, she was gradually, and gently, guided to consider the likelihood that Mike would make a full recovery within a year (i.e. the potential inaccuracy of her timeline). While care was taken to validate Jane's need to enhance her son's recovery, a focus was also placed on the costs to her and her family of the particular strategies she was using. At this point, Mike had disclosed in his individual sessions that he was experiencing frequent paranoid thoughts that others intended to harm him, which was introduced into the family sessions. Jane, Paul and Elaine had also noticed that Mike's self-care had significantly declined compared to prior to his episode. The realisation that Mike's recovery was likely to be slow came as a powerful blow to Jane. In individual sessions she returned to loss issues, especially for the relationship with the son whom she deeply loved. (Previously Jane and Mike's relationship had been extremely good, and both had enjoyed the other's company, sharing similar senses of humour.) Efforts were made to guide Jane to consider what parts of the relationship with her son remained as a way of working against her fear that she would lose Mike completely, and the message that his recovery was ongoing was revisited.

Working with Mike's substance misuse: the use of the stages of change model

In order to help the family make sense of their situation, ideas from the 'SOC' model were discussed, along with key principles of MI (Miller and Rollnick, 2002). In particular, the idea that attempting to force change on another person when they view the change to be irrelevant, or simply lacking in importance was most likely to backfire and contribute to an increase in resistance (i.e. the person rehearsing reasons why they use substances), along with a probable subsequent increase in use. The family members were quickly able to recognise the potential usefulness of these ideas, and this led onto a discussion of alternatives to direct challenge with an emphasis upon 'not acting'.

Encouraging strategic inaction

Jane's tendency to confront Mike was locking them into a vicious circle, increasing the probability of Mike's continued drug use and placing Jane at risk of potential attack. As Mike was unlikely to change his substance use at this stage, we asked Jane to step out of the pattern by not challenging her son. For many people, the idea that they may most effectively help their loved ones by not acting on their urges to directly challenge their substance use can appear nonsensical. Consequently, a considerable degree of attention was placed upon emphasising the other active strategies that would support this central approach. For example, Jane and Paul were asked to provide Mike with unambiguous messages regarding his drugs use, but to do this in a planned and gentle way (i.e. paying careful attention to the wording and intonation). They were also asked to consider how they would react if someone were to directly challenge them about something they did, which helped them to understand the common triggers for Mike's increased resistance. Due to Jane's difficulty of altering her behaviour (i.e. her fear that something would happen to her son if she did not continue to challenge), care was taken to introduce the idea of dropping direct challenges as something of an 'experiment' that could be tested out for a specific time period and reviewed.

Ground rules regarding drug use

At the same time, Jane and Paul were encouraged to increase their use of boundaries in their house regarding Mike's drug use. However, this was extremely difficult to consider due to their predictions about the potential problems of enforcing any such rules: the possibility that they could find themselves asking Mike to leave the family home. This was difficult partly due to concerns that Mike could refuse and react violently, and also due to Jane's concerns about where her son would go. She predicted that Mike would be quickly asked to leave many forms of supported accommodation, leading to either poor quality hostel accommodation or living on the street. A main concern connected to this possible scenario was that Mike could relapse, and that this would go unrecognised and untreated, increasing the possibility of Mike being 'lost' to psychosis.

At this stage Paul and Jane were in a difficult dilemma. They were struggling with living with Mike at their home, but could see no workable alternatives. However, the family agreed to introduce the ground rule of not using drugs in the house, again seeing this as an experiment to be reviewed. They discussed with Mike that they were introducing a rule in order to decrease the stress for all concerned. This was something that Mike agreed to. (This was also discussed in Mike's individual sessions.) Mike was able to follow this rule for some time, and placed effort into smoking cannabis when he was walking his dog, which Jane and Paul viewed as an attempt to compromise, which they greatly appreciated.

The indirect funding of Mike's drug use

Mike received considerable financial aid from Paul and Jane, which protected him from the reality of his financial situation. For example, he was not required to contribute to the running of the household, he was frequently given small amounts of money and he was provided with regular lifts to his friends' houses (who lived a considerable distance from the family home). In many ways, this was entirely understandable: Mike was experiencing a significant episode of depression and his concerned parents wanted to make him feel happier. However, while accepting this financial assistance from his family, Mike continued to buy considerable quantities of drugs. Consequently, we raised the idea that Paul and Jane were indirectly subsidising Mike's drug use. This appeared to be quite a revelation to them. Both parents were encouraged to consider changing the ways they helped their son in order to allow him to experience the natural negative financial consequences of substance use. We reviewed the idea that it was likely that Mike's motivation to change his use would be affected either by natural developmental changes in his life, and/or by experiencing negative consequences of his current pattern of use.

The sudden withdrawal of previously provided assistance could easily have been experienced as punishment, which would be likely to lead to negative side effects (e.g. Mike becoming angry towards Jane and Paul). Encouraging parents/partners to make changes in the way that they financially support others in the family therefore needs to be done with great care. In relation to Jane, Paul and Mike, it was suggested that this issue be discussed openly, and the subsequent individual session with Mike was used to check out how he made sense of the discussions. Although we had some concerns, Mike was able to look objectively at the situation his parents were in and accepted the rationale for limiting his funds from them. Furthermore, this discussion allowed Mike to express his wish to be more independent with his money. (Mike received regular disability allowance payments, which his parents organised for him due to their concerns that he would immediately spend all the money immediately on drugs as had happened in the past.)

When short of money (following periods of drug use) Mike continued to ask his parents to help him out, but they were encouraged to respond with clear reasons for being unable to do so. A great deal of emphasis was placed on a consistent approach with the message being conveyed in a neutral and caring way. However, some tension between Paul and Jane emerged. Paul was keen to provide small amounts of money and reduce this in a gradual way, while Jane was keen to stop this immediately. This difference in preferred pacing caused Jane considerable concerns: that the lack of a clear approach would confuse Mike, and make her appear as the 'bad guy' in the couple, further worsening their relationship.

Despite Paul providing small sums on occasions, Mike's financial support was reduced significantly. This change gradually began to have an impact. Mike was aware that if he spent all his money on drugs he would be left without enough money to go out with friends, etc. More specifically, it appeared that he was faced with the choice of using his money in order to have a binge of cocaine (potentially converting it to crack), which would be extremely enjoyable for a very short time, or using his money in order to plan out lesser drug use throughout the week (e.g. buying cans of beer and cannabis). He appeared to be being careful as to how much debt he was willing to build up. In later sessions, Jane and Paul also began to provide Mike with more control over his disability living allowance.

The family's discovery of Mike's ambivalence

As the family situation began to change, Mike was able to explore his views regarding drugs in more detail. (Individual MI sessions were provided by SB.) From this work, we were able to identify that Mike was taking a range of precautions regarding his drug use to protect his health (e.g. not injecting substances, being careful about who he bought his drugs from and managing his finances fairly well by not building his debts up with his dealer). Additionally, and very important for Mike was his principle that he would never steal or harm others to fund his drugs use. Also, and rather gradually, Mike began to explore his concerns regarding his drugs use affecting his state of mind.

Providing positive feedback to the family about Mike's self-care regarding his drug use was an important change for them. Being able to identify that ambivalence existed, and that Mike was using a range of strategies in order to stay physically healthy was an important discovery, and appeared to allow Jane, Paul and Elaine to feel a little hope about further possible changes in the future.

Mike's assault on Jane

Approximately half way through the therapy sessions, following what appeared to be a relatively straightforward family argument (not drugs related) in their house, Mike had a fight with his brother. Shortly afterwards, he walked into the kitchen where Jane was, and ignited the sprayed contents of a flammable aerosol at her face and upper body. Fortunately, she was able to just avoid the flames. The police were called and Mike was admitted to hospital.

SB visited Mike on the ward after the incident. Mike said that he regretted the fight he had with his brother and he felt ashamed of what he had done, although he was unable to recall attacking his mother. Later, in his individual sessions, early warning signs of relapse were identified in the lead up to the attack. Mike had used cocaine and alcohol that evening and had also been feeling paranoid. He also described being rejected by a girl he liked prior to the argument with his brother. He also said he believed that his brother had deleted files from his computer, and that his mother had hidden some of his clothes.

Mike's actions had a huge impact on Jane, Paul and Elaine. We shared our concerns that unless Mike was helped to move out of the family home in a positive way, it was possible that he might do something that he would later regret, which could result in family relationships breaking down permanently. The seriousness of the assault prompted Jane and

Paul to organise, and help Mike to move to his own flat relatively near the family home.

Making sense of Mike's anger

The time between the attack and the flat being ready for Mike to move into (several months) was an exceedingly difficult one for Jane and Paul. The emphasis in the sessions during this time moved to risk management. From a combination of information gathered in the individual and family sessions we were able to identify that Mike, at times, tended to be concrete in the way that he would understand communications. One part of Jane and Mike's relationship that had been previously been a source of joint enjoyment was their ability to have witty conversations, which were full of irony. It now appeared that, at times, Mike was unable to follow Jane's attempts at recapturing the previous spirit of the conversations. Jane was encouraged to reduce the level of abstraction in her comments to Mike, and to focus upon trying to make use of gentle tones. This was difficult for Jane as it reminded her of how she had needed to speak to Mike at the beginning of his psychosis, and was seen as a further sign that his recovery was likely to be a slow one.

Mike moves out

Paul and Jane spent a great deal of energy and time preparing the flat for Mike. They placed emphasis on the move being a positive step rather than his rejection from the family home and celebrated his move with a family party at the flat, which Mike was pleased about. Having his own space, in addition to Jane's lack of confrontation appeared to allow Mike to begin to consider the negative aspects of his drug use. During his individual sessions, he talked increasingly about the disadvantages of drug use (e.g. having no money to go out with, and the impact on his physical and mental health). He used the internet to gather information about the negative effects of drug use on mental and physical health, and voiced concerned about the long-term consequences of his actions. He also said that he hoped that if he ever had children he hoped they would not use drugs and could now empathise with his parents' concerns. He also talked about his values and goals: that in 5 years he wished to own a house, hold a job and be in a long-term relationship. Mike was aware that his current level of drug use was not compatible with these. Over time, Mike reduced his drug use significantly. (A formulation linking the various aspects of Mike's experience was shared with him at this stage: see Figure 5.3.) Mike also understood more about what motivated him to take drugs, quite often he felt very depressed and used drugs to lift his mood, but recognised that his mood lifted only temporarily, significantly decreasing when his 'high' had worn off. Mike's beliefs about drug use and psychosis also changed: he stated that he was certain that his drug use did lead directly to distressing psychotic experiences. This led him to avoid particular substances such as ketamine as the effects felt similar to psychosis (i.e. difficulty to distinguish between reality and unreality).

Transferring the onus of care to the community mental health team

Understandably, Jane experienced considerable difficulties with Mike no longer living in the family home, as she would have to rely upon other health professionals to take care of him. We tried to support and validate Jane's fear for her son's safety, but also emphasised the importance of the clinical team taking over increasingly large aspects of Mike's care. Unfortunately, this process was not aided by what appeared to be, at times, significant disorganisation. For example, meetings arranged by the care co-ordinator were held without a number of key professionals; and at times clear indications of Mike's reduced self-care appeared to be ignored. While these events were frustrating for us as health professionals, they caused considerable amounts of stress to Jane and Paul.

One key area that we had identified as being a priority was regular feedback to Jane and Paul from the CMHT regarding Mike's mental health, something that Mike had given his consent for. Unfortunately, little feedback was provided. Colleagues in others parts of the health service also let the family down. (For example, as Mike had run out of medication, Jane called and left messages on an answer phone of the out of hours service requesting advice on how to handle the situation. The requests for assistance were not responded to.) At a point in which we were focusing upon encouraging Jane to step back from her degree of involvement with her son, handing over his responsibility of care to other professionals, such events gave her little confidence that Mike would receive a continuously good level of care.

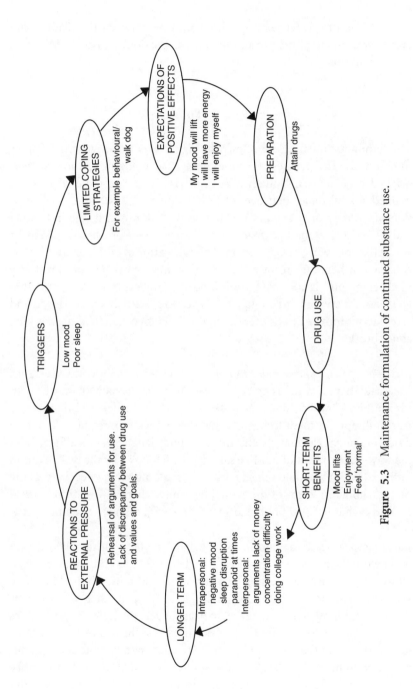

Figure 5.3 Maintenance formulation of continued substance use.

In addition to wider team involvement, it was agreed that Paul would take over as many of the prompting tasks as possible, and again Mike was happy with this.

End phase of therapy

The family formulation (as shown in Figure 5.1) was reviewed in order to emphasise the progress that the family had made in relation to their original problem list. Nonetheless, in the last phase of therapy there remained several issues that needed to be addressed. Mike and Jane's relationship was prioritised, and this theme was addressed in the individual and FI sessions. Jane had made herself step back from her involvement with Mike following his aggression. This was extremely difficult as her concerns about her son's recovery remained, but she now had no direct way of checking on his well-being. Additionally, Jane expressed concerns that Paul was not trying hard enough to convey to Mike that she still loved and cared about him (e.g. not mentioning to Mike that Jane had been asking about him).

Mike's perspective of the problems in the relationship. In individual sessions, Mike said that prior to his first episode of psychosis he had got on well with his mother. However, since the onset of psychosis he believed that he was a great disappointment to her and that she blamed him for not recovering quickly enough. He deduced this from her body language, tone of voice and the way she looked at him. Mike said that he felt upset by the deterioration in their relationship and coped with it by avoiding seeing her or speaking on the phone. In terms of the future, he wanted them to feel more relaxed around each other and be able to spend time with each other again.

Jane's perspective. In agreement with Mike, Jane felt that they had got on well before the onset of psychosis and had enjoyed spending time together. However, she was now feeling very awkward and tense about Mike. She was worried if she tried to say something she hoped Mike would enjoy, he would misinterpret it and take it to heart or get angry. Jane was therefore naturally 'closed down' with Mike. Jane's hopes for the future were for Mike to be able to visit the house and for them to chat on the phone about things unrelated to mental health. She also wanted to be able to go out for coffee with him like they used to do. Jane said that she felt sad that Mike did not currently have the things that he had hoped for in life (e.g. university or employment or a partner) and that she was disappointed for him, but clearly not with him. She explained that she acknowledged how difficult it was for Mike to reduce his drug use or attend to his self-care. Recovery, for her, was connected to Mike being happier and 'safe', rather than in relation to university or employment. She also said how impressed she had been with Mike in terms of the progress he had made over the past year. This was feedback to Mike in an individual session, which helped him understand his mother's viewpoint.

Through the communication between individual and family sessions each of the perspectives on their current relationship problems and hopes for the future were shared, helping each to see the other's understanding and preferences for the future. It made sense to both Jane and Mike that due to the Mike's episode of psychosis their relationship had been under a great deal of stress. Jane understood how Mike could feel like when she wanted to get off the phone as quickly as possible due to her awkwardness and efforts not to say the wrong thing. It also made sense to Mike that his mother was much more quiet than usual due to fears that she may say the wrong thing or provoke another assault.

For a number of sessions we then worked through specific examples of when they felt uncomfortable with each other or encountered relationship difficulties. By sharing each other's interpretations of situations we were able to test out the accuracy of their thoughts (e.g. Mike jumping to the conclusion that his mother did not want him in the family home when he rang her about coming round to the house). By working through specific examples, we established that Mike was very sensitive to his mothers' tone of voice and he often interpreted it as meaning she was disappointed or angry with him. It appeared that this played a role in aggression towards her. Sometimes Mike would ruminate about an incident for weeks, leading to an angry outburst after seemingly meaningless minor triggers. This helped Jane make sense of why Mike seemed to get disproportionately angry. By providing Mike an accurate picture of what his mother was thinking and feeling in particular situations helped him to feel less angry and resentful. Thought records were also used in individual sessions to test out the accuracy of Mike's thoughts when he and his mother encountered difficulties. This helped him to generate alternative explanations and spot any cognitive biases that were occurring.

Addressing Mike and Jane's relationship in detail was an important part of the FI. This helped them to understand the difficulties they were experiencing and what was maintaining them. Based on the formulation, through a series of home tasks they gradually started to have more contact with each other and started to meet up for coffee or go shopping and feel more relaxed around each other. They now have regular contact and things feel far less strained.

Maybe it is not all psychosis

Accepting that psychosis could have a key role in some of Mike's behaviour was initially very useful for the family. This became more complex when Mike was using drugs, as it muddied the water. However, in the latter part of the work we were also keen to focus Paul and Jane on alternative explanations for some problems. It appeared that some of Mike's behaviours demonstrated more a sense of entitlement (something that Mike agreed with in the individual sessions with SB) rather than his thinking influenced by psychosis. For example, Mike had agreed to accompany the family to a local shopping centre in order to meet and catch up with each other. However, once it became apparent that Mike was not going to be treated to a range of things (e.g. clothes) he left abruptly, making his frustration clear to others. After we had checked out that this was not influenced by psychosis in an individual session, we were able to feed this back to Paul and Jane. They were then able to make sense of this situation as Mike being overly demanding, and that it was important to react to this type of situation as Jane and Paul would have for any of their children.

Conclusion

The vicious circles the family found themselves in after Mike had experienced his psychotic episode and continued to use substances impacted on Mike's ability to consider the implications of his drug use on his life, and on the lives of those around him. Being on the receiving end of demands to change naturally led to him to resist and continue drug use as would be predicted by MI theory. From Paul and Jane's point of view the situation was excruciating, and they felt trapped. Encouraging the family to step back and reappraise their efforts in a wider context helped them to alter the strategies they were using. Working upon gradually increasing communication and support, altering the wider environment in which the drug taking was occurring (i.e. allowing Mike to experience the negative consequences) and encouraging taking a risk on helping Mike to gain more independence appropriate to his age were useful. Focusing upon a likely recovery time was also useful in helping the family members to think about pacing issues in connection to their attempts to provide care. The FI in this case required a flexible approach, moving between individual, and group work and between motivational interviewing and cognitive therapy approaches. Some months after the intervention the family continues to do well. Mike's drug use has reduced significantly and although it is possible and perhaps likely that Mike's drug use will wax and wane in terms of severity, we are confident that the family will be able to respond in a way that will minimise the stress to all concerned, subsequently maximising the probability that Mike will gradually be able to maintain these changes to his substance use due to the influence of his own values and goals.

References

Barrowclough, C. (2003) Family intervention for substance use in psychosis, in *Substance Misuse in Psychosis: A Handbook of Approaches to Treatment and Service Delivery* (eds H. Graham, K.T. Mueser, M. Birchwood and A. Coppello), John Wiley & Sons, Ltd, Chichester.

Barrowclough, C., Haddock, G., Tarrier, N. *et al.* (2001) Randomised controlled trial of motivational interviewing, cognitive behaviour therapy, and family intervention for patients with comorbid schizophrenia and substance use disorders. *American Journal of Psychiatry*, **158**, 10.

Barrowclough, C. and Tarrier, N. (1992) *Families of Schizophrenic Patients: Cognitive Behavioural Intervention*, Chapman and Hall, London.

Barrowclough, C., Ward, J., Greg, L. and Weardon, A. (2005) Expressed emotion and attributions in relatives of schizophrenia patients with and without substance misuse. *Social Psychiatry and Psychiatric Epidemiology*, **40**, 884–91.

Gilbert, P. (2005) *Compassion: Conceptualisation, Research, and Use in Psychotherapy*, Routledge, London.

Gilbert, P. and Leahy, R. (eds) (2007) *The Therapeutic Relationship in the Cognitive Behavioural Psychotherapies*, Routledge, London.

Kay, S.R., Opler, L.A. and Lindermayer, J.P. (1989) The positive and negative syndrome scale (PANSS): rationale and standardisation. *British Journal of Psychiatry*, **155** (7), 59–65.

Leventhal, H., Nerenz, D.R. and Steele, D.F. (1984) Illness representations and coping with health threats, in *A Handbook of Psychology and Health* (eds A. Baum and J. Singer.), Erlbaum, Hillsdale, NJ, pp. 219–52.

Lobban, F., Barrowclough, C. and Jones, S. (2003) A review of models of illness in mental health. *Clinical Psychology Review*, **23**, 171–96.

McGlashan, T.H. (1987) Recovery style from mental illness and long-term outcome. *Journal of Nervous and Mental Disease*, **175**, 681–5.

Miller, R.M. and Rollnick, S.R. (2002) *Motivational Interviewing: Preparing People for Change*, Guilford, London.

Mueser, K.T. and Gingerich, S. (1994) *Alcohol and Drug Abuse in Coping with Schizophrenia: A Guide for Families.* New Harbinger Publications, Oaklow.

Turner, S.M. (1998) Comments on expressed emotion and the development of new treatments for substance abuse. *Behaviour Therapy*, **29**, 647–54.

West, R. (2005) Time for a change: putting the transtheoretical (stages of change) model to rest. *Addiction*, **100**, 1036–9.

Resources

Barrowclough, C. (2003) Family intervention for substance use in psychosis, in *Substance Misuse in Psychosis: A Handbook of Approaches to Treatment and Service Delivery* (eds H. Graham, K.T. Mueser, M. Birchwood and A. Coppello), John Wiley & Sons, Ltd, Chichester.

6

Family Motivational Intervention in Early Psychosis and Cannabis Misuse

Maarten Smeerdijk, Don Linszen, Tom Kuipers and René Keet

Introduction

Cannabis use is common in people with psychosis. Based on a review of 53 treatment samples, prevalence estimates of cannabis use in people with psychosis turned out to be 42% for lifetime use and 23% for current use (Green, Young and Kavanagh, 2005). Another recent study reported that in the United Kingdom cannabis use among people with a first-episode psychosis is approximately twice that of the general population (Barnett *et al.*, 2007). The high prevalence of cannabis use among people with early psychosis is unfortunate as it has been shown that cannabis use is an independent risk factor for more hallucinations and delusions (Soyka *et al.*, 2001), more psychotic relapses, aggravation of psychotic and disorganisation symptoms (Linszen, Peters and De Haan, 2004), longer treatment duration, more re-admissions and poorer treatment compliance (Dixon, 1999; Seibyl *et al.*, 1993). For relatives of clients with psychosis it is often frustrating that the client seems unwilling to change their cannabis use, even when the negative consequences are so obvious. As a result many relatives develop a critical attitude towards cannabis use, which in turn evokes resistance in the client to change. Therefore, in the Amsterdam Adolescent Clinic we designed an innovative family group intervention that trains relatives in a motivational approach to ameliorate the interaction and to facilitate positive behaviour changes in people with early psychosis. This intervention, called Family Motivational Intervention (FMI), combines insights from motivational interviewing, psychoeducation and family interventions into one integrated approach. In this chapter, we describe a case example of a father

A Casebook of Family Interventions for Psychosis   Edited by Fiona Lobban and Christine Barrowclough
© 2009 John Wiley & Sons, Ltd

and mother (Mr and Ms Green) who participated in our family intervention after their son Martin was hospitalised with a first psychotic episode. In the first part of this chapter, we provide the context wherein our family intervention takes place, which includes a description of our clinical service, the specific issues concerning our clients and their relatives, the theoretical influences on the intervention, the style, structure and evaluation of the intervention, and the training of the therapists. The second part of the chapter deals with our case example. We describe the engagement and assessment of Martin and his parents, followed by a closer look at the components of our intervention and how they were provided to Mr and Ms Green. Next, we provide some results of the evaluation of the intervention. The chapter closes with some general considerations concerning the implementation of FMI.

Context

Our clinical service

The Adolescent Clinic is a specialist early intervention service in Amsterdam for adolescents (15–24 years) who experience episodes of early psychoses. The service is part of the department of psychiatry of the Academic Medical Center (AMC). The clients of our service receive a comprehensive clinical interview, including assessment of the history of psychotic symptoms and of lifetime and current substance use.

The standard treatment programme of our service usually starts with an inpatient phase of approximately 2 months and is followed by a varying outpatient phase till 12 months. During the inpatient phase, clients participate in a structured programme aimed at remission or stabilisation of psychotic symptoms, the establishment of optimal medication and psychoeducation about psychotic disorders. In this phase, efforts are made to create an optimal working alliance with the relatives, including individual contacts with one of our family therapists and group psychoeducation. The outpatient phase consists of a day-care programme of 3 months, followed by 9 months of community care.

Specific issues concerning our clients and their relatives

There are several issues associated with the nature of our clients and their relatives that made us decide to add a family intervention to our treatment programme. First, the combination of psychosis and substance abuse (often called dual diagnosis disorders) is associated with an increased burden on relatives and fuels interpersonal conflicts (Dixon, McNary and Lehman, 1995). For example, in our clinic a lot of clients with psychosis and cannabis use have financial problems because they spend money on drugs instead of essentials like food, clothing and rent. As a result their family members feel under pressure to give financial support. Second, in our experience most relatives consider the cannabis use as a behavioural problem for which the client is responsible. This often results in the relative saying that the client has to stop cannabis use altogether and even in blaming the client for his use. By providing psychoeducation about cannabis use in relation to psychosis, we give the relatives new insights that enable them to cope more effectively with cannabis use without experiencing demoralisation. Third, dual diagnosis disorders are associated with poor compliance to recommended treatments and medication regimes (Coldham, Addington and Addington, 2002). This lack of compliance undermines other strategies that target psychotic symptoms. Therefore strategies that indirectly influence the client are important. A family intervention has a high potential for this indirect influence, because we estimate that in our clinic more than 70% of our clients with a dual diagnosis live with family members. In addition, family members express a strong interest in psychoeducation and learning strategies of coping with the disorder (Mueser *et al.*, 1992). Fourth, adolescence is a period of psychosocial challenges and changes in the brain which can increase the probability of the onset of both schizophrenia and substance use in predisposed persons (van Nimwegen *et al.*, 2005). This calls for an early integrated intervention targeted at both psychosis and substance use. Finally, families can buffer the effects of stress on the client whereas loss or a lack of family support can markedly worsen the course of the dual disorder.

The theoretical influences on our family approach

Patients with psychosis and substance use disorders traditionally receive parallel treatments in different settings. Results are often frustrating and show that there is a need for an integrated treatment in which psychosis and drug use are treated in one programme by the same clinicians with an emphasis on reduction of harm rather than on immediate abstinence (Drake *et al.*, 1998). Motivational Interviewing (MI) is an effective evidence-based approach to overcoming the ambivalence that keeps people from making desired changes in their lives. It was developed for the treatment of addiction disorders by Miller and Rollnick (2002) and has also been applied in the treatment for dual diagnosis disorders and to increase compliance. Two controlled studies in patients with psychosis have shown the effectiveness of combined interventions for early psychosis that include MI. Firstly, Kemp showed that an adjusted MI intervention improves treatment adherence in patients with psychotic disorders (Kemp *et al.*, 1996, 1998). Secondly, Barrowclough investigated the effectiveness of an integrated programme with MI, cognitive behaviour therapy and family intervention for patients with comorbid schizophrenia and alcohol or drug abuse or dependency. The integrated treatment programme resulted in significantly greater improvement in patients' general functioning than routine care alone at the end of treatment and 12 months after the beginning of the study. Other benefits of the programme included a reduction in positive symptoms and in symptom exacerbations and an increase in the percent of days of abstinence from drugs or alcohol over the 12-month period from baseline to follow-up. (Barrowclough *et al.*, 2001).

FMI consists of two other components. First, psychoeducation lays the foundation, providing support and information. Second, Interaction Skills Training provides an experience-based training in using effective communication and problem-solving skills when confronted with problematic behaviour related to schizophrenia. In these sessions, a graphic tool is used to help relatives recognise how to define problems and decide which communication skill will be most appropriate for the situation (Gordon, 1998). The style of active listening and the non-blaming, non-judgemental approach to the problem behaviour fits well with the principals of MI.

Style and structure of the intervention

The core element of our FMI is empowerment of relatives by training them to develop a motivational attitude and apply motivational techniques to promote positive behaviour changes of clients. The main focus is on abstaining from or reducing cannabis use and increasing compliance. FMI is carried out in groups of 15 relatives, who can be parents, siblings or other members of the family who are closely involved in the upbringing of the client. The client does not attend the sessions. FMI consists of 14 group sessions scheduled every other week, each lasting 180 minutes. The intervention starts with two sessions of psychoeducation, followed by six sessions of Interaction Skills Training and six sessions of MI.

The therapists

The FMI intervention is provided by an experienced family therapist of our clinic, assisted in each part of the intervention by a therapist who is trained in that part of the intervention. There are several advantages to have a family therapist involved in all of the family sessions. First, there is already a bond between the family therapist and the relatives because of their individual contact before the start of the intervention. In our experience, this creates an environment in which the relatives are more willing to express themselves freely. Second, because of the individual contact the family therapist is aware of the family background and can anticipate issues that may arise in relation to this. Third, the family therapist can provide the other therapists with relevant information about the relatives, including the progress they are making. Before we started the FMI intervention, the family therapists were trained by certified trainers in using the interaction and motivational techniques offered in the FMI intervention. We also held several pilot sessions in which the family therapist received supervision from certified trainers who joined the sessions.

The Clinical Case

Family engagement and assessment

Background. We first came in contact with Mr Green (44 years) and Ms Green (43 years, both pseudonyms) after their 22-year-old son Martin was referred to our clinic by his general practitioner. At the time Martin was living with his parents and experienced both delusions and hallucinations. For the initial assessment we invited both Martin and his parents. Martin is the only son in the family and works in the local supermarket owned by his father. From the first day at work, Martin felt that his colleagues were constantly talking negatively about him, because he is the son of the boss and therefore in favour. He also has the strong belief that he was being spied on by some customers, and these people were planning to get him fired by his dad. These beliefs made him stop attending work 6 weeks before the referral. His mother reported that Martin spent the major part of the day in his room and that he only came out to eat and to hang out at night with other boys from the neighbourhood to smoke cannabis. She also told us that in the last month Martin complained about hearing voices inside his head that were criticising his behaviours and telling him he was a spoiled and lazy person. In the last year, the interaction between Martin and his parents was minimal, and consisted mostly of struggles about Martin's cannabis use and not attending work. Our routine assessment revealed that Martin suffered from a first-episode psychosis. Martin and his parents agreed with the treatment programme of 2 months in the Adolescent Clinic. Additionally, Mr and Ms Green had a 2-weekly face-to-face contact with one of the family therapists of the clinic. It is the family therapist who informs the clients and their relatives about our family intervention. This starts with the explanation that in our experience quitting or reducing cannabis use can significantly improve the outcome of the treatment. Next, the family therapist explains that for a lot of our clients it is very difficult to abstain from or reduce cannabis use and that family members can play an important role in supporting the client in this process of change. The family therapist then introduces our family intervention by giving a brief description of the content and the aims of the three components. Although Martin was initially not as enthusiastic as his parents, he was willing to participate when he heard that he did not have to attend the sessions himself. We then invited Martin and his parents separately for the assessment we do before the start of the intervention. A reassessment with the same battery of instruments was scheduled right after and 12 months after the termination of the intervention.

Assessment of Martin

The assessment of our clients begins with obtaining a detailed description of the pattern of the client's substance use. For this we use the Timeline Followback (Fals-Stewart *et al.*, 2000; Sobell and Sobell, 1992), which is a widely used calendar method for evaluating the pattern of substance use over the past 3 months before the hospitalisation. Like many of our clients, Martin found it difficult to accurately recall the moments in the last 3 months in which he used substances. We asked him to think of the key events that took place in the 3 months before the hospitalisation, such as birthdays, holidays, etc. It became clear that alcohol and cannabis were the only substances Martin used. Of these the cannabis use was intense: he could not remember a week without smoking cannabis and estimated that in the last 3 months he smoked cannabis at least 3 days a week, mostly with his friends from the neighbourhood.

Besides the pattern of substance use, we want to get more insight into the craving our clients experience towards their substance use. For this purpose, we use the Obsessive Compulsive Drug Use Scale (OCDUS), which measures three factors: thoughts about cannabis and interference, desire and control and resistance to thoughts and intention (Franken, Hendriksa and Van Den Brink, 2002). Martin had a high score on all of these three factors concerning his cannabis use, especially regarding the desire to use cannabis.

In the assessment, we also measure the client's experiences concerning the emotional climate with their carers. We measure this by using the Dutch short version of the Level of expressed emotion scale (LEE). The LEE scale is a self-administrated test in which the client is requested to answer questions about their relatives. It consists of 33 items which load on the following three factors: lack of emotional support, intrusiveness/control and irritability (Gerslma, Van Der Lubbe and van Nieuwenhuizen, 1992). Because parents can be very different in their attitude and response style, we let our clients complete the LEE for both relatives individually. The results showed that Martin experienced a lot of expressed emotions (EE) from his parents. Martin perceived that his father held him responsible for his condition which made him intolerant of Martin's disturbing behaviours and social impairments. On the other hand, he perceived that his mother repeatedly attempted to establish more contact with Martin and gave him a lot of unsolicited advice concerning his illness.

Assessment of Mr and Ms Green

The assessment of the relatives starts with measuring the distress and bur- den the relatives experience in relation to the client's illness. For this we use two self-report measures: the Experience of Caring Inventory (ECI) and the Family Questionnaire (FQ). The ECI measures the family members' experience of caring for a person with a serious mental illness (Szmukler *et al.*, 1996). The assessments of Mr and Ms Green reflected that they both clearly experienced difficulties in relation to the illness of their son, and that these had a negative impact on their psychological well-being. The FQ measures the relatives' perceptions of the behaviours and symptoms of clients with psychosis on three dimensions: the frequency of symptoms, the relatives' concern and their ability to cope with the symptoms (Quinn, Barrowclough and Tarrier, 2003). Both Mr and Ms Green reported experi- encing a lot of problematic behaviours and symptoms in Martin that they were concerned about and felt unable to cope with. The behaviours and symptoms with the highest score were negative symptoms, interpersonal problems and psychotic symptoms.

Since our family intervention aims to teach carers basic MI skills, we also assess the carers MI skills in the interaction with the client. We do a 10–15 minutes audiotaped role-play whereby the carers play themselves and the assessor the child. The situation in the role-play is that the child shows ambivalence to change his cannabis use, while the carers are asked to react the way they normally would do. The tape is scored by using a modified version of the Coding System for Integrity of Treatment (COSIT), which was originally developed to measure proficiency of therapist in MI (De Jonge, 2005). The MI skills of Mr Green were low overall: he constantly stressed the importance of quitting cannabis and blaming Martin for making his problems worse through cannabis use. Ms Green on the other hand showed more empathy, but had the tendency to fall into arguments and to convince Martin to quit the use of cannabis.

The Intervention in Practice

Psychoeducation (session 1–3)

The intervention started with two sessions of psychoeducation, provided by an experienced psychiatrist and a family therapist who is also involved in all following sessions. After a short introduction, the relatives were invited to report about the specific problems they experience in relation to the dual disorder of the client and the expectations they have of the family treatment programme. In our case example, Mr Green was very concise about their situation, while Ms Green expressed a lot of mourning and despair. Like most of the other participants, both Mr and Ms Green had a lot of questions about the nature of the psychotic symptoms and how to deal with them. In our experience, the need for information by relatives is especially high in the cases where the psychosis is accompanied by intensive drugs use. Following an explanation that these initial sessions are aimed at providing information and that the next sessions are about learning how to deal with the dual disorder, Mr and Ms Green became more eager to start with the programme.

The major part of the information giving sessions dealt with the aetiology and course of schizophrenia and cannabis use. Our experience is that relatives often have the tendency to regard themselves and the client as the cause of the psychosis, along with the cannabis use as a further causal factor. Mr and Ms Green were convinced that their son was to blame for the onset of his present state because of his cannabis use. By explaining the biopsychosocial model of aetiology of both psychosis and drugs use, we attempted to challenge the notion that Martin has caused the dual disorder and replace this by the concept that in both disorders, a biologically determined vulnerability plays a role. Although this evoked the statement by Mr Green that only biological interventions would be helpful for his son, the model also made him clear that they can influence the course of the psychosis with psychological and social strategies. In the following session, we taught the carers about recognising prodromal signs, psychotic symptoms and risk factors of relapse and how to manage medication use. We noticed that it was very important to incorporate enough time in the sessions for questions and discussion. Not only did this create an environment where the relatives could express freely their feelings and thoughts, but more importantly it also gave us the opportunity to correct any misinterpretation the relatives had of the sometimes complex issues that were discussed.

Interaction Skills Training (session 4–9)

The main purpose of the Interaction Skills Training is to train the relatives in using effective communication and problem-solving skills when confronted with problematic behaviour related to psychosis ('empowerment'). In this intervention we use a graphic tool called 'the Mat', which is derived from the so-called 'behaviour window' by Gordon (1998). The Mat is an oilcloth with two compartments, one green and the other red (Figure 6.1; green is shown as grey and red as black). When these two mats are joined with the green parts next to each other, it provides an instrument to observe interaction. In the centre there is a green 'area of cooperation', on the verge the red 'problem area'.

The Mat is placed in the middle of the training room, with the course members sitting around it. When observing the behaviour of the other person, there are two possibilities. Either you accept what the other does, in that case you are on the green part, or you do not accept it in which case you are in the red part. When an interaction problem is 'put on the Mat', the persons are standing opposite to each other with the Mat in between. A problem situation is explored and the trainer asks people to stand on the mat, either on the red or the green part, depending on whether they do or do not accept the behaviour of the other. During the role-play the person can move

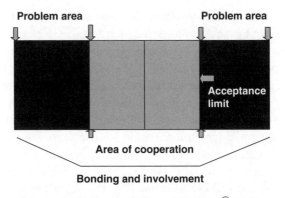

Figure 6.1 The Mat (Bureau 'The Mat'® 1992).

from one part to the other, thus visualising what is going on in the interaction process. In our case example, Mr Green said that the main problem between him and his son lies with the lack of effort by Martin to get back to work. He pointed out that there were a lot of conflicts in the last year because his son was unwilling to leave his room. We asked Mr Green to visualise on the Mat where he stands in relation to this particular behaviour of his son. Mr Green took place on the red field, which indicates that he was not accepting his son's lack of effort. Next, the therapist played the role of Martin and stood on the opposite red field. It was now visible that both parties did not accept each other's behaviour. Then Mr Green was asked what he could do to get on the green field. This question made Mr Green realise that he had been denying his own part in the problem and that forcing his son was not making any changes. Mr Green formulated the goal to communicate more often with his son about the situation instead of criticising him and telling him what to do.

In a later session, Mr Green learnt the skill to make the distinction between behaviours that Martin cannot change due to his illness and behaviours that he does not want to change ('cannot or will not'). It was reassuring for Mr and Ms Green that other carers were struggling just as much with this distinction and to learn from the trainers that this is often an area of difficulty for professionals as well. In the case of Martin, they remembered that in the psychoeducation they had learned about the so-called 'negative' symptoms, like apathy and loss of initiative. Thus, Martin's staying in his room the major part of the day was now labelled as part of the illness and not laziness, weakness or a lack of morale ('cannot').

We also used the Mat with a problem Ms Green was experiencing in relation to the illness of her son. It turned out that in the last year she gave up a lot social contacts just to be at home with him. She formulated the goal to stop centring her life around her son and to draw a line between behaviours of Martin that are acceptable and those that are not. In the next part of the training, we worked on realising the goals Mr and Ms Green and the other participants had formulated.

Mr and Ms Green participated in several more role-plays on the Mat, and learned the basic skills of communication: clearly 'transmitting', unambiguously conveying your intentions and effectively 'listening', consisting of efforts to understand the other as well as possible. During the training it became clear that Mr Green still found it very difficult to accept that his son was not capable of attending his work. We invited him again to stand on the red field of the Mat and to let him hold a bag. The bag represented the load he was experiencing concerning the problem with his son. We asked him to find out what he could do with the bag: Hold on to it and collapse? Give it away to the therapist of the clinic? Which part of the load is attributable to the illness? Which part of the load can you let go of and which part not? Mr Green realised that it was not helpful for him and his son if he were to keep carrying the bag and gave it to the therapist standing on the green field. In the same way Ms Green learned on the Mat to confront her son more effectively with his unacceptable behaviour of smoking cigarettes in bed. In an evaluation interview, Mr and Mrs Green both felt that the Interaction Skills Training had made them stronger. They were neglecting themselves less and there were fewer arguments with Martin. Mr Green pointed out that in spite of this, Martin's behaviour regarding cannabis use had not really changed at all. To his surprise however he added that it had not increased either. The thought that 'letting go' would stimulate Martin's cannabis use had always reinforced his attitude of not accepting his behaviour. Now, he acknowledged, he had 'other ways to deal with it'. This made him eager to start with the third part of the intervention, the MI.

Motivational Interviewing Training (session 10–15)

Session 1: the wheel of change. Following the Interaction Skills Training we started with the six sessions of MI. We explained to the relatives that they were going to be trained in applying communication techniques to enhance positive behaviour changes in the client, especially with respect to abstaining from or reducing cannabis use and increasing compliance with medication. Next, we explained that there would be home assignments to apply the techniques in their own living environment. At the end of the introduction all the relatives received a workbook with the information mentioned in the sessions and the forms for writing down their experiences for the home assignments. We emphasised that in our experience people were more skilled in the communication skills at the end of the programme if they practiced them in their own environment and shared their experiences with other group members. After getting an initial agreement from all the relatives to be actively involved with the training, we started with an open group discussion of how to define motivation. In our case, Mr Green defined motivation as the lack of internal drive of his son to quit his cannabis use and to get back to work. We explained to Mr Green and the other participants that non-compliance and lack of motivation are not trait characteristics of the client, but a state that can be influenced by the communication style of the relative. Mr Green told us that he had many times tried to influence the excessive cannabis use of his son, but that he never was able to motivate him to quit the cannabis use. We told him that Martin's readiness to change depends on the stage of change he is in at the moment. We explained these stages by showing on a Power Point slide the transtheoretical model of stages of changes (Prochaska, DiClemente and Norcross, 1992), which we translated to our participants as 'the wheel of change' (Figure 6.2).

When the client is in the stage of pre-contemplation, he does not perceive the behaviour as a problem and has no desire to change it. When the

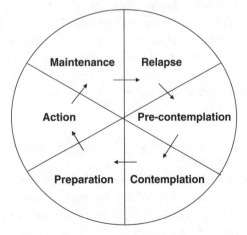

Figure 6.2   Stages of change by Prochaska, DiClemente and Norcross (1992).

client is in the stage of contemplation, he has some awareness of problems associated with the behaviour and is considering change. In the preparation stage, the client makes the decision to change and accordingly makes plans to perform the change. If the client is in the stage of action, he is actually carrying out the planned change of behaviour. The fifth stage is called maintenance, which refers to consolidation of the change and to building new patterns of behaviour to prevent relapse. The final stage is relapse, which is regarded as a common phenomenon when people try to maintain a particular behaviour change. It is our experience that a lot of relatives find it hard to make a distinction between the different stages and to recognise them. To overcome this, we walk through the wheel of change by taking a particular behaviour change that one or more of the relatives have initiated in the past for themselves (e.g. quitting smoking or losing weight). We asked Mr Green who told us earlier that she was unable to motivate her son to quit his cannabis use, in which stage of change Martin was in at the last time she was trying to motivate him to change his cannabis use. We had the following conversation:

TRAINER: You told us that you were unable to influence Martin to change his cannabis use. Can you tell us about the last time you had a conversation with Martin about his cannabis use?

MR GREEN: Well, that would be last week when he told me that he was considering reducing his cannabis use because it was making him anxious.

TRAINER: And how did you respond to that?

MR GREEN: I really want him to quit smoking cannabis, so I told him to throw away all the cannabis he still had and to go back to the clinic.

TRAINER: And how did he respond to your reaction?

MR GREEN: Like always, he got irritated and told me that I should mind my own business.

TRAINER: Right, let's look now at the wheel of change. Can you tell us in which stage of change your son probably was in at the conversation you'd just described?

MR GREEN: Well, because he showed no intention to change his cannabis use, I think he was in the pre-contemplation stage.

TRAINER: Okay, but you also told me that he expressed a wish to change his cannabis use because it was making him anxious.

MS GREEN: That's right. So at that moment he was probably thinking about changing. This means that he was in the contemplation stage.

TRAINER: I think you are right about that.

Table 6.1 Motivational Approaches to Stages of Change

Stage family member	Motivational approach by relative
Pre-contemplation	Provide objective information about the risks of the current behaviour when asked for by the person
Contemplation	Help explore the pros and cons of the current behaviour and emphasise self-efficacy
Preparation	Help define realistic goals and give confidence
Action	Give advice concerning strategies to change the current behaviour
Maintenance	Give support at difficult moments, give advice on how to maintain the behaviour change
Relapse	Give support, express confidence and emphasise self-efficacy

When we were convinced that all carers know how to interpret the different stages, we explained that each stage asks for a particular motivational approach. The approaches most effective to each stage are summarised in Table 6.1.

We told the relatives that if they are able to apply the appropriate motivational approach belonging to the stage the client is in, they can help him move to the next stage in the wheel of change. To let the relatives see the importance of applying the right approach to each stage, we continued the conversation with Ms Green who was unable to motivate her son:

TRAINER: We just talked about the conversation you had with Martin about changing his cannabis use. You told us that he was irritated by your reaction and told you to mind your own business. Is that right?

MS GREEN: Yes, that's the way he always reacts when I want to help him to quit his cannabis use.

TRAINER: In the conversation he expresses some doubt about whether or not he wants to change his cannabis use. We agreed that this means that he was at that moment in the contemplation stage. Now let's look again at the motivational approaches to each stage, can you explain why he reacted so defensively?

MS GREEN: Well probably my reaction was inappropriate at that moment because he was still doubting to change his cannabis use or not.

TRAINER: That's right. You were telling him what he should do, while he still doubted if he should change his behaviour. What would be a more appropriate reaction to his doubts?

MS GREEN: Well I could help him to define and weigh the pro and cons of his cannabis use.

TRAINER: Yes I think that's the right reaction. With this approach it is more likely that he will move to the next stage in the wheel of change.

In the next part of the first session, we explained that one of the central principles of MI is that relatives communicate acceptance and respect of the client's values and perceptions without disapproval and judgement. We emphasised that relatives should not interpret this as acceptance and approval of the family member' intolerant behaviours and that they still can draw a line in what they find acceptable and non-acceptable. Next, we discussed some central strategies of MI: expressing empathy, strengthening self-efficacy, avoiding discussions and rolling with resistance. We closed the first session by explaining the home assignment. The relatives were asked to find out the client's personal beliefs, values and goals in relation to his cannabis use and the use of prescribed medication. By means of the client's perceptions, the carers have to estimate in which stage of the wheel of change the client is in concerning his cannabis use as well as his use of prescribed medication. The main purpose of this assignment is that the relatives will focus more on the perspectives of the client instead of their own concerning cannabis and medication use.

Session 2–5. Sessions 2 till 5 had the same structure: a short review of the theory discussed in the previous session, discussion of the assigned home-work, education about one or more MI techniques, practice of interviewing techniques in role-play and assignation of new homework. In session 2, we discussed and practiced in role-play three basic communication techniques the carers can apply to develop a working relationship with the client and encourage him to explore the values and goals concerning his unhealthy behaviours (i.e. cannabis and medication use) from his own perspective. These communication techniques are asking open questions, summarising and reflective listening. Concerning reflective listening we explained that this is a method to check the meaning of what is heard and to demonstrate understanding by paraphrasing the client's message with a minimum of interpretation. When a client hears his own statements reflected back this can lead to further exploration, which helps him to develop a better under-standing of his own beliefs and behaviours. It is also a way for the relatives to get more understanding of the clients' perception and to express interest in this. After giving the meaning and aim of the techniques, we showed on Power Point slides dialogues in which the techniques are utilised. Then we started with practicing reflective listening in role-play. We know from our previous experience that many relatives find role-play scary. Therefore, it is very important to have a safe environment in which group members feel free to express themselves and are open to advice from other members. We started with a demonstration of the role-play, whereby the therapist played the carer and the co-therapist the client. Before the role-play we gave the following instructions: at the start of the play the topic of conversation should be clear, the 'client' should not make it too hard for the carer because this can interfere with the practice, let the carer who practiced the technique tell his experiences first before going to the feedback from the other participants, start always with positive feedback before giving advice about what could be done differently and repeat the role-play by using the feedback. In each of the following sessions we repeated the instructions, because from our experience they are essential for performing a role-play adequately. After the demonstration, we asked Mr Green to take the place of his son Martin so that he could experience how the therapist applies reflective listening in their situation. We agreed to play the situation in which Mr Green and his son Martin had a conversation about the cannabis use. We highlight the following part of the role-play that took place:

MARTIN: I'm not addicted, I am still able to quit smoking cannabis if I want to.

TRAINER: It doesn't cost you any effort to stop cannabis use, but you don't want to stop.

MARTIN: Well I'm not sure what I want. I know cannabis is not good for me, but it also makes me feel better.

TRAINER: That must be very confusing for you. On one hand you want to stop with cannabis because you know it's bad for you and on the other hand you feel better when you use it.

MARTIN: That's right, I can't make up my mind what to do.

TRAINER: You cannot make the choice what the best thing is for you.

MARTIN: Well, I know that quitting is better for me, because cannabis makes me more paranoid than I am already.

In the above conversation we see that the trainer gives different kinds of reflections of what Martin is saying, some that stay closer to the words of Martin and others that are more interpretations of what Martin probably is trying to say. In the interpretations the trainer even exaggerates a little the possible meaning, so Martin is challenged to explore what he really wants. When asked about his experiences of the conversation, Mr Green said that he felt interest and understanding on the side of the trainer, which made him more willing to talk freely about his own perspectives. We then switched places to let Mr Green practice the technique of reflective listening. Although he was capable of giving simple reflections (i.e. staying close to the words of the trainer), he found it difficult to give interpretations that did not contain his own convictions. After pointing this out to him we did the role-play again. We also let other relatives practice in role-play with the technique. At the end of session, we asked the relatives to practise in their own environment with the communication techniques asking open questions, summarising and reflective listening, by applying them in free conversations and/or in role-play with the partner or an acquaintance. We pointed out that the relatives should only use the techniques in conversation with the client if they were convinced that they had mastered them sufficiently. The relatives were invited to write down their experiences in the workbook.

In session 3, we went further into the technique of reflective listening, by focusing specifically on reflections of the so-called self-motivational statements by the client. Derived from Miller and Rollnick (2002) who define these self-motivational statements as 'change talk', they concern the reflections of the clients' statements that indicate a need, intent, optimism or desire to make a specific behaviour change. To help the relatives recognise the self-motivational statements of the client, we gave them examples on a Power Point slide. Then we let the relatives practice in role-play with recognising and reflecting the clients' self-motivational statements. Also in session 4 we got into the technique of giving reflection, this time as a strategy to overcome the client's resistance to change cannabis use and other unhealthy behaviour. We explained to the relatives that resistance to change is a natural and understandable reaction. Like motivation, resistance should not be regarded as a trait characteristic of the client, but a state that can be influenced by the communication style of the carer. More specifically, resistance is a signal for the relative that he should alter his approach and tune this to the stage of change the client is in. We asked Ms Green to give an example of an interaction with her son where he would react with resistance. Ms Green stated that she had a conflict with her son because he was unwilling to leave his room when she wanted to clean it. We told Ms Green that her arguments in this situation were understandable, but counterproductive as they only lead her son into more resistance. Rather than directly opposing her son's reluctance to leave his room, it is better to explore it in order to fully understand why her son is unwilling to cooperate. We discussed the strategies of simple and amplified reflections for reducing resistance. By simple reflections the relative demonstrates that he is listening by paraphrasing what the client is saying. Here the relative has to avoid the trap of reacting with counter arguments, which would only lead to more defensiveness. With amplified reflections the relative amplifies slightly what the client is saying, thereby helping the client to see the other side of what he is saying. We practiced in role-play with Ms Green how she could roll with the resistance of her son by using simple and amplified reflections. Besides giving reflections, we also used role-play to practise other techniques to overcome resistance: shifting the topic of the conversation, going along but changing slightly the direction and putting the words in another light. In session 5, we continued practicing in role-play the strategies to reduce resistance, because in our experience relatives find it difficult to apply these strategies in their own environment. In the last session, the relatives got the opportunity to practise again in role-play with one of the techniques discussed in the training that they still find hard to apply.

Feedback from the Participants

During the writing of this chapter, we were still inviting the relatives and clients for the reassessment 6 months after the termination of the intervention. Therefore, we are not able to give here any clinical outcomes. We can provide however some comments we obtained from the participants in the evaluation we held in the last session of the intervention. Overall the relatives found their participation with the intervention very worthwhile. Relatives noticed that they were more able to have elaborative conversations with their child about the problematic behaviours, without turning into discussions. Some relatives even experienced that they understood for the first time their child's motives for not giving up smoking cannabis or for not taking the prescribed medication all the time. Mr Green explained to the group that his bond with his son has become much better, because his approach to his son's problematic behaviours was more non-judgemental and less emotional than before the intervention. Concerning the different components of the intervention, visualising problem situations on the Mat and the motivational approaches to the stages of change were rated by the relatives as the most valuable. A lot of parents reported that they still find it very difficult to apply the different techniques to overcome resistance.

Therefore, we decided that in the next training we would simplify the strategies to overcome resistance and give relatives even more the opportunity to practise in role-play with these strategies. Although only one of the parents reported that her child had given up smoking cannabis during the period of the intervention, more than half of the parents (including Mr and Ms Green) told us that as a result of their use of motivational techniques, their child has become more aware of the problems associated with the cannabis use and is considering to change this use.

Some General Considerations

To our knowledge, FMI as illustrated in this chapter is the first intervention that combines empowerment of carers with a training of MI techniques to promote positive behaviour changes in clients with psychosis. At this moment we are using a randomised controlled design to compare the effect of FMI versus psychoeducation only on changes in the client concerning cannabis use and compliance with medication. There are some issues to consider when training carers in applying MI techniques. First, because our clinic consists mostly of young clients with a first psychotic episode, their relatives may not be ready for the MI skills while they are still in the process of acceptance and mourning. More specifically, the family members may not be fully motivated to adopt the MI skills, because it is difficult for them to believe that the symptoms could emerge again. Therefore, we believe that it is beneficial to precede the MI training with psychoeducation and Interaction Skills Training since these interventions aim to provide knowledge and change family attitudes. Second, the symptoms clients with psychosis experience may be an obstacle for the relatives in fostering positive behaviour changes. For example, due to negative symptoms clients may lack the internal drive to initiate behaviour change, while positive symptoms may lead them to an impaired ability to consider the possibilities for change. Third, for the consistency of the treatment programme it is important that this kind of intervention is not isolated from the rest of the care the client is receiving. Therefore, we put much effort in informing, training and supervising the doctors, nurses and psychologist of all sites involved in the project. We expect that the enthusiasm of the staff for FMI will be an important component of the future success of our family intervention.

Acknowledgements

First of all we would like to thank the relatives and the clients for sharing with us their experiences with the FMI intervention. We also would like to thank the therapists of the FMI intervention: Anouschka de Jager, Marijke Krikke and Bas van Raay.

References

Barnett, J.H., Werners, U., Secher, S.M. *et al.* (2007) Substance use in a population-based clinical sample of people with first-episode psychosis. *British Journal of Psychiatry*, **190**, 515–20.

Barrowclough, C., Haddock, G., Tarrier, N. *et al.* (2001) Randomized controlled trial of motivational interviewing, cognitive behaviour therapy, and family intervention for patients with comorbid schizophrenia and substance use disorder. *American Journal of Psychiatry*, **185**, 1706–13.

Coldham, E.L., Addington, J. and Addington, D. (2002) Medication adherence of individuals with first episode of psychosis. *Acta Psychiatrica Scandinavica*, **106** (4), 286–90.

De Jonge, J.M. (2005) *Motivation for Change in the Addictions: Studies in Assessment*, thesis Groningen University, Universal Press, Veenendaal.

Dixon, L. (1999) Dual diagnosis of substance abuse in schizophrenia: prevalence and impact on outcomes. *Schizophrenia Research*, **35** (Suppl.), S93–100.

Dixon, L., McNary, S. and Lehman, A. (1995) Substance abuse and family relationships of persons with severe mental illness. *American Journal of Psychiatry*, **152** (3), 456–8.

Drake, R.E., Mercer-McFadden, C., Mueser, K.T. *et al.* (1998) Review of integrated mental health and substance abuse treatment for patients with dual disorders. *Schizophrenia Bulletin*, **24** (4), 589–608.

Fals-Stewart, W., O'Farrell, J.T., Freitas, T.T. *et al.* (2000) The timeline followback reports of psychoactive substance use by drug-abusing patients: psychometric properties. *Journal of Consulting and Clinical Psychology*, **68**, 134–44.

Franken, I.H., Hendriksa, V.M. and Van Den Brink, W. (2002) Initial validation of two opiate craving questionnaires the obsessive compulsive drug use scale and the desire for drug questionnaire. *Addictive Behaviours*, **27**, 675–85.

Gerslma, C., Van Der Lubbe, P.M. and van Nieuwenhuizen, C. (1992) Factor analysis of the level of expressed emotion scale: a questionnaire intended to measure 'perceived expressed emotion'. *Brief Journal of Psychiatry*, **160**, 385–9.

Gordon, T. (1998) *Parent Effectiveness Training*, Penguin Putnam, New York.

Green, B., Young, R. and Kavanagh, D. (2005) Cannabis use and misuse prevalence among people with psychosis. *British Journal of Pychiatry*, **187**, 306–13.

Kemp, R., Hayward, P., Applewhaite, G. *et al.* (1996) Compliance therapy in psychotic patients: randomised controlled trial. *British Medical Journal*, **312**, 345–9.

Kemp, R., Kirov, G., Everitt, B. *et al.* (1998) Randomized controlled trial of compliance therapy – 18 month follow-up. *British Journal of Psychiatry*, **172**, 413–9.

Linszen, D.H., Peters, B. and De Haan, L. (2004) Cannabis abuse and the course of schizophrenia, in *Marijuana and Madness* (eds D. Castle and R. Murray), Cambridge University Press.

Miller, W.R. and Rollnick, S. (2002) *Motivational Interviewing. Preparing People to Change*, 2nd edn, Guilford Press, New York.

Mueser, K.T., Bellack, A.S., Wade, J.H. *et al.* (1992) An assessment of the educational needs of chronic psychiatric patients and their relatives. *British Journal of Psychiatry*, **160**, 647–80.

Prochaska, J.O., DiClemente, C.C. and Norcross, J.C. (1992) In search of how people change. *American Psychologist*, **49**, 1102–14.

Quinn, J., Barrowclough, C. and Tarrier, N. (2003) The Family Questionnaire (FQ): a scale for measuring symptom appraisal in relatives of schizophrenic patients. *Acta Psychiatrica Scandinavica*, **108** (4), 290–6.

Seibyl, J.P., Satel, S.L., Anthony, D. *et al.* (1993) Effects of cocaine on hospital course in schizophrenia. *The Journal of Nervous and Mental Disease*, **181**, 31–7.

Sobell, C. and Sobell, B. (1992) Timeline follow-back: a technique for assessing self-reported alcohol consumption, in *Measuring Alcohol Consumption: Psychosocial and Biochemical Methods* (eds R.Z. Litten and J.P. Allen), Humana Press, Totowa, NJ, pp. 41–72.

Soyka, M., Albus, M., Immler, B. *et al.* (2001) Psychopathology in dual diagnosis and non-addicted schizophrenics – are there differences? *European Archives of Psychiatry and Clinical Neuroscience*, **251**, 232–8.

Szmukler, G.I., Burgess, P., Herrman, H. *et al.* (1996) Caring for relatives with serious mental illness: the development of the experience of caregiving inventory. *Social Psychiatry Psychiatric Epidemiology*, **31** (3–4), 137–48.

van Nimwegen, L., de Haan, L., van Beveren, N. *et al.* (2005) Adolescence, schizophrenia and drug abuse: a window of vulnerability. *Acta Psychiatrica Scandinavica*, **111** (Suppl. 427), 35–42.

Resources

Bloch Thorsen, G., Grønnestad, T. and Øxnevad, A.L. (2006) *Family and Multi-Family Work with Psychosis. A Guide for Professionals*, Routledge, London and New York.

Bureau de Mat® (2006) www.demat.nl (accessed 28 November 2006).

Miller, W.R. and Rollnick, S. (2002) *Motivational Interviewing. Preparing People to Change*, 2nd edn, Guilford Press, New York.

Muesser, K.T., Noordsy, D.L., Drake, R.E. and Fox, L. (2003) *Integrated Treatment for Dual Disorders. A Guide to Effective Practice*, Guilford Press, New York.

Prochaska, J.O., DiClemente, C.C. and Norcross, J.C. (1992) In search of how people change. *American Psychologist*, **47**, 1102–14.

Further Reading

Owen, R.R., Fischer, E.P., Booth, B.M. and Cuffel, B.J. (1996) Medication non-compliance and substance abuse among patients with schizophrenia. *Psychiatric Services*, **47**, 853–8.

Pharoah, F.M., Rathbone, J., Mari, J.J. and Streiner, D. (2006) Family intervention for schizophrenia. *Cochrane Database of Systematic Reviews* (4), CD000088.

IV

Variety of Issues Arising in Working with Relatives

7

A Case of Family Intervention with a 'High EE' Family

Juliana Onwumere, Ben Smith and Elizabeth Kuipers

This chapter is focused on the delivery of family intervention within a high expressed emotion (EE) household. We have selected the case example because it illustrates the commitment shown by the client and relatives in their enduring quest to improve their circumstances and 'make things better'. It is hoped the case may serve to dispel some of the overwhelmingly negative connotations associated with high EE households and facilitate a broader understanding of their clinical presentation.

Before describing the case of 'Melanie', the chapter commences with a brief summary of EE, its measurement and the clinical presentation of 'high EE' relatives.

Context for the Intervention: Theoretical Influences of the Approach Used

EE represents a well-established method of assessing a relatives' reported attitudes and behaviour towards a client; their appraisal of the situation (Scazfuca and Kuipers, 1996). As a concept, it has been credited for the development of family work in psychosis (Bebbington and Kuipers, 1994a; Falloon, 2003). The full history of EE has been well documented (e.g. Brown, 1985; Kuipers, 1979; Leff and Vaughn, 1985).

The importance of EE in mental health has been its ability to predict clinical outcomes (Bebbington and Kuipers, 1994b; Butzlaff and Hooley, 1998); the ability of a 'social' rather than a biological measure to predict

A Casebook of Family Interventions for Psychosis Edited by Fiona Lobban and Christine Barrowclough
© 2009 John Wiley & Sons, Ltd

illness course. Thus, since the instrumental findings from Brown and colleagues (Brown, 1959; Brown, Birley and Wing, 1972; Brown *et al.*, 1962), there have been a series of worldwide studies that have replicated the relationship between high EE and poor client outcomes in psychosis (e.g. Leff and Vaughn, 1985; Moline *et al.*, 1985; Vaughn and Leff, 1976a). Furthermore, the results from meta analyses have shown significant and robust findings in support of a predictive relationship between high EE ratings and higher levels of subsequent client relapse (e.g. Bebbington and Kuipers, 1994b; Butzlaff and Hooley, 1998; Kavanagh, 1992; Vaughan *et al.*, 1992).

EE: A Measure of the Quality of Family Interaction

Brown and colleagues developed the Camberwell Family Interview (CFI) as a way of assessing the emotional climate between relatives and clients. The original CFI was modified by Vaughn and Leff (1976b) and is commonly regarded as the 'gold standard' of EE measurement (Van Humbeeck *et al.*, 2002). The CFI is a semi-structured interview and is typically administered to a client's key relative/s shortly after a relapse or onset in their condition. EE ratings are based on the content of relatives' responses and the prosodic aspects of their speech (e.g. tone and emphasis).

On the CFI there are five components of EE (criticism, hostility, emotional over involvement (EOI), warmth and positive remarks), and each have their own specified criteria for scoring. However, only the first three components (i.e. criticism, hostility and EOI) are used in the computation of the EE index because of their predictive relationship with client outcome. *Criticism* refers to an unambiguous statement, which contains an unfavourable remark or an expression of dissatisfaction about the client's behaviour or personality (e.g. 'he never got up until 3.00 pm... that really irritated me'). *Hostility* reflects extreme forms of criticism. It is expressed as a rejecting remark in the context of a critical attitude or a generalisation of a specific criticism to statements about the person rather than their behaviour (e.g. 'He's an evil person'). Hostility relies on speech content that is usually unequivocal. EOI is often described as the most complex of scales (e.g. Brown, Birley and Wing, 1972; Bebbington and Kuipers, 1994b) because it reflects different aspects of relative behaviour such as over protection, exaggerated emotional response, self-sacrifice and preoccupation with clients' illness (e.g. 'I gave up my job and visit her every day . . . she is on my mind every day'). Ratings are based on behaviours observed during the interview (e.g. crying, speech tone, dramatisation), or reports of past behaviour (e.g. self-sacrifice).

EE ratings are dichotomised and therefore relatives are rated as either high or low EE. Although exact thresholds can sometimes vary depending on the cultural group under study (e.g. Martins, de Lemos and Bebbington, 1992; Moline *et al.*, 1985; Nomura *et al.*, 2005), on the CFI relatives are normally rated high EE when they report six or more critical comments or they score 1 or more on hostility or obtain a score of 3 or above on EOI (Vaughn and Leff, 1976b).

Critical comments are usually the most common EE rating (Brown, Birley and Wing, 1972; Marom *et al.*, 2002; Raune, Kuipers and Bebbington, 2004), and relatives normally exhibit a combination of high EE behaviours. For example, hostility and critical comments are highly correlated (Hooley and Licht, 1997; Yang *et al.*, 2004). EOI has a curvi-linear relationship with criticism and hostility. Therefore, high levels of criticism and hostility can be associated with high or low EOI (Brown, Birley and Wing, 1972).

Although it was not used in the EE index because it overlapped with EOI, and was not itself predictive, Brown and colleagues also recognised the importance of the *warmth* component. Warmth reflects expressions of understanding, empathy, sympathy and concern for the client. It comprises features such as enjoying the company of the client and engaging in shared activities together (e.g. 'we get on really well'), and is based upon a positive voice tone. Brown and colleagues found that high levels of warmth, in the absence of high EE behaviours, were associated with lower relapse rates (Brown, Birley and Wing, 1972). Indeed, in a handful of studies the results have shown that warmth appears to provide protection against relapse (Leff, 1989; Leff and Vaughn, 1985; Lopez *et al.*, 2004; Ivanovic, Vuletic and Bebbington, 1994).

The prevalence of high EE and its clinical presentation

In most studies of relatives, high EE can be found in over 50% of samples. For example, 61% (Barrowclough *et al.*, 2005); 68% (Barrowclough *et al.*, 2003); 74% (Woo, Goldstein and Nuechterlein, 2004). Similar rates are also found in relatives of patients with early psychosis, for example 60% (Patterson, Birchwood and Cochrane, 2005). Although low EE is more characteristic within traditional cultures and less industrialised nations, high EE has been identified in diverse cultural and ethnic relative groups including those from *Israel* (Marom *et al.*, 2002), *China* (Ran *et al.*, 2003) and *Iran* (Mottaghipour *et al.*, 2001).

Attribution studies

The EE index has been investigated alongside different client and relative attributes. Some of the most interesting results have tended to emerge from studies that have focused on the attributions relatives report about the illness and client behaviours.

Attribution theory proposes that negative emotions (e.g. anger, criticism) towards another person are more likely when a *bad* event is attributed to a cause perceived as controllable by that person (Weiner, 1986). In contrast, beliefs about uncontrollability tend to be associated with favourable emotions such as pity and compassion (Weiner, 1993, 1995). Evidence confirms that high EE critical relatives tend to attribute more control to clients for their symptoms and behaviour compared to low EE/EOI carers (Barrowclough and Hooley, 2003; Brewin *et al.*, 1991; Hooley and Campbell, 2002; Lopez *et al.*, 1999; Weisman *et al.*, 1993; Weisman *et al.*, 1998; Wendel *et al.*, 2000; Yang *et al.*, 2004). Furthermore, attributions of controllability appear to be more common for negative rather than positive symptoms of psychosis (Harrison and Dadds, 1992; Hooley *et al.*, 1987; Provencher and Mueser, 1997; Weisman and Lopez, 1997).

High EE critical and/or hostile relatives are also more likely to report 'responsibility attributions'. Therefore, these relatives are inclined to attribute the illness and related difficulties to factors within the client that are *internal, personal* and *controllable* (Barrowclough, Johnston and Tarrier, 1994; Hooley and Licht, 1997). Thus, they are more likely to believe that clients are able to control their behaviour if they wanted to, but their decision not to do so reflects a specific flaw within their character. This is in contrast to low EE or EOI relatives, who are more likely to attribute the client's behaviour to the illness and/or external factors. Recent data have also suggested that relatives reporting higher levels of self-blaming attributions (i.e. attributing the cause of a client's illness and behaviour to self), are more likely to obtain higher ratings of EOI compared to those attributing blame elsewhere (Bolton *et al.*, 2003; Peterson and Docherty, 2004).

The effects of EE

Researchers such as Hooley (1985) have suggested that high EE behaviours may be better understood as a relative's attempts to control the situation at home. Thus, critical and/or hostile relatives who are more inclined to judge the client's behaviour as being within their own control, will attempt to change their situation through criticism and pressure. In contrast, EOI relatives, who are more likely to perceive the client as having no control over their behaviour, and in fact blame themselves for the illness and feel guilty, may also try to control the situation themselves and protect the client from any further difficulties.

High levels of criticism in relatives have also been associated with lower levels of knowledge about the illness (Harrison, Dadds and Smith, 1998). There is also evidence to suggest that high EE relatives tend to experience higher levels of burden and distress compared to low EE carers (Barrow-clough and Parle, 1997; Raune, Kuipers and Bebbington, 2004; Scazufca and Kuipers, 1996; Shimodera et al., 2000). They are more likely to engage in avoidant coping (Raune, Kuipers and Bebbington, 2004; Scazufca and Kuipers, 1999) (which in itself is associated with higher levels of distress), and perceive themselves as not being able to cope with client symptoms (Barrowclough and Parle, 1997; Karanci and Inandilar, 2002; Smith et al., 1993). Thus, in addition to labouring under the belief that clients are able to control their symptoms and behaviour, these groups of carers are also reporting higher levels of distress and experience difficulties in coping with it (Kuipers et al., 2006).

Low EE relatives are often characterised as being sensitive to the needs of clients, tolerant and non-intrusive in their manner in contrast to high EE relatives, who are reported to display greater intolerance of clients' problems and have less flexibility in their management approaches (Leff and Vaughn, 1985).

Style and structure of the intervention

One of the primary aims of the Kuipers, Lam and Leff (2002) model of family intervention is to specifically reduce levels of criticism, hostility and emotional overinvolvement within high EE families, as well as increase warmth and by doing so, reduce the risk of future relapse. This is partly achieved through attempts to increase a relative's understanding and tolerance of a client's symptoms, with a particular focus on facilitating cognitive reappraisal of negative symptoms, negotiated problem solving and improving communication. Promoting independence for clients and their relatives, improving coping and defusing the innumerable emotions that psychosis engenders in families, also forms part of the primary aims.

Similar to other evidence-based models of FI (Barrowclough and Tarrier, 1992; Falloon, Boyd and McGill, 1984), Kuipers, Lam and Leff (2002) model draws upon a stress–vulnerability framework for understanding the development of psychosis and its relapse. Intervention sessions are focused on current problems, and the strengths of the family unit are explicitly acknowledged and utilised. Overall, the style of the intervention requires therapists to possess a *genuine* and *positive* regard for families. Therefore, family members are enlisted as supportive therapeutic allies.

The Kuipers, Lam and Leff (2002) model of family intervention is delivered by two trained family workers rather than a single practitioner. The advantages of coworking have been well documented (Leff and Gamble, 1995). The intervention sessions are normally conducted within the family home. Evidence-based FIs are currently part of the UK National Institute of Clinical Excellence recommended treatment guidelines for schizophrenia (NICE, 2003).

'Melanie': A Case Example

Clinical setting

Melanie was seen as a part of a UK based FI clinical trial. In accordance with the model of intervention (i.e. Kuipers, Lam and Leff, 2002), and the trial protocol, all sessions took place in the family home and were audio taped. The family received 20 hour-long sessions on a fortnightly basis over a period of 12 months.

The therapists

The therapists were both research clinical psychologists (BS and JO), who had considerable experience of working with psychosis. They were trained and supervised in family intervention by professors Elizabeth Kuipers and Julian Leff.

Both therapists were very familiar with each other's clinical work and clinical style. Indeed, prior to their work with Melanie, the two therapists had jointly delivered FI with other families within the clinical trial. As part of their work, BS and JO always set aside time prior to and following the FI sessions to run through their plans and individual roles within the session.

Clinical background

At assessment, Melanie was a 25-year-old woman who had been diagnosed with schizophrenia when she was 19 years old. During this period (i.e when aged 19 years) she was studying away from home at University in the South of England. Shortly before the Easter break during his first year of studies, Melanie was brought home by her parents after her friends raised serious concerns about her mental health, and the college had failed to respond appropriately. Following a few unsuccessful attempts by the family to encourage a voluntary admission, Melanie was eventually admitted, under section, to a local inpatient facility close to her family home. She spent 6 months as an inpatient. Melanie was prescribed anti-psychotic medication and anti-depressants, and over time her symptoms gradually remitted.

Not long after her discharge, Melanie completed her degree via a distance-learning programme. The decision to complete her higher education through distance learning was made at the request of her parents, who were fearful for their daughter's mental health and did not want her to leave home again. Melanie had not moved out of the family home other than the brief spell at university. She lived at home with both her parents (Alec and Dorothy) who were in their 60s, and her younger sister (Sally) aged 23 years.

In the run up to her first admission, Melanie's main psychotic symptoms were delusions of persecution and reference. She believed that strangers spoke to one another about her (in a very derogatory manner) just out of her earshot, although sometimes she was able pick up the odd word. It was these paranoid symptoms that precipitated problems at university. Melanie had also experienced symptoms of depression.

Having remitted in her psychosis for over 2 years, Melanie was slowly taken off all medication. However, following some recent stressful incidents in a new work place, Melanie slowly became unwell and experienced a complete return of her previous paranoid symptoms and low mood. She was admitted for 5 months, under section, to the local inpatient facility.

During this admission, Melanie was placed on a relatively high dose of anti-psychotic medication.

The whole family was shocked and considerably upset that Melanie had relapsed. Melanie's previous mental health problems had been perceived as an isolated incident. Alec and Dorothy described the relapse as a 'huge personal blow', and were angry with themselves and self-blaming that they had not responded to changes in Melanie's behaviour much sooner. They reported that they were devastated when Melanie's mental health team had recently told them that she would probably have the 'illness' for many years and may always be reliant on medication.

Following her recent admission, Melanie was compliant with her medication, but continued to experience residual symptoms. Despite this, she had secured herself a part-time job, which took her out of her home most days for a few hours in the afternoon. She was also slowly making plans about how to pursue a career in the profession that she had studied for at university. Melanie enjoyed a wide circle of friends that she had known since her days at college.

Melanie's sister, Sally, was a full time drama student. She led quite a busy life and often divided her time between going to college, attending auditions and seeing her boyfriend. Alec and Dorothy were both retired and tended to spend their time looking after the house, gardening and preparing family meals. Dorothy also spent a couple of hours each week volunteering at her local church.

Prior to the illness, Sally and Melanie had always shared a relatively close relationship and were able to talk about 'most things' with one another. Melanie also shared a particularly close relationship with both of her parents. All family members had talked about Melanie in a very loving and warm fashion. She was described as a generous and thoughtful young woman, and there was a general sadness about Melanie developing the illness.

Clinical assessment

On the CFI (Vaughn and Leff, 1976b), Melanie's father (Alec) was rated as high EE on account of scoring above threshold on EOI. His score on the criticism component fell just one short of the high EE threshold. Alec obtained a score of 38 on the General Health Questionnaire (GHQ-28; Goldberg and Williams, 1988). Scores on the GHQ-28 can range from 0 to 84; with higher scores indicating higher levels of symptomatology. On the

Beck Depression Inventory (BDI=II; Beck, Steer and Brown, 1996), Melanie scored 30, which fell within the *severe* range.

Overview of Family Intervention

It is important to note that the nature of FI work has meant there is always a tendency for different aspects of the intervention to overlap. Thus, sessions given over to psychoeducation may also comprise elements of problem solving, facilitating communication and working with the emotional reactions to psychosis. Consequently, there are rarely discrete aspects of the intervention. The intervention is reported around the following main areas.

Initial session: setting ground rules to improve communication

In accordance with Kuipers, Lam and Leff (2002) treatment manual, in the initial session the therapists outlined what FI usually involved. BS (therapist) explained that the family, alongside the therapists, would be encouraged to solve problems related to different aspects of Melanie's psychosis. Also, that up-to-date information on psychosis would be shared with them and that they would be encouraged to talk through any issues that arose and that were especially pertinent to them as a family. The family were reassured that there were up to 20 FI sessions available so there was no rush to cram everything into the first few sessions. With the purpose of ensuring that the session was able to run smoothly and the discussions were not dominated by one family member, in this initial session the therapists also developed the 'ground rules' by which all sessions were expected to run. Thus, all family members were asked to ensure that *only one person spoke at a time.* As part of the rules, each family member was to be given *equal talking time* and their flow of speech was to be protected from interruption. In addition, members were asked to *speak directly to, and not about, others* in the room. The therapists' explicitly gained the consent of all family members to ensure that the ground rules were followed over the course of the sessions. At the end of each individual session, all family members were specifically asked how they had found the session particularly any difficult aspects, and whether they had any questions for the therapists.

Engagement and establishing the individual aims of family intervention

Melanie, Sally and Alec were keen to give the FI sessions a try. However, Dorothy questioned the usefulness of the sessions and remarked that 'I will never feel better' until her daughter is cured. Throughout the FI sessions, but particularly in the first two to three sessions, the therapists actively focused on trying to engage and join with each family member. They were aware that it was equally important to engage each family member with the process of therapy *and* with both therapists. They were mindful of potential areas of difficulty within engagement such as the relative youth of the two therapists, compared to the parents. It was possible that Melanie's parents may have felt concerned about the type of input the therapists could offer. Notwithstanding these potential issues, the engagement process was principally achieved through the therapists actively listening to each family member, validating their reports, normalising their concerns, empathising and ensuring adherence to the session 'ground rules'. As part of the engagement process, an 'aim' rather than a 'problem' list was collaboratively developed, which reflected the views of Melanie, Sally, Alec and Dorothy. The aims list for each family member was as follows.

Melanie
1. To explain to the others exactly what my paranoia is like and how bad it can be.
2. To learn how to cope with paranoia when out and about (and at home sometimes).
3. Not to be seen as mad and weird by the others and to get my parents to understand the stigma of mental illness.
4. For my parents not to quiz me about my illness all the time.
5. To avoid knee-jerk reactions from my parents if I was to become unwell again, and to avoid another hospital admission.
6. To recover and to get a proper job.

Sally
1. To ease some of the tension at home.
2. To help support Melanie as best I can.
3. To learn as much as I can about the illness.

Alec
1. To do anything I can to help my daughter with her paranoia.
2. To get Melanie to open up to us more.
3. For Melanie to get up in the morning and go to bed earlier.
4. For Melanie to chip in and help out more around the house.
5. To find out lots about schizophrenia research particularly the cure.

Dorothy
1. Above all else to keep Melanie safe and well.
2. For Melanie to recover.
3. To get Melanie to talk to us about how she is feeling.
4. To find out lots about schizophrenia research particularly the cure.

The individual aims were summarised and fed back to the family, and a discussion was conducted about what areas they could address during the initial, middle and latter phases of the intervention. As part of this discussion, the therapists encouraged the family to see that many of their aims appeared to complement each other. For example, Melanie was keen to talk about her experiences and her family were keen to understand and learn more about the illness. Similarly, Melanie was keen to recover and Dorothy was also keen to assist Melanie in that process.

Psychoeducation: Cognitive Reappraisal of Difficulties

Sally, Alec and Dorothy all reported that they wanted to learn more about the 'illness'. Although family members were familiar with the term 'schizophrenia', there was evidently less understanding of the varied phenomena that comprised the condition. For example, from his earlier reports the therapists learnt that a source of frequent tension between Melanie and her father often related to what Alec perceived as Melanie's 'unwillingness' to go to bed at a reasonable hour and wake up when everyone else did. He believed that if Melanie 'did more' during the day then she was more likely to go to sleep and wake up at a suitable hour. Alec firmly believed that Melanie needed to 'try harder' to fit in with everyone else's routine in the home. He also felt that Melanie was not active enough and needed to do more around the house to help out, even with minor tasks. He found it hard to accept her reports that the medication caused her to feel drowsy in the morning, and acknowledged that this made him annoyed. Alec often made reference to other people who were known to him or were in the public eye and had disabilities, but were leading productive lives. In contrast, Dorothy appeared to be less irked about the time Melanie went to bed but, like her husband, wanted her daughter to show some more motivation and commitment to getting things done around the house and with her career.

The sessions that focused on psychoeducation were primarily designed to disentangle the myths of psychosis from the facts (e.g. laziness vs. negative symptoms and depression). Conducted collaboratively, sensitively and at an appropriate pace, psychoeducation can provide a platform for discussion of pertinent issues such as family members' appraisals about symptoms and Melanie's experience of specific symptoms. In the context of Melanie's personal experiences and symptoms, the therapists systematically worked through a clear information leaflet that was specifically designed for use with relatives and clients, together. The leaflet was comprehensive and covered a wide range of issues including diagnosis, symptoms, causes, therapies, recovery, impact on relatives and relapse prevention. Each section of the information leaflet was discussed with the family and all members were encouraged to provide their own perspective, and comment on the information they heard from the therapists and from each other.

Understanding the experience of paranoia

It was evident that Alec and Dorothy were keen to understand Melanie's experience of the illness and wanted her to talk more about issues that were bothering her. In turn, Melanie wanted to share her feelings with her parents. She was increasingly learning that she always felt considerably better when she was allowed to talk through an upsetting incident with someone she trusted. However, although she wanted to, she found it difficult to talk to her family and was concerned that they would misinterpret her comments and perceive her as 'mad and weird'.

Melanie's family knew that she sometimes experienced troublesome thoughts, but they were not aware of their content or the impact these thoughts had on different aspects of her functioning. Sally was more familiar with her sister's low mood but remained unsure of how best to interact with Melanie and was scared about saying something 'wrong'. Consequently, they discussed very little about the illness and Melanie's feelings.

All the family reported that they found it difficult to have these conversations (they would often get curtailed quickly) and reported that they had had very few of them in the past.

As part of the psychoeducation process, Melanie was encouraged to talk about her disturbing ideas and unusual experiences. In turn, the family were encouraged to actively listen, empathise and comment on how Melanie's reports made them feel. For example, in session 3 Melanie spoke candidly (for the first time) about a recent experiences of paranoia whilst travelling on a train. All family members were visibly moved by Melanie's account and reported that they actually found it difficult to 'hear' what Melanie was saying because it was so painful. Alec acknowledged that he struggled to understand his daughter's experience though he often reported that he was 'desperate' to help her in any way. He frequently tried to interrupt Melanie's account with practical suggestions of how to cope. Alec had a tendency to suggest, in a critical tone, that Melanie should try harder to ignore her paranoid ideas and distract herself (e.g. 'we all get paranoid sometimes, so I just don't understand why you can't just dismiss it like everyone else'). In response, Melanie stopped her description of the paranoia she experienced and agreed to implement the various distraction strategies that Alec suggested. However, Sally noted that they were the same strategies that had been raised and tried on previous occasions, but had always been met with little success.

Based on the coping suggestions he had made, the therapists focused on praising Alec for the commitment he showed towards supporting Melanie in her recovery. This was followed by the therapists' commenting that there appeared to be a pattern in the families' response to Melanie's reports of her symptoms. Thus, it appeared to be the case that Melanie would mention a difficult situation involving her paranoid experiences. This was typically met by her family immediately suggesting coping strategies and Melanie rapidly agreeing to these. However, this functioned only to limit any further discussion of her distressing experiences and left everyone feeling they wanted more from one another.

Improving communication

In order to facilitate communication in the family about Melanie's paranoia, the therapists explicitly brought the conversation back to Melanie and asked her to continue with her description. The therapists encouraged the family to report on how they *felt* about Melanie's account. Interestingly, although both parents reiterated that the content was emotionally difficult to hear, they noted that, for the first time, they felt they had achieved a deeper understanding of how powerful and distressing paranoia could be. When questioned, Melanie reported that she was pleased that she had been able to 'explain herself'. She was reassured by the reaction she received from her family and reported that she felt understood. Based on Melanie's suggestion, the family agreed to watch a film that depicted paranoia with the aim of Alec, Dorothy and Sally trying to empathise with the main protagonist.

As the psychoeducation sessions progressed, Melanie became increasingly more relaxed and open about her symptoms and specific disturbing beliefs. Many of these experiences were new to her family and the therapists. For example, Melanie reported that the source of some of the derogatory comments that she heard was her family. This represented a considerable shock to Melanie's family. However, they were able to explicitly acknowledge how difficult it must be for Melanie to interact with the family at home given her beliefs. In an anticipated fashion, Dorothy tearfully reported that she found all the 'new' information and the extent of Melanie's belief systems 'depressing'. She doubted the prospect of Melanie fully recovering. In response, Melanie sadly reported that she was acutely aware of the emotional impact her illness had on her family, and this had always inhibited her from talking about her experiences with them. The family began to see that they had a common desire to have an open discussion about the illness but also wanted to avoid feeling overwhelmed by the emotional impact. They were able to agree, however, that their discomfort was outweighed by the benefits Melanie experienced from talking openly.

As part of the psychoeducation sessions, further discussions were also held about the impact of psychosis on the beliefs Melanie had about herself. Melanie explicitly stated that she perceived herself as 'mad' and a 'nutter'. In response, both Alec and Sally clearly communicated to Melanie that, in their view, she was nothing of the sort. With facilitation from the therapists, Alec and Sally were able to work together to bolster Melanie by saying that she had experienced challenges that most other people never had to deal with, and her beliefs did not mean she was 'mad'. Sally reflected that her sister's paranoia sounded very similar to the fears and worries that 'anyone' might have. She even suggested that her paranoia sounded like 'insecurity' and disclosed that she herself shared some of those insecurities. Melanie was very moved by the responses from her family, and particularly those from her sister. She reported that it was important to hear their comments as it made her feel less 'odd and different'.

The different meanings of recovery

A significant part of the psychoeducation comprised family discussions about the meanings attached to Melanie's recovery. Alex and Dorothy had stated very clearly that only a 'cure' for their daughter would improve their own well-being. Both parents reported that they were prepared to do anything to ensure that Melanie was cured including selling their home (e.g. 'we would sell the house; of course we would . . . we would do anything to get her better of course we would'). They candidly talked about their frustration with regard to the pace of Melanie's recovery; Alec stated, 'You just want to click your fingers and get rid of all this . . . but you can't.' However, although Melanie and Sally noted that a cure would be ideal, they also thought that Melanie could feel better and lead a productive life even if some of her symptoms were still present. Melanie was able to share with her family her own frustration and fears about the speed and course of her recovery. However, during emotional disclosure to her parents, Melanie reported that waiting for a cure put a lot of pressure on her to 'get better', which, in turn, negatively affected her mood and paradoxically, could make symptoms worse.

It was important for the therapists to normalise the family's concerns about the pace of recovery, and to draw their attention to the role of time in Melanie's recovery. This was spontaneously supported by comments from Sally, who actively drew Melanie's attention to the varied and significant improvements she had made since her recent inpatient discharge.

Relapse prevention

Since her recent relapse, Melanie reported that her parents, particularly her mother, frequently questioned her about the presence of any symptoms (e.g. 'Are you still feeling paranoid Melanie?' or 'Have you heard anything odd today Melanie?'). Their questions were often raised during family meals or at other social gatherings. To ease her discomfort and minimise any distress to her parents, Melanie regularly felt compelled to 'lie' and therefore report that her symptoms were not present when they were. Melanie was encouraged by the therapists to explain to her parents how their questions and their timing made her feel. She was able to say directly to her parents that although she felt they were probably trying to be helpful, she sensed that they wanted reassurance that she was all right rather than an opportunity to talk about any specific details or her emotional response, which is what she would have preferred. She found it hard trying to reassure her parents and was often left feeling isolated at home, which everyone recognised as a risk factor in her relapse.

It was evident that Melanie's reports of concealing or downplaying her symptoms had surprised her parents and Sally. Dorothy reported that she was unaware that Melanie found it stressful to be questioned during the family meals. She admitted that she frequently tried to look out for signs of illness in Melanie, and wanted to be prepared if Melanie were to become unwell again. Melanie was keen to reassure her mother that she was not about to become acutely unwell again although she still experienced ongoing distressing symptoms.

The therapists tried to draw attention to the 'pressure' and 'responsibility' that Dorothy and Alec most likely experienced as part of their attempts to ensure that Melanie was well. Their discussions prompted Melanie's family to experiment with a new strategy that was negotiated with the help of the therapists. Thus, Alec and Dorothy were encouraged to assume that the symptoms were present and were to ask Melanie about other dimensions of her experiences such as levels of distress and preoccupation. In this way, Melanie had invitations to talk about her experiences if she chose to do so, and was asked in a manner that meant she was less likely to conceal her experiences (e.g. How have you been feeling today? How have you coped with things today? Would it be helpful to talk through things?) This 'new way of doing things' was practiced over many weeks before family members, particularly Dorothy, became more familiar with it.

With reference to her recent relapse, the therapists learnt that Melanie's parents and sister were aware that her behaviour was becoming increasingly disturbed, but did not feel confident enough to share their concerns with anyone including Melanie. They kept hoping that the situation would improve. Melanie also reported that there was a time, at the beginning of her problems, when she was aware that she was finding it difficult to cope with life. However, she was fearful that if she disclosed too much to her parents about her symptoms, then this would trigger a 'knee-jerk reaction' and she would find herself in hospital again. Consequently, she was reluctant to share her concerns with anyone.

The sessions focused on reviewing in detail the potential triggers and the early signs of relapse. All family members were encouraged to contribute to the group discussion. One of the main and early signs of relapse identified by Melanie and her family related to her emotional and social withdrawal and irritability. It was important for the therapists to explicitly acknowledge the difficulty for Melanie and her family in trying to differentiate an 'off day' from a 'bad week', 'bad two weeks' and 'bad month'. It was also necessary to draw attention to how commendable it was that Melanie and her family had all tried to cope with the previous relapse, and the strength of character it required. For example, Sally mentioned that during the lead up to Melanie's recent admission, she tried to keep out of her sister's way to ensure that she did not unintentionally upset her. The family was led in discussions about how they would do things differently if similar circumstances were to arise again. From Melanie's description, the therapists were able to introduce the idea that there were different stages of the relapse and therefore, different responses might be required. Having accepted the stage conceptualisation of relapse, Melanie reported that during the initial stages, when she was more likely to be aware of the early signs, then she would welcome the opportunity to talk about what was worrying her without her parents immediately assuming it was the start of a major relapse.

In discussions of what responses were best suited to the later stages of a relapse, Melanie reported that she was keen to enlist the help of her sister to mediate any 'disproportionate' response from her parents. All family members agreed that during a crisis, Sally always maintained a neutral relationship with Melanie. She was more likely to remain calm and should therefore be involved in any discussions about hospital admissions. Melanie was also keen to secure greater involvement from her sister, as she had not been allowed to see her when she was an inpatient.

Problem Solving

Problem solving is an essential part of the Kuipers, Lam and Leff (2002) model. It comprised an important feature of FI with this family. Different problems were negotiated and reviewed as a running theme throughout and across sessions. Problem solving was structured, focused and specific. All problems were broken down into smaller parts, and were discussed in a specific here-and-now manner. One specific aspect of a problem was attempted at each family meeting, and homework set if indicated. All family members were encouraged to adopt a realistic approach to outcomes and the pace of change. The areas addressed included the following: the family's understanding of the illness, Alec's 'annoyance' about Melanie not doing *more* around the house, helping Melanie to improve her life skills (e.g. cooking) and relapse prevention.

One of Dorothy's stated aims was to (above all else) keep Melanie safe and well. In session 7, a discussion took place about whether Melanie should inform some of her inner circle of friends about the extent of her mental health problems. All family members recognised that the decision of whether Melanie should disclose or not, served as a continual source of tension and disagreement within the family and often escalated at times when Melanie was due to go out with her friends. The therapists were told that Melanie's friends were aware that she had experienced some difficulties in the past; they were unaware, however, that she had been diagnosed with 'schizophrenia' and was receiving medication.

Dorothy and Alec were adamant that Melanie's friends should be told. It was their belief that if Melanie's friends were informed about her condition, then they would know what to do when Melanie 'fell ill' in their company. Both parents were able to spontaneously offer numerous situations in which Melanie could suddenly fall ill in the company of her unknowing friends and the danger it presented. In addition, Alec and Dorothy tended to seek visual and verbal reassurance from the therapists that their suggestion for Melanie to disclose to friends was both reasonable and necessary. Melanie talked to her parents about the stigma attached to mental illness amongst young people and why she did not want to feel so different from her friends. Sally reported that she would also be reluctant to disclose to *all* her friends if she had similar experiences because of issues relating to stigma and privacy. However, she would probably talk to one of her friends. Interestingly, this served as a very powerful comment from Sally, as she was often perceived by her parents as being informed about young peoples' attitudes.

Emotional Processing

The therapists acknowledged the dilemma facing the family about the disclosure issue, and the level of distress it was causing them all. The therapists highlighted the concern that Alec and Dorothy had about Melanie's welfare and the efforts they made to ensure her safety to date. In accordance with the therapy model, they chose to focus on the feelings that lay behind Alec and Dorothy's need to *pressure* Melanie to disclose her illness to friends. With encouragement, Alec and Dorothy explained to Melanie that they wanted her to tell her friends about her problems because they loved her, and were frightened about something terrible happening to her and no one being around who could help. It was clear to both therapists that Alec and Dorothy remained haunted by incidents that had occurred in the run up to Melanie's first episode, whereby she had found herself in situations where her safety had been compromised. Their recollection of previous incidents also lay behind their desire to know where Melanie was at all times and their sense of uneasiness if she was out late. The therapists spent time trying to elicit what their worst fears were.

All family members were asked to consider alternative ways in which Alec and Dorothy could feel reassured about the safety of Melanie outside of the family home, rather than Melanie feeling that she 'had to' tell everyone about her experiences (i.e. Were there other ways in which Melanie could reassure her parents about her safety?). It was eventually negotiated that Melanie could inform one of her trusted friends about her situation. With Dorothy and Alec in mind, the therapists also raised the issue of relative support groups. It was mentioned that for many relatives, the support and confidence obtained from other parents and siblings in similar roles, was invaluable. They explained that the groups also served as an excellent resource for obtaining information about different aspects of the illness, which is something they all wanted to do.

The Final Sessions

As we approached the end of the intervention, Melanie and her family were in the process of trying to organise their own family meetings, where they could continue to meet and discuss issues in the same way they did with the therapists. All family members believed that the opportunity to discuss concerns together, on a regular basis, were beneficial to Melanie and themselves.

The final two sessions were spent reviewing the areas that were covered in the previous sessions and reflecting on the process of therapy, and the achievement of each member. For example, in response to questioning, Melanie reported that she had found the sessions invaluable, while Sally reported having learnt 'loads'. Dorothy reported tearfully that it was useful to learn about Melanie's experiences and although she would miss the regular visits of the therapists, the therapy process had not made her feel *any* different. Alec wondered openly about why FI was not more widely available, and why they as a family had not been able to access the intervention in the past.

The therapists shared with the family their own observations of how 'close and supportive' they were of each other, and how common and understandable their struggles were.

Conclusions

Family intervention based on the treatment model outlined by Kuipers, Lam and Leff (2002) can be effectively applied to the difficulties experienced within a high EE household. This work highlights the significant contribution that healthy siblings can offer to the therapy process. In many ways, Sally often served as an 'ally' and was able to comment on the family, and bring information that the therapists were not able to access. Although this family was 'high EE', their concerns were indistinguishable from other families; that a son/daughter may be vulnerable to relapse, that the family may not react appropriately to such a relapse, and that the family would need help and support. There was a considerable reluctance to discuss the painful reality of Melanie's experiences, a fear of making things worse and/or saying the 'wrong' thing. A key feature of FI is that therapists facilitate painful discussions in a family setting. This can allow difficult emotions to be experienced, not as overwhelming but as appropriate sadness and loss, which, once identified, can be used as motivation to drive change. In this situation, Melanie, by discussing her difficulties with the rest of her family, and not having them try to jump in with coping ideas that were too superficial to be useful, was able to negotiate new and more effective behavioural change.

By the end of the intervention, the family was able to deal more effectively with a range of difficulties. Melanie had not experienced another relapse and continued to take her medication and go to work. While symptomatic, she was able to access help with her experiences, feel supported and avoid triggers that exacerbate her symptoms. Dorothy reported still being worried, but was not as visibly distressed as when therapy began. Post-therapy assessment showed that Melanie's father obtained a low EE rating on the CFI (Vaughn and Leff, 1976b). In addition, his original score of 38 on the

GHQ-28 fell to 23. On the BDI (Beck, Steer and Brown, 1996), Melanie's original of 30 (*severe range*) dropped to 18, which fell within the *mild* range.

Critical Reflection

In carers of clients with relatively shorter illness histories, the links between feelings of loss and higher levels of EE (specifically EOI) have recently been documented (e.g. Patterson, Birchwood and Cochrane, 2005). Feelings of loss and grief can often manifest themselves in innumerable emotions including anger and frustration, which were evident in some of the behaviours and comments from Melanie's parents. Alec and Dorothy rejected our suggestion to attend a relative's support group, often an ideal environment for relatives to talk about their feelings of sadness and loss and be supported. It may also have been fruitful to address those issues more directly within the family sessions or within one or two supplementary sessions with the parents on their own, or by offering booster sessions over a longer time period, for example up to 2 years.

Melanie was offered FI as part of a clinical trial and at the close of the sessions reported that she had benefited a great deal from the experience. FI therapists must ensure that all family members are involved within the sessions rather than conducting an individual session with a family member within a group format. However, the therapists were aware that there were specific issues that suggested that Melanie might also have benefited from individual (one-to-one) sessions provided either in parallel or concurrently. In the current National Health Service climate, where few people are afforded routine access to evidence-based psychological treatments for psychosis (e.g. FI or cognitive behavioural therapy), this may not have been possible, but adding individual sessions to FI would often be indicated clinically.

All identities have been anonymised and the situation described has been disguised. The leaflet is available on request from the authors.

References

Barrowclough, C. and Hooley, J.M. (2003) Attributions and expressed emotion: a review. *Clinical Psychology Review*, **23** (6), 849–80.

Barrowclough, C., Johnston, M. and Tarrier, N. (1994) Attributions, expressed emotion, and patient relapse – an attributional model of relatives response to schizophrenic illness. *Behavior Therapy,* **25** (1), 67–88.

Barrowclough, C. and Parle, M. (1997) Appraisal, psychological adjustment and expressed emotion in relatives of patients suffering from schizophrenia. *British Journal of Psychiatry,* **171**, 26–30.

Barrowclough, C. and Tarrier, N. (1992) *Families of Schizophrenic Patients: Cognitive Behavioural Intervention,* Chapman and Hall, London.

Barrowclough, C., Tarrier, N., Humphreys, L. *et al.* (2003) Self-esteem in schizophrenia: relationships between self-evaluation, family attitudes, and symptomatology. *Journal of Abnormal Psychology,* **112** (1), 92–9.

Barrowclough, C., Ward, J., Wearden, A. and Gregg, L. (2005) Expressed emotion and attributions in relatives of schizophrenia patients with and without substance misuse. *Social Psychiatry and Psychiatric Epidemiology,* **40** (11), 884–91.

Bebbington, P. and Kuipers, L. (1994a) The clinical utility of expressed emotion in schizophrenia. *Acta Psychiatrica Scandinavica,* **89**, 46–53. *Archives of General Psychiatry,* **52** (8), 679–87.

Bebbington, P. and Kuipers, L. (1994b) The predictive utility of expressed emotion in schizophrenia – an aggregate analysis. *Psychological Medicine,* **24** (3), 707–18.

Beck, A.T., Steer, R.A. and Brown, G.K. (1996). *Manual for the Revised Beck Depression Inventory,* Psychological Corporation, San Antonio, TX.

Bolton, C., Calam, R., Barrowclough, C. *et al.* (2003) Expressed emotion, attributions and depression in mothers of children with problem behaviour. *Journal of Child Psychology and Psychiatry and Allied Disciplines,* **44** (2), 242–54.

Brewin, C.R., Maccarthy, B., Duda, K. and Vaughn, C.E. (1991) Attribution and expressed emotion in the relatives of patients with schizophrenia. *Journal of Abnormal Psychology,* **100** (4), 546–54.

Brown, G.W. (1959) Experiences of discharged chronic schizophrenic mental hospital patients in various types of living group. *Milbank Memorial Fund Quarterly,* **37**, 105–31.

Brown, G.W. (1985) The discovery of expressed emotion: induction or deduction? in *Expressed Emotion in Families* (eds J. Leff and C. Vaughn), Guilford, New York, pp. 7–25.

Brown, G.W., Birley, J.L.T. and Wing, J.K. (1972) Influence of family life on the course of schizophrenic disorders – a replication. *British Journal of Psychiatry,* **121** (3), 241–58.

Brown, G.W., Monck, E.M., Carstairs, G.M. and Wing, J. (1962) The influence of family life on the course of schizophrenic illness. *British Journal of Preventive Social Medicine,* **16** (2), 55–68.

Butzlaff, R.L. and Hooley, J.M. (1998) Expressed emotion and psychiatric relapse – a meta-analysis. *Archives of General Psychiatry,* **55** (6), 547–52.

Falloon, I.R.H. (2003) Family interventions for mental disorders: efficacy and effectiveness. *World Psychiatry*, **2** (1), 20–8.

Falloon, I.R.H., Boyd, J.L. and McGill, C.W. (1984) *Family Care of Schizophrenia*, Guildford Press, New York.

Goldberg, D. and Williams, P.A. (1988) *A Users' Guide to the General Health Questionnaire*, NFER-Nelson, Windsor.

Harrison, C.A. and Dadds, M.R. (1992) Attributions of symptomatology – an exploration of family factors associated with expressed emotion. *Australian and New Zealand Journal of Psychiatry*, **26** (3), 408–16.

Harrison, C.A., Dadds, M.R. and Smith, G. (1998) Family caregivers' criticism of patients with schizophrenia. *Psychiatric Services*, **49**, 918–24.

Hooley, J.M. (1985) Expressed emotion – a review of the critical literature. *Clinical Psychology Review*, **5** (2), 119–39.

Hooley, J.M. and Campbell, C. (2002) Control and controllability: beliefs and behaviour in high and low expressed emotion relatives. *Psychological Medicine*, **32** (6), 1091–9.

Hooley, J.M. and Licht, D.M. (1997) Expressed emotion and causal attributions in the spouses of depressed patients. *Journal of Abnormal Psychology*, **106** (2), 298–306.

Hooley, J.M., Richters, J.E., Weintraub, S. and Neale, J.M. (1987) Psychopathology and marital distress – the positive side of positive symptoms. *Journal of Abnormal Psychology*, **96** (1), 27–33.

Ivanovic, M., Vuletic, Z. and Bebbington, P. (1994) Expressed emotion in the families of patients with schizophrenia and its influence on the course of illness. *Social Psychiatry and Psychiatric Epidemiology*, **29** (2), 61–65.

Karanci, A.N. and Inandilar, H. (2002) Predictors of components of expressed emotion in major caregivers of Turkish patients with schizophrenia. *Social Psychiatry and Psychiatric Epidemiology*, **37** (2), 80–8.

Kavanagh, D.J. (1992) Recent developments in expressed emotion and schizophrenia. *British Journal of Psychiatry*, **160**, 601–20.

Kuipers, E., Bebbington, P., Dunn, G. *et al.* (2006) Influence of carer expressed emotion and affect on relapse in non-affective psychoses. *British Journal of Psychiatry*, **188** 173–9.

Kuipers, E., Lam, D. and Leff, J. (2002) *Family Work for Schizophrenia: A Practical Guide*, Gaskell Press, London.

Kuipers, L. (1979) Expressed emotion: a review. *British Journal of Social and Clinical Psychology*, **18**, 237–43.

Leff, J. (1989) Controversial issues and growing points in research on relatives' expressed emotion. *International Journal of Social Psychiatry*, **35** (2), 133–45.

Leff, J. and Gamble, C. (1995) Training of community psychiatric nurses in family work for schizophrenia. *International Journal of Mental Health*, **24**, 76–88.

Leff, J. and Vaughn, C. (1985) *Expressed Emotion in Families*, Guildford Press, London.

Lopez, S.R., Hipke, K.N., Polo, A.J. *et al.* (2004) Ethnicity, expressed emotion, attributions, and course of schizophrenia: family warmth matters. *Journal of Abnormal Psychology*, **113** (3), 428–39.

Lopez, S.R., Nelson, K.A., Snyder, K.S. and Mintz, J. (1999) Attributions and affective reactions of family members and course of schizophrenia. *Journal of Abnormal Psychology*, **108** (2), 307–14.

Marom, S., Munitz, H., Jones, P.B. *et al.* (2002) Familial expressed emotion: outcome and course of Israeli patients with schizophrenia. *Schizophrenia Bulletin*, **28** (4), 731–43.

Martins, C., de Lemos, A.I. and Bebbington, P.E. (1992) A Portuguese/Brazilian study of expressed emotion. *Social Psychiatry and Psychiatric Epidemiology*, **27**, 22–7.

Moline, R.A., Singh, S., Morris, A. and Meltzer, H.Y. (1985) Family expressed emotion and relapse in schizophrenia in 24 urban American patients. *American Journal of Psychiatry*, **142** (9), 1078–81.

Mottaghipour, Y., Pourmand, D., Maleki, H. and Davidian, L. (2001) Expressed emotion and the course of schizophrenia in Iran. *Social Psychiatry and Psychiatric Epidemiology*, **36** (4), 195–9.

National Institute of Clinical Excellence (NICE) (2003) *Schizophrenia; Full National Clinical Guidelines on Core Interventions in Primary and Secondary Care*, Gaskell Press, London.

Nomura, H., Inoue, S., Kamimura, N. *et al.* (2005) A cross-cultural study on expressed emotion in carers of people with dementia and schizophrenia: Japan and England. *Social Psychiatry and Psychiatric Epidemiology*, **40** (7), 564–70.

Patterson, P., Birchwood, M. and Cochrane, R. (2005) Expressed emotion as an adaptation to loss: prospective study in first-episode psychosis. *The British Journal of Psychiatry*, **187** (48), s59–s64.

Peterson, E.C. and Docherty, N.M. (2004) Expressed emotion, attribution, and control in parents of schizophrenic patients. *Psychiatry-Interpersonal and Biological Processes*, **67** (2), 197–207.

Provencher, H.L. and Mueser, K.T. (1997) Positive and negative symptom behaviors and caregiver burden in the relatives of persons with schizophrenia. *Schizophrenia Research*, **26** (1), 71–80.

Ran, M.S., Leff, J., Hou, Z.J. *et al.* (2003) The characteristics of expressed emotion among relatives of patients with schizophrenia in Chengdu, China. *Culture Medicine and Psychiatry*, **27** (1), 95–106.

Raune, D., Kuipers, E. and Bebbington, P.E. (2004) Expressed emotion at first-episode psychosis: investigating a carer appraisal model. *The British Journal of Psychiatry*, **184** (4), 321–6.

Scazufca, M. and Kuipers, E. (1996) Links between expressed emotion and burden of care in relatives of patients with schizophrenia. *British Journal of Psychiatry*, **168** (5), 580–7.

Scazufca, M. and Kuipers, E. (1999) Coping strategies in relatives of people with schizophrenia before and after psychiatric admission. *The British Journal of Psychiatry*, **174** (2), 154–8.

Shimodera, S., Mino, Y., Inoue, S. *et al.* (2000) Expressed emotion and family distress in relatives of patients with schizophrenia in Japan. *Comprehensive Psychiatry*, **41** (5), 392–7.

Smith, J., Birchwood, M., Cochrane, R. and George, S. (1993) The needs of high and low expressed emotion families – a normative approach. *Social Psychiatry and Psychiatric Epidemiology*, **28** (1), 11–6.

Van Humbeeck, G., Van Audenhove, C., De Hert, M. *et al.* (2002) Expressed emotion – a review of assessment instruments. *Clinical Psychology Review*, **22** (3), 321–41.

Vaughan, K., Doyle, M., Mcconaghy, N. *et al.* (1992) The relationship between relatives expressed emotion and schizophrenic relapse – an Australian replication. *Social Psychiatry and Psychiatric Epidemiology*, **27** (1), 10–5.

Vaughn, C.E. and Leff, J.P. (1976a) The influence of family and social factors on the course of psychiatric illness. A comparison of schizophrenic and depressed neurotic patients. *The British Journal of Psychiatry*, **129** (2), 125–37.

Vaughn, C.E. and Leff, J.P. (1976b) Measurement of expressed emotion in families of psychiatric-patients. *British Journal of Social and Clinical Psychology*, **15**, 157–65.

Weiner, B. (1986) *An Attributional Theory of Motivation and Emotion*, Springer, New York.

Weiner, B. (1993) On sin versus sickness – a theory of perceived responsibility and social motivation. *American Psychologist*, **48** (9), 957–65.

Weiner, B. (1995) *Judgements of Responsibility: A Foundation for a Theory of Social Conduct*, Guildford Press, New York.

Weisman, A.G. and Lopez, S.R. (1997) An attributional analysis of emotional reactions to schizophrenia in Mexican and Anglo American cultures. *Journal of Applied Social Psychology*, **27** (3), 223–44.

Weisman, A., Lopez, S.R., Karno, M. and Jenkins, J. (1993) An attributional analysis of expressed emotion in Mexican-American families with schizophrenia. *Journal of Abnormal Psychology*, **102** (4), 601–6.

Weisman, A.G., Nuechterlein, K.H., Goldstein, M.J. and Snyder, K.S. (1998) Expressed emotion, attributions, and schizophrenia symptom dimensions. *Journal of Abnormal Psychology*, **107** (2), 355–9.

Wendel, J.S., Miklowitz, D.J., Richards, J.A. and George, E.L. (2000) Expressed emotion and attributions in the relatives of bipolar patients: an analysis of problem-solving interactions. *Journal of Abnormal Psychology*, **109** (4), 792–6.

Woo, S.M., Goldstein, M.J. and Nuechterlein, K.H. (2004) Relatives' affective style and the expression of subclinical psychopathology in patients with schizophrenia. *Family Process*, **43** (2), 233–47.

Yang, L.H., Phillips, M.R., Licht, D.M. and Hooley, J.M. (2004) Causal attributions about schizophrenia in families in China: expressed emotion and patient relapse. *Journal of Abnormal Psychology*, **113** (4), 592–602.

Resources

Kuipers, E., Leff, J. and Lam, D. (2002). *Family Work for Schizophrenia. A Practical Guide*, 2nd edn, Gaskell Press, London.

Kuipers, E. and Bebbington, P. (2005) *Living with Mental Illness: A Book for Relatives and Friends*, 3rd edn, Souvenir Press, London.

Jones, S. and Hayward, P. (2004) *Coping with Schizophrenia: A Guide for Patients, Families and Caregivers*, Oneworld publications, London.

www.rethink.org (accessed 5 January 2009).

www.mentalhealthcare.org.uk (accessed 5 January 2009).

www.carersonline.org.uk (accessed 5 January 2009).

www.understandingpsychosis.com (accessed 5 January 2009).

8

Coming to Terms with Mental Illness in the Family – Working Constructively through Its Grief

Virginia Lafond

The ripple effects of mental illness will not go away, and we will continue to rail, rage, cry, and mourn. But in between, maybe we can try to find meaning by doing a good deed, experiencing something deeply, and trying to bring some identity and meaning to the suffering (Mona Wasow – Mental Health Practitioner, Researcher, Family Member).

Introduction

This chapter focuses on grief work with families when psychosis (usually leading to many other subsequent losses) presents itself via a member of the family. Rather than focusing on assisting the person with the mental health problem, it will attempt to illustrate how work with the grief endured by other family members can be effectively approached so that they can 'have a life' and still remain the caring, loving family they want to be. In pursuing this focus, it is hoped that further steps are taken to steer this important aspect of the family's experience from its historical 'orphan' status so that it becomes a phenomenon that is both recognised and affirmed as *normal emotional process* to be worked with. In this chapter, family members are regarded as living through and coping with their emotional process in the face of the loss of mental health in a relative – and not as simply presenting with difficult negative and/or static expression or behaviour. It is actually from this view of the family member that a definition of the family

A Casebook of Family Interventions for Psychosis   Edited by Fiona Lobban and Christine Barrowclough
© 2009 John Wiley & Sons, Ltd

member's grief process has been developed: the thoughts, feelings, actions and other experiences of relatives related to their perceptions of loss resulting from a family member's mental health problem. Put simply, our working philosophy is that the grief of mental illness is *normal resulting emotion* that is to be worked with (even cultivated) so as to bring family members to a point of having come to terms with the illness of a family member so as to regain good quality of life and peacefulness. The grief work model presented in this chapter has its origins in the Schizophrenia Programme, Royal Ottawa Mental Health Centre (ROMHC), Ottawa, Canada. We have found that identification of the family's grief process and coaching as to how to work with it can be helpful to families in resolving distress in the 'here and now'. Because this work may produce lasting paradigm shifts in family members, it also serves to help family members avoid potential problems in the future, which might otherwise show themselves as complications of grief expression. A detailed case example[1] will describe commonly presenting grief expressions in a family and how this grief work model can be used.

Context for Case Presentation

Specific issues associated with working with the grief of mental illness in families

Conceptualising mental illness as a disenfranchised loss (Doka, 1989; Pine *et al.*, 1990) is central to our work. Because little is known about grief and the experiences of loss in this context – that is, precisely because it and they are not recognised – there is a need to provide family members with basic education about the subject. However, this oftentimes flies in the face of what families say they want. What families usually seek first is treatment (if not an outright cure) for their relative and then later comprehensive services for him or her. In most cases they ask nothing for themselves. We see this to be the case even when family members are obviously entrenched in particular phases of their grieving process. But, when gently prompted, family members will allow that they do feel stuck in a seesaw grieving

---

[1] The case example described in this chapter has been pieced together from casework experience. While it is representative of our work and its results, the clients are fictionalised so as to safeguard confidentiality.

dynamic moving from anger to sadness and back to anger, and so forth to an extent that they do not ever consider that they can work to come to peaceful terms with their illness-related losses. Another abiding issue relating to the practical application of this model is figuring out how and when to open up the subject of the grief of mental illness in order to introduce education we consider essential to the family's well-being. We have found some answers in using public educational forums and also, when doing individual family work, in purposely looking for entry points (e.g. when a family member breaks into tears or expresses anger, including when they scold themselves about their emotional expression). We have also learned through practice that to begin working with the family requires on our part shifting beyond simply assessing the family's emotional expression. The shift requires normalising the grieving process in the context of families where a member has a mental health problem. Then examining the process of 'to be expected' grieving of each member of the family becomes the therapeutic task at hand.

Theoretical influences

Besides our observations from clinical practice of the emotional expression and behaviour of family members which have led us to believe that grief is always present whenever a family member contracts a mental health problem, our approach has been enriched from the study of several sources in the literature. These include those with a focus on normal grief reaction (Kübler-Ross, 1969; Lindemann, 1944; Parkes, 1972; Raphael, 1983); disenfranchised loss and grief (Doka, 1989; Pine *et al.*, 1990); critical analysis of grief and trauma theory (Averill and Nunley, 1988; Prigerson *et al.*, 1995; Summerfield, 2000; Wortman and Silver, 1989); and grief reaction of families when mental illness is present in a family member (Atkinson, 1994; Godress *et al.*, 2005; Hatfield and Lefley, 1989; Miller *et al.*, 1990; Ozgul, 2004; Perera, 2003; Solomon and Draine, 1996; Wasow, 1995). First-person accounts by family members (e.g. Button, 1996; Deveson, 1992, 2003; Govig, 1994; Lachenmeyer, 2000) have also been studied. We have also taken into account suggested implications for practice offered by researchers and practitioners in the area of loss and grief (e.g. Boss, 1999; Hatfield, 1989; Miller, 1996; Terkelsen, 1987; Wasow, 1995; Worden, 1982). Our model has also been informed by the wisdom of practitioner philosophers – in particular, Frankl (1997), particularly his conclusion arrived at through concentration camp experience, i.e. the human being always has choice – the choice of choosing one's attitude, and Kabat-Zinn (1990) on mindfulness. As well, though it may at first appear curious, we have found that the practice wisdom of laughter therapists has been of service in developing this model. (See MacDonald (2004) for laughter therapy overview.) Other valuable influences in developing the approach are derived from the principles and practice of cognitive behaviour therapy (as previously noted in Lafond (1998, 2002); particularly in Appendix II).

Style of intervention

In the main, the style of our intervention is a mix of supportive listening, conveyance of didactic 'gentle but firm' educational information, group educational presentations, as well as cognitive behavioural work. We have found that cognitive behaviour therapy (CBT) is especially helpful as family members like most people often exhibit constricted and painful takes about many human activities including about grief and the grieving process – so much so that they often tend to avoid grief work. We also incorporate the use of bibliotherapy whenever this would appear to be helpful.

The initial presentation of the family is always considered a window which permits an important if imperfect glimpse of how family members are grappling with their respective grieving processes. The particular direction and form of therapy is based on the findings of the initial assessment and continues to be informed by ongoing assessment. This grief work model is always adapted to match the particular needs of the family as a whole and the needs of individual members within a family unit. In short, it sets out to (1) meet family members exactly where they are at, emotionally and otherwise, (2) take a compassionate look at what their situation is and (3) offer the family guidance and tools to manage their grieving journey.

Therapists and therapy

At the ROMHC, psychiatrists, psychologists, nurses, social workers, occupational therapists and recreation therapists comprise the multidisciplinary teams of its various programmes. Depending on the presenting need of the family, one therapist, sometimes together with a psychiatrist, works with family members. Most of our professional staff have been introduced to this grief work in the family context through in-service educational sessions, either on this model specifically or on other therapeutic approaches including CBT for schizophrenia/psychosis. One module of our CBT for schizophrenia/psychosis series is devoted to work with the grief of mental illness. Prerequisites for this work are:

- Knowledge of the grief of mental illness experience and willingness to use this as a cornerstone framework for approaching families.
- An attitude of compassionate sensitivity to the family's experience.

In terms of doing the actual work, we suggest that workers

- anticipate grief's presence whenever psychosis occurs in a member of the family;
- never skip the basics – alert and otherwise educate family members about grief's presence and their consequent need for grief work;
- in the case where denial is predominating, take the time to outline in detail the normal dynamics of the grieving process accompanying mental illness, emphasising its component of denial as well as denial's potential hazards;
- early on, encourage conscious and constructive engagement in the grieving process by explaining to family members that they can 'have a life' or 'take their lives back' by engaging with their grief rather than having their lives driven by the status of the family member's mental health problem.

In addition, it is highly recommended that therapists choose their grief work language carefully. We have found that it is not effective to use always or exclusively words or phrases like 'grief' or 'grieving process'. With many, it is more helpful to make mention of such words but to move on to other language, for example, 'You've had so much to deal with around his/her problems. Have you been able to take time to look at how you are doing?'; or 'Others have found the coming to terms with this kind of problem is really tough. Have you been able to work at coming to some peace for yourself?'

The clinical service

In the majority of cases at ROMHC's Schizophrenia Programme, social workers are assigned to work with families though other members of the team interact with clients and their families as well – this, whenever possible and always with the permission of the client. (If the client withholds consent for communication with his or her family, social workers will still take calls from family members and document the family's input but not give any information about the client.) Following assessment, families can be offered service on an individual family basis. As well, all are invited to twice monthly family information and support group meetings which are open to the public.

The number of sessions for grief work with family members varies. What we have discovered is that there is a marked difference in the number of sessions required depending on whether family members attend our group meetings in which the grief work rendered in individual family sessions is purposely interspersed with other subject matter. On average, the number of individual sessions for families who attend group meetings ranges from 4 to 6. The number required for those who do not is at least doubled.

Case Example: Barbara and Clement, Parents in Marital Distress

The following case example illustrates a family situation mental health practitioners frequently observe – relationship distress developed and/or exacerbated more or less in tandem with each family member's experience of loss when a mental health problem develops in a family member.

Barbara and Clement, a married couple in their later 40s, are the parents of Rania, age 21, who left home at the age of 19 to attend a college diploma course in design outside of Ottawa. Always a good student, she chose to attend this particular course because she had been offered a scholarship for it. Though she had succeeded fairly well through most of her first year, her year-end marks were not as high as her parents had anticipated. That summer a job in an elite coffee shop did not work out. Her parents recounted that they remembered Rania complaining once or twice that her boss 'has it in for me' and that this was just before she suddenly quit the job in midsummer. Clement added, 'She might have been fired. We don't know.'

Though Barbara and Clement had some concerns about her return to school given her *laissez-faire* attitude as summer wound up, they supported her return to school including financially. Not too long after the Christmas/New Year break they were called by one of Rania's school acquaintances who first said that she herself had a sibling who had a diagnosis of schizophrenia. She hesitated but nonetheless said that Rania was reminding her of her sister. This young woman gave details: 'Rania is holed up in her room, sleeping through all her classes, and not mixing with others because she says, "They are out to get me." ' Barbara and Clement immediately went into action. They were successful in persuading Rania to seek help at the college's student health services. However, as time went on, they questioned the pace and adequacy of this service. Their concerns understandably increased when at school year's end Rania returned to them but remained in bed in her room, did not return her friends' calls and hardly communicated with her parents.

Referral

We first encountered Barbara and Clement when they attended the family information and support group meetings and then later through Barbara's telephone outreach to one of the group's facilitating social workers. Barbara and Clement had attended three of six meetings over the course of 3 months.

When Barbara and Clement came to our attention at their first family information and support meeting they did not appear to be exhibiting an exceptional level of distress. In fact, they both seemed comfortable during the opening of the meeting when they along with other group participants responded to our routine invitation to briefly introduce themselves. Clement explained that their daughter, now an inpatient in our centre, had just been diagnosed with a mental illness and that they were feeling relief that she was finally in the hands of competent help. He added that they were now beginning to hope for a successful outcome so that she could get on with her life and even possibly return to school. Barbara added that they were glad to have found out about these meetings because they were feeling the need for 'something for ourselves'.

Family engagement methods/issues

The Royal Ottawa's family information and support group meetings are open to anyone who is a family member or friend of someone who may have a psychiatric problem. We offer education about a range of topics, that is from treatments, self-care, resources for both patients and family and this sometimes by way of guest presenters including mental health professionals and also family caregivers. We also mention that the facilitating social work team is open to taking calls from anyone attending the family meetings even if the one in the family with a mental health problem is not a registered patient of one of our services.

Along with other participants in the family group meetings, Barbara and Clement took part actively by asking for clarification and also by volunteering information about ways they communicate with each other when in distress. Their participation was such that the workers facilitating the sessions had no outstanding concerns about the couple's situation except that it had been noticed that Clement had been uncharacteristically silent during the last session the couple attended. Barbara's telephone call came about three months after the couple's last attended group meeting. She explained that she and her husband were in need of some assistance: 'We've had our rough patches in our thirty year relationship but we've always gotten through. Now, we seem to have turned into a very dark corridor. With Rania not getting better it's as if our world has been turned up-side-down. Now Clem hardly speaks to me. I know he thinks Rania's not even trying to get better. But we don't know. I think she is so stunned herself by all this. Anyway, she's not talking to him or to me or to anyone else for that matter. I know we're not seeing eye-to-eye about this.'

We have learned through our clinical practice that we need to often remind family members about the basic points of grief work. We suppose this to be necessary because it is not unusual for family members to be engaged with a number of issues, some at crisis level and sometimes unrelated to the person with the mental health problem. As well, there is the factor of the tasks of conscious and constructive engagement with this grief not being at the forefront of anyone's awareness or agenda. Returning to the case example, the therapist gently but firmly interrupted Barbara, attempting first to offer reassurance. She began this by normalising their plight. The dialogue between Barbara and the worker went as follows:

THERAPIST: Barbara, may I stop you there? What I'm hearing from you is something that happens in many families at times like this.

BARBARA: It does?

THERAPIST: Yes, it does. You and Clement are both dealing with a lot as far as Rania is concerned and, like most people do, you are both going about this according to your individual insights about her. It is not uncommon that parents have different feelings and then different points of view. You and Clement are perceiving Rania's health problem differently and therefore you're each reacting differently. Individuals always grieve at their own pace and in their own ways. We see this as the normal, if painful, grief reaction pattern in families.

BARBARA: I hadn't thought of it like that lately but I think that's sure true about us. I mean though we've disagreed before we've been able to compromise – at least eventually. Right now, Clement isn't the same and I'm afraid to speak up – though I know I need to – for fear of making matters worse for him. (As she made this last statement, Barbara broke into tears.) Therapist, after a pause to convey appreciation of Barbara's emotional expression: 'We offer our services to people who come to the groups outside of the group sessions. Would you want to come in with Clement?'

When family members indicate their desire to come in for counselling session, it is the routine in our service to notify the psychiatrist attending the family member and other members of the team.

Assessment formulation/reaching a shared understanding of problems

The next week Barbara and Clement came in exhibiting none of the hopeful and relaxed manner they had when they attended the family group meetings. Clement looked guarded and Barbara somewhat anxious. The therapist's first goal was to hear Clement's viewpoint and more of Barbara's and then to facilitate discussion between the couple – this towards developing a shared formulation of problems to work on. Her opening comments, 'I understand you've been having some difficulties. Barbara, you did not go into detail on the phone last week. You were mostly expressing emotional distress', were followed by both Clem and Barbara describing their individual experiences. Clem admitted to being 'sullen' and explained that this was because 'I feel dread at the pit of my stomach. I was hopeful for a while there about Rania when she first came here but I'm not any more. What's it been? Three, maybe four, months and she's still not facing the fact that she has a problem. From what I've been able to gather from people in the groups and the bit of reading I've done, there isn't much chance that things will turn around quickly. I'm really afraid for her. I feel the daughter I knew is lost to us and this whole thing is ruining our lives – hers and ours.' Barbara followed with: 'I feel it's still early yet. From what I've learned in the group meetings, it can be slow going at first because many people begin by denying that they have a problem, but eventually they do come around.'

As this first assessment session continued the therapist attempted to elicit more information about how Barbara and Clement thought they were fairing as a family in the face of their family's problem. Once both had been heard, the therapist then offered an assessment formulation and asked if they agreed with the formulation. Once there was consensus about the formulation, an offer to assist the family was made:

THERAPIST: I hear both of your concerns about Rania and also about the difficult times you've been having emotionally and otherwise. It sounds like you've both been going through what we call a grieving process and if you are like most people you've each been trying to get through on your own. Though this is what we've come to see as a usual way of reacting on the part of the family members we work with, we think that there can be great benefit all around if people grasp an understanding of this as grief process and commit to working with it . . . Do you understand what I mean? Would you agree?

Once the couple's agreement on the formulation was secured, the therapist then suggested that they 'look together at a recent particular problem they've had and how you individually and as a couple managed that. We can then move on to considering how you might handle the same problem in light of a mini refresher course in working with the grief of mental illness.'

Barbara responded first, citing an incident which had occurred on a recent weekend when she had 'on the spur of the moment' purchased tickets for the three of them to a chamber music festival. She explained that she had done this to see if she could reignite Rania's interest in classical music as well as to maybe pleasantly surprise Clement who had in the past responded with delight to surprises like her impulsive concert ticket purchases. But this time, as she explained in the session, her initiative backfired to the extent that Rania simply retreated once more to her room and Clement told her in no uncertain terms that she should not have bought the tickets. Clement, in his turn, said that he felt 'pressured and put upon' and that he really didn't 'want to go anywhere that used to be a place Rania enjoyed because it would just remind me of her situation now'.

From this kind of account, using a grieving mental illness lens, it became obvious to the therapist that Clement and Barbara were in their respective throes of unrecognised grieving. As in most cases when recent experiences of dysfunctional communication are explored through this lens, issues that come to the fore include

- communication difficulties as each is expressing himself or herself differently given the experience of unrecognised loss or, perhaps, recognised loss but the person is without language to express himself/herself about the loss;
- behaviour change in a negative direction – from healthy or relatively healthy interpersonal behaviour to dysfunctional behaviour; in our case example, the uncharacteristic rejection of Barbara's initiative by Clement is an example of this phenomenon.

The therapist's agenda at this point was threefold: (1) review with the couple her understanding of their feelings and behaviour in an attempt to reach a more robust and accurate shared formulation of the problems, (2) continuation of normalisation and (3) reintroduction of points about working with the grief of mental illness:

THERAPIST: What seems to be happening between the two of you since Rania became ill is what happens in many families. Communication glitches often develop when something unusual and unpleasant happens. Each of you has been affected emotionally by Rania's mental health problem – including Rania herself. Now, I know that you both have heard something at the family group meetings about the benefits of knowing about the grief process that comes when someone in the family has a mental health problem. Most people find it is helpful to have some review of that material here in these sessions. If you are in agreement I would be happy to discuss this further with you so that you might be able to make use of it for yourselves now.

Intervention

The therapist had identified in Barbara and Clement's situation evidence of a common problematic dynamic: family members acting unilaterally in accord with their individual unconscious grieving processes, without much (if any) sensitivity to what other family members are thinking and feeling. The therapeutic tasks focused on expansion of the shared assessment formulation to include this problematic dynamic, validation of each family member's grieving process expression and conveyance of heuristic points about engagement with the grieving process:

THERAPIST: You both have your individual feelings and your own ways of dealing with these – as anybody would have. I think we agree that Rania's mental health problem affects both of you differently. We've found through our experience that when family members, and patients too, identify and take the time to look at their own individual grieving process they can better appreciate what they are going through emotionally – and not just as individuals. As well, they also come to understand and appreciate what other family members are going through. We find these new understandings make for a decrease in communication breakdowns and family conflicts. These new understandings about emotions in the face of mental illness can actually help family members adopt compassionate attitudes towards themselves and to others in the family.

The therapist continued by building a persuasive case for appreciating their grieving or 'coming to terms' process. Basic points discussed over a number of sessions included the following:

- Whenever a mental health problem occurs in a member of a family, each person in the family who becomes aware of the problem is affected by its presence.
- The mental health problem is a loss, that is a loss of mental health, which is usually the vanguard of other losses (e.g. changes in terms of jobs, education and career pursuits, financial income, expenses, residential accommodation) to the person and his/her family members.
- When we experience loss, we humans grieve.
- Depending on a range of factors, including the particular presentation of the psychosis and the family member's relationship with the person with the psychosis (both in terms of closeness and quality), individual reactions differ. But once aware of the mental health problem being suffered by the relative, family members find themselves in varying degrees of distress – in shock, denial, fear, anger, sadness.
- Grieving in reaction to any loss is a *normal human reaction.* It is considered well within the realm of normalcy to experience more than one grief emotion at any one time and/or to be feeling one of its components one day and feeling another the next, only to have the first feeling return, *et cetera.* Once aware of their grieving process, most people make

their way through their various grief 'journeys' to a point where they have found peace, or as Parkes (1972) put it, to the point where a 'new identity [emerges] from the altered life situations' (p. 122).

- Loss associated with mental illness can be seen as a disenfranchised loss – a loss which is unrecognised by society, that is endured without ritual and in other ways is unsupported with the result that the grieving which ensues is also disenfranchised (Doka, 1989). In addition, the losses about mental illness and its ensuing grief are compounded because of stigmatisation of the circumstances of those with mental health problems in our society.

After reviewing these points, the therapist returned to the recent communication difficulty described by the couple and asked how they might approach each other now in light of greater awareness of their respective grieving processes. Clement was clear: 'Now, I see that I had been dealing with Rania's situation by retreating into myself and I was at a point that I wasn't giving a care for or about what Barbara was going through. In that sense, I was actually making matters worse.' Barbara was clear also: 'I learned a lot here. I now know that I've got to be more sensitive in practical ways towards Clem and Rania. Knowing what I do now about individual grieving process, I can see that I'd better from now on approach Clem and Rania before doing things like buying concert tickets. Besides that I am learning how important it is to take care of myself during this coming to terms process.'

Sessions 3–5 were spent first reviewing Barbara and Clement's progress and their difficult moments. Also, because both Barbara and Clement were evidencing misinterpretation of each other's words and actions, in session 3 it was decided to introduce the thought record analysis technique (TRA) from Beck's CBT model as a way of buttressing the grief work. This was done by affirming progress made ('From what I can see you are both making successful efforts to be more aware and respectful of your partner's emotions') and then moving on to the TRA introduction along the following lines:

I am concerned that on both of your parts there may be a tendency still to misinterpret each other's words or actions in a way that is somewhat narrow and negative – and thus doing neither of you any real good. I have a suggestion for you from cognitive behaviour therapy. I'd like to take a few minutes to explain this to you as many family members we have worked with have found that doing homework exercises with certain CBT techniques has proven truly helpful.

Following the initial CBT introduction, the therapist introduced and then coached the couple in the technique of TRA. A sheet of common cognitive distortions was given as well. She then proposed to Barbara and Clement that they might try to use this CBT technique if possible three times before their next session.

When the couple returned for their fourth and fifth sessions, they took turns to explain that they found the instruction both in understanding their individual grief processes and in CBT had been of real assistance. In part, Clement said: 'Though we are still very concerned about Rania because she is still not really improving – at least noticeably – and she does give us both hardship, we are now supporting each other. I'm not just looking out for myself – cocooned up like I used to be. And with these [CBT] exercises, I think I find that I am correcting my misjudgements or, as you call them, cognitive distortions. I'm still learning even about facing my grief . . . which to be honest, I had been avoiding. I actually feel less hurt now.' And in her turn, Barbara's evaluation of her progress was similar: 'Now, with these exercises, I catch myself. I might first think "There he goes again walking off, leaving me alone. He's rejecting me" but then I look at that list [of cognitive distortions] and realise I'm making the mistakes of jumping to conclusions and catastrophising. When I take the few minutes to do the exercises you suggested I come to remind myself that Clem is doing what he needs to do at the moment for himself. I now respect and honour that.'

Outcome

It was about 6 months before we had another session, which was devoted to the couple's need to know what was available in terms of affordable housing for Rania. This was taken as an opportunity to ask how they themselves were doing. Their positive feedback – that is that though they were still concerned about their daughter, they had maintained their gains as a couple and as individuals – is not atypical of the feedback we receive about the application of this model of work with the grief of mental illness.

Critical reflection

In hindsight, the successful outcome of the application of grief work in the foregoing case example appears to have as much to do with the cooperation of the client family members as with the skilful grief work coaching of the worker. These circumstances beg obvious questions, for example what about when family members remain in a stance of 'I just can't get over what's happened' or, when they are predominantly focused on finding better resources for their relative rather than getting into engaging with their own emotional process? There is no doubt that movement through and with the grieving process can be slowed down to the point of there being no perceptible changes even following skilful grief work attempts. Progress can also be confounded by other factors such as those which stem from a scarcity of resources. At the end of the day, we believe that it remains important to open a door nonetheless so that family members are exposed to potential new possibilities for themselves – like being able to achieve deserved and needed peacefulness.

Conclusion

Over 30 years ago, Colin Murray Parkes, after studying grief reactions of both death and non-death losses, opined: 'Willingness to look at the problems of grief and grieving instead of turning away from them is the key to successful grief work . . .' (p. 213). The development of our grief model in the Schizophrenia Programme at the Royal Ottawa has been spurred by the advice of Parkes and also that of others, including researcher/practitioners who have studied family grief when a mental health problem affects a family member (Miller, Wasow, Boss, Perera, Godress *et al.*, and Ozgul). We have also been compelled in our work by the ever-present needs of the families with whom we work. We are profoundly grateful for the feedback families have given us.

Is our model as presented adequate? Outcome evaluations, garnered through focus groups and end of therapy feedback, are encouraging. Feedback ranges from 'It's simply good to have someone who understands to talk this over with' to 'My life has changed permanently for the better' and 'I/we have a life now'. That being the case, we realise there is much more work to be done to address the phenomenon of family grief. Now, for one example, we are looking at and thinking about how best to work with the family expression of denial – including apparent arrest in denial – when it functions to put obstacles in the way of recommended treatment for the family member. As we continue our work in this vein, we invite others who are doing similar work to enter into dialogue with us.

Acknowledgements

Many thanks to the editors of this book, Dr Fiona Lobban and Professor Christine Barrowclough, both for the opportunity to focus on family grief work and for their excellent editorial guidance. Also, to Alain Labelle, MD, FRCP, Clinical Director, Schizophrenia Programme, Royal Ottawa Mental Health Centre, and Raymond D. Lafond, MSW, RSW, for their counsel and editorial assistance – thanks very much!

References

Atkinson, S.D. (1994) Grieving and loss in parents with a schizophrenic child. *American Journal of Psychiatry*, **151** (8), 1137–9.

Averill, J.R. and Nunley, E.P. (1988) Grief as an emotion and as a disease: a social-constructionist perspective. *Journal of Social Issues*, **44** (3), 79–95.

Boss, P. (1999) *Ambiguous Loss: Learning to Live with Unresolved Grief*, Harvard University Press, Cambridge, MA.

Button, M. (1996) *The Unhinging of Wings*, Oolichan Press, Lantzville, BC.

Deveson, A. (1992) *Tell Me I'm Here*, Penguin Books, Hawthorn.

Deveson, A. (2003) *Resilience*, Allen & Unwin, Sydney.

Doka, K.J. (1989) *Disenfranchised Grief: Recognizing Hidden Sorrow*, Lexington Books, Lexington, MA.

Frankl, V.E. (1997) *Man's Search For Meaning*, Simon & Schuster, London.

Godress, J., Ozgul, L., Owen, C. and Foley-Evans, L. (2005) Grief experiences of parents whose children suffer from mental illness. *Australian and New Zealand Journal of Psychiatry*, **39**, 88–94.

Govig, S.D. (1994) *Souls Are Made of Endurance: Surviving Mental Illness in the Family*, Westminster John Know Press, Louiseville.

Hatfield, A.B. (1989) Families as caregivers: a historical perspective, in *Families of the Mentally Ill: Coping and Adaptation* (eds A.B. Hatfield and H.P. Lefley), Guildford, New York.

Hatfield, A.B. and Lefley, H.P. (eds) (1989) *Families of the Mentally Ill: Coping and Adaptation*, Guildford, New York.

Kabat-Zinn, J. (1990) *Full Catastrophe Living: Using the Wisdom of your Body and Mind to Face Stress, Pain, and Illness,* Bantam Doubleday Dell Publishing Group, Inc., New York.

Kübler-Ross, E. (1969) *On Death and Dying,* Tavistock, London.

Lachenmeyer, N. (2000) *The Outsider: A Journey into My Father's Struggle with Madness,* Random House, New York.

Lafond, V. (1998) The grief of mental illness: context for the cognitive therapy of schizophrenia, in *Cognitive Psychotherapy of Psychotic and Personality Disorders* (eds C. Perris and P.D. McGorry), John Wiley & Sons, Ltd, Chichester.

Lafond, V. (2002) *Grieving Mental Illness: A Guide for Patients and Their Caregivers,* 2nd edn, University of Toronto Press, Toronto.

Lindemann, E. (1944) Symptomatology and management of acute grief. *American Journal of Psychiatry,* **101** (2), 141–8.

Miller, F., Dworkin, J., Ward, M., and Barone, D. (1990) A preliminary study of unresolved grief in families of seriously mentally ill patients. *Hospital and Community Psychiatry,* **41** (12), 1321–5.

Miller, F.E. (1996) Grief therapy for relatives of persons with serious mental illness. *Psychiatric Services,* **47** (6), 633–7.

MacDonald, C.M. (2004) A chuckle a day keeps the doctor away: therapeutic humor and laughter. *Psychosocial Nursing and Mental Health Services,* **42** (3), 18–25.

Ozgul, S. (2004) Parental grief and serious mental illness: a narrative. *Australian and New Zealand Journal of Family Therapy,* **25** (4), 183–7.

Parkes, C.M. (1972) *Bereavement: Studies of Grief in Adult Life,* International Universities Press, New York.

Perera, K. (2003) An investigation of the relationship between intensity of grief and coping patterns of parents of individuals affected by psychotic disorders. MSW Thesis, Curtin University of Technology, http://adt.curtin.edu.au/theses/available/adt-WCU20041123.145802 (accessed 13 February, 2006).

Pine, V.R., Margolis, O.S., Doka, K. *et al.* (eds) (1990) *Unrecognized and Unsanctioned Grief: The Nature and Counseling of Unacknowledged Loss,* Charles C Thomas, Springfield, IL.

Prigerson, H.G., Frank, E., Kasl, S.V. *et al.* (1995) Complicated grief and bereavement-related depression as distinct disorders: preliminary empirical validation in elderly bereaved spouses. *American Journal of Psychiatry,* **152** (1), 22–30.

Raphael, B. (1983) *The Anatomy of Bereavement,* Basic Books, New York.

Solomon, P. and Draine, J. (1996) Examination of grief among family members of individuals with serious and persistent mental illness. *Psychiatric Quarterly,* **67** (3), 221–34.

Summerfield, D. (2000) War and mental health: a brief overview. *British Journal of Psychiatry,* **321**, 232–5.

Terkelsen, K.G. (1987) The meaning of mental illness to the family, in *Families of the Mentally Ill: Coping and Adaptation*, (eds A.B. Hatfield and H.P. Lefley), Guildford, New York.

Wasow, M. (1995) *The Skipping Stone: Ripple Effects of Mental Illness on the Family*, Science and Behavior Books, Inc., Palo Alto, CA.

Worden, J.W. (1982) *Grief Counseling and Grief Therapy: A Handbook for the Mental Health Practitioner*, Springer, New York.

Wortman, C.B. and Silver, R.C. (1989) The myths of coping with loss. *Journal of Consulting and Clinical Psychology*, **57** (3), 349–57.

Resources

Barrowclough, C. and Tarrier, N. (1992) *Families of Schizophrenic Patients: Cognitive Behavioural Intervention*, Chapman and Hall, London.

Deveson, A. (2003) *Resilience*, Allen & Unwin, Sydney.

Lafond, V. (2002) *Grieving Mental Illness: A Guide for Patients and Their Caregivers*, 2nd edn, University of Toronto Press, Toronto.

Wasow, M. (1995) *The Skipping Stone: Ripple Effects of Mental Illness on the Family*, Science and Behavior Books, Palo Alto, CA.

Further Reading

Anderson, C.M., Reiss, D. and Hogarty, B. (1986) *Schizophrenia and the Family: A Practitioner's Guide to Psychoeducation and Management*, Guildford, New York.

Barrowclough, C. and Tarrier, N. (1992) *Families of Schizophrenic Patients: Cognitive Behavioural Intervention*, Chapman and Hall, London.

Falloon, I.J.R., Boyd, J.L., McGill, C.W. *et al.* 1982. Family management in the prevention of exacerbations of schizophrenia. *New England Journal of Medicine*, **306**, 1437–40.

9

Interventions with Siblings

Jo Smith, Gráinne Fadden and Michelle O'Shea

Overview

> Sibling relationships . . . outlast marriages, survive the death of parents, resur-
> face after quarrels that would sink any friendship. They flourish in a thousand
> incarnations of closeness and distance, warmth, loyalty and distrust (Erica E.
> Goode, 'The Secret World of Siblings', U.S. News & World Report, 10 January
> 1994).

Introduction and rationale

This chapter will consider the impact of psychosis from a sibling perspective
and their needs for intervention and support arising from this. The rationale
for including siblings in family work is straightforward: the majority of
young people will still be living within the family home when they first
develop a psychosis, in many cases with siblings. It is difficult to conceive
that family work can occur without the involvement of siblings both in
terms of the unique importance of the sibling relationship, an emerging
literature documenting the pervasive impact of psychosis on sibling lives,
and siblings' own increased vulnerability to psychosis.

Yet, within the field of psychosis, research and clinical practice has predominantly focused on parents, spouses and offspring and has neglected
siblings' needs (Fisher, Bordass and Steele, 2004). Access to services and
support is limited and frequently achieved indirectly through the client or

---

A Casebook of Family Interventions for Psychosis   Edited by Fiona Lobban and Christine Barrowclough
© 2009 John Wiley & Sons, Ltd

their parents. Anecdotal evidence suggests siblings rarely receive specific information and support although they themselves identify the need for both (Mulder and Lines, 2005). There is a dearth of literature on the impact on and needs of siblings and few models, even within the general health literature, as to how best to address successfully sibling needs across the age range (Curson and Sharkey, 2006). Interventions for siblings coping with long-term physical illness have ranged from specific information leaflets, therapeutic games, peer support groups, activity camps and short breaks (Curson and Sharkey, 2006).

We could not find any published interventions with siblings in the mental health field. This is surprising in view of the unique characteristics that define most sibling relationships: they tend to be of longer duration than most other relationships that we share including those with our parents, partners, peer friendships and our children. Sibling relationships tend to persist with varying degrees of intimacy and investment throughout the life cycle (Dunn, 2000) and are often renewed when children mature and leave home (Shanas, 1979). They also become important in old age both in maintaining morale (Wood and Robertson, 1978) and providing emotional and practical support (Cicerelli, 1991). During childhood and adolescence, when a psychosis is most likely to manifest in a family, sibling relationships provide companionship, emotional support and direct service to one another (Goetting, 1986). The onset of psychosis in late adolescence or early adulthood may be critical in terms of the potential disruption to this relationship and potential mutual loss of an important reciprocal relationship.

We are not aware of published data on the numbers of siblings who may be coping with psychosis in their family. Unpublished audit data from Worcestershire early intervention (EI) service (Smith, 2006; personal communication) revealed a total of 113 siblings in a caseload of 66 first episode individuals, where 89% of individuals had siblings. Although the majority of siblings (68%) were aged 19 years or older, there was a broad age span where 4.4% were under 10 years, 9.7% were aged between 10 and 14 years and a further 17.7% were aged 15–18 years. Unpublished audit data from Berkshire EI service (Sin, 2006; personal communication) confirmed a similar picture.

At the moment therefore, the extent of resources available for siblings consists of information leaflets providing information and coping advice specifically targeting siblings living with psychosis and a small but growing number of sibling-specific web sites (see 'Resources'). Family intervention has often been regarded as the vehicle for whole family support but in practice, practitioners tend to be better at talking to parents and spouses and not necessarily the *whole* family to ensure that everyone is included. This is also reflected in the published family intervention studies which have largely targeted 'key relatives', and where few siblings are identified within family intervention samples.

This chapter will summarise the literature that exists in relation to the impact on siblings and through a detailed clinical case study that provides an insight from a sibling perspective of the impact of psychosis and how sibling needs may be addressed through family intervention. The case study was chosen to highlight some of the issues that can arise when there are children of different ages in the family. Topics such as the appropriate pitch of information, available information materials (particularly for the younger age group), attention span and concentration limitations, different levels of understanding and potential contribution to family discussion will be addressed.

It will also provide some critical reflection as to how family work might be developed to provide more sensitive and specific support to siblings.

Case Context

Impact of psychosis on sibling relationships

Despite the importance of the sibling bond, little is known about how siblings are affected by the onset of psychosis in the family. The majority of studies to date have either been retrospective asking siblings to recall feelings and events over 20 years previously (Gerace, Camilleri and Ayres, 1993; Kinsella, Anderson and Anderson, 1996), studies where siblings are a subset of a larger sample of key relatives (Magliano *et al.*, 1999) or studies of the impact on siblings coping with long-term psychosis (Lukens, Thorning and Lohrer, 2002; Marsh *et al.*, 1993). Studies that have included siblings of people with severe mental health problems have found that siblings report a pervasive impact on their lives (Marsh *et al.*, 1993) and experience similar levels of subjective burden as parents and offspring (Solomon and Draine 1995). The literature identifies commonly occurring themes including profound sadness and guilt (Titleman and Pysk, 1991) and grief and loss (Kristoffersen and Mustard, 2000; O'Shea, 2000). Siblings have also consistently been found to struggle with worries of becoming unwell (Samuels and Chase, 1979), survivor guilt, stigma, anger and shame (Bank and Kahn,

1982; Harris, 1988), feel neglected by their parents (Gerace, Camilleri and Ayres, 1993) and fear that their children will inherit the disorder. They can also feel a pressure to compensate for the shortcomings of their sibling who is unwell and express anxiety that they may become the primary caretakers in the future (Johnson, 1988). Many opt to distance themselves from the affected sibling by withdrawing from or leaving the family environment (Kinsella, Anderson and Anderson, 1996).

UNAFAM (Union Nationale des Amis et Familles de Malades Psychiques) carried out a questionnaire survey of their membership (Davtian, 2003). The 600 respondents highlighted three periods of greatest vulnerability for siblings: the onset of the problem where stress levels are considerable, the aging of parents where siblings start to feel anxious over responsibility for their affected sibling and when their own children reach the age at which their brother or sister became unwell. Siblings highlighted that they were often the first to recognise changes as well as providing a social link for their affected sibling. They reported lacking information, adverse effects on their own health, fears about developing mental health difficulties and anxieties about future burden without adequate preparation to cope with it. Their principal sources of information were family and the media.

Another large membership survey of siblings was carried out by Rethink (Canning, 2006) generated 264 respondents and had similar findings. The majority rated access to advice and support as inadequate. They were concerned about the impact of mental health problems on the family as a whole and also mentioned stigma. Siblings were seeking accessible information, including sibling-oriented information packs, dedicated sibling web site space and publications by service users on how they could be supported by siblings. As would be expected from a group of young people, they suggested a range of media including newsletters, web-based chat rooms and discussion forums and the opportunity for direct contact with other siblings through a local support group or web-based sibling network. In addition to the findings of these two surveys, Fisher, Bordass and Steele (2004) found that first-episode siblings reported a neglect of personal needs, difficulties in sustaining friendships and impaired academic performance. They felt they were ignored by mental health services, and wished to be more involved in the care of their affected sibling.

These findings appear to be consistent across cultures: a recent sibling guide to psychosis produced by the Canadian Mental Health Association (Mulder and Lines, 2005) responding to local needs suggested ways of dealing with these various difficulties.

Specific issues for siblings

There are a number of important foci for intervention when working with siblings. Siblings are requesting information to aid their understanding of psychosis and to inform coping and support to the family member with psychosis. It is also important to raise and address concerns about their own health related to potential genetic vulnerability as a higher risk group with an emphasis on taking care of their own health and well-being. This needs sensitive handling to avoid inadvertently raising anxiety levels by over-sensitising naïve siblings to potential genetic risk. A similar balance needs to be struck in identifying and mobilising their support related to caring for their affected sibling and helping siblings hold reasonable boundaries in relation to the demands that might be placed upon them. It is equally important to help siblings maintain their emotional well-being, sustain friendships and role performance and address their personal needs and goals.

Working with families can raise the complex issue of confidentiality and relies to some degree on how much the affected sibling wants their family, particularly their peer siblings, to know or be involved directly with their difficulties. This can be difficult for an individual who understandably wishes to preserve their independence, autonomy and privacy while also acknowledging that their difficulties can have a direct impact on family life, relationships and well-being of other family members. This requires skilful negotiating in relation to the involvement of siblings and flexibility to hold sessions where siblings may or may not be present as appropriate. Offering concurrent individual and family support options can be helpful, as can identifying needs which may best be addressed individually from those who may benefit from family involvement. In the case study described, this was achieved by involving the case manager as a cotherapist in family intervention who was able to identify issues that were more appropriately addressed in individual work with the client.

Style of intervention and theoretical influences on style used

The notion of specifically intervening with siblings coping with psychosis is relatively new, and there are no clinical studies to date describing or evaluating the delivery of sibling-specific support in practice. The model used in the case study is broadly based on the behavioural family therapy (BFT) approach developed by Falloon *et al.* (2004). BFT provides a structured framework for intervention based on the assessed needs. The intervention, although structured, allows considerable flexibility in its delivery to respond to expressed and identified needs and is designed to be collaborative in terms of agreeing goals for intervention, exploring whether sessions have been useful and negotiating further family meetings on a session by session basis (Fadden and Smith, 2008; Stanbridge *et al.*, 2003).

Therapists' training, role and attributes

A number of specific training and service issues arise when working with siblings. These include the following:

- *Working with siblings who may be children or adolescents* which can be novel for staff who are often trained and working in adult services. While the majority of siblings will be adults, one can expect approximately a fifth who are under 16 years with a small but significant number still in their primary years. This presents a challenge when working with families who have siblings across a very wide age range (from primary, through teenage to early 20s in some cases).
- *Remembering to include siblings in family assessment processes:* In the course of collecting the siblings demographic data described above, we observed that when we asked case managers about sibling details for individuals on their caseloads, some were unaware whether some of their clients had siblings, suggesting that siblings had not been included in family assessment at inception into the service or included in routine family intervention. Psychoeducational family intervention offers a format of individual assessments prior to meeting a family which lends itself well to formally assessing the impact on individual siblings and the opportunity to speak with siblings directly rather than basing assumptions about their needs on indirect conversations with parents or the affected sibling. Interestingly, informal conversations with parents revealed that many parents may avoid even asking about the impact on siblings for fear of increasing their sense of burden and having to extend their already stretched capacity beyond the affected family member. Equally, in similar discussions, siblings acknowledged that they hold back on revealing the true impact on themselves for fear of increasing burden and responsibilities on their parents.

- *Ensuring availability of specific resources for siblings:* Services need to have a range of resource materials available for siblings appropriate for different age groups as well as information about sibling web sites, books and other resources (see 'Resources').

Clinical service constraints on intervention

Even in a well-resourced service, there are limits on resources to meet all family needs identified particularly in relation to capacity to offer dedicated individual or group support to siblings in addition to family intervention. In a family-centred service, there should be both capacity and flexibility to offer a range of support as required including individual sessions, access to a psychoeducational group and peer support opportunities as well as family intervention. Realistically, most support to siblings will be in the context of broader family support through the medium of family inter- vention. However, the limits of providing only one mode of support also needs to be acknowledged particularly as a 'one size fits all intervention' which may be tricky for younger age children, individuals who tend to be less confident or comfortable in family group situations and the capacity of a group-based intervention to target specific individual needs. This is clearly illustrated in the following case study where the youngest children (aged 7) understandably struggled to maintain attention and to follow all of the discussion, where another of the siblings (aged 14) struggled with family group situations, by nature was avoidant and had to be coaxed to participate in sessions. At the end of the family intervention, while acknowl- edging its value for family well-being and outcomes, one of the siblings (aged 16 years) noted that it still failed to address his needs in relation to meeting other siblings in similar situations or in offering sibling-specific support.

Clinical Case Example

The following case study illustrates some of the issues that can arise when working with siblings. For the purpose of this chapter, the case study will specifically focus on the needs and contributions of the siblings rather than the family as a whole.

Context and referral

The family were under the care of an EI Service following their eldest son Martin developing a first-episode psychosis when aged 17. The mum had spoken to Martin's case manager about the need for family work, in the context of a carer's assessment, where she explained, 'because the family appear to cope, we have been left to cope, although, in reality, the family has been placed under great strain by Martin's problems.' The outcome was that the family was offered family intervention and seen for family sessions in their home. All family members attended.

The client. He was a 17-year-old man who had developed a first-episode psychosis over the previous 12-month period. This occurred in the context of a number of stressors affecting the family including the following: his brother's poor physical health which had led to him being hospitalised on several occasions in the past year; his father's business being in financial difficulties which had placed a considerable emotional and financial strain on the family; Martin was studying for his GCSE examinations. Martin had experienced command auditory hallucinations which he had acted upon, contributing to aggressive outbursts in the home including a recent occasion where he had hit his mother. He was also extremely paranoid, refusing to eat meals with the family, and had gone missing on a number of occasions causing considerable worry to his parents. He had become increasingly withdrawn, isolating himself from the family by spending considerable amount of time in bed. He was also truanting from school. His self-care was poor and he required considerable prompting to wash and change his clothes.

Parents. Both parents were in their mid-40s and were working full time. Although the mother, Karen, would like to reduce her hours, the threat to her husband's business made her reluctant to do so. She carried the burden of responsibility for supporting the family and managing the home. At the start of intervention, mum was reporting feeling afraid for herself and the children related to Martin's aggressive outbursts. Dad (Derek) was finding work stressful, and worked long hours in an attempt to keep the business solvent. He noted that Martin's problems arose in the context of other family difficulties which had increased the strain upon the family.

Siblings. Martin had four younger siblings who were all living at home. Simon aged 16 had diabetes, which has led to repeat hospitalisations in the past year. When the family work started, Simon was 17 years old studying for AS level qualifications. Louise, aged 14, had been referred and seen within Child and Adolescent Mental Health Services (CAMHS) in relation to an eating disorder and episodes of self-harming over the previous year since Martin had been unwell. Twins, Matthew and Cerys aged 7 were at primary school. Mum noted that the twins found Martin unpredictable and tended to push him away when he tried to play with them.

Assessment

The assessment phase of intervention was carried out over a single extended session (lasting a couple of hours) and was conducted with the whole family group present, including Martin. Information was elicited using both direct questions to individuals and circular questioning involving other family members present offering perspectives on the impact that Martin's difficulties had on individual family members and the family unit as a whole. There are benefits and risks with conducting family assessments in this way. It does enable information to be gathered quickly and efficiently from family members and provides the opportunity to create a shared perspective on difficulties, collectively constructed by all of the family. However, the process has the potential to both allow negative comments to be articulated directly in an unprocessed and insensitive manner (e.g. 'Martin smells') and to become a forum for group scapegoating. Careful and sensitive handling is required from the therapist particularly to ensure that overtly critical comments are converted into positive requests for change that individuals or the family as a whole are seeking as outcomes from family work, and to ensure that discussion is balanced and not unduly negatively biased towards one family member.

Family unit

The assessment of the family unit revealed a family under considerable strain, experiencing frequent arguments and where there was overt tension, conflict and at times, aggression between family members. The family tended to be very critical of each other with few positive comments. They described some shared activities between family members including holidays (without Martin), an interest in sport and going to music gigs (Martin and Louise).

The siblings identified a number of specific concerns in relation to their brother's difficulties. They noted that he dominated control over the television and computer, and was often aggressive or threatening to get his own way. He played his music too loudly and often late into the night, which disturbed their studies and kept them awake at night. They commented on the level of aggression they had witnessed and were concerned for their own and their parent's safety, particularly mum. The youngest siblings commented that they were afraid of their brother.

They all made comments in relation to Martin's self-care and poor hygiene. Cerys comments that 'Marin smells', while the older siblings talked about their embarrassment and reluctance to bring friends home and their struggles to explain their brother's difficulties to peers. They all commented on the adverse impact of Martin's difficulties on family relationships and routines particularly the disruption to family mealtimes, family time together, shared holidays and having friends to stay.

Individual sibling needs

Simon had long standing physical health difficulties which necessitated frequent repeat hospitalisations. He was studying for AS levels and described being under considerable pressure to meet course work demands. He described himself as closest to Louise, whom he was concerned about and had taken under his wing. He felt he was subject to a lot of criticism from Martin with whom he felt he was often competing for attention. Simon wanted to complete his A levels successfully and to go to university.

Louise was 14 years old and under the care of a CAMHS psychiatrist related to incidents of self-harming (superficial cuts to her arms and stomach) and an eating disorder resulting in substantial weight loss. Her dad viewed Louise as presenting more of a problem to the family than Martin.

Louise described a marked change in her relationship with Martin since he had developed psychosis. Prior to the onset of psychosis, they used to spend a lot of time together with a shared interest in music and bands. She tended to disengage from the family and stay in her bedroom and there were some concerns from her parents as to whether she was becoming depressed. Louise wanted 'everyone off my back' and 'to be left alone'.

The twins were in year 2 at primary school. Cerys enjoyed Brownies and dance classes outside of school, while Matthew loved football. Cerys struggled with Martin's unpredictability and as a consequence, was wary of him and kept him at arms length. Matthew equally tended to avoid Martin and refused to play with him or to be in close contact with him. Mum was particularly concerned about the adverse emotional impact of the family difficulties on the twins who both said they wanted Martin to move out of the house.

Formulation/shared understanding of problems

Martin's difficulties appear to have developed in the context of a number of stressors which had impacted and placed strain on the family including dad's business concerns, financial pressures and family ill health. These stressors had contributed to the disruption of family routine and put pressure on the family, particularly dad who had been suffering with stress prior to the onset of Martin's difficulties. There also was a family history of psychosis which increased Martin's potential vulnerability to developing psychosis.

The family were all trying to cope with these difficulties but the stress and pressure they were experiencing was manifest in the tensions described between family members, in terms of frequent arguments and attention-seeking behaviour as well as the impact on individual family member's well-being including dad and Simon's poor physical health, Louise's self-harming attempts and Martin's mental health difficulties. There appeared to be some blaming of Martin, a tendency to ostracise him: the family wanted him to move out of the family home in an attempt to restore family balance and remove stress.

Sibling engagement methods and issues

How do we as family workers respond to the concerns raised by Martin's siblings and engage them in family work to try and address these?

The following may serve as general guidance to assist in the engagement process:

- *Normalising without minimising some of the difficulties that were identi-fied* as natural tensions and concerns which might arise within families and among siblings of different ages, regardless of mental health problems in the family, for example concerns about Martin playing his music too loudly, fights between siblings over who watches what television programme or uses the computer and reflecting natural dominance hierarchies that might exist within families where an older brother might seek to secure his own way among his junior sibling peers.
- *Showing genuine concern for what the family has had to deal with* in trying to cope with serious mental health problems in the family without any specialist education or training, and handling aggressive outbursts which appear unpredictable and have generated understandable fear and anxiety in family members.
- *Involving all of the siblings in the discussion and seeking to hear and understand their different perspectives* on the difficulties facing the family. Cerys when asked what she had noticed had happened in the first family session helpfully observed that '*mum said most*'. This served as a helpful prompt to remind the therapist to ensure that all family members have a voice and an opportunity to express their views and opinions so that no individual dominates, feels left out, is excluded or alienated in the discussion.
- *Tailoring session length to suit the age of the siblings present.* This is particularly important when working with siblings as young as 7, who struggled to maintain attention in sessions lasting an hour. Setting tasks for the youngest siblings such as holding a watch to act as timekeeper and enlisting them to help hand out information materials were used as tactics to keep them included in the process. Similarly, using visual materials (including asking them to draw pictures) to support verbal discussion is another helpful strategy to engage younger age children.
- *Providing suitable information materials for siblings to support the discussion.* In this particular case, we gave a copy of a siblings information booklet for the older siblings to read and suggested that mum adapt the Young Minds information story book 'Wise Mouse' (Ironside, 2003) to describe concerns about a brother (rather than a mother's ill health) and read it to the younger siblings at bedtime to create the opportunity to talk about what had been discussed in family sessions.

- *Getting all family members to identify positive outcomes they would like to see emerging from family work* both individually and for the family unit as a whole, particularly seeking to convert critical comments such as 'Martin smells' into more constructive goals for change, for example 'I would like Martin to bathe more regularly and take more care of his appearance and hygiene.'
- *Being flexible (within reasonable limits!) in both the timing of and venue for family sessions:* Arranging family meetings at home at the end of the day and fitting around family routines such as the evening meal, regular school and homework demands and personal social commitments to facilitate attendance of siblings.
- *Acknowledging and positively reinforcing attendance at family meetings,* for example commending the younger sister, Louise, whose opening line in the initial session was '*I didn't want to be here*', for attending the majority of the sessions and producing small treats for the youngest siblings for helping and contributing to the family sessions.

Intervention

Session 1. This initial family session focused on engagement of the family in family work. The initial part of the session explored their attitudes to family intervention and the potential goals and outcomes they were seeking from it.

The later part of the session started the process of psychoeducation to develop a shared understanding of psychosis and how it relates to their personal experiences and observations. The session was supported by information materials 'Back on Your Feet' psychosis information booklet (Jackson and Reading, 2001) and Worcestershire EI Service Siblings booklet (Maynard and Smith, 2003) which the family were encouraged to read prior to the next session.

Issues for Therapist

- Concentration and attention span limits of younger children and ways to engage younger children meaningfully in the discussion.
- Ambivalence of the younger female sibling in relation to being present for the family session and passive undermining, including saying she did not want to be there, not actively contributing to discussion and

stating that she had learnt nothing at end of session. The sibling was commended for coming and staying for the whole session even though she had not wanted to be there.

- Dealing with anger and overt criticism such as when Cerys stated openly that 'Martin smells' and all four siblings voiced that they wanted Martin to leave the family home and suggesting that this might be more helpfully converted into positive requests about what they would like to change to enable Martin to continue to live at home.

Session 2. The initial part of the session continued the psychoeducational process and reviewed their understanding of psychosis from the previous session and the information materials they had read between sessions.

The second part of the session introduced the notion of early warning signs and the family were encouraged to identify early warning signs that they had observed prompted by an early warning signs family card sort exercise (Smith, 2001).

Issues for Therapist

- Reflecting on what each sibling had understood and taken from the information materials to assist in making sense of and affirming personal observations they had made and placing these in a meaningful context of typical experiences when someone develops a psychosis.
- Using a card sort as a tool to engage the family in discussion about early signs and to facilitate discussion about what they had individually and collectively observed and their different perspectives on what was happening to inform observations made by the siblings such as why had Martin gone missing or why had he walked out of the house in his pyjamas on another occasion (both observations made by Matthew).

Session 3. This session reviewed and refined the early signs card sort list identified in the previous session and sought a consensus agreement on both the nature and time order of appearance of signs leading up to the initial episode of psychosis.

Issues for Therapist

- Need to review and refine early signs observations allowing time in between sessions for reflection on the preliminary signs identified in the previous session. It is to be noted, however, that when subsequently reviewing the family work sessions there was some frustration expressed by the father that this review had felt unnecessary.

Session 4. The initial part of this session introduced the notion of relapse risk and relapse prevention strategies based on a stress–vulnerability model. This included discussion about potential risk factors and triggers, and ways to manage vulnerability and maintain well-being. The discussion about vulnerability included discussion around family history and the potential increased risk of psychosis for siblings. The importance of maintaining personal well-being was emphasised.

Issues for Therapist

- Providing the opportunity for siblings to discuss their own anxieties about genetic risk and their potential to develop a psychosis. Consistent with the findings from Fisher, Bordass and Steele (2004), this was new information for the siblings who, up to this point, had not considered their personal risk of developing similar difficulties.

Session 5. On arrival at the family home for the start of the family session, the therapist heard raised voices and doors slamming. On further exploration with the family, this related to an incident where Martin had spilt coffee over his brother's homework, on purpose according to Simon, and this had led to a heated argument. In response to this situation, the focus of the session was on handling conflict and disagreements. The siblings used the incident as another example of the problems that Martin was presenting and justification as to why Martin should move out of the family home. The therapist sought to explore why the incident might have occurred and how it might be prevented from happening again. The therapist sought to shift the balance of family attention from focusing on 'problems' and criticism to looking for positives and supporting and encouraging more appropriate behaviour. The principles of communication skills training were introduced, particularly around the skills of both giving and receiving positive comments.

Issues for Therapist

- Arriving at the family home to witness family conflict raised the issue of whether to ignore what had been heard or being responsive to working with the 'here and now', using a current example of conflict. This facilitated both problem solving alternative ways of dealing with a situation and the exploration of why conflicts such as negative attention seeking arise. This was used as an opportunity to discuss ways to avoid conflict in the future.

- The use of homework tasks where family members were tasked with 'catching one another being good' and noting any observations (no matter how small) and where everyone was also encouraged to try doing 'good' things to see if these are noticed and commented on, to be fed back at the next family meeting.

Session 6. The initial part of the session reviewed the homework task in relation to developing positive family communication skills.

The second part of the session introduced the skill of problem solving to tackle Martin's difficulties with medication compliance which it was felt may be contributing to some of the aggressive outbursts that had been occurring and which had been identified as problematic for all family members.

Issues for Therapist

- Keeping the family focus on improvements, progress and positive changes by differentially paying attention to and reinforcing positive comments and observations made by family members.
- Mobilising family ideas and resources for solving problems. In this instance various options to aid adherence were discussed. The solution which the family agreed to try was that mum would buy some card and Louise and Cerys would produce coloured medication prompt cards which would be strategically placed where Martin might read them to encourage him to remember to take his medication.

Session 7. This session continued the focus on problem-solving principles both in relation to continuing to support medication compliance but also to address other problem areas identified including managing Martin's current low mood and maintaining his activity levels over the college summer break by introducing the notion of activity scheduling using the family calendar.

Issues for Therapist

- Mobilising sibling involvement in generating ideas to help Martin maintain activity levels. For example, Simon offered to lend Martin his bike to get out to do some exercise and to support him seeing college friends. He also suggested Martin could walk the dog daily. Matthew offered to accompany Martin in walking the dog and invited him to attend his sports day at school as both parents were unavailable to attend.

Session 8. The initial part of the session reviewed progress in relation to activity scheduling. The later part of the session used problem-solving principles to address: how the parents and youngest siblings might have a break away leaving the older siblings at home, constraints of relying on public transport to get out and about which particularly affected the two eldest siblings and Martin's financial concerns which affected his ability to fund social activities.

Issues for Therapist

- Dealing with the absence of siblings from the session. On arrival at the family home for the start of the session, the therapist was told Louise was 'asleep' and, despite repeated prompting to get up, would not wake to join the session. How far do you push to secure full attendance and involvement from siblings at family sessions balanced against their needs for autonomy, control and the opportunity to withdraw? On this occasion, the therapist decided not to make an issue of Louise's non-attendance but instead, commented at the end on the absence of Louise's problem-solving ideas which had been so helpful in the previous sessions (when she eventually appeared towards the close of the family session).
- Acknowledging inequities that can arise between siblings; for example, Simon was supplied with money for taxis to assist him with his transport needs related to his severe physical health difficulties, yet Martin perceived his support needs for transport were equal or potentially greater. Similarly, Louise had been able to secure paid holiday work while Martin was currently unable to work and struggling to manage financially.

Session 9. The initial part of the session reviewed progress with goal setting. The session continued with discussion and further goal setting relating to Martin moving to independent accommodation and starting driving lessons.

Issues for Therapist

- The therapist specifically sought siblings' observations on progress in relation to current goals and in identifying further goals for intervention both for themselves and for Martin.

Session 10. The session started with a progress review and discussed Martin returning to college.

The later part of the session involved a review of the family intervention outcomes to date.

Issues for Therapist

- The family reported marked improvements in family relationships but noted that this had also significantly altered family dynamics so that Martin and Louise were now relating much better and spending more time together while Simon was left feeling the loss of the increased contact he had previously enjoyed with Louise prior to this development.

Session 11. The initial part of the session reviewed progress in relation to goals set.

The later part of the session discussed family assessment and care planning processes and additional sibling support needs. This included trying to identify a peer sibling e-mail contact for Simon who was leaving home to go to university and liaising with the CAMHS service in relation to securing an external mentor for Louise.

Issues for Therapist

- Louise 'pretending to be asleep' in the session. The parents observed that as Martin's difficulties had improved, the family focus had shifted to Louise's behaviour and problems. This raised the dilemma as to whether family intervention was the appropriate vehicle to address wider family difficulties or specifically those related to psychosis?
- Acknowledging the limitations of a family intervention approach in meeting all sibling needs and problem solving how unmet needs might be met in other ways such as providing peer support contact with other siblings (Simon) and addressing specific individual support

needs by securing mentoring support for Louise for her current difficulties.

Outcome evaluation

Following 11 sessions of family intervention, the family felt they had adjusted their expectations and accommodated Martin's difficulties. They all described themselves as being in a different place to when they had first started family intervention. The whole family were reporting feeling less tense and stressed, both individually and collectively. They noted that there had been a marked reduction in family conflict and incidents of aggression. They were also reporting that they no longer felt afraid or dreaded coming home.

Martin felt his family had benefited from family intervention and noticed more positive family attitudes towards him and a generally more supportive family environment. There was a marked shift in the later family sessions from negatives (describing what Martin was not doing) to positive comments about him and what he was achieving. The family were noting improvements in Martin's medication adherence, self-care and social functioning by the end of family intervention. There was also no longer any pressure from the family on Martin to leave the family home or on the EI service to find alternative accommodation for him.

Matthew reported that he was getting on well with Martin and no longer felt scared of him. Cerys equally was observed sitting on Martin's knee, being tickled and laughing during several of the later family sessions.

Martin and Louise were enjoying each others' company again and were observed laughing and chatting together in their bedrooms. They had started going to concerts together again and were getting on well together.

Simon was the only family member who described a negative outcome from family intervention. He reported a loss of his closeness with Louise, as Louise's relationship with Martin had improved. He acknowledged that family intervention had addressed Martin's needs and improved family functioning but felt it had failed to address his specific needs as a sibling in relation to meeting other siblings in a similar situation or in offering him sibling-specific support. This was subsequently partly addressed by setting up a peer support e-mail arrangement with another sibling of a similar age within the service which was reported to be mutually beneficial by both siblings.

Critical reflection

The case study provides an insight into family work with siblings and raises a number of issues when thinking about family work with siblings:

- *Assessment.* Changes are often required in the service clinical assessment procedures, for example requiring the completion of a simple family genogram at baseline assessment to reveal numbers, names and ages of all siblings whether living at home or not. Services need to develop a family-centred culture, which recognises and acknowledges a broader impact on families and where the needs of siblings in relation to information, coping and support are routinely assessed.
- *Spanning a wide sibling age range (ages 7–19 years).* How do you talk meaningfully to a 7-year-old about psychosis? How can we ensure all members of the family are involved and informed and how do we pitch the family work and discussion to maximise engagement of all family members, even very young siblings?
- *Recognising the valuable role of siblings and the resources they have to offer.* Siblings who share the same room, attend the same school, share the same friends or interests are often the first to observe changes in behaviour and functioning and awareness that something is wrong. They can also be important social allies and provide considerable social support.
- *Getting the balance right in addressing sibling needs and difficulties.* There is an implicit assumption when offering family work where a member of the family has psychosis that siblings do not have major difficulties of their own (either independent or secondary to Martin's difficulties). In this family, Simon had serious physical health problems and Louise was engaging in self-harming behaviours and both were involved with specialist services for their own difficulties. Although the care team's involvement may be related to the affected sibling, it is important to view the family from a broader perspective: while recognising that siblings can have a potentially important support function it is important to bear in mind their limitations and need for distance and to ensure that parents (and services) are not making demands on them to be involved or available to provide support at the expense of their own needs for care themselves.
- *Working with minors.* How to successfully engage very young siblings in family intervention by making it fun, creating games, assigning tasks,

rewards, finding age appropriate information materials, using drawing and practical tasks (e.g. sorting and reading out early signs card sort cards to keep their attention).

- *Addressing the peer support needs of teenage siblings.* Providing peer sibling e-mail contacts, directing them to young people and sibling web sites, providing contact details for linking with national sibling networks and groups.
- *Providing sibling-specific information materials and guidance.* Supplying copies of information materials specifically developed for siblings to support family psychoeducation sessions.
- *Flexibility in timing of family sessions.* Fitting family intervention around day-to-day family routines and commitments including family mealtimes, school timetables, after school activities and clubs and homework demands (Simon and Louise were both in year groups sitting public examinations and with considerable coursework assignment demands).
- *Ensuring the sibling voice and opinions are heard.* Trying to keep a balance in the family discussion so that everyone is encouraged to express their views as well as listen to the views of others and particularly ensuring that family intervention is not dominated by parental narrative and views.

Questions for services to reflect on

When considering the ideas explored within this chapter, it may be helpful to reflect on current practice within your service in relation to engaging and working with siblings:

- How does your service currently respond to siblings concerns?
- Do you routinely include siblings in your family assessment processes?
- What are you doing to engage siblings in family intervention processes and to encourage their attendance and participation in family meetings?
- Do you provide specific written materials for siblings or provide information about sibling resources and web sites?

Conclusions

Working with siblings presents challenges to service in terms of broadening the scope of routine assessment and intervention to include support to siblings, potentially offering support to siblings who may be children or young adolescents and providing access to appropriate information materials and resources. This also raises a number of important issues relating to confidentiality, raising awareness about but not sensitising siblings to potential personal vulnerability for psychosis and striking an appropriate balance between mobilising sibling support while also encouraging siblings to hold appropriate boundaries and giving them permission to address their personal needs and goals and preserve their emotional well-being.

The UNAFAM siblings study (Davtian, 2003) highlights the 'no man's land' that siblings often find themselves in where they face three paradoxes:

- They have too little information yet they know too much.
- They are often involved but without a defined role or knowing what is expected of them.
- They experience difficulties but asking for help may risk making themselves more vulnerable.

They also often find themselves in the dilemma of choosing either 'compassion or abandonment'.

Services (and parents) need to be aware of and validate siblings' experiences and difficulties. We need to provide siblings with accurate information about what they are dealing with and address their anxieties and support needs. While acknowledging the potential resources and support that siblings can provide, we also need to be mindful of setting appropriate limits on responsibilities, ensuring that sibling needs for distance are supported and siblings are protected from undue burden of care.

References

Bank, S.P. and Kahn, M.D. (1982) *The Sibling Bond*, Basic Books, New York, NY.

Canning, L. (2006) *Rethink Siblings Survey*, Rethink, London.

Cicerelli, V. (1991) Sibling relationships in middle and old age, in *Sibling Relationships: Their Causes and Consequences* (ed. G.H. Brody), Ablex, Norwood, NJ, pp. 47–73.

Curson, D. and Sharkey, S. (2006) 'Out of the mouths of babes': drawing upon siblings' experiences to develop a therapeutic board game for siblings and children with a chronic illness. *Clinical Psychology Forum*, **159**, 36–8.

Davtian, H. (2003) UNAFAM study of the needs of siblings. *EUFAMI Newsletter*, **11**, 14–6.

Dunn, J. (2000) State of the art: siblings. *The Psychologist*, **13** (5), 244–8.

Fadden, G. and Smith, J. (2008) Family work in early psychosis, in *A Casebook of Family Interventions for Psychosis* (eds F. Lobban and C. Barrowclough), John Wiley & Sons, Ltd, Chichester.

Falloon, I.R.H., Mueser, K., Gingerich, S. *et al.* (2004) *Family Work Manual*, Meriden Family Programme, Birmingham.

Fisher, H., Bordass, E. and Steele, H. (2004), Siblings' experience of having a brother or sister with first-episode psychosis. *Schizophrenia Research*, **70** (Suppl. 1), 88.

Gerace, L.M., Camilleri, D. and Ayres, L. (1993) Sibling perspectives on schizophrenia and the family. *Schizophrenia Bulletin*, **19** (3), 637–47.

Goetting, A. (1986) The developmental tasks of siblingship over the life cycle. *Journal of Marriage and the Family*, **48**, 703–14.

Harris, E.G. (1988) My brother's keeper: siblings of chronic patients as allies in family treatment, in *Siblings in therapy: Life Span and Clinical Issues* (eds D. Kahn and K.G. Lewis), W.W. Norton, New York, pp. 314–38.

Ironside, V. (2003) *The Wise Mouse*, Young Minds, London.

Jackson, C. and Reading, B. (2001) *Getting Back on Your Feet: Understanding and Recovering from Psychosis*, Birmingham Early Intervention Service, Birmingham.

Johnson, J.T. (1988) *Hidden Victims: An Eight Stage Healing Process for Families and Friends of the Mentally Ill*. Double Day, New York, NY

Kinsella, K., Anderson, R. and Anderson, W. (1996) Coping skills, strengths and needs as perceived by adult offspring and siblings of people with mental illness: a retrospective study. *Psychiatric Rehabilitation Journal*, **20** (2), 24–32.

Kristoffersen, K. and Mustard, G. (2000) Towards a theory of interrupted feelings. *Scandinavian Journal of Caring Sciences*, **14** (1), 23–8.

Lukens, E., Thorning, H. and Lohrer, S. (2002) How siblings of those with severe mental illness perceive services and support. *Journal of Psychiatric Practice*, **8** (6), 354–64.

Magliano, L., Fadden, G., Fiorillo, A. *et al.* (1999) Family burden and coping strategies in schizophrenia: are key relatives really different to other relatives? *Acta Psychiatrica Scandanavica*, **99**, 10–5.

Marsh, D., Dickens, R., Koeske, R. *et al.* (1993) Troubled journey: siblings and children of people with mental illness. *Innovations and Research*, **2** (2), 13–23.

Maynard, C. and Smith, J. (2003) *Information About Psychosis for Brothers and Sisters*, South Worcestershire Early Intervention Service, UK.

Mulder, S. and Lines, E. (2005) *A Sibling's Guide to Psychosis. Information, Ideas and Resources*, Canadian Mental Health Association, Toronto, Canada.

O'Shea, M. (2000) *The Impact on Siblings of Psychosis within the Family: A Comparison with Key Relatives*. Unpublished Doctoral Clinical Psychology Thesis, University of Birmingham.

Samuels, S. and Chase, L. (1979) The well sibling of schizophrenics. *American Journal of Family Therapy*, **7**, 24–35.

Shanas, E. (1979) Social myth as hypothesis: the case of the family relations of old people. *The Gerontologist*, **19**, 3–9.

Sin, J. (2006) Berkshire EI service siblings audit data.

Smith, J. (2001) *Early Signs Self Management Training Manual for Individuals with Psychosis*, Worcestershire Community and Mental Health Trust, Worcester.

Smith, J. (2006) Worcestershire EI service siblings audit data.

Solomon, P. and Draine, J. (1995) Subjective burden among family members of mentally ill adults: reactions to stress, coping and adaptation. *American Journal of Orthopsychiatry*, **65** (3), 419–27.

Stanbridge, R.I., Burbach, F.R., Lucas, A.S. and Carter, K. (2003) A study of families' satisfaction with a family interventions in psychosis service in Somerset. *Journal of Family Therapy*, **25**, 181–204.

Titleman, D. and Pysk, L. (1991) Grief, guilt and identification in siblings of schizophrenic individuals. *Bulletin of the Menninger Clinic*, **55**, 72–84.

Wood, V. and Robertson, J.F. (1978) Friendship and kinship interaction: differential effect on the morale of the elderly. *Journal of Marriage and the Family*, **40**, 367–75.

Resources

Educational Materials

Information booklets

Almond, D. (2007) *My Dad's a Birdman*, Walker Books Ltd, London. (A novel about a parent's mental health problems but which can be adapted for young siblings).

Froggatt, D. (2001) *Leave my Stuff Alone – A Story for Young Teen Siblings*, WFSAD, Canada.

Horn, K. and Howe, D. (2002) *For Brothers and Sisters, Information About Psychosis*, Young People and Early Psychosis Intervention (YPPI) Centre Australia.

Ironside, V. (2003) *The Wise Mouse*, Young Minds, London. (For aged 5–11 years).

Lloyd, H. (2002) *Children Can Understand*, The Meriden Family Programme, West Midlands.

Maynard, C. and Smith, J. (2003) *Information About Psychosis for Brothers and Sisters*, South Worcestershire Early intervention Service, UK.

Mulder, S. and Lines, E. (2005) *A Sibling's Guide to Psychosis: Information, Ideas and Resources*, Canadian Mental Health Association, Canada.

NSF Scotland (2005) *It's About You Too!* (Age 8–10 years), www.nsfscot.org.uk (accessed 1 October 2008).

NSF Scotland (2005) *Need to Know*. (Age 11–14 years), www.nsfscot.org.uk (accessed 1 October 2008).

NSF Scotland (2005) *Making Time to Talk* (for parents with a mental illness wanting to talk to children about mental illness), www.nsfscot.org.uk (accessed 1 October 2008).

Sherman, M.D. and Sherman, D.M. (2006) *I'm Not Alone: A Teen's Guide to Living with a Parent Who Has Mental Illness*, www.seedsofhopebooks.com (accessed 1 October 2008).

Schizophrenia Society of Ontario (2006) *When Your Brother or Sister Has Schizophrenia*, www.schizophrenia.on.ca (accessed 1 October 2008).

Further Reading

Lamb, W. (1998) *I Know This Much Is True*, HarperCollins Publishers, London. (This is a novel about twins where one has schizophrenia, and may be helpful for staff in understanding the impact on siblings. Not suitable for children.)

Loudon, M. (2006) *Relative Stranger: A Sister's Story*, Canangate Books.

Neugeboren, J. (1997) *Imagining Robert: My Brother, Madness and Survival*, William Morrow and Company, New York.

Safer, J. (2003) *The Normal One: Life With a Difficult or Damaged Sibling*, Delta Books.

Secunda, V. (1997) *When Madness Comes Home: Help and Hope for the Children, Siblings and Partners of the Mentally Ill*, Hyperion Books.

Simon, C. (1998) *Mad House: Growing Up in the Shadow of Mentally Ill Siblings*, Penguin.

Web sites

'Sibs': www.sibs.org.uk (accessed 1 October 2008).
Generic web site for siblings producing information sheets, regular newsletter, will take calls from siblings, runs workshops.

Rethink Siblings: www.rethink.org/siblings (accessed 1 October 2008).
New on-line national network for siblings to share experiences and get support set up by Rethink mental health charity.
Champs: http://www.easternhealth.org.au/champs/champs.shtml (accessed 1 October 2008).
For children aged 5–12 years who have an adult family member with a mental illness.

10

Family Intervention with Ethnically and Culturally Diverse Groups

Juliana Onwumere, Ben Smith and Elizabeth Kuipers

This chapter is focused on the application of evidence-based family intervention in psychosis to ethnically and/or culturally diverse groups. It begins with a brief review of the relationship between ethnicity and mental ill health, with a particular focus on how caregiving experiences can vary across groups. The second half of the chapter presents case material that illustrates the application of family intervention with a UK Black African family. In line with other published reports (e.g. Department of Health, 2005; NIMHE, 2003), this chapter uses the term Black and Minority Ethnic (BME), unless otherwise specified, in reference to individuals with minority ethnic status, to non-white groups and to people of Irish origin. It does not, however, seek to imply homogeneity between the groups; their heterogeneity and unique characteristics are acknowledged.

Background

Differential rates of psychosis have been reported in BME groups when compared to rates found within indigenous populations (e.g. Brugha *et al.*, 2004; Cantor-Graae and Pedersen, 2007; Selten *et al.*, 2001; Zolkowska, Cantor-Graae and McNeil, 2001). For example, there is compelling and robust evidence which attests to higher incidence rates of schizophrenia and other psychoses in Black Caribbean and Black African groups living in the United Kingdom (Cantor-Graae and Selten, 2005; Fearon *et al.*, 2006; Sharpley *et al.*, 2001). Although different factors have been highlighted such

A Casebook of Family Interventions for Psychosis   Edited by Fiona Lobban and Christine Barrowclough
© 2009 John Wiley & Sons, Ltd

as early parental loss and separation, social adversity and discrimination (e.g. Cooper, 2005; Hutchinson and Haasen, 2004; Mallet *et al.*, 2002; Morgan *et al.*, 2007; Selten and Cantor-Graae, 2005), definitive reasons for the increased incidence remain unclear (Sharpely *et al.*, 2001). However, what the evidence does appear to suggest is that Black African and Black Caribbean service users have a more negative experience of psychiatric services (e.g. Cochrane and Sashidharan, 1996; Parkman *et al.*, 1997), and are less likely to be offered 'talking therapies' (Callan and Littlewood, 1998).

Caregiving in psychosis: ethnic and cultural diversity

The importance of expressed emotion (EE) to client outcomes is widely acknowledged and has been well documented (e.g. Bebbington and Kuipers 1994; Butzlaff and Hooley, 1998). EE has been widely studied, particularly within the United States and Western Europe (e.g. Wearden *et al.*, 2000). High EE has been reported within different ethnic and cultural groups and from groups drawn from less industrialised or developing nations including Egypt, Iran, Israel, Bali, Japan and Singapore (e.g. Fujita *et al.*, 2002; Hashemi and Cochrane 1999; Healey, Tan and Chong, 2006; Kamal, 1995; Kopelowicz *et al.*, 2006; Kurihara *et al.*, 2000; Marom *et al.*, 2002; Mottaghipour *et al.*, 2001). However, the evidence consistently suggests that these groups have lower rates of high EE when compared to Caucasian groups from America and Western Europe (e.g. Jenkins and Karno, 1992; Karno *et al.*, 1987; Ran *et al.*, 2003a).

Although issues around ethnicity have tended to attract less attention, in recent years there has been a developing body of research which has sought to examine the role of ethnicity and/or culture on family functioning and EE (e.g. Kopelowicz *et al.*, 2002; Lopez *et al.*, 2004; Moline *et al.*, 1985; Rosenfarb, Bellack and Aziz, 2006a, 2006b; Rosenfarb *et al.*, 2004; Tompson *et al.*, 1995; Wuerker, Hass and Bellack, 1999). This has confirmed that the predictive relationship between high EE and relapse rates in psychosis appears to be less clear within non-Caucasian groups. Lopez *et al.* (2004) found that family criticism was a significant independent predictor of relapse for Anglo-American clients but not for Mexican Americans. In contrast, a lack of family warmth was a risk factor for relapse for Mexican Americans but not for their Anglo-American counterparts. Recently, Rosenfarb, Bellack and Aziz (2006b) reported that higher levels of critical and intrusive behaviours from relatives were actually associated with better outcomes for

African-American clients. In a UK study, whilst high EE was associated with relapse in White client–relative dyads, no links were found in British born Asian client–relative dyads (Hashemi and Cochrane, 1999).

The negative impact of caregiving (burden) is also known to differ according to ethnicity. Much of this work has been undertaken in the United States and comparisons have generally been made between White, African–American and Hispanic caregivers, often in the absence of matched groups. Nevertheless, data from these studies have tended to consistently suggest that African–American caregivers, compared to their White peers, are more likely to report significantly lower levels of burden and emotional distress despite undertaking similar or higher levels of caregiving duties (e.g. Guarnaccia and Parra, 1996; Horwitz and Reinhard, 1995; Stueve, Vine and Struening, 1997).

Thus far, the relatively limited literature in this area suggests that affective attitudes that can be predictive of illness course in psychosis, and the negative impact of caregiving (i.e. burden), might also differ according to ethnic and/or cultural membership.

Family Intervention in Psychosis (FIP): Ethnicity and Cultural Diversity

To date, there have been only a small number of studies that have examined the application of family intervention with diverse ethnic and cultural groups. Some of these studies have included families from China (e.g. Chien and Chan, 2004; Ran *et al.*, 2003b) and Spanish-speaking migrants to the United States (e.g. Telles *et al.*, 1995; Weisman, 2005; Weisman *et al.*, 2006). Whilst further studies are indicated, the preliminary findings suggest that evidence-based models of family intervention require flexibility and some modification in their delivery and/or content if they are to be successfully applied to different ethnic and cultural groups (e.g. Telles *et al.*, 1995).

In the United Kingdom an ever changing demographic profile (see Census, 2001), particularly within urban settings, increases the likelihood that family interventions, as recommended by the NICE treatment guidelines for schizophrenia (NICE, 2003), will need to be offered to ethnically, racially, culturally and linguistically diverse migrant (including refugee) groups (e.g. Leavey *et al.*, 2004). Therefore, the common needs associated with caregiving for a relative with psychosis have to be met alongside more specific cultural needs such as language, family composition and illness conceptualisation. For example, the English language may not be adequately spoken or understood by service users and/or relatives. This might necessitate the use of interpreters who can, inadvertently, introduce a new layer of complexity into family meetings. Where there is availability, interpreters will need to be suitably qualified, with sufficient comprehension of both languages (Bhui *et al.*, 2003). In addition, they should have some understanding of mental ill health (although this is not always guaranteed), and be independent of that particular family and not from a competing ethnic group, in order to guarantee confidentiality and trust. Unfortunately, many of these requirements will not be met, and has to be considered in the context of whether it does increase or decrease understanding in FIP. Alternatively, the family may be composed around a specific socio-economic and religious structure with an associated set of traditional beliefs and values (e.g. deference to parents or grandparents; Lin and Cheung, 1999; Tseng, 2004), which will influence patterns of behaviour and communication styles within sessions. BME groups may also hold specific beliefs about mental ill health and its treatment, which will affect the content and efficacy of the intervention (Lin and Cheung, 1999; Millet *et al.*, 1996; Perkins and Moodley, 1993). For example, although family members of individuals with psychosis are known to endorse psychosocial factors (e.g. Angermeyer, Klusmann and Walpuski, 1988; Holzinger *et al.*, 2003; Srinivasan and Thara, 2001) and/or biological explanations as the likely causes of the illness (Esterberg and Compton, 2006; Holzinger *et al.*, 2003; Magliano *et al.*, 2001; Phillips *et al.*, 2000; Srinivasan and Thara, 2001), BME family members are also likely to endorse esoteric causes involving magic or spirits (e.g. demons, sorcery, evil spirits; Jacobson and Merdasa, 1991; Papadopoulos *et al.*, 2004; Quinn, 2007; Srinivasan and Thara, 2001). These esoteric explanations may require specific interventions (e.g. herbal remedies, prayer, contact with 'spirits') that are more likely to be provided by non-healthcare personnel (e.g. traditional healer, religious leader or community elder) and may sometimes appear incompatible with mainstream Eurocentric-based interventions (e.g. Jacobson and Merdasa, 1991; Quinn, 2007; Papadopoulos *et al.*, 2004). Further, given the high levels of religious and spiritual activity noted within some BME groups (e.g. Musgrave, Allen and Allen, 2002; Weisman, Gomes and Lopez, 2003; Weisman and Lopez, 1996), specific religious and/or spiritual beliefs may enable families to cope with the illness and make sense of their difficulties (Weisman *et al.*, 2006; Weisman, Gomes and Lopez, 2003).

Overall, the current evidence points towards the importance of under-standing the meaning and impact of psychosis within a specific cultural context, of providing models of interventions that are culturally sensitive and syntonic (Leavey *et al.*, 2004; Rosenfarb, Bellack and Aziz, 2006b; Telles *et al.*, 1995), and of being aware of how one's own cultural background and family background as a therapist may bias interpretations of another fam-ily's functioning (e.g. APA, 1990, 2002). However, irrespective of the ethnic or cultural background of the service user and their relative, the content of FIP should always be matched to the specific needs of the family.

In the second half of this chapter, we have selected specific aspects of a case example to illustrate the manner in which some key features of FIP (e.g. *engagement, psychoeducation and facilitating communication*) might require modification in order to meet the culturally specific needs of an individual family. The intervention was based on the Kuipers, Leff and Lam (2002)[1] model of family intervention and was delivered by two trained therapists as part of a psychological therapy trial of FIP. The male and female therapists were of White British and Black African origin, respectively. In accordance with the trial protocol, the family were offered a maximum of 20-hour-long sessions over 9–12 months. As part of the Kuipers, Leff and Lam (2002) model, intervention sessions were normally held fortnightly within the family home and with the client and their relatives both present. The sessions were structured; therapists tried to ensure that only one family member talked at a time; that each family member was given equal time, and that family members talked directly to each other rather than about each other.

Case Example

The following case has been based on our clinical experience; all names and any identifying features have been changed to ensure confidentiality.

Background

Sade, a 25-year-old woman, had a 2-year history of paranoid schizo-phrenia. At the start of her illness-related difficulties she experienced

---

[1] Full details of this model have been reported in this chapter of this book.

paranoid thoughts regarding work colleagues, specifically that they were laughing at her behind her back and spreading rumours. These thoughts were extremely anxiety provoking for Sade and made life at work almost intolerable for her. She eventually left her job as a personal assistant in order to escape from the perceived laughter and ridicule of her colleagues. Following a similar incident whilst she was working in a short-term temporary job, together with paranoid beliefs about people in her local area, Sade started to doubt her original paranoid thoughts. She then felt extremely embarrassed and ashamed at having left her job under such circumstances. Sade rapidly became depressed and reported 'I am useless and tired, I am not strong or confident enough to work' and 'I am a fool for getting so scared and weird at work – they really must be laughing at me now'.

Sade had always lived in the family home, which she shared with her parents and younger sister, Adeola (23 years). She had one elder sister and brother, who were both married and lived in America and Germany, respectively. Her mother (Eunice) and father (John) both worked full-time in the catering industry. Adeola completed an undergraduate degree and had recently started a demanding administration job in which she often worked long hours. The family were of West African origin; John and Eunice were economic migrants to the United Kingdom from Nigeria and had arrived during the late 1960s. The family were self-defined as Christians; Eunice and John were heavily involved in the evangelical movement as fundraisers and event organisers. Sade and Adeola had stopped being involved in church-related activities since their late teens.

At the beginning of our contact with the family, Sade was not working and regularly spent long periods of time on her own at home. She had been feeling depressed, embarrassed and ashamed for over 11 months, the period in which she had not worked. Sade scored 43 on the Beck Depression Inventory (BDI=II; Beck, Steer and Brown, 1996), which fell within the *severe* range. Her psychiatrist felt that she was 'slipping very fast' into the negative symptoms of schizophrenia and was encouraging Sade to increase her activity levels, something she was struggling to do. Sade was keen to 'get back to normal – I can't carry on like this' but wanted her family and services to know that she was, despite initial appearances, doing all that she could to return to her previous level of functioning. In family meetings, Sade often sat with her head lowered and tended to avoid eye contact with the therapists and her family. Although they were distressed with Sade's situation and wanted to see a return to normal functioning for their daughter, Eunice and John were clear that her recovery could not be rushed; its speed and trajectory were not controlled by Sade or themselves. They had a strong belief that their daughter's recovery 'would happen' but only when the time was right; when 'God' rather than individuals (i.e. the medical profession, Sade and the family) considered that the time was right. Eunice and John expressed doubt about the usefulness of the family meetings but agreed, following some encouragement from the therapists, to attend a few trial sessions and then reconsider. Adeola wanted to help her sister to get 'back on to her feet again'. She was keen to find out more about 'why the illness had come to Sade' and had affected her so much.

It is worth noting that ambivalence towards FIP sessions is common in most families and is not specific to particular ethnic groups. The therapists were mindful that the family might have had some concerns about interventions *per se* and therefore spent some time talking this through. Collaboratively, it was agreed that an *initial* focus of our sessions would be on learning more about what had happened to Sade, and indeed about psychosis more widely. These sessions were structured around slowly moving through prepared psychoeducative information on psychosis, taking time to relate the information to Sade's particular situation. All family members were encouraged and supported to express their views.

Issues around engagement and communication

From the initial stages of the intervention, the therapists recognised and appreciated the role that the family's specific cultural and religious practices could play in the sessions. For instance, John, and Eunice in particular, were always very concerned that we, as therapists, were made to feel welcome in their home. As John often reminded us, we were guests in their home and therefore, we must drink *and* eat something. While this is not culturally specific, it was more challenging than usual to refuse this kindness. In the first two sessions, Eunice spent 15 minutes preparing refreshments for the therapists. This was despite an earlier compromise in which the therapists had declined an offer of food but accepted an offer of beverages. Interestingly, when the drinks arrived, it was still accompanied by a broad selection of food items. The therapists recognised the benefits the parents experienced by their provision of refreshments to the therapists (e.g. feeling more relaxed, pride), and the role it played in facilitating engagement with the entire family. However, they were also aware of the valuable session time that was lost and how, with some families, preparing refreshments might also serve as an opportunity to avoid the business of the sessions (Kuipers, Leff and Lam, 2002). After sharing their dilemma with the family (i.e. time for refreshments vs. time for session), and stating very clearly that the warm welcome and extra efforts of Eunice were most sincerely appreciated, it was agreed that Eunice could make considerably less effort as the therapists were becoming better known to the family. Further, as a workable compromise, the therapists developed a system with the family where they arrived 5 minutes earlier for each session and were therefore able to accept an offer of tea/coffee, without compromising the 60-minute appointment.

Initially, within sessions, Sade (and her sister to a lesser degree) was noticeably reluctant to express views that contradicted anything her parents, particularly her father said. A pattern soon developed where Sade would often backtrack on her opinions if it subsequently became obvious that her parents held a different view. As part of their supervision, the therapists wondered whether this was out of respect for the views of her parents (especially in front of guests) rather than a genuine shift in her opinion. The deference meant that it was often hard to access what Sade's thoughts really were and her parents opinions dominated. Engagement with *all* family members is a prerequisite of any successful FIP. Similar to their work with many other families, the therapists found themselves frequently 'walking a tightrope' between establishing and maintaining good initial engagement with the family and removing barriers to the open permissive conversations in families that tend to characterise powerful and successful interventions. The therapists always encouraged each family member to comment on issues and planned the questions so that Sade was often the first to reply. By doing this, the family and the therapists were more likely to form an accurate idea of what she was thinking.

Psychoeducation: beliefs about cause and recovery

In FIP, the psychoeducative component is individualised (i.e. based upon the clients' personal experiences and history) and is employed as a tool to extricate some of the inaccuracies and misattribution that families can often have about psychosis (e.g. the client is being lazy vs. the client is affected by considerable negative symptoms and depression; the client caused their illness; Barrowclough and Tarrier, 1998). The psychoeducative information leaflet, used as part of the intervention, covers broad issues relating to psychosis including diagnosis, symptoms, causal theories, treatments and recovery, relapse prevention and stress management for carers. Psychoeducation, as part of FIP, is designed to be interactive rather than didactic or dogmatic. Thus, as part of the introduction to the psychoeducation material, the therapists were keen to emphasise that the leaflet was not a definitive version about 'how we should all think about psychosis'. Instead, it reflected some of the current thinking in the area, and the most important outcome from the sessions was the opportunity for everyone to share information and listen to each other.

The sessions commenced with family discussions about how they understood the difficulties that Sade had and what, if any, names they had given it. All family members, including Sade, were most relaxed when they talked about her experiences in terms of 'being down' and having 'no spirit'. Although they had heard terms such as psychosis, it was not something they considered relevant to Sade's circumstances. However, Eunice said that she was aware of many young people near the church that she attended who had serious drug and mental health problems. This led to further discussions about the 'levels' of mental health problems in Black people in the United Kingdom. The therapists commented that higher levels of illnesses that are normally classified under the generic heading of psychosis have been recorded in Black African and Black African–Caribbean groups, and highlighted that the reasons for the excess remain unclear. Adeola wondered if it was to do with drug abuse, whilst Sade said that she was unsure and had not given it much thought. Interestingly, Eunice and John thought that it had something to do with the stresses and strains of living in the United Kingdom and what 'doctors diagnosed as mental illness'. They briefly talked about the difficulties that tended to face young black people living in England and the many obstacles they experienced in terms of employment and educational opportunities. They reported that beliefs about mental illness were different between African countries and the United Kingdom. According to Sade's parents, individuals in the United Kingdom were often perceived as mentally unwell for minor things (e.g. the way in which they expressed their religious beliefs or for talking about issues that people were not familiar with). Further, they believed that the medical profession in the United Kingdom was too quick to tell patients that they were sick and prescribe medication. Although both therapists tried to relate these reports to their own circumstances with Sade, for example '[I]s that what you believe happened with Sade? Was that similar to your experience with Sade?' John and Eunice appeared somewhat resistant to this line of questioning and tended to feel more comfortable discussing ethnicity and diagnosis in a very general manner. It was however important that the therapists understood this parental belief as it was likely to impact on the view they took (and support they gave) to Sade's recovery.

On the basis of the information that Sade and her family provided, the therapists began to develop hypotheses about some of the factors that were maintaining Sade's low mood, inactivity and sense of shame. In the context of initial paranoid thoughts in the workplace, Sade had experienced intense anxiety and had abandoned her career. Back at home she had plenty of time to dwell on what had happened, which made her feel even more embarrassed and ashamed and gave rise to a vicious cycle. This account was palatable for Sade and her sister, and prompted discussions between the sisters about episodes of 'anxiety' that both girls experienced periodically during their adolescence, especially around times of exams. When Sade's parents were encouraged to comment on the therapists' hypotheses, John said that he attributed his daughters' difficulties to something that others had done to 'frustrate' their family and impede their development. When John was asked to elaborate, he informed the therapists that this type of activity was common practice where he came from. However, he believed that God would not allow Sade and their family to be defeated by others who wished to witness the demise of his family. Despite invitations, John and Eunice refrained from adding any specific details about their experiences of being 'frustrated'. The therapists were trying to accurately assess the extent to which these beliefs were shared in the family, and their implications for (potentially hindering) Sade's recovery. Sade and Adeola were unable to offer any further details when they were asked to comment on their parents' reports, although they mentioned that it was an account that they had heard on previous occasions. Nevertheless, John and Eunice were able to agree with the therapists' summary that Sade's difficulties, according to their own knowledge, were due to the malevolent acts of known or unknown others. Further, it was a practice they were familiar with but something that could be recovered from in time, with 'God's' input.

John, in agreement with Eunice, believed that the best option for ensuring Sade's recovery was to not overload her mind, to rest and 'wait' for God's guidance and intervention. Further, they believed that God's intervention could be facilitated through religious and spiritual activities such as prayer and fasting. In response to careful questioning from the therapists, Sade was able to report that her parents' perspective on her problems and its treatment was in contrast to the messages and information that she received from her Community Mental Health Team (CMHT). It was, depending on how she was feeling, also in contrast to her own opinions. Adeola empathised with her sister's position and openly wondered whether at times she felt 'lost' with the conflicting advice about her recovery. It soon became clear to all family members that Sade was currently 'stuck' waiting to feel and get better, rather than being able to actively participate in her recovery. Her passivity was being further compounded by the vicious cycle of low mood, inactivity and negative thinking. Eunice and John acknowledged that it was a pattern that they had not considered before.

In response to a discussion of the benefits (for some people) of talking treatments that also involve behavioural elements such as activity scheduling, Adeola asserted that she knew of individuals, from her time spent at university, who had benefited from such treatments when they had been suffering with depression. John and Eunice were sceptical about whether such an approach would be of any benefit to 'someone like our daughter' and the type of problems that she had (i.e. problems inflicted on the family by 'others'). They believed that Sade's difficulties required a much deeper and powerful intervention that was provided by 'God' and their faith. Both parents believed that mental health services ignored (or dismissed) the power and the healing qualities of God, and of one's faith. Eunice described two recent cases in their church where families had been healed from their difficulties. It saddened her that her two younger daughters were not involved in the church movement like they once were.

With the support of the therapists, Adeola was encouraged to comment on her parents' views. This was a conscious decision on the part of the therapists. It seemed that the passive approach to recovery advocated by Eunice and John, and borne out of their culturally informed understanding of Sade's problems, was potentially very limiting to Sade. Thus, the therapists thought it would be useful to explore the different perspectives within the family, with a view to evaluating their benefits and potential limitations for Sade's recovery and for the family. Adeola spoke out in favour of talking treatments pointing out that although Sade had a strong faith, she was also very depressed and did not appear to be improving. Tearfully, Adeola said that the family needed to consider different ways to help Sade, and wittily stated, 'God helps those who help themselves.' This was met with an acknowledging smile from her father.

The therapists spent considerable time reinforcing the benefits of such open conversations, the mutual concern that they *all* had for Sade and the importance of respecting their different perspectives. Following further discussions, Sade agreed with her sister's point of view and accepted her offer (with assistance from the therapists) to help her look into options to directly help with her low mood. As an interim measure Sade also agreed, with the verbal support of all family members, to meet with the occupational therapist from the CMHT to work on issues of activity scheduling. This was an important development because to date, this was an offer that she had always previously declined.

Working with the emotional impact of psychosis and relapse prevention issues

In addition to psychoeducation, subsequent sessions with the family addressed issues around the emotional impact of the illness on family members, relapse prevention and improving Sade's activity levels. It remained an ongoing challenge to encourage both parents to identify and/or comment on the emotional impact of the illness on themselves and their daughters. It was evident that religion and faith played a central role in how they coped with Sade's difficulties. However, John and Eunice had a tendency to reframe or equate negative emotions (e.g. sadness, fear) that might be associated with the impact of Sade's difficulties as a sign of diminishing faith. It was important for the therapists to explicitly acknowledge their coping styles and its effectiveness, whilst also highlighting and normalising the range of emotions they might have in relation to being a parent of a young daughter who was experiencing difficulties, irrespective of their beliefs about causality. The therapists found it useful to draw on their own experience of having worked with many families and the similar concerns they tended to encounter.

Unknown to Sade and her parents, it appeared that Adeola was particularly affected by her elder sister's condition. Because of their similarities, Adeola reported that Sade's difficulties had led her to question the status of her own mental health and worry about becoming unwell. Previously, Adeola had not felt confident in raising this concern herself. She knew that her parents' beliefs about the cause of Sade's problems would mean her own concerns may be dismissed. These concerns were normalised by the therapists and Adeola's attention was brought to data documenting family links with psychosis, and the type of issues and problems that siblings tend to grapple with.

Although they participated in the discussions on relapse prevention, Sade's parents remained clear throughout the sessions that the 'wrong' that had been done to their family would not occur again; their prayers and faith had ensured this. They wondered about the usefulness of concentrating on the negative issues from the past particularly as Sade was beginning to improve. As with many families, it was important for both therapists to normalise their concerns about relapse. Interestingly, when Sade and Adeola were asked to comment, it was clear that both women, to varying degrees, held similar views to their parents. For Sade and Adeola, there was a sense that talking about things getting difficult in the future, at a time when Sade was slowly improving, was somewhat overwhelming and pessimistic. Both therapists worked hard to really emphasise the developments that Sade and her family had made over the sessions. This naturally led to the therapists emphasising the importance of trying to ensure those developments were maintained by having a plan about what to do if (rather than when) Sade were to experience any difficulties in the future. Notwithstanding some of their concerns, all the family were able to work with a straightforward model of relapse prevention, which primarily focused on the family's role in identifying *and* responding, without too much delay, to incipient signs in Sade of low mood and/or expressed concern about what 'other' people were saying about her. Although they reiterated that it was unlikely to happen again, Sade's parents reported that, if faced with a similar set of difficulties, they were unlikely to do anything differently. Thus, they would highlight the importance of prayer and rest to her recovery. The therapists carefully led the family into a broad discussion of the merits of trying to respond early and of developing additional coping strategies at times when things appeared to get difficult. Adeola reported that she had greater confidence in asking her sister about how she was feeling. Further, because of Sade's developments in her recovery, she would be keen to try and engage her sister in activities rather than complying with her requests to be left alone. By doing this, Sade was less likely to dwell on the things that were upsetting her and led her to feel worse. Interestingly, although she understood her parents' response, Adeola reported that she was highly likely to contact Sade's mental health worker if she became really worried about her. Sade agreed with her sisters' strategy.

As the sessions progressed, it was clear to the therapists that Sade became more vocal and spent considerably less time with her head lowered. From the 11th session, Sade had begun to attend a weekly social group that was facilitated by her team. The group was primarily designed to minimise social isolation amongst young adults with psychosis. Although they were slightly cautious in the initial stages, Eunice and John were very supportive of their daughters' attendance and had begun to notice 'little signs of improvement'. By the end of the intervention (16 sessions) Sade and Adeola had become members of a local gym and Sade was working towards undertaking part-time voluntary work for two mornings and one afternoon a week. In our final sessions, Sade and Adeola both spoke about the rewards of being able to 'talk as a family' and admitted that they had been sceptical about the purpose of the meetings at the beginning. Interestingly, neither John nor Eunice was able to specify any individual benefits from the intervention. However, they were keen to inform the therapists that the recovery of the family was underway, as they had initially predicted; it was their faith and 'God's' power that had led to these important changes. Post therapy, Sade's score on the BDI (Beck, Steer and Brown, 1996) had decreased from 43 to 8, which fell within the *minimal* range.

Critical Reflection

The case was randomly allocated to the therapists as part of a psychological intervention trial. To date, it remains unclear to what extent therapist gender and/or ethnic background might have affected the content and process of the intervention. It is possible that some members of the family might have felt inhibited to talk about their experiences in the presence of therapist who was of similar ethnic origin. Alternatively, the presence of a Black African therapist may have been perceived as a benefit and facilitated engagement.

Although the therapists made a conscious effort to modify family intervention sessions in response to the individual cultural needs of the family, it is difficult to evaluate how far this succeeded. Modifications to interventions are necessarily individualised and reactive, thus making planning and thinking ahead more difficult. Certainly, issues of culture and ethnicity featured heavily in the therapists' ongoing supervision. At the end of the intervention, the therapists remain concerned that a *passive* recovery style associated with 'waiting for Gods' input', as advocated by Eunice and John, would be (inadvertently so, and with the best of intentions) imposed on Sade should she relapse in the future. With hindsight, the therapists wondered whether they should have given far greater attention to the role of spiritual coping, and made more explicit attempts to integrate the area into their overall intervention. In recent months within the United States, models of culturally informed FIP have been published. Working with the families' spiritual and/or religious beliefs as they relate to illness and recovery forms a central feature of the intervention. However, the data on the efficacy for this approach remain in the infancy (see Weisman *et al.*, 2006).

Conclusion

The aim of this chapter was to highlight some of the issues related to the provision of FIP with ethnically and culturally diverse families. We provided some background on the general experience of ethnic minority groups within the UK statutory mental health services and the evidence which indicates that the impact of psychosis on families may differ depending on ethnicity. Through presenting particular aspects of a case example we tried to highlight some of the areas (e.g. *engagement, psychoeducation and facilitating communication*) in which modifications might be needed when working with ethnically diverse groups (e.g. Carra *et al.*, 2007). However, more research is needed on what type of approaches will work best with particular groups.

From our own experience, providing family interventions across ethnically diverse groups can be both exciting and challenging. It is important to note that within all ethnic groups (e.g. White British, Black Caribbean, Black African and South Asian), mental health service users are entitled to services and interventions that are culturally informed and capable. This demands a workforce that has relevant skills and knowledge, and access to appropriate training (Bhui, 2003; NIMHE, 2003). BME groups may be more inclined to seek talking therapies and continue with the intervention, if the interventions are modified to take account of their specific language and cultural needs (Weisman *et al.*, 2006). However, care must be applied to ensure that everything about the client with psychosis and their relatives is not solely attributed to ethnicity and culture or conversely, that issues around ethnicity and culture are completely denied and ignored (Waheed, Hussain and Creed, 2003). A healthy balance, and a flexible, open approach based on the specific needs of the family, is always required.

References

American Psychological Association (APA) (1990) *Guidelines for Providers of Psychological Services to Ethnic, Linguistic, and Culturally Diverse Populations,* American Psychological Association, Washington, DC.

American Psychological Association (APA) (2002) Guidelines on multicultural education, training, research, practice, and organizational change for psychologists. *American Psychologist,* **58**, 377–402.

Angermeyer, M.C., Klusmann, D. and Walpuski, O. (1988) The causes of functional psychoses as seen by patients and their relatives. 2. The relatives point of view. *European Archives of Psychiatry and Clinical Neuroscience,* **238**, 55–61.

Barrowclough, C. and Tarrier, N. (1998) The application of expressed emotion to clinical work in schizophrenia. *In Session-Psychotherapy in Practice,* **4**, 7–23.

Bebbington, P. and Kuipers, L. (1994) The predictive utility of expressed emotion in schizophrenia – an aggregate analysis. *Psychological Medicine,* **24**, 707–18.

Beck, A.T., Steer, R.A. and Brown, G.K. (1996) *Manual for the Revised Beck Depression Inventory,* Psychological Corporation, San Antonio, TX.

Bhui, K. (2003) Psychiatric services for ethnic minority groups: a third way? Reply. *British Journal of Psychiatry,* **183**, 563.

Bhui, K., Mohamud, S., Warfa, N. *et al.* (2003) Cultural adaptation of mental health measures: improving the quality of clinical practice and research. *British Journal of Psychiatry,* **183**, 184–6.

Brugha, T., Jenkins, R., Bebbington, P. *et al.* (2004) Risk factors and the prevalence of neurosis and psychosis in ethnic groups in Great Britain. *Social Psychiatry and Psychiatric Epidemiology,* **39**, 939–46.

Butzlaff, R.L. and Hooley, J.M. (1998) Expressed emotion and psychiatric relapse – a meta-analysis. *Archives of General Psychiatry,* **55**, 547–52.

Callan, A. and Littlewood, R. (1998) Patient satisfaction: ethnic origin or explanatory model? *International Journal of Social Psychiatry,* **44**, 1–11.

Cantor-Graae, E. and Pedersen, C.B. (2007) Risk of schizophrenia in second generation immigrants: a Danish population-based cohort study. *Psychological Medicine,* **37**, 485–94.

Cantor-Graae, E. and Selten, J.P. (2005) Schizophrenia and migration: a meta-analysis and review. *American Journal of Psychiatry,* **162**, 12–24.

Carra, G., Montomoli, C., Clerici, M. and Cazzullo, C.L. (2007) Family interventions for schizophrenia in Italy: randomized controlled trial. *European Archives of Psychiatry and Clinical Neuroscience,* **257**, 23–30.

Chien, W.T. and Chan, S.W.C. (2004) One-year follow-up of a multiple-family-group intervention for Chinese families of patients with schizophrenia. *Psychiatric Services,* **55**, 1276–84.

Cochrane, R. and Sashidharan, S.P. (1996) Mental Health and Ethnic Minorities: A Review of the Literature and Implications for Services. NHS Centre for Reviews and Dissemination Social Policy Research Unit, Report 5, York, University of York.

Cooper, B. (2005) Immigration and schizophrenia: the social causation hypothesis revisited. *British Journal of Psychiatry*, **186**, 361–3.

Department of Health (2005) *Delivering Race Equality in Mental Health: A Summary. An Action Plan for Reform inside and outside Services and the Government's Response to the Independent Inquiry into the Death of David Bennett*, Department of Health.

Department of Health NHS Modernisation Agency, National Institute for Mental Health in England (2003) *Inside outside: Improving Mental Health Services for Black and Minority Ethnic Communities in England*, NIMHE, London.

Esterberg, M.L. and Compton, M.T. (2006) Causes of schizophrenia reported by family members of urban African American hospitalized patients with schizophrenia. *Comprehensive Psychiatry*, **47**, 221–6.

Fearon, P., Kirkbride, J.B., Morgan, C. *et al.* (2006) Incidence of schizophrenia and other psychoses in ethnic minority groups: results from the MRC AESOP study. *Psychological Medicine*, **36**, 1541–50.

Fujita, H., Shimodera, S., Izumoto, Y. *et al.* (2002) Family attitude scale: measurement of criticism in the relatives of patients with schizophrenia in Japan. *Psychiatry Research*, **110**, 273–80.

Guarnaccia, P.J. and Parra, P. (1996) Ethnicity, social status and families' experiences of caring for a mentally ill family member. *Community Mental Health Journal*, **32** (3), 243–60.

Hashemi, A.H. and Cochrane, R. (1999) Expressed emotion and schizophrenia: a review of studies across cultures. *International Review of Psychiatry*, **11**, 219–24.

Healey, F., Tan, V.L.M. and Chong, S.A. (2006) Cross-cultural validation of expressed emotion in caregivers of Chinese patients with first episode psychosis in Singapore: a qualitative study. *International Journal of Social Psychiatry*, **52**, 199–213.

Holzinger, A., Kilian, R., Lindenbach, I. *et al.* (2003) Patients' and their relatives' causal explanations of schizophrenia. *Social Psychiatry and Psychiatric Epidemiology*, **38**, 155–62.

Horwitz, A.V. and Reinhard, S.C. (1995) Ethnic differences in caregiving duties and burden among parents and siblings of persons with severe mental illnesses. *Journal of Health and Social Behaviour*, **36**, 138–50.

Hutchinson, G. and Haasen, C. (2004) Migration and schizophrenia – the challenges for European psychiatry and implications for the future. *Social Psychiatry and Psychiatric Epidemiology*, **39**, 350–7.

Jacobson, L. and Merdasa, F. (1991) Traditional perceptions and treatment of mental-disorders in western Ethiopia before the 1974 revolution. *Acta Psychiatrica Scandinavica*, **84**, 475–81.

Jenkins, J.H. and Karno, M. (1992) The meaning of expressed emotion – theoretical issues raised by cross-cultural research. *American Journal of Psychiatry*, **149**, 9–21.

Kamal, A. (1995) Variables in expressed emotion associated with relapse: a comparison between depressed and schizophrenic samples in an Egyptian community. *Current Psychiatry*, **2**, 211–6.

Karno, M., Jenkins, J.H., Delaselva, A. *et al.* (1987) Expressed emotion and schizophrenic outcome among Mexican-American Families. *Journal of Nervous and Mental Disease*, **175**, 143–51.

Kopelowicz, A., Lopez, S.R., Zarate, R. *et al.* (2006) Expressed emotion and family interactions in Mexican Americans with schizophrenia. *Journal of Nervous and Mental Disease*, **194**, 330–4.

Kopelowicz, A., Zarate, R., Gonzalez, V. *et al.* (2002) Evaluation of expressed emotion in schizophrenia: a comparison of Caucasians and Mexican-Americans. *Schizophrenia Research*, **55**, 179–86.

Kuipers, E., Leff, J. and Lam, D. (2002) *Family Work for Schizophrenia: A Practical Guide*, 2nd edn, Gaskell, London.

Kurihara, T., Kato, M., Tsukahara, T. *et al.* (2000) The low prevalence of high levels of expressed emotion in Bali. *Psychiatry Research*, **94**, 229–38.

Leavey, G., Gulamhussein, S., Papadopoulos, C. *et al.* (2004) A randomized controlled trial of a brief intervention for families of patients with a first episode of psychosis. *Psychological Medicine*, **34**, 423–31.

Lin, K.M. and Cheung, F. (1999) Mental health issues for Asian Americans. *Psychiatric Services*, **50**, 774–80.

Lopez, S.R., Hipke, K.N., Polo, A.J. *et al.* (2004) Ethnicity, expressed emotion, attributions, and course of schizophrenia: family warmth matters. *Journal of Abnormal Psychology*, **113**, 428–39.

Magliano, L., Guarneri, M., Fiorillo, A. *et al.* (2001) A multicenter Italian study of patients' relatives' beliefs about schizophrenia. *Psychiatric Services*, **52**, 1528–30.

Mallett, R., Leff, J., Bhugra, D. *et al.* (2002) Social environment, ethnicity and schizophrenia – a case-control study. *Social Psychiatry and Psychiatric Epidemiology*, **37**, 329–35.

Marom, S., Munitz, H., Jones, P.B. *et al.* (2002) Familial expressed emotion: outcome and course of Israeli patients with schizophrenia. *Schizophrenia Bulletin*, **28**, 731–43.

Millet, P.E., Sullivan, B.F., Schwebel, A.I. and Myers, L.J. (1996) Black Americans' and white Americans' views of the etiology and treatment of mental health problems. *Community Mental Health Journal*, **32**, 235–42.

Moline, R.A., Singh, S., Morris, A. and Meltzer, H.Y. (1985) Family expressed emotion and relapse in schizophrenia in 24 urban American patients. *American Journal of Psychiatry*, **142**, 1078–81.

Morgan, C., Kirkbride, J., Leff, J., *et al.* (2007) Parental separation, loss and psychosis in different ethnic groups: a case-control study. *Psychological Medicine*, **37**, 495–503.

Mottaghipour, Y., Pourmand, D., Maleki, H. and Davidian, L. (2001) Expressed emotion and the course of schizophrenia in Iran. *Social Psychiatry and Psychiatric Epidemiology*, **36**, 195–9.

Musgrave, C.F., Allen, C.E. and Allen, G.J. (2002) Spirituality and health for women of color. *American Journal of Public Health*, **92**, 557–60.

National Institute of Clinical Excellence (NICE) (2003) *Schizophrenia: Full National Clinical Guidelines on Core Interventions in Primary and Secondary Care*, Gaskell Press, London.

Papadopoulos, I., Lees, S., Lay, M. and Gebrehiwot, A. (2004) Ethiopian refugees in the UK: migration, adaptation and settlement experiences and their relevance to health. *Ethnicity and Health*, **9** (1), 55–73.

Parkman, S., Davies, S., Leese, M. *et al.* (1997) Ethnic differences in satisfaction with mental health services among representative people with psychosis in South London: PRiSM Study 4. *British Journal of Psychiatry*, **171**, 260–4.

Perkins, R. and Moodley, P. (1993) The arrogance of insight. *Psychiatric Bulletin*, **17**, 233–4.

Phillips, M.R., Li, Y.Y., Stroup, T.S. and Xin, L.H. (2000) Causes of schizophrenia reported by patients' family members in China. *British Journal of Psychiatry*, **177**, 20–5.

Quinn, N. (2007) Beliefs and community responses to mental illness in Ghana: the experiences of family carers. *International Journal of Social Psychiatry*, **53** 175–88.

Ran, M.S., Leff, J., Hou, Z.J. *et al.* (2003a) The characteristics of expressed emotion among relatives of patients with schizophrenia in Chengdu, China. *Culture Medicine and Psychiatry*, **27**, 95–106.

Ran, M.S., Xiang, M.Z., Chan, C.L.W. *et al.* (2003b) Effectiveness of psychoeducational intervention for rural Chinese families experiencing schizophrenia – a randomised controlled trial. *Social Psychiatry and Psychiatric Epidemiology*, **38**, 69–75.

Rosenfarb, I.S., Bellack, A.S. and Aziz, N. (2006a) A sociocultural stress, appraisal, and coping model of subjective burden and family attitudes toward patients with schizophrenia. *Journal of Abnormal Psychology*, **115**, 157–65.

Rosenfarb, I.S., Bellack, A.S. and Aziz, N. (2006b) Family interactions and the course of schizophrenia in African American and White patients. *Journal of Abnormal Psychology*, **115**, 112–20.

Rosenfarb, I.S., Bellack, A.S., Aziz, N. *et al.* (2004) Race, family interactions, and patient stabilization in schizophrenia. *Journal of Abnormal Psychology*, **113**, 109–15.

Selten, J.P. and Cantor-Graae, E. (2005) Social defeat: risk factor for schizophrenia? *British Journal of Psychiatry*, **187**, 101–2.

Selten, J.P., Veen, N., Feller, W. *et al.* (2001) Incidence of psychotic disorders in immigrant groups to The Netherlands. *British Journal of Psychiatry*, **178**, 367–72.

Sharpley, M., Hutchinson, G., McKenzie, K. and Murray, R.M. (2001) Understanding the excess of psychosis among the African-Caribbean population in England – review of current hypotheses. *British Journal of Psychiatry*, **178** S60–8.

Srinivasan, T.N. and Thara, R. (2001) Beliefs about causation of schizophrenia: do Indian families believe in supernatural causes? *Social Psychiatry and Psychiatric Epidemiology*, **36**, 134–40.

Stueve, A., Vine, P. and Struening, E.L. (1997) Perceived burden among caregivers of adults with serious mental illness: comparisons of Black, Hispanic, and White families. *American Journal of Orthopsychiatry*, **67**, 199–209.

Telles, C., Karno, M., Mintz, J. *et al.* (1995) Immigrant families coping with schizophrenia. Behavioural family intervention vs. case management with a low-income Spanish-speaking population. *The British Journal of Psychiatry*, **167**, 473–9.

Tompson, M.C., Goldstein, M.J., Lebell, M.B. *et al.* (1995) Schizophrenic-patients perceptions of their relatives attitudes. *Psychiatry Research*, **57**, 155–167.

Tseng, W.S. (2004) Culture and psychotherapy: Asian perspectives. *Journal of Mental Health*, **13**, 151–61.

Waheed, W., Hussain, N. and Creed, F. (2003) Psychiatric services for ethnic minority groups: a third way? Correspondence. *British Journal of Psychiatry* **183**, 562–3.

Wearden, A.J., Tarrier, N., Barrowclough, C. *et al.* (2000) A review of expressed emotion research in health care. *Clinical Psychology Review*, **20**, 633–66.

Weisman, A. (2005) Integrating culturally based approaches with existing interventions for Hispanic/Latino families coping with schizophrenia. *Psychotherapy*, **42**, 178–97.

Weisman, A., Duarte, E., Joneru, V. and Wasserman, S. (2006) The development of a culturally informed, family-focused treatment for schizophrenia. *Family Process*, **45**, 171–86.

Weisman, A.G., Gomes, L.G. and Lopez, S.R. (2003) Shifting blame away from ill relatives – Latino families' reactions to schizophrenia. *Journal of Nervous and Mental Disease*, **191**, 574–81.

Weisman, A.G. and Lopez, S.R. (1996) Family values, religiosity, and emotional reactions to schizophrenia in Mexican and Anglo-American cultures. *Family Process*, **35**, 227–37.

Wuerker, A.K., Haas, G.L. and Bellack, A.S. (1999) Racial and gender differences in expressed emotion and interpersonal control in families of persons with schizophrenia. *Family Process*, **38**, 477–96.

Zolkowska, K., Cantor-Graae, E. and McNeil, T.F. (2001) Increased rates of psychosis among immigrants to Sweden: is migration a risk factor for psychosis? *Psychological Medicine*, **31**, 669–78.

Further Reading and Resources

1. www.nafsiyat.org.uk: Nafsiyat provides individual and family psychotherapy for clients from diverse backgrounds.
2. Diverse Minds: http://www.mind.org.uk/About+Mind/Networks/Diverse+Minds.
3. Mental Health Foundation: http://www.mentalhealth.org.uk/information/mental-health-a-z/black-minority-ethnic-communities/ (accessed 5 January 2009).
4. Kareem, J. and Littlewood, R. (2000) *Intercultural Therapy*, 2nd edn, Blackwell Science, London.
5. Tribe, R. and Hitesh, R. (2003) *Working with Interpreters in Mental Health*, Brunner-Routledge, Hove.

V

Working in Different Contexts

11

Multiple Family Groups in Early Psychosis: A Brief Psychoeducational and Therapeutic Intervention

David Glentworth

Introduction

This chapter describes a brief group intervention for the families and other key supporters of clients in an early intervention service. Although the statutory framework for services in the United Kingdom (e.g. DoH, 2001) emphasises the importance of engaging families in early intervention services with the aim of improving outcomes for both clients and families, there is little empirical evidence available to inform the choice of intervention at this stage. The author has been involved with a team that used empirically based theoretical models of relatives' reaction to illness and clinical experience of the needs of families in first-episode psychosis to develop a short group for families that is sustainable in a routine service setting.

The chapter considers briefly the empirical literature but in the main concentrates on the practical issues involved from the therapist's and from the service perspective, of establishing and maintaining the intervention and of maximising therapeutic gains. The author has found that one of the biggest challenges is achieving effective and lasting engagement with families and the chapter describes the strategies, rationales, therapist characteristics and skills that have evolved to address this. Examples of therapeutic strategies used to illustrate this are drawn from actual cases. They show how embedding the process of family intervention within a service as a default mode of operation avoids pathologising families and how flexibility of approach in therapists' approaches can be vital.

A Casebook of Family Interventions for Psychosis Edited by Fiona Lobban and Christine Barrowclough
© 2009 John Wiley & Sons, Ltd

The structure and content of the five-session programme is presented in some detail. Content has been developed to meet informational needs of families and the chapter shows how this can be adjusted to meet the needs of each group. Finally, attention is paid to the non-specific therapeutic processes that occur within groups and why these are important to consider and to foster. Family members themselves often value the normalising and validating messages that they get from other carers. Therapist strategies suitable for encouraging the growth of these through the five sessions are outlined.

Service Context

The intervention for relatives to be described is part of the early intervention service, or IMPACT team (Investigating the Merits of Psychoeduation and Cognitive Therapy) in Salford, Greater Manchester, UK. IMPACT is a specialist therapeutic service for clients experiencing a first episode of psychosis. Originally a research trial, IMPACT has been funded in Salford since 2000 by the National Health Service (NHS). Clients are usually referred by specialist mental health services within the NHS, and the majority will be in receipt of care coordination under the Care Programme Approach. The service also welcomes clients who are not in contact with specialist mental health services, and self-referral is encouraged.

Clients are offered assessment within a maximum of 4 weeks of referral by an IMPACT therapist, at which point a therapeutic 'plan' will be negotiated. The goals at assessment in relation to family work are to identify a key relative or other carer or supporter, to provide the client with a rationale for involving the family arm of the service and to obtain consent to contact the key relative(s) and perform an assessment.

The family service is staged with more complex aims for each level of contact. At Stage 1 or first contact, the aim is to simply develop an initial 'meaningful' contact. Stage 2 involves 'Assessment and Triage' and the aims are assessment, identification of main needs, provision of/facilitation of access to information and support and signposting to suitable services (e.g. voluntary and non-statutory agencies). Stage 3 is directed at delivering a specialist psychosocial intervention. We aim to give access to a suitable structured psychoeducational intervention and provide interpersonal support through the multiple group intervention. Through this we hope to ensure early identification of family problems and to provide long-term structured family interventions where appropriate.

Why a Multiple Family Group?

Multiple family psychoeducational groups are the central plank of the family service and are offered to the families of all clients who consent. The intervention consists of five sessions, conducted weekly to which both family members, friends (and anyone identified by the client as being important to them) plus the client themselves are invited. The programme is designed as a series of discrete psychoeducational packages that can be offered by any reasonably experienced mental health professional. This helps give it good face validity in the eyes of potential participants as it meets a commonly expressed need by relatives in early psychosis for information about the disorder and advice on how to cope. It also takes advantage of knowledge that is ingrained in professionals and the framework helps to develop staff's sense of competence in dealing with groups and with families by allowing them to make short didactic presentations without having to be a facilitator for a whole 'therapeutic' group. Moreover, there is substantial empirical evidence that multiple group formats are an acceptable and effective way of delivering structured psychoeducational and therapeutic interventions to families. Such approaches have been developed and evaluated in several different cultural and service settings, for example in China (Chien and Chan, 2004), North America (Dyck *et al.*, 2000), Mediterranean Europe (Montero *et al.*, 2001) and the United Kingdom (Leff *et al.*, 1990). The model that has been most widely disseminated and evaluated is that of McFarlane in the United States (McFarlane, 2002). A series of empirical studies have demonstrated variously an equivalence with (McFarlane *et al.*, 1996), and an advantage over (McFarlane *et al.*, 1995), single family treatments in the prevention of relapse.

Organisational Requirements

Given the evidence suggesting that family intervention services are often not implemented (Fadden, 1997), the service has found it an advantage to design and evolve an intervention that is practicable to deliver and sustainable over time by routine services. Thus, the programme is a discrete package of care, its modular nature uses staff time economically, it is easy to cost and to identify resources, it makes use of and builds on staff's existing skills.

Theoretical Influences – Why a Group? Why This Model?

The service has therefore been configured to take account of the following themes in the literature:

(1) *Phase specificity.* In the first episode of psychosis, clients are often at major development and change points in their lives and this places an extraordinary load on families and strains their resources and coping abilities. It often requires of them not only love and dedication and the usual parenting practices but also additional knowledge and some new and possibly counterintuitive skills.

It is my experience that families often ask searching questions such as that posed by Mrs Lester:

> Where were you when my son was first admitted to hospital?

Delay in offering assessment and intervention can not only jeopardise engagement with families but it also runs the risk of contributing to the development of delayed or unsatisfactory adjustment to the often distressing impact of first episode and the entrenchment of unhelpful coping responses and attributions towards the client. Thus, the intervention needs to be made available frequently enough to guarantee that access to it is relatively close to an acute event.

(2) *Generation of positive perceptions of services.* The engagement and intervention process must be sensitive to the nature of the difficulties they are facing, the natural reactions, coping styles and processes of accommodation and change and to the cultural and contextual factors that surround families and inform all of these elements.

(3) *Responsiveness to clinical need.* There is a growing literature surrounding the impact of early psychosis on family and carers and the intervention should be configured in order to address the major issues that

families face. Poor outcome for clients, for example is associated with the establishment of an adverse emotional and interpersonal environment (Kuipers *et al.*, 2006) and the intervention has been established to address the range of attributions that relatives make that are associated with such coping responses (Raune, Kuipers and Bebbington, 2004). Brief interventions that consist of psychoeducation alone do not always demonstrate effectiveness in altering relatives' perceptions (Pekkala and Merinder, 2000). The group is a potentially powerful mechanism for generating and considering a range of perspectives about clients' illnesses and changes in behaviour. Evaluation and feedback from relatives who have been through the intervention supports existing literature on therapeutic groups that demonstrate that participants often value the support and suggestions of other participants above that of the group facilitators (Buksti *et al.*, 2006).

Poor outcome for relatives, such as psychiatric morbidity, for example is most often associated with sense of burden, sense of stigma, loss of social network and social support. The intervention provides a normalising and supportive social network at a crucial time. It also aims to socialise relatives to models of coping and behaviour that are constructive and minimise stress and to introduce a model of client and family recovery that instils a realistic degree of hope.

Furthermore, it is clear from the literature that some families develop coping strategies characterised by high expressed emotion in response to changes in client behaviour that occur during a long period of untreated illness (Miklowitz, Goldstein and Falloon, 1983). Within the total population of families presenting to services, however, there is an enormous heterogeneity of coping response. Expressed emotion 'status' is unstable and often reverts spontaneously to 'Low' as the client's recovery progresses. In addition, Linszen *et al.* (1996) found that Behavioural Family Management Approach, an intervention having demonstrable effect in high expressed emotion, was found to be difficult to implement in early onset families. The multiple family intervention therefore has been designed to be appropriate and acceptable to as wide a range of families as possible.

(4) *Be acceptable to the broad range of service users.* This intervention has been developed in order to have high levels of face validity and to meet the needs of families in first episode as they themselves express them. It is 'marketed' as being centred on the provision of information from

professionals and the opportunity to learn about services so that they might advocate effectively for themselves and their relatives.

(5)   *Socialisation to the model of working.* Although most clients will achieve an acceptable recovery, some families continue to adopt a caring role. The group intervention is important in socialising families to a model of the care process that positions them as integral to it, having both rights and the need for adequate information so that they can advocate for themselves and their relatives.

Working with Groups of Families in Early Intervention

The following sections will attempt to outline the content and process of the group sessions using case illustrations to describe some of the key issues and themes that emerge. Rather than providing a separate section on therapists' required experience and attributes, the case scenarios raise some of the therapeutic challenges likely to be encountered. It is hoped that the illustrations will convey the knowledge and skills required to develop good working relationships with relatives and to get the most out of the group intervention.

Engagement and provision of a rationale

Rationales for the intervention include descriptions of how the group is designed to meet the most common needs expressed by relatives. They include getting information on the symptoms and signs of psychosis, medical and non-medical treatments, helping with recovery, getting information on services and how to access help for themselves and their relatives. The service is presented or 'marketed' in literature by clinicians as a high value and distinctive 'brand' and adjectives such as 'up to date', 'the best' and 'essential' are used to describe the information available within the intervention.

Where possible, clinicians will attempt to illustrate to relatives how the group might answer their own particular questions or help to resolve any uncertainties. The case of the Burns family illustrates, for example how families' particular needs for information can be used to inform a rationale.

At their assessment appointment, Mr and Mrs Burns expressed some doubts about whether the service could be helpful to them. Their son

Danny had been admitted to hospital several weeks previously and was making only slow progress:

MRS BURNS: I don't really see the point of us getting involved and coming to the group. The only thing that would help us is for our son to get better. It doesn't really matter what we say or do, it's not us that needs help.

THERAPIST: At the moment your son is really unwell and I'd like you to consider what response you would expect from the staff in the hospital if he had become suddenly ill with another kind of problem that is common at this stage in life, such as diabetes perhaps. I know that if it were my son I would want to get all the information I could that might help me understand what was going on and how best I could help him.

MR BURNS: I'm pretty sure that all he needs at present is to stay in hospital where he is safe and to take the medication that they give him.

THERAPIST: I hope that your Danny is feeling better really soon, you must be really worried about him. It sounds as if, like a lot of people in his position, that he might need quite a bit of help when he comes home and as his recovery progresses. Like any other concerned parents you must have lots of questions about the kind of help and support he will need and how best you can contribute to this. These are the kind of questions that the group is designed to address.

The therapist went on to explain that one of the most common questions that relatives ask is 'Why?' Why my child? Why now? And that the information and discussions within the group are designed to address the question 'What causes psychosis?' Mr Burns was eager to state that their opinion was that Danny's drug use had precipitated his admission to hospital and that they were concerned that unless this was impressed upon him he would remain vulnerable to illness. The therapist was able to assure him that this is a common concern expressed by parents and that the possible links between drug use and psychosis are discussed in depth in the group.

As well as ensuring clinicians present the intervention as of being both routine and of high value, delivery of a rationale incorporates references to the family as having a right and entitlement to help, support and advice. Some families, like Mr and Mrs Park, for example may need to be invited to consider that they themselves have needs that are potentially different and separate to those of the client.

Sally Park had treatment as an inpatient for a severe depressive disorder with psychosis. As a result of her illness and admission her partner left and her parents took responsibility for caring for her young child and arranging her affairs.

Mr and Mrs Park had recently retired and expressed the concern at assessment, with some anger, that the approach represented an attempt by mental health services to recruit them as long-term carers. The therapist detected that some of Mr and Mrs Park's fears were related to their sense of feeling powerless in relationships with statutory services. The therapist was able to allay these fears both by emphasising that one of the focuses of the group is to share information that will enable the family to advocate for themselves in their relationship with services. One of the group meetings, for example is attended by the local Making Space worker who can act as an independent advocate for families (Making Space is a local voluntary organisation that supports carers and service users).

The Park family were also clearly worried that the therapist's approach indicated that it was believed that there was something 'wrong' with them and that they must have been in part responsible for their daughter's illness. This latter phenomenon is common and can be conceptualised as part of a normal process of attempting to find meaning and to attribute cause for an adverse and unexpected event (Ferriter and Huband, 2003). It was essential in this case that the therapist made an unambiguous statement that this attributional style is normal but that this model of causality is not shared by the therapist or by services.

One of the most effective means of engaging relatives' attention and improving uptake of the intervention is to utilise existing and previous consumers of the service.

Mrs Burns, who even towards the end of the initial assessment and re-cruitment interview was expressing doubts about the programme's potential usefulness was given a leaflet about the group which included statements that had been made by previous attendees.

Mrs Burns' attention was drawn to statements such as

The information was useful . . .

It's good to meet other people who are going through the same thing . . .

It's good to know you're not the only one . . .

I learned more about the system . . .

Mrs Burns reported that these statements matched up with needs that she herself was developing an awareness of and that due to this and the credibility that the statements from other relatives had that she decided to attend the group.

Secondly, the involvement of relatives as consultants in the service in general and in the delivery of the intervention itself can lend substantial credibility. Mr and Mrs Burns, for example had at assessment expressed considerable concern about one of their other children, Jack. They explained that Jack was currently in the third year of his degree but had become reluctant to return to the family home in the holidays saying that he 'could not cope' with the illness of his brother. He had reservations about accepting the offer of a meeting with one of the professional workers in the team but he did agree to an initial telephone contact from the service's Young Carer Worker. She herself was an undergraduate whose brother had experienced his first episode of psychosis when she was 17 years old. Although ultimately Jack chose not to attend the group, regular email and telephone contact from a person of a similar age who had gone through similar circumstances gave him access to an informal support network and a hopeful model of family adjustment and recovery.

Interventions to increase uptake of intervention based upon individual assessment/formulation

Clinicians avoid attempts to persuade or coerce relatives into attending the group. Interview or telephone contact, however, with a relative who is expressing doubts or uncertainty about attending can be managed in ways that can afford the therapist opportunities to identify and address negative beliefs and predictions about family work and to explore ambivalence and identify goals and values which might act as motivators for participation.

The McDaniel family reported at assessment that they had a series of unfortunate experiences with services that had left them understandably reluctant to enter into an intervention:

MRS
MCDANIEL: Elliot was completely uncontrollable and had threatened me and punched a hole in his bedroom door ... they sent him home from work the week before because he had a row with the boss. He had accused him of being on his case and had wanted to call the police because he thought the other workers had been putting something into his brews. I took him down

to the doctor's who sent us to the A and E . . . Elliot just didn't say anything and all they did was send us home.

THERAPIST:　That must have been so frustrating. Like any good mum you knew that something was badly wrong with Elliot and you were doing your level best to get him help. Not everyone would have recognised that him being so worked up was a sign of illness. I'm not sure if that had been one of my children I would have known that the violence was not just bad behaviour or have just put it down to drugs.

The therapist was trying to validate their experiences and strong emotions. This is an important process as it impresses upon relatives that they are being listened to and that the gravity of their concerns and the impact of events on their lives are being fully appreciated. Similarly, the therapist was careful to recognise and to place high value upon their caring efforts.

It can be important to identify relatives' key values and motivators, both personal and in relation to the client.

Key values and motivators that we all share to some extent, such as the need to be wanted and valued by others, the need to understand and find meaning in adverse life events, the need to express and find resolution for feelings of distress, and the desire to solve problems and exercise control of the future, can all be employed as motivators for involvement in the intervention.

Mrs McDaniel seemed to be the key decision maker in the family and the therapist was keen to harness particular aspects of her current experience in the formulation of a rationale for her. Factors that seemed of greatest importance were her high levels of distress, anger at 'inadequate' response from services and lack of confidence in their expertise, desire to 'make Elliot take his medication' and the desperate wish that her son achieved the best possible recovery. The therapist offered the suggestion, that the intervention might help her and her husband cope better with the problems and challenges of caring, by offering access to the best, up-to-date information and advice. Also, that they might learn from other relatives how to get the best out of services and what approaches towards encouraging compliance with medication might be most helpful. With hindsight, however, it appeared that the factor that 'clinched the deal' for the McDaniels family was the therapist having the confidence to 'challenge' them to test the service out. It was suggested that they find out for themselves whether it would be as inept and inadequate as they felt the services for her son had been and the therapist asked them to consider whether making the investment to come and try out the treatment would be worth making given the potential gains for them.

Finally, therapists sometimes find themselves trying to recruit families to the group who have already researched the subject of psychosis well, express competence or confidence or state that they have learned how to deal with problems through experience. Mr and Mrs Park, for example saw themselves as competent 'survivors' of a difficult journey. The therapist was very quickly able to validate their feelings of competence and expertise by judicious use of summary and feedback to them of the descriptions of events they had encountered, the sacrifices they had made and the strategies they developed in the course of their daughter's illness. The therapist then went on to say how impressed she was with the strengths and skills they had shown and how their story might inspire and give useful information to other people who were at a much earlier stage of their journey with their relative. This seemed to be an important factor in their decision to take part in the group.

Finally, as in all therapeutic processes it is the ability of the worker to engage the client at the interpersonal level that is often the best predictor of engagement.

The worker not only requires the necessary interpersonal 'therapy' skills but also sufficient knowledge about the effects of psychosis on the family, in order to be able to anticipate, understand and normalise relatives' reactions and to be able to adopt the necessary theoretical/causal model of psychosis. The recent promulgation of models of the cause and onset of psychosis in which trauma, abuse and early experiences are implicated (e.g. Read *et al.*, 2005) and older yet radical psychiatric models (Laing and Esterson, 1964) have the potential to inform therapists' internal models of psychosis and prejudices about families in ways that mitigate against the recognition of families' needs and the open, genuine and empathetic approach that is required for successful engagement.

In short, successful family workers are able to adopt a mental framework for understanding psychosis that does not automatically pathologise the family.

Assessment

Assessment takes the form of as a minimum, a clinical interview with the key relatives as identified by the client and the administration of a number of self-report measures to all relatives who express an interest in attending the group.

Assessment interview

This is a semi-structured interview which assesses the following:

1. The composition of the household and key relationships with the client.
2. *Assessment of development of the clients' difficulties and the family's re-sponse.* Duration of untreated psychosis is also assessed/confirmed. It is essential for some relatives to give adequate space to listen to the 'story' of how the client became ill and entered treatment.

For Mrs Burns, the observation of and attempts to slow the decline of her son and the insidious onset of his psychosis had been a particular time of distress and difficulty. This had not been recognised by services and she had not been able to share the experience with anyone previously. The recognition of its importance for Mrs Burns was a significant factor in the building of a therapeutic alliance with her.

Without a clear model to explain the changes in their son or daughter, some relatives develop unhelpful attributions and coping strategies. Simi-larly, relatives who have observed the client experiencing an acute onset – perhaps with entry to treatment via the Mental Health Act, Criminal Justice System or them acting out high-risk behaviours – might be undergoing an adaptation or coping process akin to a trauma-type reaction. Assessors of course need to be sensitive to such reactions as they may include such features as avoidance of memories of events and feelings accompanied by a minimisation or underplaying of significance of the illness process that can be conceptualised as 'sealing over'. This phenomenon can be a barrier to assessment and engagement, as families will understandably be disposed to regard a resolving first episode as a 'one-off'.

3. *Assessment of current difficulties.* The completed Family Questionnaire (Quinn, Barrowclough and Tarrier 2003) and Experience of Caregiving Inventory (Szmukler *et al.*, 1996) are used to elicit key changes in patient behaviour and well-being that have affected the family and/or demanded a caring response. It is essential at this point that some family attempts at coping and managing the disorder such as patterns of employment and social networks that might be obstacles to families' regaining normal functioning and recovery in due course are identified.
4. *Assessment of knowledge and beliefs about illness and the client's treat-ment.* The purpose is not to gauge the extent of relatives knowledge

against an absolute 'standard' but to investigate their explanatory model of the clients difficulties and whether they make attributions concerning clients' behaviour that might ultimately be associated with behavioural strategies such as control, coercion, self-sacrifice and neglect of other relationships and social activities.

The main features of explanatory models and attributional styles that might predict such behaviours are relatives' explicit beliefs about the locus of control for client's difficulties. Mr and Mrs McDaniels, for example believed that drug use was a primary cause of their son's illness and saw him as having substantial control over and responsibility for both onset and outcomes of his disorder. This information was used to 'fine-tune' the intervention group that they attended – special attention was paid to the role of drugs in psychosis and the pros and cons of a range of potential family coping responses.

A substantial minority of families present with unusual or overwhelming difficulties – these include having another family member with mental illness or substance use problems or having relationship difficulties (including divorce).

With these types of difficulties the clinician may have to make substantial efforts to engage families who might anticipate that services would take a negative or judgemental view of their circumstances and may have already experienced or have anticipated experience of stigma, blame or censure.

> Mrs Burns, for example revealed at a second assessment session that she has a half-brother who has 'chronic schizophrenia' and who, in middle age, still lives with his mother. Not only did Mrs Burns have an understandable pessimistic rather than hopeful model of 'illness' and recovery, she was aware that her parents' experiences with services had been generally negative. She perceived mental health services suspiciously and was motivated to avoid them. As previously described in this chapter, recommendations from previous group attendees and provision of help for her other son were important in her and her husband's decision to 'give the service a chance'.

The intervention

The IMPACT multi-family group psychoeducation programme is a five-session programme aiming to meet families (and clients) needs for information, social networks, destigmatisation and interpersonal support. It is aimed at clients and their families during the acute and recovery stages of first-episode psychosis. It consists of five meetings over five consecutive weeks, each taking $1^1/_2$ hours.

Approximately 12–15 clients and family members are invited to each group. Attrition that occurs tends to take place at or before the first two sessions. The ideal numbers for the group is between 6 and 12 participants and clinicians have learned from experience to slightly 'over recruit' to the group.

Close attention is paid to location, type of venue and time and duration of sessions. After some experimentation we have found that the best time for the groups is early evening and we run them from 18:00 to 19:30. This seems to be an appropriate time as it enables people to both get home from work and leave the session in time for kick off in televised football matches!

Content of the intervention by session

Week 1	Introduction and welcome
	'A Carer's Story'
	What is psychosis?
Week 2	What causes psychosis?
	Drug treatments
Week 3	Local services
	Psychosocial treatments
Week 4	Substance use and psychosis
	Stress management (1)
Week 5	Stress management (2)
	Group evaluation and feedback

An agenda is negotiated with the participants with suitable time identified for the discussion of issues that they identify, summary and feedback.

Session 1

Introduction and 'A Carer's Story'. It is important at the first meeting that the following conditions are met to ensure that relatives and clients come back for future sessions:

(1)   Attendees feel welcome.
(2)   Attendees perceive that sessions will meet some of their need(s).

(3) Facilitator is perceived as a knowledgeable helpful 'expert'.
(4) Attendees perceive they have something in common with other group member(s).

The following factors are particularly important at the first session:

(1) *Setting the room up.* We have experimented with several different formats, some of which have been imposed by venue, but the most successful has been for participants to be seated in easy chairs, roughly arranged in a circle. Availability of refreshments and reading material is especially helpful at the first meeting as it enables the more anxious participants to engage in a normal range of safety behaviours and other diversions.
(2) *Facilitators 'modelling' social behaviour.* It is important at the first session that facilitators are prepared to both set the tone as far as interpersonal behaviours are concerned and also attempt to facilitate social interactions amongst people. Therefore facilitators welcome people as they enter the room, make introductions and offer refreshments; in effect be the perfect host.

Structure and facilitation style. The first session is necessarily the most didactic and although facilitators ensure that they pay attention to eliciting feedback from participants and establishing an atmosphere of collaboration, for example by giving a choice as to whether there ought to be a 'comfort break' during the session, it is important that they establish a degree of authority and presence.

Finally, the therapist must be able to draw participants together in a sense of shared purpose by framing the challenges that both clients and relatives face in a way that affirms the resolve, courage and other strengths that have already been demanded of them and the investment that they have made in the future by being involved in the programme and attending the group. Even when participants attend with reluctance or display some discomfort or even hostility, it is best at this stage to ascribe to them the most altruistic and noble of motives. Even if appearing outwardly sceptical, for most people a clear statement of recognition and acknowledgement of value in their character and behaviour will produce a degree of 'resonance'.

A Carer's Story

Group evaluations have repeatedly shown that participants who are relatives rate the presentation by a carer 'expert' as the most valuable of the whole programme.

To be of greatest value the carer needs to be able to describe a story, or recovery journey that to some degree resembles the circumstances of the participants, but also provides a substantial degree of hope. Rachel Morrison (real name) was aged 17 when her brother was first admitted to hospital experiencing psychosis. As a 'carer' she is able to describe for the group her family's 2-year journey from being scared, confused and worried to being confident about being on a road to recovery. Within this she describes a process of going from being apprehensive about the group to enjoying it and finding support and friendship. This helps to normalise other participants' feelings and gives them a hopeful model of a recovery journey and models some of the participant behaviours (such as vicarious learning from other people receiving support, making friendships) that seem to be predictive of good outcomes.

Sessions 1 and 2: 'psychoeducation'

Information is presented in the first two sessions as three separate discrete 'packages'. The modular nature of the programme enables cofacilitators to practise specific skills particular to families and groups whilst presenting material with which they are familiar and comfortable. Our goal is to give clients and their families access to a hopeful, recovery orientated and multifactorial model of psychosis and its treatment. We believe that this model is able both to accommodate most lay or psychiatric models and to add richness and detail to them. Furthermore, we hope that the information we share would challenge any potentially unhelpful or stigmatising models or beliefs participants held, such as families being to blame.

Moreover, the group nature of the intervention enables families to learn from one another's experience. In particular, families' experiences add richness to discussion of behavioural changes and deficits that are not always easy to recognise and often misattributed as within the client's personal control. Mr and Mrs McDaniel were interested to find out, for example that many other people had observed their children to be withdrawn, disinterested, lacking in motivation and 'lazy' in the aftermath of psychosis. This led them to reconsider their view that their son Elliott must have made a conscious decision to 'give up' and live on benefits.

Sessions 3 and 4 psychoeducation – moving into contentious areas

The general aims for the sessions that cover psychosocial interventions, services and substance misuse are to encourage debate and the sharing of stories, experiences and coping responses. With this in mind the facilitators will increasingly encourage the participants to share more of their personal experiences. This is often done by therapists modelling such behaviour, for example by sharing their own anxieties about their children being exposed to drugs as they grow older, or by describing a case from their clinical experience such as a client achieving a reduction of distress due to 'hearing the voice of the devil' after considering a more benign range of explanations.

Specific areas covered in the sessions are as follows:

Psychosocial interventions. The presentation has two primary aims: to share information on the range and effectiveness of interventions such as individual cognitive behaviour therapy (CBT), relapse prevention, supportive counselling and structured family work that will enable participants to make an informed choice when presented with the opportunity to receive or to take part in such interventions (and perhaps advocate on their own or relative's behalf for such treatments to be made available). Secondly, to socialise participants to a CBT model of human distress (e.g. as in Greenberger and Padesky, 1995) that will inform their understanding of their own emotional life, their understanding of the nature and degree of distress experienced by the person with psychosis and form a backdrop to succeeding work on the importance of appraisal and belief in understanding common difficulties in caring for the person with psychosis. The session is made as interactive as possible and where possible, illustrated with the use of humorous examples. The use of a clip of video to illustrate the effect on a character's understanding and emotions of 'jumping to conclusions' often goes down well for example.

Local services. The primary aim is to increase participants' knowledge of the system of care coordination and the care programme. The session is increased enormously in effectiveness when it is delivered by professional or manager from a local Community Mental Health Team. It can often then become a focus for the expression of distress and dissatisfaction associated with the care and treatment of the clients and can illustrate the variability of service quality. Moreover, having acted as a focus for dissatisfaction and to demystify psychiatric services it often becomes a stimulus for relatives to become involved as carers representatives on consultative groups and to advocate for themselves and clients more vocally and effectively.

Substance use. The main aims of the presentation on substance use concern attempts to prevent or ameliorate unhelpful attributions (and associated attempts to control or manage) clients' substance use and associated behaviour. It is acknowledged in the material that is presented that substance use may be a contributory factor in both onset and relapse of psychosis for those who are vulnerable. The majority of the presentation, however, concentrates on the prevalence of substance use amongst the general population and young people with mental health problems and uses the transtheoretical model of change (Prochaska *et al.*, 1992) to illustrate how particular attempts to 'help' a substance user change might actually be counter productive.

The use of 'live' examples to demonstrate how direct challenge or confrontation of substance use behaviours can be counterproductive is especially effective. An excellent example of how criticism of substance use can evoke resistance and further 'rebellion' was given in the group by a minister of the Church who attended the group.

> According to him a fellow man of the cloth who was walking to church when he came upon a boy he knew smoking in the street. Shocked and disappointed he stopped the boy and remonstrated with him saying:
>
> 'Surely you are aware of how dangerous to your health it is to smoke? You are a stupid boy!'
>
> The boy replied, somewhat cheekily:
>
> 'But vicar, weren't you saying just the other day that Jesus cares for everyone, even the stupid!'

Such real examples of the failure to 'match' the intervention with the stage of change (Prochaska *et al.*, 1992) and its effect on interpersonal relationships help to normalise the difficulties that individuals and families face and stimulate the disclosure of their own difficulties and help generate a range of alternative strategies.

> The assessment and engagement of the McDaniels family showed how much importance they attributed to the role of drug use in their son's illness. During the discussion of substance use Mrs McDaniels made statements such as 'I have to keep him in to make sure that he doesn't take drugs' or '[t]here's absolutely nothing you can do about it apart from clamp down as hard as you can'.

The therapist was able to invite comments from the other group members with questions such as 'Has anyone else come up against that kind of problem?' 'What happened when you tried that strategy?' and 'Has anyone tried any other strategy other than trying to clamp down hard?'

Sessions 4 and 5: stress management

There are two separate didactic sessions that can be delivered in weeks four and/or five. They are:

> 'A model of stress management' – which describes a model of individuals' stress reaction and normalises the experience of stress.

and

> 'Looking after yourself, coping with stress' – which acts as a 'directory' of stress management techniques. It starts with teaching a simple relaxation technique (guided imagery) and encompasses advice about family meetings and problem solving.

Where possible, however, and especially when the group is functioning well, these sessions act as a framework for discussion of participant families' individual problems. Therapists specifically aim to illustrate how unhelpful attributions and behaviours develop (and how normal they are!) in the context of responding to the challenge of psychosis and to facilitate the group in discussing alternative strategies.

One of the key aims for the final session is for participants to learn that it is common for clients to emerge from an acute episode with persistent and unwelcome behavioural changes (negative symptoms) and that it is normal for them to evoke in parents and partners efforts to remedy them. Unfortunately, these deficits can be almost intractable and normal parenting behaviours such as punishment and reward can be ineffective.

The Use of Role-Play and Demonstration

A role-play demonstration is used to both illustrate and normalise the intrapersonal and interpersonal processes that occur when attempts to control or change a young person's behaviour are unsuccessful. In the role-play one facilitator takes the role of a parent, the other that of his or her child. The parent identifies a problem, such as a recent deterioration in the child's academic performance. The child's brief is to be a typical teenager, that is not to give in or to agree with the parent and a familiar exchange develops with the parent resorting to increasingly draconian punishments in an attempt to coerce the child into doing homework for example.

The group participants are then asked to comment on the role-play. Good questions to ask of participants are:

How did the parent's and young person's emotion change. How did that effect their behaviour and decisions?

Could the parent have achieved a better outcome? If so, how.

How did the young person respond to being criticised and told off?

One of the most powerful effects of the exercise is that it vividly demonstrates differences in parenting style between participants. After viewing the demonstration Mrs McDaniel expressed a great deal of sympathy for the 'parent', going so far as to endorse to a degree their controlling, bullying and hectoring style. She perceived that the parent had been given no 'choice' in his selection of strategies due to the intransigence of the teenager. The facilitator normalised the variability and efficacy of a range of parenting approaches and used the group as a whole to examine whether or not this approach may have its weaknesses and what might represent a more optimal strategy.

In general, however, the facilitator(s) should aim through a process of guided discovery to enable the group to endorse a number of more benevolent practices and principles, such as the following:

Maintenance of good relationships within the family is a desirable goal in itself.

Expression of warmth, friendship and love should not be conditional.

Families should make extra effort to recognise and reward even the smallest effort and positive change.

Maximising Therapeutic Processes and Learning within the Group

Although at five $1^1/_2$-hour sessions the programme is relatively short for a therapeutic group, post-treatment evaluations and focus groups have shown that customary therapeutic processes (as outlined for example by Bloch, Crouch and Reibstein, 1981 and Yalom, 1995) can still be identified. Participants have particularly identified the sense of universality, cohesion, guidance and altruism as having been important and valuable to them. Facilitators should be aware of the value that group members place upon these processes and adjust their behaviours so as not to interrupt them and to encourage them where they are slow to develop.

'Universality' is prevalent where participants learn that they are not the only one with a particular type of problem, that it is not just they who have made mistakes in parenting and in life generally, that they are not the only one who has bad thoughts, is not a perfect mother, father or partner. Each of us has problems that we struggle to overcome. From the outset, because it is such a short process, it is important that the facilitators are able to model self-disclosure. Not in terms of being nervous or having doubts about their ability to manage the group or to contain others' feelings, but to weaknesses in personal and parental efficacy. At the end of one particularly memorable session Mrs Burns announced:

Until I started coming to the 'classes' I thought that, because my son got ill there must be something wrong with me. I look around and I see that you are all nice, normal people. That makes me think that I'm probably normal too.

In the absence of clear statements from participants that they are experiencing this sense of universality the facilitator can use suitable questions such as 'Did anyone else have that experience/worry/problem?' or 'I have often shouted at my kids and then regretted it. Is that something we all do from time to time?' The sense of cohesion can also be built upon using similar strategies of modelling and self-disclosure. The process of sharing embarrassing information and acknowledging faults is also key to building a sense of cohesion and common purpose.

Evaluation and Conclusions

It is somewhat chastening to learn that participants, unless directly asked with the expectation of a positive response, rarely state that the information, guidance and advice from the facilitators are of particular value. They do, however, value advice, suggestions and guidance of others and the chance that they themselves get to give help, support and advice. Facilitators must quickly learn the skill of knowing how to give up some control of the content and process of the group to the members themselves and to support the process with both appropriate questioning. In addition, as alluded to earlier, it is an important feature of a responsive and learning organisation to recognise and utilise the expertise and enthusiasm of carers.

During the life of the IMPACT family service, over 80 relatives have taken part in the programme of whom just over half have attended a whole series of family meetings. It is clear that although it is not a suitable vehicle for the delivery of psychosocial and supportive interventions to all relatives in early psychosis (a substantial minority choose not to take the intervention) that for some families it represents a valuable component of a flexible and responsive service. Moreover, it has been sustained in routine services without substantial new investment in family work and has utilised staff time and expertise economically. It has been effective in engaging and maintaining families in an intervention and has proved to be a catalyst for the formation and development of informal and formal supportive networks of carers.

References

Bloch, S., Crouch, E. and Reibstein, J. (1981) Therapeutic factors in group psychotherapy. A review. *Archives of General Psychiatry*, **38** (5), 519–26.

Buksti, A.S., Munkner, R., Gade, I. *et al.* (2006) Important components of a short term family group programme. From the Danish National Multicenter Schizophrenia Project. *Nordic Journal of Psychiatry*, **60** (3), 213–9.

Chien, W.T. and Chan, S.W. (2004) One year follow-up of a multiple family-group intervention for Chinese families of patients with schizophrenia. *Psychiatric Services*, **55** (11), 1276–84.

Department of Health (2001) *The Mental Health Policy Implementation Guide*, Crown Copyright.

Dyck, D.G., Short, R.A., Hendryx, M.S. *et al.* (2000) Management of negative symptoms among patients with schizophrenia attending multiple-family groups. *Psychiatric Services*, **51** (4), 513–9.

Fadden, G. (1997) Implementation of family interventions in routine clinical practice: a major cause for concern. *Journal of Mental Health*, **6**, 599–612.

Ferriter, M. and Huband, N. (2003) Experiences of parents with a son or daughter suffering from schizophrenia. *Journal of Psychiatric and Mental Health Nursing*, **10**, 552–60.

Greenberger, D. and Padesky, C.A. (1995) *Mind Over Mood: A Cognitive Therapy Treatment Manual for Clients*, Guilford Press, New York, NY.

Kuipers, E., Bebington, P., Dunn, G. *et al.* (2006) Influence of carer expressed emotion and affect on relapse in non-affective psychosis. *British Journal of Psychiatry*, **188**, 173–9.

Laing, R.D. and Esterson, A. (1964) *Sanity, Madness and the Family. Families of Schizophrenics*, Tavistock, London.

Leff, J., Berkowitz, R., Shavit, N. *et al.* (1990) A trial of family therapy versus a relatives' group for schizophrenia. Two-year follow-up. *British Journal of Psychiatry*, **157**, 571–7.

Linszen, D., Dingemans, P., Van Der Does, J.W. *et al.* (1996) Treatment, expressed emotion and relapse in recent onset schizophrenic disorders. *Psychological Medicine*, **26** (2), 333–42.

McFarlane, W.R. (2002) *Multifamily Groups in the Treatment of Severe Psychiatric Disorders*, Guilford Press, New York, NY.

McFarlane, W.R., Dushay, R.A., Stastny, P. *et al.* (1996) A comparison of two levels of family-aided assertive community treatment. *Psychiatric Services*, **47** (7), 744–50.

McFarlane, W.R., Link, B., Dushay, R. *et al.* (1995) Psychoeducational multiple family groups: four-year relapse outcome in schizophrenia. *Family Process*, **34** (2), 127–44.

Miklowitz, D.J., Goldstein, M.J. and Falloon, I.H.R. (1983) Premorbid and symptomatic characteristics of schizophrenics from families with high and low levels of expressed emotion. *Journal of Abnormal Psychology*, **92** (3), 359–67.

Montero, I., Asencio, A., Hernandez, I. *et al.* (2001) Two strategies for family intervention in schizophrenia: a randomized trial in a Mediterranean environment. *Schizophrenia Bulletin*, **27** (4), 661–70.

Pekkala, E. and Merinder, L. (2000) Psychoeducation for schizophrenia. *Cochrane Database of Systematic Reviews*, (2), CD002831.

Prochaska, J.O., DiClemente, C.C., Velicer, W.F. and Rossi, J.S. (1992) Criticisms and concerns of the transtheoretical model in light of recent research. *British Journal of Addiction*, **87** (6), 825–8; discussion 833–5.

Quinn, J., Barrowclough, C. and Tarrier, N. (2003) The Family Questionnaire (FQ): a scale for measuring symptom appraisal in relatives of schizophrenic patients. *Acta Paychiatrica Scandinavica*, **108** (4), 290–6.

Raune, D., Kuipers, E. and Bebbington, P.E. (2004) Expressed emotion at first episode psychosis: investigating a carer appraisal model. *British Journal of Psychiatry*, **184**, 321–6.

Read, J., van Os, J., Morrison, A.P. and Ross, C.A. (2005) Childhood trauma, psychosis and schizophrenia: a literature review with theoretical and clinical implications. *Acta Psychiatrica Scandinavica*, **112** (5), 330–50.

Szmukler, G.I., Burgess, P., Herman, H. *et al.* (1996) Caring for relatives with serious mental illness – the development of the Experience of Caregiving Inventory. *Social Psychiatry and Psychiatric Epidemiology*, **31**, 134–48.

Yalom, I.D. (1995) *The Theory and Practice of Group Psychotherapy*, 4th edn, Basic, New York, NY.

Resources

Early Psychosis; A Workbook for Clients, Families and Friends. Compiled by D. Glentworth, M. Campbell, F. Chapman and I. Lowens. Available from the author.

12

Meeting the Needs of Families on Inpatient Units

Chris Mansell and Gráinne Fadden

Overview

Family work has traditionally been associated with community settings and is not seen as a primary activity for staff working within inpatient services. However, large numbers of service users who are admitted to inpatient units with acute mental health difficulties have relatives, families and friends who find the experience of having a loved one admitted to hospital traumatic (Kok and Leskela, 1996). Frequently, they have been facing enormous pressures prior to the admission and have to deal with emotions such as guilt, fear, relief and anxiety (Hardcastle *et al.*, 2007). Compared to relatives of people who are not admitted, they are more likely to have experienced threats, temper outbursts and physical assault as the service user commonly has severe difficulties (Vaddadi *et al.*, 1997). There are consequences for their own mental health, and they may have to deal with disturbing experiences such as being part of the client's delusional system.

Mental health inpatient facilities can often appear strange and intimidating, and families need help to understand what is happening and how the system works. These families play a very important role in supporting and caring for their loved one during admission and after discharge and require support and information to do this.

Inpatient staff play a vital role in engaging families. A positive experience of services at this point can make it much more likely that families will continue with family work post-discharge. Inpatient staff are often in the unique position of having contact with the service user and their family at the most difficult and distressing stages of their mental health difficulties

A Casebook of Family Interventions for Psychosis Edited by Fiona Lobban and Christine Barrowclough
© 2009 John Wiley & Sons, Ltd

and are thus in a position to build very effective relationships. However, basic pre-registration training for most groups of staff primarily addresses issues relating to services and the individual and as a result staff often do not have the skills or confidence they need to work with families.

Our experience in the Meriden Programme has been that inpatient staff need to see themselves as part of the whole mental health care system, and to see their role in that context. Training must be adapted to help them to understand how they can apply family work principles in ward settings, and the crucial role they play in engaging families, allaying their anxieties and providing them with essential information to help them to understand and cope with what is happening in their lives. Lack of confidence is a big factor, as is the difficulty of reconciling difficult roles, most notably those of supporting the individual and working simultaneously with the family. Rivett *et al.* (1997) discuss the concept of membership roles and the struggles faced by staff, for example in relation to when to use knowledge from one role in another. Similarly, McCann and Bowers (2005) discuss the difficulty for staff in disengaging psychologically from their other ward duties.

The focus of this chapter will be on the issues that arise when ward staff attempt to deliver family work. The benefits that result from this will be highlighted, as well as the challenges posed for staff. The client in question is fairly typical of those who get admitted to inpatient units with a range of difficulties including psychosis and drug use. The fact that she has a young child introduces further challenges. Common themes such as confidentiality and information sharing will also be discussed. Some of the challenges in delivering family work are linked with the way ward systems run and traditional patterns and practices. This case study will highlight the fact that family situations are not always as complex as they seem if the family has time to talk and someone to listen to the differing perspectives of family members.

Context

Specific issues relating to families and inpatient units

Staff from inpatient services appear to have difficulty accessing or being freed from their other duties to attend training to prepare them for delivering therapeutic approaches such as working with families (Jones, 2005). Similarly, there are difficulties delivering family work following receipt of training

(Fadden and Birchwood, 2002). The reasons for this are complex. There is a large organisational agenda for mandatory training such as risk assessment, fire safety, moving and handling, physical restraint and infection control. These are seen as crucial for inpatient settings where more violence and self-harm occurs, where there is a detained population who do not wish to be there, and where in the United Kingdom currently, there is a strong emphasis in all residential settings on infection control. Brennan, Flood and Bowers (2006) articulate very well the preoccupation on acute psychiatric wards with risk assessment, adherence to legal requirements such as the Mental Health Act and to policy, no matter how much this interferes with therapeutic outcome.

In addition to this, there is currently much pressure on inpatient wards in relation to insufficient staffing levels (Brennan, Flood and Bowers, 2006; Buchan and Seccombe, 2002; Garcia *et al.*, 2005). The issues of staffing and training are interrelated: in the risk-aversive culture that prevails on inpatient units, and where staffing levels are low, resources are not set aside to ensure that staff receive training in therapeutic skills. There is not an equal emphasis on mandatory training as described above, and on training in therapeutic skills. When it comes to the crunch, training in therapeutic skills will be cancelled. We have had numerous experiences of this in the Meriden Programme over the past 10 years where well-planned training programmes with inpatient staff are cancelled, frequently at short notice.

The importance of providing more effective and comprehensive care on inpatient units was identified 10 years ago (Sainsbury Centre for Mental Health, 1998), and although recommendations have been made including those relating to 'family-sensitive practice and engagement' (Clarke, 2004), difficulties remain, and care is often far from ideal. National bodies such as the Royal College of Psychiatrists have also recently set standards to provide staff with clear descriptions of best practice on inpatient wards and a clearly defined accreditation process (McGeorge *et al.*, 2006).

Problems with issues of confidentiality and the provision of information are common. This can lead to situations where families are not involved in the care process and are unclear about the nature and purpose of various treatments. The result is often isolation of the service user from their family and social role (Clarke, 2004), which is counterproductive in terms of their recovery and results in further distress for the family. Many of these issues have been highlighted in recent UK study conducted by Rethink (Slade *et al.*, 2007) in relation to adults with psychosis where issues such as mental capacity and refusal of consent can arise.

Theoretical influences on the approach used

Little attention has been paid by proponents of family work to the delivery of interventions on inpatient units or where staff are in contact with the client over short periods of time (Olfson, Glick and Mechanic, 1993). This issue has become more pronounced as the length of acute hospital admissions has decreased over time, either because of the development of 24-hour community services such as home treatment teams as is the case in the United Kingdom or because of fiscal considerations such as those imposed by insurance companies in the United States. Keefler and Koritar (1994) described how they had to modify their comprehensive programme which included a number of elements of family work while the relative was an inpatient including inpatient crisis groups for relatives, inpatient family counselling and psychoeducational workshops, because of the trend towards shorter hospital admissions. In their report of family group work for hospitalised clients, Lemmens *et al.* (2007) talk about people and their families not joining the group sometimes until their fourth week after admission. However, in many countries now, admission times are shorter, leaving staff with the view that little can be achieved therapeutically with families.

The other strand of literature that informs this area is the work on expressed emotion (EE). Whatever one thinks of the construct of EE, we know that the relatives of those families with high levels of EE are more likely to experience relapse and readmission to hospital (Vaughn and Leff, 1976). These families are therefore likely to be in need of advice and support to help them to cope with the situation. However, in crisis and emergency situations, the necessary support is not always provided, with family support being listed as one of the services that is often not available (Carpenter *et al.*, 2005). Involvement of families is more likely to occur in adolescent inpatient units than on acute adult wards (Rivett *et al.*, 1997), although the need for it is as great.

In terms of what the content of family interventions should be in inpatient settings, very few studies have actually explored this. A psychoeducational approach reported on over a 9-year period (Clarkin *et al.*, 1990; Glick *et al.*, 1993; Glick *et al.*, 1985; Haas *et al.*, 1988; Spencer *et al.*, 1988) emphasised the reality of the disorder and methods of coping with current and future stressors. The intervention was associated with clinically significant improvement at discharge, especially for female clients, and those with long-term schizophrenia and bipolar disorder. The results were maintained

6 months after admission before attenuating at the 18-month time point. The effect was not found with males with these diagnoses, though effects were positive for males with other disorders. This study suggests that applying family interventions in these settings may be quite complex, with a range of factors influencing outcome. The authors conclude that the impact of inpatient family intervention may be limited and they suggest the need to extend family intervention into the outpatient treatment phase.

Keefler and Koritar (1994) emphasise the importance of addressing the emotional impact psychosis has on the family, and their coping strategies. They suggest that until the anxiety experienced by families during the admission and diagnostic period is addressed, there is little point in providing educational interventions, as information is not retained. Timing therefore is crucial. They also describe the challenge posed by their estimate of about 5% of families who deny the presence of a disorder in their relative. They emphasise the importance of all families being offered help immediately on admission, addressing social functioning of both the client and family, continuity of care from admission to post-discharge, and a nominated family clinician who acts as an ombudsman for the family. They highlight the need for protocols for care and regular meetings of all staff involved with the care of the individual and the family.

Lemmens *et al.* (2007) describe some promising early findings of a brief multi-family group intervention, although the results of the clinical trial are not yet available. They recommend between four and seven families as the optimal number in the group. They have previously highlighted the importance of family discussion groups being embedded in the therapeutic programme of the unit (Lemmens *et al.*, 2005). Other issues they describe as needing consideration include the challenge of having children with a wide variation of ages in the group. Another model that has been proposed for use with clients and their families in inpatient settings is a solution-focused therapy approach used with clients and their families (Kok and Leskela, 1996). The authors describe the benefits of this model that emphasises the clients' and families' strengths and resources, viewing them as competent and resourceful, thus creating a context of hope and expectation for change, with hospitalisation becoming a time of transition and opportunity.

What is most striking overall, however, is how little research is carried out into what approaches are most effective, especially since the mid-1990s. It appears as if there was an expectation that inpatient facilities would form a very small part of the care system, and that with shorter admission lengths, it was not clear what could be offered to families therapeutically in a short time-frame. Where interventions have been offered, this has tended to be as part of a research programme rather than delivered by regular ward staff, although this issue applies equally to other psychosocial approaches delivered in acute settings (Drury, Birchwood and Cochrane, 1996a, b), and is not specific to family work.

Therapist attributes, training and service issues

The difficulty in implementing family work in acute settings is part of a wider systems issue. The history of care in these settings was focused on treatment of the individual using predominantly physical treatments with some attention to occupational activities. A number of reports have highlighted the low levels of nurse–client interactions on wards which obviously makes it difficult for any therapeutic interventions to be delivered. Low levels of staffing have resulted in demoralisation of those that remain in acute settings, as colleagues leave wards to work on what are often perceived as more glamorous functionalised teams in the community.

The disappointing results reported by McCann and Bowers (2005) in their attempts to introduce psychological therapies onto acute settings are attributed to two factors – lack of effective leadership and management and insufficient or lack of stable staffing. Similarly, the recently published report of the Royal College of Psychiatrists (Cresswell *et al.*, 2007) identifies low staff numbers and high use of non-permanent staff as contributing directly to the lack of availability of psychological therapies on inpatient wards. One of their recommendations is that it should be a national priority that the availability of these therapies is increased for those receiving inpatient care. Anyone providing training in this area, however, needs to be aware that tackling the systemic issues is as important as addressing the development of skills.

Case Example

Context

The family was identified as needing support after Sarah had been an inpatient for 4 weeks. She was admitted under Section 3 of the Mental Health Act (1983). She has a partner, Peter and they have a 5-year-old daughter, Emily who was cared for by Peter while Sarah was in hospital.

Sarah was experiencing delusional beliefs that a group of people were going to harm her daughter and she felt that Peter was involved with this group. Their relationship was becoming strained and there was concern that Peter may not be able to support Sarah because he did not fully understand what she was experiencing. She had also been using cannabis and this was adding to his frustration. Because of his concerns and Sarah's attitude towards him, Peter was reluctant to allow Sarah to have contact with their daughter. He frequently sought information from the staff about Sarah's condition and progress.

The staff did not appear to understand Peter's concerns and viewed his behaviour with suspicion. They were concerned about his motives for wanting information, fearing that he might be trying to seek custody of Emily. They were reluctant to answer his questions or share information with him because they felt that this might compromise Sarah being able to see her daughter. They felt that their prime responsibility was towards Sarah. This resulted in Peter feeling very angry, unsupported and unwilling to attend review meetings as he felt there was no point. He was also reluctant to have Sarah home for periods of leave. The consultant psychiatrist was becoming concerned about Sarah's lack of contact with her family and the fact that she was unable to go home on leave. This was discussed at a clinical review meeting and it was felt appropriate for the Deputy Ward Manager, who was trained in behavioural family therapy (Falloon, Boyd and McGill, 1984; Falloon *et al.*, 2004) to see if family work would help.

The family

Sarah (aged 28) achieved well at school and attended university. She began to experience paranoid ideas and hear voices when she was 20 years old. She received help from the Community Mental Health Team and was able to finish university. She joined a firm of solicitors and worked as a senior administrator until the birth of her daughter 4 years later when she became unwell again. She recovered well and took on the day-to-day responsibilities of caring for Emily. Over the previous 18 months she appeared to have found this role more difficult. She became increasingly paranoid and preoccupied, spending long periods of time outside of the family home. She shows a great deal of affection towards Emily and appears able to relate well to her.

Peter (aged 30) had worked in car sales and had a good salary with commission, but resigned to provide childcare as Sarah became more unwell.

He is currently enrolled on a part-time web design course. He has secured a grant for his course and was using savings to support the family since giving up his job. On reflection, this was a decision he regretted because financially they were finding things difficult and with support from his parents he could have continued to work.

Sarah and Peter met at a friend's wedding. They lived together for 2 years and then decided to get married and have a child because they were in a good financial position. Sarah had made Peter aware of her previous difficulties. Neither had any concerns and did not think that she would become unwell again.

Emily (aged 5) is doing very well at school, although she appears to have difficulty concentrating at times. She gets upset when her parents argue, but she appears to respond well to her mother and enjoys being with her.

Peter's parents have been taking some responsibility for caring for Emily over the last 18 months. They do not have a great deal of understanding of Sarah's mental health issues and find her use of cannabis very frustrating. Peter takes Emily to his parent's home to visit. Sarah does not have a great deal of contact with them.

Engagement with the family

Peter and Sarah were invited by the Deputy Ward Manager to attend an initial meeting within the inpatient unit. Both Sarah and Peter were very keen to meet. Emily was at school and so did not attend.

During the first meeting, Peter expressed a lot of anger and frustration about his contact with the ward. He felt that he was being excluded from decisions about Sarah's care and that he was not being kept up to date with progress. It was hard for him to make decisions about whether it would be suitable for her to spend time with their daughter. He also felt that he wanted to support her and be close to her, but did not know how to do this. He stated that when he visited, staff avoided contact with him and if he approached them, they appeared reluctant to talk. When he did approach staff, he was referred to the consultant psychiatrist. When he telephoned, he found staff were very evasive saying that they could not discuss what was happening because of confidentiality. He talked about not understanding Sarah's difficulties and behaviour. He appeared very keen to engage in family work. Sarah stated that she was happy to be involved in any process that would enable her to have more contact with her daughter.

She also felt that Peter did not understand her difficulties and that he was unsupportive. She was very keen on the idea of family work to help increase Peter's understanding.

The Deputy Ward Manager, in taking on the role of family therapist was faced with pressures from the expectations of both the psychiatrist and the family in helping to increase understanding and communication. The psychiatrist was looking for improvements in communication between Peter and Sarah as an indication for discharge. The Deputy Ward Manager also had to manage the concerns of the staff team in relation to Peter's motives. He needed to balance his role in providing support to the staff and challenging some of their views and concerns. He also needed to listen to Peter express anger and frustration about his colleagues and respond to comments, which could potentially be very critical.

Another factor was the expectation from staff that he would be present on the ward during busy periods. It was unusual for inpatient staff to work outside the ward environment. He would need to access family work supervision, which could lead to the ward staff feeling that he was avoiding responsibilities and leaving them to cope with the workload. Some of the team had felt criticised by Peter's angry responses and this could result in further resentment if the Deputy Ward Manager was offering support to Peter when they felt that he should be on the ward. In taking on the family work therefore, he had many conflicting views to manage.

The assessment process

Note. The Deputy Ward Manager who took on the family work will be referred to from here on as the family worker. Readers are asked to keep in mind, however, the dual roles that he had and the issues that this gave rise to as were discussed previously.

Individual assessments

Peter and Sarah were each seen by the family worker for an individual assessment. This is often the first opportunity a family member has to talk about how they feel, their issues in relation to the mental health problem, how their lives have been affected and things they would like to change. The individual assessment also provides an opportunity for the therapist to begin building a relationship with each person and for them to 'check out' the therapist, to ask questions in private and discuss issues that they may not feel comfortable talking about in front of other family members.

It did not seem appropriate to do a formal assessment with Emily because of her age, but Sarah and Peter both wanted her involved in the therapy. They were keen that she was present when they met so that she would see the process as a normal activity and not something that mum and dad were doing that was secretive. They felt that it was important that Emily did not become embarrassed by her mother's health issues. It was agreed that the family worker would have a chat with Emily in the presence of either her mum or dad when he visited them at home. He also observed how Emily responded with her mother at each meeting. The involvement of Emily was a further challenge facing the family worker as he felt he lacked experience working with children because of specialising in Adult Mental Health.

Sarah

Sarah felt that Peter did not understand what she had been experiencing and how difficult it had been for her to cope. She felt that at times he expected too much from her and then at other times he would not let her take any responsibility for their daughter. She felt very sad about not being able to work and would like to find employment, especially now that Emily was at school. Although she had given up work to look after Emily, she felt this had been influenced by not feeling confident after being unwell. She talked a little about her mental distress. She had never discussed in detail with anyone what happens when she is unwell because she feels scared by her experiences. She talked very briefly about her cannabis use. She feels that it helps her to relax and helps when she is feeling very unwell. She has tried to discuss this with Peter, but the conversation usually ends in an argument. She feels that Peter's parents do not understand what she has been through, acknowledging that they offer a lot of support to Peter, but worrying that they may be very negative about her. She did not feel that she wanted them involved in the family meetings at this point. She enjoys her relationship with her daughter and feels that Emily gives meaning to her life. Sarah wanted them to spend more time together as a family and have family outings. She also wanted to reduce the arguments between herself and Peter.

Peter

Peter wants to support Sarah, feels that Emily needs a mother and that he has a responsibility to ensure Emily has contact with her mother. However, he feels very frustrated by Sarah's behaviour and feels that she does not appreciate his efforts or the sacrifices he has made. He feels that her use of cannabis leads to her being more unwell, and whilst he does not feel that she has any choice in having a mental health problem, she does have a choice about using drugs. This makes him feel very angry, especially when she smokes in front of Emily. He described the strain of feeling responsible for Emily, and that he would never forgive himself if anything happened to her. He had concerns about Sarah having Emily on her own, either because of her lack of concentration or her sometimes unpredictable behaviour. He felt that Sarah was concealing what she was really thinking, therefore he did not know if he could trust her.

He reported that his parents did not understand Sarah's difficulties, questioning why he offers so much support. This results in him feeling very torn as he needs their help. He felt that they were not ready yet to develop their understanding and that it would not be helpful for them to be involved in the family meetings at this point. He wanted to be able to complete his web design course and spend some time with his friends. He also stated that he would like Sarah to be able to have visits home from the ward so that Emily could spend time with her.

Emily

When the family worker went to the family home to assess the family, he talked briefly with Emily in the presence of both parents. She was quite shy but talked with encouragement from her parents. She said that she missed her mum and would like her to be home again. She also said that she did not like when mum and dad shouted at each other, and that she usually cried when this happened. The other thing she said she did not like was when her grandparents said things that were not nice about her mum. She liked school, her teacher, and wanted to get a pet rabbit because her friend had one.

Assessment of the family unit

The family worker then talked with Sarah and Peter together to assess how they discussed day-to-day problems and how they communicated with each other to deal with issues that arose. This assessment took place in the family home, which provided an opportunity to see how Peter and Sarah communicated with each other outside the ward in a more relaxed environment. This assessment was organised during an afternoon when there was a higher number of staff on duty so that he could have some time away from the ward, and conduct the assessment without fear of being interrupted.

After talking with Emily, it was agreed that she would play in the room whilst the assessment took place. She appeared very pleased to see her mother at home and soon became very relaxed alternating between playing with toys on the floor and climbing on to her mother's knee.

Sarah and Peter both felt that they used to talk a great deal about many topics and that if they had issues to discuss they used to talk over a meal in the evening. They both felt that this had changed a little when Emily was born because there was less time, and they were often tired. They felt that in the last year when they tried to discuss issues, they usually ended up arguing. In the last few months they had not been discussing any issues, with Peter making decisions on his own. They were both conscious about the effects of their arguing on Emily.

The family worker asked them to discuss an issue that was current and relevant to both of them. They agreed to try and plan getting Emily to and from school when Sarah was discharged from hospital. The conversation soon became tense with Sarah feeling that Peter was making all the decisions and not giving her chance to explain herself properly. Peter appeared to become frustrated with Sarah not being keen to get up in the mornings to take Emily to school. They both agreed to end the conversation without reaching an agreement so that Emily did not become distressed. They both felt that this reflected their normal pattern of discussion.

Formulation

The family worker arranged for this meeting to take place on the ward to accommodate staffing levels. He would have preferred to see them in their own home but they were happy to come to the ward to facilitate the meeting.

The purpose of this meeting was to give feedback to the family on the outcome of the assessment, discuss the issues and agree what the process of the family work would be. The meeting began with the family worker giving a lot of positive feedback to both Sarah and Peter about how well they had worked together to support Emily with all of the pressures that they had been under. Even with the lack of support from both family and services they were still trying to support each other and were prepared to engage in family work. Peter talked about how difficult he had found things at times and Sarah spoke about the fact that she felt she was putting Peter under pressure, and felt guilty.

They agreed that they would like help with the way that they communicated with each other. They both felt they would like to go back to a situation where they could sit down and talk together. They both wanted more information about the diagnosis and treatment and Peter wanted to talk about Sarah's cannabis use. They agreed to meet weekly initially for a period of 6 weeks and then review progress. It is generally better to agree a short number of sessions initially, as this gives the family a chance to see if the approach is producing benefits for them. When people are in a crisis situation as is often the case following an admission, asking for a long-term commitment can put them under pressure at a time when they face many uncertainties, and may prevent engagement. Long-term commitment for inpatient staff may also be problematic. A period of 6 weeks will allow information sharing to take place, and to help the family to develop some strategies to deal with the most pressing issues they face. It is also likely that the member of staff will be able to fulfil this type of short-term commitment.

Both wanted to meet at home but agreed to be flexible because of the family worker's shift patterns. The meeting time was between 2.00 and 3.00 p.m., which was during the staff handover period, which would facilitate the family worker being able to leave the ward. This would mean that Emily would be collected from school earlier on days when she was attending family meetings.

Session 1: information sharing, reaching a shared understanding

It was agreed that Emily would not attend the sessions on information sharing, but that the family worker would explain issues to her in a simple way once her parents had agreed what information would be appropriate for her to have. In many ways, the family worker felt more comfortable with this because of his lack of experience with children's issues. The first session focused on helping Sarah and Peter understand each other's experience of Sarah's psychosis. Peter was keen to understand more about what Sarah was experiencing and how this affected the way she behaved. Sarah was very happy that there was an opportunity to discuss issues in a calm environment.

The family worker began by giving a very brief overview of psychosis and some of the experiences people have. Then acknowledging Sarah as the expert in her own difficulties, he encouraged her to talk about what she experienced when she was feeling unwell. She spoke about hearing voices telling her that her daughter was going to be harmed. She also described hearing Emily crying and asking for help, and about how scared and helpless she felt. She spoke about feeling overwhelmed by thoughts that something dreadful was going to happen to Emily and this made her feel very low and unmotivated. She stated that she felt so consumed by these feelings that she found it difficult to think about anything else. Peter became upset at this point. He stated that they had never talked about the nature of her experiences and he did not realise they were so distressing. The family worker used this opportunity to acknowledge how difficult it is for people to talk about such distressing issues and explained further some of the symptoms of psychosis.

Sarah went on to say that when the voices are very frequent she feels very suspicious of people and thinks that family members are going to harm Emily. This includes Peter and his parents. Peter initially appeared very shocked by this, but when he was encouraged to reflect, he said that it helped him to understand why Sarah behaved so suspiciously towards him. He shared with her that at times he felt he could not trust her, and that for different reasons to her, he was concerned that Emily could come to harm when she was with her. Sarah then became upset saying that she would never harm Emily who was the most important person in her life. They both said that they felt closer than they had done for a long time, and that they both knew deep down that neither of them would ever do anything to harm Emily.

The session had been emotional for both, and they said they would like to discuss something practical. They spent time discussing ways to respond when Sarah was feeling unwell and things that they would both find helpful. Peter asked if using cannabis could make her symptoms worse.

They agreed to discuss the use of cannabis at the next meeting. This session felt very positive and Sarah stated that she found it helpful just to talk about her experiences. Peter felt that he had got a much better understanding.

Session 2: information sharing – use of cannabis

The meeting took place at home and the family worker and Sarah travelled home together as it had been arranged for Sarah to spend the evening at home after the meeting.

The family worker recapped on the issues covered in the previous session and checked to see if there were any issues that needed clarifying. He then provided some basic facts around the prevalence of drug use amongst people with mental health problems. Peter then spoke about his frustration towards Sarah when she smokes cannabis. He felt that cannabis made her more unwell and withdrawn and he was also concerned about possible effects on Emily. He stated that by talking in last week's session he was able to understand more about her experiences. He did not feel that she had a choice in this but felt she made a choice to use cannabis.

Sarah appeared to become withdrawn but the family worker encouraged her to talk about her use of cannabis. She explained that she had used cannabis when she was a student and had started again when she became unwell after Emily's birth. She had not smoked since until she was admitted to hospital. She had found that smoking cannabis when she was feeling unwell helped her to feel less stressed and sometimes helped with the voices. She said that when she was feeling very unwell it was a great relief and she did not know of other ways to get this relief. She spoke about feeling very isolated and feeling that she had no one she could talk with so cannabis seemed like the only option. Peter stated that he had not realised that smoking cannabis had helped when she was feeling unwell but that he was still concerned about the possible effects on Emily. Sarah said that as she had not smoked while in hospital, she could probably agree not to smoke in front of Emily.

The family worker gave Sarah positive feedback for being able to talk about this sensitive subject in such a detailed way. He acknowledged Peter's concerns and spent some time normalising these. The family worker highlighted that as they developed more skills through the family work they could come back and talk about this again.

Comment. Prior to this session the family worker had spoken with a member of staff from the substance misuse team for some advice on how to respond to issues that may be raised.

The family worker felt that this was a very positive session. Even though Sarah had not made any agreement to address her use of cannabis they had both been able to talk about how they had felt in a safe way and this was the first time they had been able to discuss this sensitive issue.

After these two sessions, the family worker and parents agreed what information would be helpful for Emily. They decided that some simple explanations about her mum getting very worried sometimes and not feeling well, and being in hospital to make her feel better would be the most appropriate. Sarah and Peter said that they would chat to Emily together on one of Sarah's visits home. Mostly, they felt they wanted to reassure her that her mum was beginning to feel better and would be home soon.

Session 3: communication skills training

Note. It was half term and leave had been agreed for Sarah, so she was already at home when the family worker arrived. The plan for this session was to focus on communication skills. The atmosphere appeared tense and they stated that they had been arguing. Sarah stated that the leave had gone well for the first couple of days but that she felt she was being criticised by Peter. Peter stated that all his efforts were taken for granted and they began to argue. The family worker reminded them both of the ground rules they had set at the commencement of family work. To attempt to try and alleviate some of the tension, the family worker decided to facilitate a problem-solving session. Problem solving would usually be introduced after communication skills training, but the family worker felt facilitating a problem-solving session may be a useful way of addressing the current situation.

Sarah and Peter were encouraged to identify the issue. Peter stated that he felt taken for granted and that all his efforts were not appreciated. Sarah felt that she was always being criticised and was unsure why. They were both encouraged to think about it in more detail and they identified that the trigger was Sarah spilling tobacco over the floor after Peter had cleaned the flat in the morning before he went to college. After considering the options it was agreed that Sarah would roll all of her cigarettes for the day in the morning outside the front door. They agreed that they would try this for a week and review the outcome at the next family meeting. They also agreed to focus on communication skills because it had not been appropriate at this meeting.

Comment. The family worker was very pleased with this session because it demonstrated that often small issues can cause a great deal of distress to families, but by following a method of problem solving the family can identify ways of resolving situations themselves. Sarah and Peter both appeared much more positive at the end of the session.

Sessions 4–7: communication skills training

These four sessions addressed the issues of the family being able to say positive things to each other, ask for things in a constructive way, express difficult feelings and how to listen effectively. These sessions went very well. Both Sarah and Peter were able to identify how using these skills would be helpful to them and were able to demonstrate use of the skills during the session. They also focused on their personal goals, Peter had completed work for his web design course and they had been spending more time together as a family. Emily participated in parts of these sessions, though alternating between sitting on her mum's lap, running in and out of the room and colouring on the back of family work prompt sheets!

Comment. The family had initially agreed to six sessions of therapy. At the sixth session this was discussed briefly. The family felt that the meetings were helping them, and that there were still some areas that they wanted further help with, so they wanted to continue for another couple of sessions. This is quite common that a family may be reluctant to commit to a long period of therapy until they see what it is like and how they relate to the therapist. The behavioural family therapy model is very flexible and responsive to the needs of the family, and extensions to the number of sessions will often be done informally when it is clear to the worker and family that progress is being made and all are happy with the content and conduct of sessions.

Session 8: problem solving/goal achievement

The family met at home to focus on problem solving and goal achievement. The family worker had introduced the concept to Sarah and Peter in a previous session where he had taken on the role of facilitator to address an issue that was causing tension. The resulting action plan had worked very well and they were both keen to practice using the Six Step Method of problem solving independently. They decided to focus on the issue of getting Emily to school in the morning. They were able to define the goal, and with encouragement were able to identify possible solutions and choose the best option. They decided on a plan and agreed to try it out before the next meeting. Sarah reported that she felt included and listened to. Peter felt that this process had enabled them to reach an agreement without arguing. They decided that it would be helpful to use the problem-solving method outside of the meeting in relation to collecting Emily from school.

Session 9: ending and outcome

At the last session, Sarah stated that she felt they had gained all they could from the family work at present. She had been discharged from hospital and she wanted to settle back into family life. Peter was happy with this and they agreed to meet once more with the family worker to review how things had gone and think about contingency plans. Sarah's discharge was prompted by the improvement in Sarah's mental state and the obvious improvement in the way the couple were relating to each other.

Time was spent reflecting on how the work had been helpful for them. Peter stated that he felt he understood more about Sarah's experiences and her anxieties when she was unwell. Although he still found things difficult he felt he would have more understanding if she became unwell again. He also felt that he had a better understanding of her use of cannabis. He still did not agree, but understood why she may need to use illicit substances.

Sarah felt that she was less stressed at home and she was having a large input into Emily's day-to-day care. She felt that she had a better understanding of how the psychosis impacted on Peter.

They both agreed that they were communicating more effectively. When there were periods of tension, concentrating on the communication skills helped to reduce arguments. They also found the problem solving extremely effective. They felt they were now able to deal with difficult issues in a constructive way.

Peter stated that the most helpful and valuable part of the family work was being included and listened to. Being provided with an opportunity to ask questions and given information reduced his stress levels. He felt that the initial lack of involvement had put a great deal of pressure on their relationship and affected his ability to support Sarah.

They both felt that they understood Sarah's care plan and they could contact her care coordinator if they needed help. It was agreed that the family worker would contact the Community Mental Health Team and give an outline of their work and the skills they had developed and explain that they had agreed to end the family meetings. He discussed with them the fact that people sometimes find that when they return home that issues arise that they had not anticipated. It can also be difficult to put skills into practice when facing the ordinary stresses and strains of day-to-day living, and that people sometimes like the chance to go over the skills learned again. The family worker agreed that he could be contacted in the first instance should they require any booster sessions. He explained that in that instance they could look together at whether longer term support from the community team was needed, and if so, that he would organise some joint handover sessions with them and a family worker from the community team.

Comment. In this instance, the ending of therapy coincided with discharge, but this is not always the case. Sometimes inpatient staff argue that they should not begin family work if they cannot see it through to completion. However, many families do not want to wait indefinitely during an uncertain length of admission when their needs are greatest to receive any help or support – they want it when they are most distressed. As we noted earlier, inpatient staff need to see themselves as part of a broader system. Their role may be to engage the family on behalf of the service, even if the bulk of the family work may be carried out by other teams in the system. In other situations, depending on the length of admission, they may also provide information, or introduce the family to a range of other skills. There should not be an issue of continuity into the community if the service as a whole has adopted a family-based approach to care. It is much more likely that community staff are trained in family work, so a handover joint session with the community worker who is taking on the care of the family can be arranged. It is preferable if the inpatient member of staff can remain involved, especially if they have done quite a bit of work with the family as this means that the family do not need to go over the same material a second time.

The argument that inpatient staff cannot offer any sessions post-discharge is also spurious: the implications for staff cover are the same whether the inpatient member of staff is seeing the family on the ward or in their home. The argument that staff need to be available for crises that arise is not valid unless one sees it as acceptable for staff to rush out of a family meeting whenever something happens on the ward – this is hardly therapeutic – so this idea is linked more with attitude and perception rather than reality. All of these issues are linked with the way systems are managed which is why we emphasise that any attempt to implement family work in inpatient settings needs to influence service systems. In the services within the Meriden Programme, there are many excellent examples of flexible shift patterns and inreach and outreach working and split posts between inpatient and community services to ensure that the needs of families are met.

Response of ward staff

Ward staff were initially sceptical about the Deputy Ward Manager delivering family work because of staffing levels. However, they appeared to become used to the idea that he would be away from the ward once per week to meet with the family and after the first few meetings it no longer appeared to be an issue.

The Deputy Ward Manager provided a brief overview to the team after each meeting. This helped staff to consider how Sarah and her family had been affected by her becoming unwell and her admission to hospital. Staff noticed that Peter appeared much more relaxed when he visited and communicated much more with Sarah. He was also much less demanding of staff time. Several members of the team expressed an interest in working with families and applied to train in behavioural family therapy having seen the positive benefits for this family. We have found that demonstrating the benefits to staff in this way and modelling what can be done to effect change in the way families communicate is much more effective than trying to challenge attitudes directly which tends to produce a defensive reaction in a staff group that frequently comes under criticism from many sources.

Critical Reflection

The family work described highlights a number of issues that readers may wish to reflect on:

- The family worker in this situation was able to have a number of meetings with this family, possibly because of his commitment and seniority.

Ward staff may not be able to do such extensive work, but as can be seen, even the two educational sessions would have been very useful for this family.

- Inpatient staff can play a key role in engagement and assessment, which is beneficial throughout their contact with services.
- The question of who to involve in therapy – in this family, the grandparents were very involved with the family, but neither the client nor her partner felt it was the right time to involve them in the family meetings.
- Involving young children can pose a number of challenges depending on their age. There are issues around visiting on wards, confidentiality issues around sharing of information necessary for childcare, decisions around safety and their capacity to understand complex mental health issues. There are also issues around the confidence of mental health staff on adult wards in dealing with children.
- The value of working with the family is highlighted. If this is not done, there is a danger of seeing just one part of the picture. Seeing the person who is unwell at home in an environment that is relaxed also allows a more detailed assessment and helps to clarify their interactions with others in the family and to make decisions on safety issues.
- If ward staff are to work with families, they need the support of their colleagues, and managers play a key role in ensuring that this happens.
- Confidentiality – inpatient staff are often anxious about sharing information in the hierarchical systems that often prevail on wards. These staff often come straight from training onto wards and therefore lack exposure to the broader social context in the way that community staff have. There is a strong message in the ward milieu that their responsibility is to the individual, therefore they find confidentiality conflicts particularly difficult and need training in how to manage them. The Rethink organisation is acting on the results of their recent survey and is currently developing training materials on this topic. They are aware of the need to make these accessible to inpatient staff.

Conclusion

Inpatient staff clearly have a key role to play in the delivery of family work, but their work conditions, especially low staffing levels and lack of permanent staff clearly interferes with this. Support of management is crucial if this is to work effectively. Recent research is lacking in terms of what the content of family interventions in inpatient settings should be. However, earlier research has indicated that the emotions of families at this stressful time need to be addressed, information needs to be provided and coping skills need to be attended to. Family groups may be beneficial. Any training must address issues in the system in order to be successful.

References

Brennan, G., Flood, C. and Bowers, L. (2006) Constraints and blocks to change and improvement on acute wards – lessons from the City Nurses project. *Journal of Psychiatric and Mental Health Nursing*, **13**, 475–82.

Buchan, L. and Seccombe, I. (2002) *Behind the Headlines: A review of the UK Nursing Labour Market in 2001*, Royal College of Nursing, London.

Carpenter, L.L., Schecter, J.M., Underwood, J.A. *et al.* (2005) Service expectations and clinical characteristics of patients receiving psychiatric emergency services. *Psychiatric Services*, **56**, 743–5.

Clarke, S. (2004) *Acute Inpatient Mental Health Care: Education, Training and Continuing Professional Development*, Department of Health Publications, London.

Clarkin, J.F., Glick, I.D., Haas, G.L. *et al.* (1990) A randomised clinical trial of inpatient family intervention. V. Results for affective disorders. *Journal of Affective Disorders*, **18**, 17–28.

Cresswell, J., Bevan, M., Baskind, R. and Lelliot, P. (2007) *Accreditation for Acute Inpatient Mental Health Services (AIMS): Pilot Phase Report, July 2006–July 2007*, Royal College of Psychiatrists, London.

Drury, V., Birchwood, M. and Cochrane, R. (1996a) Cognitive therapy and recovery from acute psychosis: a controlled trial. I. Impact on psychotic symptoms. *British Journal of Psychiatry*, **169**, 593-601.

Drury, V., Birchwood, M. and Cochrane, R. (1996b) Cognitive therapy and recovery from acute psychosis: a controlled trial. II. Impact on recovery time. *British Journal of Psychiatry*, **169**, 602–7.

Fadden, G. and Birchwood, M. (2002) British models for expanding family psychoeducation in routine practice, in *Family Interventions in Mental Illness – International Perspectives* (eds Lefley, H.P. and Johnson, D.L.), Praeger, Connecticut.

Falloon, I.R.H., Boyd, J.L. and McGill, C.W. (1984) *Family Care of Schizophrenia*, Guilford, New York.

Falloon, I.R.H., Fadden, G., Mueser, K. *et al.* (2004) *Family Work Manual*, Meriden Family Programme, Birmingham.

Garcia, I., Kennett, C., Quraishi, M. and Duncan, G. (2005) *Acute Care 2004: a National Survey of Adult Psychiatric Wards in England*, Sainsbury Centre for Mental Health, London.

Glick, I.D., Clarkin, J.F., Haas, G.L. and Spencer, J.H. (1993) Clinical significance of inpatient family intervention: conclusions from a clinical trial. *Hospital and Community Psychiatry*, **44** (9), 869–73.

Glick, I.D., Clarkin, J.F., Spencer, J.H. *et al.* (1985) A controlled evaluation of in-patient family intervention. I. Preliminary results of the six-month follow-up. *Archives of General Psychiatry*, **42**, 882–6.

Haas, G.L., Glick, I.D., Clarkin, J.F. *et al.* (1988) Inpatient family intervention. II. Results at hospital discharge. *Archives of General Psychiatry*, **45**, 217–24.

Hardcastle, M., Kennard, D., Grandison, S. and Fagin, L. (eds) (2007) *Experiences of Mental Health In-patient Care: Narratives from Service Users, Carers and Professionals*, Routledge, London.

Jones, M. (2005) Supporting the application of psychosocial interventions in adult inpatient services. *Mental Health Practice*, **9**, 42–4.

Keefler, J. and Koritar, E. (1994) Essential elements of a family psychoeducational program in the aftercare of schizophrenia. *Journal of Marital and Family Therapy*, **20** (4), 369–79.

Kok, C.J. and Leskela, J. (1996) Solution-focused therapy in a psychiatric hospital. *Journal of Marital and Family Therapy*, **22**, 397–406.

Lemmens, G., Eisler, I., Heireman, M. and Van Houdenhove, B. (2005) Family discussion groups with patients with chronic pain and their family members: a pilot study. *Australian and New Zealand Journal of Family Therapy*, **26**, 31–2.

Lemmens, G., Eisler, I., Migerode, L. *et al.* (2007) Family discussion group therapy for major depression: a brief systemic multi-family group intervention for hospitalized patients and their family members. *Journal of Family Therapy*, **29**, 49–68.

McCann, E. and Bowers, L. (2005) Training in cognitive behavioural interventions on acute psychiatric inpatient wards. *Journal of Psychiatric and mental Health Nursing*, **12**, 215–22.

McGeorge, M., Cresswell, J., Beavon, M. and Chan, D. (2006) *Accreditation for Acute Inpatient Mental Health Services (AIMS): Standards for Acute Inpatient Wards and Accreditation Process*, Royal College of Psychiatrists, London.

Olfson, M., Glick, I.D. and Mechanic, D. (1993) Inpatient treatment of schizophrenia in general hospitals. *Hospital and Community Psychiatry*, **44**, 40–4.

Rivett, M., Tomsett, J., Lumsdon, P. and Holmes, P. (1997) 'Strangers in a familiar place': the evolution of a family therapy clinic within an in-patient adolescent unit. *Journal of Family Therapy*, **19**, 43–57.

Sainsbury Centre for Mental Health (1998) *Acute Problems: A Survey of the Quality of Care in Acute Wards*, Sainsbury Centre for Mental Health, London.

Slade, M., Pinfold, V., Rapaport, J. *et al.* (2007) Best practice when service users do not consent to sharing information with carers. *British Journal of Psychiatry*, **190**, 148–55.

Spencer, J.H., Glick, I.D., Haas, G.L. *et al.* (1988) A randomised clinical trial of inpatient family intervention. III. Effects at 6-month and 18-month follow-ups. *The American Journal of Psychiatry*, **145** (9), 1115–21.

Vaddadi, K.S., Soosai, E., Gilleard, C.J. and Adlard, S. (1997) Mental illness, physical abuse and burden of care on relatives: a study of acute psychiatric admission patients. *Acta Psychiatrica Scandanavica*, **95**, 313–7.

Vaughn, C. and Leff, J. (1976) The influence of family and social factors on the course of psychiatric illness: a comparison of schizophrenic and depressed neurotic patients. *British Journal of Psychiatry*, **129**, 125–37.

Resources

Training resources

- *The Journey Begins: Supporting Carers on an Acute Admission Ward.* A training resource for use with staff working in inpatient services. Lu Duhig (Lu.Duhig@csip.org.uk). Avon and Wiltshire Mental Health Partnership Trust.
- *Family Awareness Training for Staff Working in Inpatient Services.* A three-stage training programme for inpatient staff. Also the Meriden Special Interest Group for Family Work in Inpatient Services.

  Meriden West Midlands Family Programme, www.meridenfamilyprogramme. com (accessed 21 November 2008).

- *Partnerships in the Making: Carers in Mental Health. Carers DVD and Training Pack.* A training pack that aims to address issues for acute staff around working with carers within inpatient settings enhanced by BME focused DVD to integrate BME carers issues into mainstream acute staff training. DRE and Acute Care Programme CSIP SW. Francine.bradshaw@nimhesw.nhs.uk
- *Keeping the Family in Mind.* A training resource with a DVD aimed at anyone who works with parents with mental health difficulties, their children and their families and is designed to raise awareness of the issues they face. Clare.Mahoney@csip.org.uk
- *An Information Pack for Relatives and Friends Who Care for People with Mental Health Problems.* Avon and Wiltshire mental Health Partnership NHS Trust.
- *Parents in Hospitals: How Mental Health services Can Best Promote Family Contact When a Parent Is in Hospital.* A report offering guidance on contact arrangements between parents in mental health settings and their children, http://www.barnardos.org.uk/parentsinhospital (accessed 21 November 2008).

- *Being Seen and Heard: The Needs of Children of Parents with Mental Illness.* A video and DVD training pack for professionals which has some descriptions of the experiences of families when their parents are in hospital. Book Sales: Royal College of Psychiatrists, 17 Belgrave Square, London, SW1X 8PG, http://www.rcpsych.ac.uk/publications.aspx (accessed 21 November 2008).

Web site
Reports on the Rethink survey on confidentiality and information sharing with carers, http://www.sdo.nihr.ac.uk/sdo542003.html (accessed 21 November 2008).

Books and Further Reading

Hardcastle, M., Kennard, D., Grandison, S. and Fagin, L. (eds) (2007) *Experiences of Mental Health In-patient Care: Narratives from Service Users, Carers and Professionals*, Routledge, London.
Heru, A. and Drury, L. (2007) *Working with Families of Psychiatric Inpatients: A Guide for Clinicians*, The Johns Hopkins University Press, Baltimore.
NIMHE (2008) *Acute Care and National Workforce Programmes: More Than Just Staffing Numbers*, http://www.southwest.csip.org.uk/silo/files/more-than-just-staffing-numbers–a-workbook-for-acute-care-workforce-redesign-and-development.pdf (accessed 21 November 2008).
Commission for Healthcare Audit and Inspection (2008). *The Pathway to Recovery: A Review of NHS Acute Inpatient Mental Health Services*, Commission for Healthcare Audit and Inspection, London, http://www.healthcarecommission.org.uk/db/documents/Thepathwaytorecovery200807251020.pdf (accessed 21 November 2008).

Systems for improving experiences on inpatient units
Star Wards, www.starwards.org.uk.
Accreditation for Acute Inpatient Mental Health Services (AIMS), Royal College of Psychiatrists, London, AIMS@cru.rcpsych.ac.uk.

VI

Service Related Issues

13

Setting Up a Family Interventions (FI) Service – A UK Case Study

Frank Burbach and Roger Stanbridge

It was an invaluable service.

Without the help I don't think we'd have been in business. I don't think we'd have been able to carry on normally.

They gave you hope and another view of the situation.

It is a must to have a service like this . . . there must be a support service for families.

Background

Although evidence for the efficacy of family interventions (FI) when a family member experiences psychosis/schizophrenia is robust (see reviews of randomised controlled trials by Bustillo *et al.*, 2001; Dixon, Adam and Lucksted, 2000; Mari and Streiner, 1996; Pharoah, Mari and Streiner, 2002; Pitschel-Walz *et al.*, 2001), and FI has been included in national policy (e.g. National Institute for Clinical Excellence (NICE) Guidelines, 2002; Department of Health (DoH), 1999), it has not led to the widespread establishment of family intervention services in routine clinical settings (Brooker, 2001; Dixon *et al.*, 2001; Fadden, 1998).

A comprehensive review of the literature by Brooker and Brabban (2004) concluded that there has been a 'measured success' in implementing psychosocial interventions (PSI), such as family work for people with

A Casebook of Family Interventions for Psychosis   Edited by Fiona Lobban and Christine Barrowclough
© 2009 John Wiley & Sons, Ltd

psychosis. This review highlighted a number of well-designed studies 'which reported similar barriers to the implementation of FI training' (p. 8), particularly difficulties relating to clinicians' inability to prioritise family work due to the service environment. Specific issues included not having sufficient time for FI, difficulties in integrating it with other responsibilities, lack of support from colleagues and a lack of appropriate supervision. In addition, many studies identified a difficulty in finding and engaging with 'appropriate families', which appears to have implications for the type of training provided.

It was against this background that, rather than consider sending staff members on external FI training courses, we decided to develop FI services by means of an in-house whole-team training approach (Burbach and Stanbridge, 1998, 2006).

Aims

In this chapter, we aim to describe how we set up an FI service in the light of the research into the barriers to implementation of FI training. We will explore the strategies used in Somerset with a particular reference to the three factors highlighted in the Brooker and Brabban (2004) review – team training, supervision and organisational ownership/support. In addition, we would add to this list the need to address the prevailing individually focused service culture and the importance of developing more family sensitive mainstream clinical practice.

We will describe how we have developed the FI services in Somerset by means of accredited *in situ* whole-team training. Our 1-year training course teaches a range of skills which have enabled our trainees to successfully engage and work with a wide range of families. We will evaluate the service development approach we have used and reflect on key issues relevant to establishing FI Services.

Context

Somerset is a rural county in the South West of England with a population of half a million. In the mid 1990s, as in other areas of the United Kingdom, large Victorian hospitals were replaced by community care teams and locally accessible units. In this context, the needs of families where a member has severe mental health problems was beginning to be recognised. However, mental health services retained their focus on individually based treatment. Fortunately, in Somerset there were a number of family therapy clinics in operation and there were people who had developed skills in working with families with a wide range of mental health problems, including psychosis (Brennan and Challenger, 1996; Procter, 1985, 1986; Procter and Pieczora, 1992; Procter and Stephens, 1984). As with other forms of psychological therapy, however, the availability of these specialist services was limited and dependent on the enthusiasm of particular clinicians.

At the same time, our mental health trust had become aware of FI in psychosis training initiatives (Thorne; behavioural family therapy) which had been developed following the randomised controlled trials which demonstrated the efficiency of FI (for a summary of the evidence base at this time see Mari and Streiner, 1996). A small number of staff had attended these courses but this had not led to families being seen.

In 1994, following publication of UK Department of Health's Mental Illness Key Area Handbook, our trust management consulted senior family therapists including the authors regarding the provision of family work for psychosis. Having recently researched this area (Burbach, 1995, 1996) and having successfully implemented a short ($2^1/_2$ day) whole-team training programme in 'behavioural principles' across the six rehabilitation units in Somerset (Quarry and Burbach, 1998), we put forward proposals to develop a new in-house FI in psychosis training programme – the FI (Research, Skills, Theory) in psychosis course (FIRST).

Our initial idea was to develop a local service with a multi-disciplinary group of colleagues drawn from different parts of the mental health services. The authors began to work together seeing families where someone was experiencing psychotic symptoms but found it difficult to involve others due to the constraints of their existing roles. The solution to this was to propose a more formal 1-year training programme, but to design this in a way which would lead to the establishment of a service. The key to this was the plan to begin work with local families halfway through the course.

We argued that this proposal made use of existing skills and that an in-house whole-team training package would overcome the implementation difficulties experienced subsequent to other FI training courses. Managers investigated other training options and then decided to support our proposal. The cost of putting on the course was largely absorbed within the existing trust budgets – besides a small amount of start up money to facilitate the development of course materials. We have not received any additional funding to cover staff time (tutors and trainees) to establish the service. In further meetings with trust management we developed these local proposals into a trustwide 5-year development strategy and went on to gain accreditation with our local university (60 credits at degree or diploma level) and the Association of Family Therapy.

Over a period of 5 years we consecutively took the course to the four service areas in Somerset. Teaching sessions were delivered by two tutors drawn from successive course teams, each consisting of the authors and two others. In order to maintain the service we have provided a series of 'top-up' courses in subsequent years. Our most recent courses have included staff from the child and adolescent mental health services which has enabled teams to intervene early with a younger age group (i.e. age 14 and over).

Key Features of the *In Situ* Whole-Team Training Approach and Family Interventions Service

We invite applications from interested members of staff in the relevant locality and then consider the applications in conjunction with the appropriate line manager. We select staff only with the clear agreement of their line manager that they will be able to devote a minimum of half a day per week to providing the service when the course finishes. In essence this is a process of selecting a team and we therefore carefully consider team composition. We seek to have a range of professions (which have included art therapists, family therapists, nurses, occupational therapists, psychiatrists, psychologists, social workers and support workers) and also seek to recruit staff from each part of the local mental health service (e.g. inpatient unit; Community Mental Health Teams; assertive outreach team).

The 1-year course comprises three modules, and approximates to a half day per week. This establishes a level of commitment which is required to provide the service subsequent to the course. Having this structure is particularly important for staff who work according to staff rotas (e.g. inpatient units) but this level of clarity also assists community staff who are able to adjust their workload in order to participate in the FI service. The *in situ* whole-team training approach allows us to accept referrals from the local services and trainees begin to see families half way through the course (using live supervision from course tutors). In addition, the local 'Family Support Service' (this is the name we have adopted for our FI service) becomes established part way through the course.

The three modules focus on systemic practice, FI and cognitive approaches with psychosis. The first module covers systemic theory, research and basic practice skills. Systems thinking, the importance of context, and the way in which problems arise/are maintained, are introduced from a 'cognitive-interactional' perspective. The family lifecycle, family beliefs/ narratives, the individual's/caregivers' experience of psychosis and the stress–vulnerability model are introduced. Clinical skills relevant to the various stages of therapy are developed by means of role-play. The second module critically examines the systemic family therapy and psychoeducational FI approaches to psychosis and further develops their integration. Theory and research about early intervention, ethical issues and risk are also examined. Behavioural family therapy skills and systemic interviewing skills are developed in role-play and in supervised work with families. The third module further develops clinical skills through direct supervision and considers their application in the service context. The focus is on cognitive behaviour therapy techniques for psychosis and relapse prevention strategies. In addition, solution focused/narrative approaches to working with families are further developed.

Evaluation of the training approach

Although the most important measure of the efficacy of our training approach is the fact that we have successfully established four FI teams, we have also conducted a study into the ability of FIRST trained staff to implement the approach. This is significant in the light of previous studies (Brennan and Gamble, 1997; Fadden, 1997; Kavanagh *et al.*, 1993) which found that staff trained in FI had great difficulties in implementing the approach in routine clinical practice and saw few families post-training (e.g. 1.7 families (9–42 months post-training) and 1.4 (6–26 months) seen in the Fadden and Kavanagh studies, respectively). Fifteen therapists who had completed the FIRST course participated in the study which involved questionnaires used in previous studies and focus groups (Bailey, Burbach and Lea, 2003). All reported working with families using the Family Support Service approach since completing the FIRST course. The average number of families seen since completion of training (an average of 26 months, range 3–35 months) was 3.5. Eighty per cent of the graduates reported 'little or no difficulties' in implementing the approach, and no one found they were unable to offer the intervention following training. These findings compare very favourably with the findings of other reported studies of post-training implementation (Fadden, 1997; Kavanagh *et al.*, 1993).

In common with previous studies the two main areas of difficulty reported were having sufficient time to do the work and its integration with caseload and other responsibilities at work. However, in contrast with the previous studies the Somerset staff did not experience any difficulty in tailoring their approach to the needs of individual clients and families, nor in accessing consultation and supervision.

In the focus groups, staff identified a number of specific aspects of the service which enabled successful work with families. In particular, they highlighted the flexible nature of the service, the multi-disciplinary nature of the teams, the use of co-working and regular supervision as being beneficial.

The Somerset family interventions service

The Family Support Service uses a competency-based approach which integrates psychoeducational/cognitive behavioural and systemic approaches. The service is available to people who are in regular contact/living with their family members or significant others (e.g. carers) who are experiencing psychotic symptoms (including prodromal symptoms). We aim to intervene as early as possible and encourage early referral which may be during the acute phase and before a diagnosis has been made. Although the evidence base for FI was originally developed with people with enduring symptoms who were vulnerable to relapse, our service works with a wider spectrum of people with psychosis. This is in line with national initiatives to develop early intervention in psychosis services (DoH, 1999; IRIS, 2001) and our FI service works closely with the recently established early interventions in psychosis service, prioritising those with first and second episode psychosis (Burbach, Fadden and Smith, 2009). The procedure is for two therapists to meet with individual families in the location most conducive to engagement. The aim is to collaboratively negotiate with each family a therapeutic contract which reflects their particular needs and to continue supporting them as long as required.

Whilst the main focus of the work is often described as seeking to improve outcome and quality of life for the person experiencing psychotic symptoms, our systemic thinking leads us to place emphasis on relationships and there-fore the needs of all family members (Pearson, Burbach and Stanbridge, 2007). Our aim is to improve quality of life and well-being for the whole family. A range of interventions may be used such as those aiming to increase competency in problem solving and communication within the family, and developing more realistic expectations of the person's functioning. Whereas information sharing may be helpful in this, in itself it has not been shown to be sufficient to significantly effect clinical outcome (Lam, 1991; NICE, 2003). In most cases, an exploration of feelings (e.g. guilt, loss) and inter-actional patterns and beliefs which maintain problems is required in order to effect change in attitudes and behaviour. For further details regarding the Family Support Service, see Burbach and Stanbridge (1998, 2006).

Evaluation of the service

Whereas the efficacy of FI is now evident, relatively few services have been established in routine clinical settings and evaluation of the approach is particularly difficult in such circumstances. Nonetheless in Somerset we have evaluated the Family Support Service in a number of ways in order to improve the service we offer.

We routinely collect data on all cases, which enable us to monitor our service and provide feedback and thereby influence the wider mental health system. This includes the following: referral rates, demographics of fam-ilies referred, information about diagnosis and onset/episode of psychosis, attendance figures, dropout rates, details of which family members attend sessions, feedback from families and caseloads of therapists. We have also conducted an in-depth study of families' satisfaction with the first Family Support Service to be established (Stanbridge *et al.*, 2003). Fifteen of the first 22 referrals to the service agreed to take part in semi-structured in-terviews regarding family satisfaction, clinical outcome and the therapeutic alliance. All family members expressed satisfaction with the service overall, 10 families rated themselves as 'very satisfied' and 3 families as 'partially sat-isfied'. The other two families were unable to evaluate the service as they felt they had been referred 'too late' (i.e. on their son's discharge from hospital when their situation had already improved) but reported that they would have welcomed the service if it had been offered earlier. These high levels of satisfaction are the more reassuring given that 73% of the sample reported feeling apprehension prior to being seen in the Family Support Service.

This study highlighted some of the ingredients which may be associated with successful outcome. Satisfaction was related to families' needs being met (e.g. coping with symptoms, problem solving, improved communication in the family, better liaison with the services), family members developing new perspectives, as well as feeling listened to in the context of an empathic, non-judgemental therapeutic relationship. A number of factors specifically emphasised in the Somerset Family Support Service appeared to contribute to the establishment of a positive therapeutic relationship and be particularly valued by families, namely mutually agreed therapeutic aims, regular evaluation of the usefulness of sessions and the opportunity for open discussion. These factors reflect the service's broad, flexible therapeutic approach which enables clinicians to offer a range of interventions suited to different families' specific needs. These findings are perhaps best summed up by one family members' response to the question regarding their overall satisfaction with the service:

> Surprised and satisfied. The most important thing was that they listened and responded to the family's needs, not followed their own agenda, and that happened.

The Importance of Supervision

Supervision is crucial in the maintenance of the service and also in ensuring its quality. Besides Somerset-wide 'study days' and local team supervision sessions, each pair of therapists also reflect on their clinical work before, during and after each family session. Whilst one of the functions of this range of approaches to clinical supervision is to ensure safe and ethical practice, the prime function is to facilitate reflective practice (Schön, 1983) and thereby enhance the effectiveness of therapy. We have found that the range of supervision processes is important to support staff carrying out this at times complex and demanding work.

Trustwide study days

Our quarterly study days bring together all members of our trustwide service. These days have a number of functions including continuing professional development, clinical governance and service development/ maintenance. The study days include case presentations and a consultation slot for difficult clinical situations.

The format of the days varies, covering a range of topics and speakers, but they all focus on service improvement and clinical reflection. For example, a mother spoke to the group about her son's emerging psychosis and the family's experience of services. In addition to increasing our understanding of such traumatic experiences, a number of difficulties were highlighted which resulted in further discussion. Initially, care was provided by the mental health services in another part of Somerset to which her son had only recently moved. The family struggled to transfer his care to a team in the area where the family lived. As a result they experienced difficulty in accessing appropriate information and support. The Family Support Service clinicians were concerned to hear about these difficulties and, in addition to doing what they could to ensure that the family received a better service, highlighted issues with colleagues and managers and emphasised the importance of early referral to the FI service.

Team supervision meetings

The monthly team peer supervision meetings contain an organisational element (e.g. referral/allocation process) but reflecting on cases/clinical issues is the main focus. In particular, clinicians are expected to report back on the assessment phase and to refine a case formulation in consultation with the group (e.g. see Table 13.1). Another key function of these group supervision meetings is to help the therapists to generate new ideas.

Complex situations are often usefully discussed on a case-by-case basis in the supervision group. For example, deciding whom to involve in family sessions if a young person's parents have separated acrimoniously. In some cases it is helpful to meet with different combinations of family members (e.g. client and mother; client and father), whereas in others it may be more appropriate to bring together all of the family members. Supervision meetings can help the therapists to explore the implications of intervening in the family structure and to develop appropriate therapeutic strategies.

Although some issues regarding the therapeutic process/therapeutic alliance can be addressed within family sessions by the co-therapists, other more complex/personal issues for the therapist are best explored within post-session discussions or team supervision meetings. For example, a

Table 13.1 Example of Case Formulation

A 34-year-old man with bipolar disorder was referred to the Family Support Service at the point at which he was being discharged from an inpatient unit to live with his parents. The following formulation was agreed with him and his family:

> James' present episode of illness and hospitalisation has interrupted his sense of direction and achievements in life and he now finds himself temporarily living with his parents and having lost his job and girlfriend. This has left James feeling demoralised, frustrated and angry. James is a sensitive, articulate, energetic person with a lot to offer, who is vulnerable to believing that he cannot meet societal and family expectations. It is good that James is part of such a close supportive family who are able to talk about issues and support him during this transition period. This situation puts understandable strain on all family members but it is positive that all are aware of unhelpful patterns and want to change them.

recently qualified female therapist who had grown up in a farming family with rigid gender-based roles did not realise that she was taking sides with a mother in the family sessions. She struggled to understand the positions of the young man with psychosis and his father, found it difficult to develop a systemic formulation, and did not realise that the male members of the family were beginning to disengage from therapy. Reflecting on this in supervision enabled her to subsequently explore, in a non-judgemental way, how the various roles (especially the husband's socially defined role) had developed in this family, enabling them to make some adjustments. This also allowed further helpful conversations about the son's future role within the family business.

Pre-session discussion

Our practice is for the two therapists to meet before and after their session with a family. The pre-session meeting (± 15 minutes) enables the therapists to orient themselves – they review the previous session, assimilate any new information entered in the clinical notes, and plan for the session. This plan would involve the identification of potential themes and hypotheses to explore, as well as following up agreed goals and tasks. In addition, the therapist would consider process issues, both in terms of how the family operates and respective therapist roles (e.g. who will take the lead or explore particular topics). This is an opportunity to consider family dynamics and the nature of the therapeutic alliance between the therapists and the family members. This would of course be elaborated in other supervisory contexts, where issues such as the therapist's use of personal experience as well as wider contexts such as gender, race and culture are considered in greater depth.

Post-session discussion

Post-session there are a number of practical tasks to complete (e.g. writing up notes, communicating with colleagues) as well as spending some time reflecting on how the session has gone and noting issues to pick up on at the next family meeting.

We often find that it is difficult for busy clinicians to safeguard the time for pre- and post-session discussions; however, this is an essential part of effective family work. It enables therapists to compare views on significant moments in therapy and the effectiveness of particular therapeutic interventions, and to remain focused on the goals of therapy. It also allows therapists to debrief after sessions and to deal with any difficult feelings which the session may have evoked in them. Of course many therapists are also parents and therefore particularly affected by, for example, traumatic accounts of the effects of psychosis in young people.

Reflection between therapists during sessions

Besides reflecting on therapy sessions in supervision groups as well as before and after each session, reflection between the therapists during family meetings is an important part of our way of working. An advantage of the co-therapy model is that in part it is like having a supervisor in the room. Whilst one therapist is engaged in talking with the family the other therapist is able to observe the process and intervene where appropriate. The co-therapist can help to keep the therapy on track, introduce new ideas and help their colleague should they feel 'stuck'.

At times during the meeting it may be helpful for the therapists to have a brief reflective conversation with each other in which they may comment on the way in which the meeting has progressed and options for the rest of the session, share observations and tentatively offer alternative perspectives. For example, in a session with a young man (James[1]) experiencing psychosis and his parents, the therapists had the following conversation after concerns were raised about possible relapse and evidence that James was exhibiting pressure of speech and tending to dominate the session:

CO-THERAPIST: Hearing James talk when he feels passionate about something makes me wonder how Anne and Charles respond when James talks late into the night.

THERAPIST: Yes, it must be difficult for Anne and Charles to know how best to respond. On the one hand they are interested in James' views but on the other they may be concerned that if he doesn't get enough sleep he may become unwell again.

CO-THERAPIST: Perhaps we could ask James how he would like his parents to respond when he is in full flow late at night.

Whilst this is in keeping with our aim of wishing to work in a manner which is as transparent as possible, it is also an effective way of influencing the process of sessions. It is an unusual experience for families to hear themselves being talked about and this can effectively interrupt unhelpful interactions as they stop to listen. In addition, families value these opportunities to reflect upon themselves and consider new perspectives. These reflective conversations are not instructive or directive in nature but are conducted in a tentative manner, where a range of ideas is offered for the family to consider, comment on and incorporate where they seem appropriate. These conversations need to be brief, genuine and positive in nature, use language which is easily understood by the family, emphasise solutions rather than problems, and be respectful and valuing of the family. These conversations can be highly effective if conducted sensitively (Andersen, 1995; Lax, 1995) but this approach does not suit all families (Jenkins, 1996) and it is important to seek the family's feedback as to its value.

Reflections on Establishing a Service

This chapter has outlined the way in which we have equipped staff with a range of knowledge and skills to successfully engage and work with

---

[1] All names have been changed to ensure anonymity.

families. We have done this by developing a new training paradigm (Burbach, Donnelly and Stanbridge, 2002) in which an *in situ* whole-team training approach is used to establish trustwide services consisting of local teams.

As with any model, there are benefits and drawbacks. In this section, we will consider these as well as wider organisational issues which are essential in the establishment of FI services. In addition, we will consider the importance of developing more family sensitive mainstream clinical practice.

Benefits and drawbacks of our service development approach

Trainees find it far less stressful to attend a local course with their colleagues, with no additional time lost due to travel. This leads to high levels of attendance and a low course dropout rate. Working together throughout the year also helps to develop a strong team spirit which continues as the course becomes the service.

Unlike other trainees who have to return to their workplace and set up a service, our trainees establish the service during the course. They are able to use their local knowledge to develop referral pathways, educate other colleagues and problem-solve any operational difficulties. In addition, the fact that there is ongoing clinical work with families at the point at which the course ends means that the newly trained team is already operational.

The team training approach conveys additional benefits for the ongoing service. Having a group of eight trained staff in each locality provides the necessary critical mass to influence the local culture. We would agree with Fadden (1997) on the importance of achieving a critical mass of trained staff in order to enable the implementation of FI. In our services the team of like-minded colleagues is able to provide the necessary initial support and encouragement to sustain this demanding work. The establishment of a team also enables the maintenance of service quality through the establishment of clinical supervision, audit procedures and continuing professional development.

Focusing training on service development conveys a number of advantages in that the knowledge and skills taught are clinically relevant. Providing this training in-house to whole teams is clearly a robust way of ensuring the transference of these skills into an effective service. That this was achieved in Somerset without significant additional funding may be seen as an advantage, however, in an ideal world this would have been a funded plan rather than a 'reconfiguration' dependent on goodwill. A related drawback is that our staff will have a limited time devoted to FI as opposed to having people employed specifically to provide FI. Although we would strongly argue the benefits of having FI team members integrated into other teams/services we would advocate that some dedicated FI time should be funded (e.g. trainers and coordinators of the FI teams). This has been the approach adopted in another Trust in our region where they have also established area-based teams using our training course and model. Here, they have established half-time FI team coordinator posts and a research assistant post, and have funded some of the trainer/trainee backfill costs. Whereas we have found that our training approach and flexible collaborative family-needs led model has resulted in good engagement rates and high levels of satisfaction with the service, we are aware that some managers in other areas may baulk at the extensive 1-year training course. Another potential disadvantage of the more extensive range of approaches/skills taught on our course is that it is more difficult to measure fidelity subsequent to training.

Wider organisational issues

The establishment of FI services has required both the championing of FI as well as achieving support and ownership throughout the organisation. We approached this by establishing partnerships across the organisation. It was essential to have the formal endorsement of the trust board and to have the establishment of the service included in the Trust's business plan. However, it was also vital to collaborate with local team and service managers as their support enabled the reconfiguration of services to allow staff to devote a portion of their working week to the training and subsequent service. We promoted the project through a range of presentations in order to raise awareness at a senior management level as well as to motivate staff to consider embarking on the training. Achieving accreditation for the course with Plymouth University and the Association for Family Therapy provided additional incentives for staff to undertake the training.

It has also been essential to consider the maintenance of the service from the start of the project. Besides maintaining organisational support (e.g. via annual reports, audits, presentations) we have been aware of the need to maintain staff motivation and to ensure the quality of the service. The whole-team training naturally facilitates mutual support, which is formalised in team clinical supervision on a monthly basis. The co-therapy model also enables supervision and support in the clinical situation. We have also found that quarterly trustwide study days have enabled mutual support and the updating of knowledge and skills.

Influencing mainstream clinical practice

When setting up a specialist FI service it is important to take into account the baseline level of experience of staff in working with families. We have found that the majority of staff have low levels of experience and confidence in working with families as this did not form part of their initial professional training. Working with the workforce as a whole to increase their levels of knowledge and skills in engaging and working with families as part of their routine clinical practice can provide a helpful platform for developing specialist family services. A family sensitive workforce is likely to be more supportive of specialist FI and to make more appropriate referrals.

In Somerset we have developed a strategy to enhance working partnerships with families and carers in order to raise the general awareness of family sensitive practice (Stanbridge and Burbach, 2004). This has involved the development of a multi-professional, multi-agency steering group which includes service user and carer representatives in order to guide the implementation of the strategy. This group has developed best practice guidelines regarding confidentiality and information sharing, reviewed trust policies and facilitated the provision of information and support for carers. In addition, we have provided a trustwide staff training programme for inpatient and community staff which explores how clinical services might develop working partnerships with families and enhances skills to enable the routine inclusion of families/carers in the assessment and treatment processes as part of the care programme approach (Stanbridge and Burbach, 2007a; Stanbridge, Burbach and Leftwich, 2008).

Whereas clinical practice in mental health services still predominantly focuses on the individual, recent national policy guidance (Department of Health, 2002; NICE Guidelines for Schizophrenia, 2002) has signalled a shift towards increased partnership working with family and carers (Simpson and Benn, 2007). We have found that the combination of both the specialist FI and the general working with families training programme has helped to begin to shift the organisational culture to a more family inclusive way of working (Burbach and Stanbridge, 2008). An important element of this has been the involvement of carers in delivering the training (Stanbridge and Burbach, 2007b).

Conclusions

This chapter has described our experience of setting up an FI service. Our service was developed in a particular context – a small specialist Health and Social Care Mental Health Trust serving a population of 500 000 in a rural setting. There are some advantages to working in an organisation of this scale. Senior clinicians are perhaps able to have a greater influence throughout the organisation through closer links with trust management. The disadvantages have largely concerned the lack of availability of funding. The rural nature of the area has necessitated the development of four smaller FI teams, rather than a larger, central team. This could have the potential vulnerability to fragmentation, gradual loss of staff and deterioration in quality. We have, however, taken these issues into account and developed a network of services by means of our training approach and subsequent focus on service maintenance.

Although we developed our approach in Somerset, we have found that it is also possible to implement this whole-team training approach to service development in other trusts. Another rural trust in the South West of England has used our package to develop a trustwide FI service consisting of three area teams, suggesting that the approach is transferable and may have wider applicability.

Other FI services in the United Kingdom have been developed using somewhat different models. At a recent conference (NIMHE Implementation of PSI Conference, 2004) four FI services were described – West Midlands, Avon and Wiltshire, Dorset and Somerset. The Meriden programme in the West Midlands (Fadden, 2000) employed a strategic approach with trusts in the region to deliver training and develop supportive supervision structures post-training. This project provides a short (5 day) training for a large number of mental health professionals, leading to widespread raising of skills and awareness regarding the needs of families with psychosis, although the number of families seen per therapist post-training is proportionally lower than in our service. In Avon and Wiltshire (Smith and Velleman, 2002) the employment of local 'champions' has enabled co-working, supervision and the coordination of staff trained in FI. In Dorset (Kelly and Newstead, 2004) strong links have been created between the local University Thorn programme and the mental health services, involving regular meetings between course graduates, their line managers and the trainers. Whilst there are other FI services in the United Kingdom, these examples reflect the range of solutions which have been employed.

Anyone who wished to set up an FI service would have a range of examples to draw on, but the key to success will be to identify an approach which is appropriate to the local service setting and which emphasises the link between training and service provision. Once established, the service will have to focus on maintenance and ensuring that it remains well embedded in the management and clinical structures.

We would hope that an enthusiastic clinician reading this chapter would not be daunted by the scale of the task. Our experience is that developing partnerships between clinicians, managers and families can create a momentum towards the development of FI services. Anyone wishing to develop FI services today would benefit from the presence of supportive national policy and increasingly well-developed carer/family organisations. Listening to the experiences of families struggling with the influence of psychosis it is clear that appropriate help for families should be routinely available. The quotes at the beginning of this chapter demonstrate that families who have experienced FI are particularly compelling advocates for these services.

References

Andersen, T. (1995) Reflecting processes; acts of informing and forming, in *The Reflecting Team in Action: Collaborative practice in Family Therapy* (ed. S. Friedman), Guildford, New York.

Bailey, R., Burbach, F.R. and Lea, S. (2003) The ability of staff trained in family interventions to implement the approach in routine clinical practice. *Journal of Mental Health*, **12**, 131–41.

Brennan, J. and Challenger, A. (1996) Talking to ourselves. *Context*, **24**, 15–22.

Brennan, G. and Gamble, C. (1997) Schizophrenia, family work and clinical practice. *Mental Health Nursing*, **7** (4), 12–5.

Brooker, C. (2001) A decade of evidence-based training for work with people with serious mental health problems: progress in the development of psychosocial interventions. *Journal of Mental Health*, **10** (1), 17–31.

Brooker, C. and Brabban, A. (2004) Measured Success: A Scoping Review of Evaluated Psychosocial Interventions Training for Work with People with Serious Mental Health Problems. *NIMHE/Trent WDC*.

Burbach, F.R. (1995) Services for Families which include a 'psychotic' person. *Context*, **24**, 22–8.

Burbach, F.R. (1996) Family based interventions in psychosis – an overview of, and comparison between, family therapy and family management approaches. *Journal of Mental Health*, **5**, 111–34.

Burbach, F.R., Donnelly, M. and Stanbridge, R.I. (2002) Service development through multi-disciplinary and multi-agency partnerships. *The Mental Health Review*, **7** (3), 27–30.

Burbach, F.R., Fadden, G. and Smith, J. (2009) Family interventions for first episode psychosis, in *Promoting Recovery in Early Psychosis* (eds P. French, M. Read, J. Smith *et al.*), in press.

Burbach, F.R. and Stanbridge, R.I. (1998) A family intervention in psychosis service integrating the systemic and family management approaches. *Journal of Family Therapy*, **20**, 311–25.

Burbach, F.R. and Stanbridge, R.I. (2006) Somerset's family interventions in psychosis service: an update. *Journal of Family Therapy*, **28**, 39–57.

Burbach, F.R. and Stanbridge, R.I. (2008) Training to develop family inclusive routine practice and specialist family interventions in Somerset. *Journal of Mental Health Workforce Development*, **3** (2), 23–31.

Bustillo, J.R., Lauriello, J., Horan, W.P. and Keith, S.J. (2001) The psychosocial treatment of schizophrenia: an update. *American Journal of Psychiatry*, **158** (2), 163–75.

Department of Health (1994) *Mental Illness Key Area Handbook*, Department of Health, London.

Department of Health (1999) *The National Service Framework for Mental Health. Modern Standards and Service Models*, Department of Health, London.

Department of Health (2002) *Developing Services for Carers and Families of People with Mental Illness*, Department of Health, London.

Dixon, L., Adam, C. and Lucksted, A. (2000) Update on family psychoeducation for schizophrenia. *Schizophrenia Bulletin*, **26**, 5–20.

Dixon, L., McFarlane, W.R., Lefley, H. *et al.* (2001) Evidence-based practices for services to families of people with psychiatric disabilities. *Psychiatric Services*, **52**, 903–12.

Fadden, G. (1997) Implementation of family interventions in routine clinical practice following staff training programs: a major cause for concern. *Journal of Mental Health*, **6** (6), 599–612.

Fadden, G. (1998) Research update: psychoeducational family interventions. *Journal of Family Therapy*, **20**, 293–309.

Fadden, G. (2000) *Implementing family Interventions at a Regional Level: A Cascade Training Model*. Presentation to conference "Working with families: making it a reality", Stratford-upon-Avon.

IRIS (2001) *Initiative to Reduce the Impact of Schizophrenia: Clinical Guidelines and Service Frameworks – Toolkit*, Kaleidoscope (National Schizophrenia Fellowship).

Jenkins, D. (1996) A reflecting team approach to family therapy: a Delphi study. *Journal of Marital and Family Therapy*, **22**, 219–38.

Kavanagh, D.J., Piatkowska, O., Clarke, D. *et al.* (1993) Application of cognitive-behavioural family intervention for schizophrenia in multi-disciplinary teams: what can the matter be? *Australian Psychologist*, **28**, 181–8.

Kelly, M. and Newstead, L. (2004) Family intervention in routine practice: it is possible! *Journal of Psychiatric and Mental Health Nursing*, **11**, 64–72.

Lam, D.H. (1991) Psychosocial family intervention in schizophrenia: a review of empirical studies. *Psychological Medicine*, **21**, 423–41.

Lax, W.D. (1995) Offering reflections: some theoretical and practical considerations, in *The Reflecting Team in Action: Collaborative Practice in Family Therapy* (ed. S. Friedman), Guildford, New York.

Mari, J. and Streiner, D. (1996) The effects of family intervention on those with schizophrenia, in *Schizophrenia Module, Cochrane Database of Systematic Reviews* (eds C. Adams, J. Anderson and J. Mari), BMJ Publishing, London.

National Institute of Clinical Excellence (2002) *Schizophrenia: Core Interventions in the Treatment and Management of Schizophrenia in Primary and Secondary Care*, Clinical Guideline 1, National Institute for Clinical Excellence, London.

National Institute for Clinical Excellence (2003) *Schizophrenia: Full National Clinical Guideline on Core Interventions in Primary and Secondary Care*, Gaskell and The British Psychological Society, London.

Pearson, D., Burbach, F.R. and Stanbridge, R.I. (2007) Meeting the needs of families living with psychosis: implications for services. *Context*, **93**, 9–12.

Pharoah, F.M., Mari, J.J. and Streiner, D. (2002) Family intervention for schizophrenia (Cochrane Review), in *The Cochrane Library*, Issue 3, Update Software, Oxford.

Pitschel-Walz, G., Leucht, S., Bauml, J. *et al.* (2001) The effect of family interventions on relapse and rehospitilization in schizophrenia: a meta-analysis. *Schizophrenia Bulletin*, **27**, 73–92.

Procter, H.G. (1985) A construct approach to family therapy and systems intervention, in *Personal Construct Theory and Mental Health* (ed. E. Button), Croom Helm, Beckenham, Kent.

Procter, H.G. (1986) Change in the family construct system: the therapy of a mute and withdrawn schizophrenia patient, in (eds R. Neimeyer and G. Neimeyer), *A Casebook in Personal Construct Therapy*, Springer, New York.

Procter, H.G. and Pieczora, R. (1992) A family oriented community mental health centre, in *Using Family Therapy in the 90's* (eds A. Treacher and J. Carpenter), Blackwell, Oxford.

Procter, H.G. and Stephens, P.K.E. (1984) Developing family therapy in the day hospital, in *Using Family Therapy* (eds A. Treacher and J. Carpenter.), Blackwell, Oxford.

Quarry, A. and Burbach, F.R. (1998) Clinical consultancy in adult mental health: integrating whole team training and supervision. *Clinical Psychology Forum*, **120** (October), 14–7.

Schön, D.A. (1983) *The Reflective Practitioner: How Professionals Think in Action*, Basic Books, London.

Simpson, A. and Benn, L. (2007) *Scoping Exercise to Inform the Development of a National Mental Health Carer Support Curriculum*, City University, London/DOH, http://www.citypsych.com/docs/Carersfinal.pdf (accessed 2 October 2008).

Smith, G. and Velleman, R. (2002) Maintaining a family work service for psychosis service by recognising and addressing the barriers to implementation. *Journal of Mental Health*, **11**, 471–9.

Stanbridge, R.I. and Burbach, F.B. (2004) Enhancing working partnerships with carers and families in mainstream practice: a strategy and associated staff training programme. *The Mental Health Review*, **9** (4), 32–7.

Stanbridge, R.I. and Burbach, F.B. (2007a) Developing family inclusive mainstream mental health practice. *Journal of Family Therapy*, **29**, 21–43.

Stanbridge, R.I. and Burbach, F.B. (2007b) Involving carers Part 1: including carers in staff training and service development in Somerset, U.K., in *Families as Partners in Care: A Guidebook for Implementing Family Work*, Worldwide Fellowship for Schizophrenia and Allied Disorders, Toronto, chapter 5.

Stanbridge, R., Burbach, F. and Leftwich, S. (2008) Establishing family inclusive acute inpatient mental health services: a staff training programme in Somerset. *Journal of Family Therapy* (accepted for publication).

Stanbridge, R.I., Burbach, F.R., Lucas, A.S. and Carter, K. (2003) A study of families' satisfaction with a family interventions in psychosis service in Somerset. *Journal of Family Therapy*, **25**, 181–204.

Resources

www.earlydetection.csip.org.uk (accessed 2 October 2008).
www.eppic.org.au (accessed 2 October 2008).

www.hearingvoices.org (accessed 2 October 2008).

Barrowclough, C. and Tarrier, N. (1992) *Families of Schizophrenic Patients: Cognitive Behavioural Intervention*, Chapman & Hall, London.

Bertolino, B. and O'Hanlon, W.R. (2002) *Collaborative, Competency-Based Counselling and Therapy*, Allyn and Bacon.

Carr, A. (2000) *Family Therapy: Concepts, Process and Practice*, John Wiley & Sons, Ltd, Chichester.

Chadwick, P., Birchwood, M. and Trower, P. (1996) *Cognitive Therapy for Delusions, Voices and Paranoia*, John Wiley & Sons, Ltd, Chichester.

Falloon, I., Mueser, K., Gingerich, S. *et al.* (2004) *Family Work Manual*, Meriden West Midlands Family Programme.

14

Overcoming Barriers to Staff Offering Family Interventions in the NHS

Gráinne Fadden

It is an interesting concept to write a chapter on overcoming obstacles to delivering family work in a publication that is, in fact, a casebook outlining how to work with families: the book itself directly addresses one of the obstacles by equipping clinicians with knowledge about how to work therapeutically with families. However, we know from existing research that implementation of family work in routine clinical services is often difficult to achieve (Fadden, 1997; Kavanagh et al., 1993). This is in spite of the existence of many powerful drivers supporting the delivery of 'whole family' approaches to care. These include a robust evidence base (Bustillo et al., 2001; Pfammatter, Junghan and Brenner, 2006; Pilling et al., 2002; Pitschel-Walz et al., 2001) and in the United Kingdom a range of national policies and guidelines. Several of these refer directly to family work, such as Standard 6 of the National Service Framework for Mental Health (Department of Health, 1999), the NICE guidelines for schizophrenia (National Institute of Clinical Excellence, 2002) and the government white paper, Our Health, Our Care, Our Say (Department of Health, 2006).

However, as well as drivers, there are a wide range of complex factors that impede the delivery of family interventions. These are a combination of potential obstacles that are associated with those delivering family work, the recipients or the context in which the interaction between them takes place. The author of this chapter has described these drivers and impediments in greater detail in recent publications that readers may wish to refer to (Fadden, 2006a, 2006b).

It is intended that this chapter will help those at different levels in organisations to manage some of the difficulties they encounter in NHS (National

A Casebook of Family Interventions for Psychosis   Edited by Fiona Lobban and Christine Barrowclough
© 2009 John Wiley & Sons, Ltd

Health Service) settings when attempting to make services to families of those with psychosis more readily available. The reasons for the limited availability of family work are complex. Any attempt to tackle barriers to implementation therefore must be multi-faceted and imaginative. Readers will be provided with guidance on how to assess the factors that are blocking change towards more family-sensitive services. They will then be taken through a range of strategies for bringing about the type of change in the culture of organisations and the attitudes of staff that will facilitate the delivery of family work. This is an organisational change or organisational development model where, in a way, the organisation is the 'family' to be assessed and provided with an intervention. It may help the reader to think about the issues in that way in keeping with interventions described in the other chapters of the casebook.

Key issues addressed in the chapter include training, ongoing supervision, the role of managers at different levels in organisations, leadership, therapist attributes and how family members themselves can contribute to the development of services. Illustrations from organisations will be used when outlining strategies, and although these are taken from experiences in the United Kingdom we anticipate that the examples will be relevant to all readers. To create a realistic context for the reader, the interventions at an organisational level will be described in the context of a typical mental health Trust, with a range of changing issues and personnel with differing degrees of interest and motivation over time.

Context

Specific issues relevant to the implementation of family work

A question that is frequently asked in relation to family interventions is why implementation is so poor given the strong evidence base supporting them. This assumes of course that those charged with implementing family approaches place value on the concept of an evidence base. McFarlane *et al.* (2001) point out that publication of clinical trials in prestigious journals has a limited impact on clinicians' and organisations' practices when the individuals involved are not part of an academic setting. Indeed in my own experience in the West Midlands, I have encountered individuals at a senior level who comment that they know what the research evidence says, but that they do not believe a word of it! It is clear that proof of effectiveness of an intervention is necessary but not sufficient for its adoption in practice. The same applies in relation to policy – policy in itself will not produce change unless there is ongoing audit and performance management of implementation.

Rogers (1976) described the criteria that are relevant if a new innovation is to be diffused rapidly. These include factors such as compatibility with the theoretical training of clinicians, that it offers an advantage over existing treatments, that it is not more complex than existing treatments, that it can be tried out in a brief and easily evaluated form, and that the outcomes are observable in the short term. These factors help to explain why dissemination of family work has not always been successful. While family interventions clearly offer an advantage over standard treatments in mental health, they are complex to deliver, they must be delivered over a long time frame to be effective, the results occur in the long term, and they do not fit with the training that many clinicians have received.

Working with families and social networks challenges the culture of individual models of care that are dominant historically in most mental health services. Collaborative work practices that are implicit in family work challenge the ethos and culture of many services where there are clear power structures, and the voice of family members articulating their needs is not heard. In terms of training, one of the key issues for clinical staff is that they have not received any training in family work, with surveys showing that 70–80% of clinicians do not have training to work with families prior to undertaking any of the few in-service training post-qualification courses that exist (Fadden and Birchwood, 2002; Stanbridge and Burbach, 2007). This results in a lack of confidence, and a reluctance to take on family work. When this is combined with a lack of management commitment resulting in time not being allocated for this activity or for supervision, then the likelihood of people receiving family support is minimal.

Theoretical influences and style of approach used

The theoretical backdrop to family work implementation draws from the literature on organisational change such as models of driving and restraining forces for change (Lewin, 1951), and seminal papers challenging the ineffectiveness of hero-innovators and suggesting other strategies such as developing a supportive culture prior to conducting training and the importance of the organisational context (Georgiades and Phillimore, 1975). There are more recent publications on these topics that discuss how research evidence can be translated into practice (Iles and Sutherland, 2001; Palmer and Fenner, 1999; Ywye and McClenahan, 2000).

There is now a sufficient body of knowledge to guide us in relation to the implementation of family work specifically, and core principles can be derived from the current literature. It is clear that a key factor in effective implementation is input at an organisational level. Georgiades and Phillimore (1975) were clear that it is not possible to bring about change by changing individuals. They talk about working at an organisational level and developing a supportive host culture for any new innovation prior to introducing training. All of the services where family work has been implemented successfully have adopted this approach, and have worked with managers as well as clinicians (Burbach and Stanbridge, 2006; Fadden and Birchwood, 2002; Kelly and Newstead, 2004; Repper and Brooker, 2002; Smith and Velleman, 2002). Work at an organisational level includes strategies such as

- getting approval at senior management or board level;
- training of managers at lower levels such as team managers;
- the development of family work policies and implementation plans;
- whole team training or the establishment of a critical mass of trained workers;
- writing family work into job descriptions and annual plans;
- linking the reporting of implementation into organisational structures such as clinical governance committees;
- establishing regular audits.

Where family work has not been successfully implemented, or where family services have been unable to continue, lack of support from managers is often cited as a key difficulty either directly (Baguley et al., 2000) or through raising issues such as competing demands and high caseloads (Hughes et al., 1996).

Another key factor that emerges from this literature is the role of leaders and champions. The importance of having skilled, knowledgeable and supportive people in leadership roles is clear from the general literature on change management (Department of Health, 2004). It is recognised as crucial in family work implementation (Corrigan et al., 2001), whether this is achieved through appointing experienced people in coordinator roles (Smith and Velleman, 2002) or as experienced trainers and supervisors

(Fadden and Birchwood, 2002). Support from colleagues is also seen as key, whether this is achieved through whole team training (Stanbridge and Burbach, 2007), co-working (Smith, Gregory and Higgs, 2007) or through bringing those trained together into geographical groups (Fadden and Birchwood, 2002). Supervision and regular training updates are also crucial.

Therapist training and attributes of change agents

We are aware that there are certain therapist characteristics such as humanity and flexibility that facilitate family work being implemented (James, Cushway and Fadden, 2006). The characteristics of effective change agents have also been described. These include credibility, high levels of energy, ability to communicate and work effectively in multiple environments and a willingness to confront difficult issues (Hemmelgarn, Glisson and James, 2006; Rogers, 1995). A detailed account of issues relating to family work training can be found in the Fadden (2007) chapter in the recent publication from the World Fellowship for Schizophrenia and Allied Disorders (Froggatt *et al.*, 2007).

The clinical service

The climate and culture of a service influences the type of service that clients receive (Hemmelgarn, Glisson and James, 2006). All services will have both internal and external demands placed on them. Attention must therefore be paid to the broader organisational context when introducing any new programme. Strategies for how to do this have been described in the organisational change literature and include creating a sense of urgency, having a vision that is communicated well and institutionalising new approaches (Kotter and Schlesinger, 1979), with others emphasising factors such as strong leadership and having an implementation plan (Kanter, Stein and Jick, 1992). These have been adapted for application to the implementation of family work (Leggatt, 2007).

The crucial role played by family members has also been emphasised (Corrigan *et al.*, 2001; Woodhams, 2007). Cleary, Freeman and Walter (2006) and Fadden, Shooter and Holsgrove (2005) have highlighted the need for training and preparation of staff to ensure they work effectively with family members or carer consultants and trainers.

Constraints on the intervention

The main issue here is sustainability – it is easy enough to get something started but making sure that this is maintained over time tends to need continued commitment from people who champion this type of work – otherwise achievements are likely to be lost. A second constraint is that this model is not likely to be applicable to developing countries.

Organisational Case Study

Context

In the United Kingdom, health services are delivered in geographical areas with their own management and financial structures known as Trusts. The mental health Trust in which this intervention took place, serves a population of 500 000, with a range of community teams and some inpatient facilities. The geographical area includes urban centres, some with areas of high deprivation and a rich cultural mix and other rural areas with primarily farming communities, some in quite remote areas. The community services were offered through functionalised teams, including assertive outreach teams, crisis/home treatment teams, primary care liaison teams and some rehabilitation and recovery services. Over the course of the work in the Trust, an early intervention service was developing.

There was a Chief Executive and a Board of Directors, but most of the responsibility for operationalising service delivery was devolved to the Mental Health Services Manager and to the Head of Nursing. There was a training department, though this did not appear to operate in a very coherent manner. Different people in the organisation set up training events, although this did not fit in with any clear organisational plan, and there was no follow through of training and its implementation.

The initial thrust for the intervention that will be described at an organisational level came from the Chief Executive who was keen to ensure that the recommendations of the NICE Guidelines on Schizophrenia (National

Institute of Clinical Excellence, 2002) were implemented in the organisation. In relation to family work, the guidelines recommended that 100% of people with schizophrenia who were in contact with their families should receive family support. The Trust had come out badly on measures of numbers of carer's assessments that had been offered since this had been stipulated by the Department of Health (1999) as an entitlement for anyone caring for someone with severe mental health difficulties. Only 10% of families in the area had received assessments. He was also becoming irritated and concerned by the number of complaints from families about particular aspects of the service they were dissatisfied with. There was also lobbying from local carers' groups. He therefore decided that the Trust was underperforming in relation to services to families, and wanted to change this so that the Trust would, in his terms, become a 'Model Organisation' in relation to services to families that others would look to for ideas on how to provide excellence in this area. An external family work consultant was therefore called in to assess the situation, to advise on what needed to be done, to help with bringing about change and to monitor and report on progress over time to the Board of the Trust. It is important that this person has credibility, a genuine interest in bringing about change and a willingness to see the process through. The Chief Executive anticipated that the situation would be changed within a year, so the initial contract with the external consultant was for a 12-month period.

Year 1: months 1–6: engagement methods and issues

The Chief Executive nominated the Mental Health Services Manager as a link person for the family work consultant in terms of planning how to take things forward. The consultant met with this manager to gather information on the Trust, to identify what was happening already and to begin to identify key people who would facilitate the process of making the delivery of family work more consistent, as well as those who may be likely to block changes. It was agreed that as a starting point it would be useful to bring together all those who were relevant and interested in the implementation of family work for a half-day workshop. This included managers and senior clinicians from both health and social care, as well as representatives from voluntary agencies, in particular representatives from carers' groups. The consultant met with a small number of key people individually prior to the workshop. Among these were the Head of Nursing, the Medical Director, two members of nursing staff who had been running carer support groups for a number of years, a systemic family therapist employed in the Trust, and some family members who were particularly vocal about the lack of good services. It is always important to have meetings like this prior to going into a group setting – you need to know the views of key people so that you have time in advance to think about how to respond to issues that might be raised, and also to know who your allies are if things become difficult during the meeting.

The meeting was well attended (60 people) as the importance of attending was emphasised in the invitation which came jointly from the Chief Executive and Mental Health Services Manager. The family work consultant presented the research evidence supporting family work as well as government policy relating to the needs of families, including those relating to parental mental ill health. A coffee break allowed the participants to chat informally to each other. The group was then broken into five smaller groups and were asked to discuss what assets the Trust had in terms of implementing family work, and what were the likely hindrances. This formed part of the assessment that will be discussed in the next section. There was then an attempt at bringing together the ideas that had been shared, and some targets were agreed in terms of how to begin to make progress towards the goal of having more widespread availability of family work. These will be discussed in the formulation section.

Assessment

There are a number of models that are helpful in terms of assessing an organisation, and how to progress a goal such as that outlined above. The force-field model (Lewin, 1951) is probably one of the simplest but most useful in that it is helpful in identifying both driving and restraining forces for change. There are other simple techniques such as listing down key players and categorising them in terms of which are key in making things happen, who are more passive but need to be on-side, and who are the people who stop things happening (Appendix 1). It is then possible to come up with strategies for helping people to shift categories so that they are more strategically positioned to bring about change. This technique has been adapted from the work of Colville (2002; personal communication).

In the Trust in question, the driving and restraining forces were identified as follows:

Driving forces	Restraining forces
• Commitment of the Chief Executive • Family members already have a voice in the Trust • Some staff genuinely interested in family issues, for example those who were running the carer support groups • Systemic family therapist already employed in Trust • Mental Health Services Manager identified as responsible manager • Lot of committed staff willing to receive training and improve their skills • Out of hours working system already in place • Training facilities available in the Trust	• Training department had no coordinated plan in relation to family work training • Budgetary issues meant little money available for training or backfilling posts • Supervision not prioritised • Very few staff with any training in family work • Poor audit results in relation to services to families • Rivalries between different teams • Inpatient staff have limited access to training because of low staff numbers • Uncertainty about how much time the mental health services manager could commit to this initiative

During the initial assessment period, and through meetings following the workshop, the family work consultant was able to identify the key assets in the Trust, and also the factors that were likely to get in the way. It was clear from conversations with clinical staff that this was on the whole a committed workforce, keen to do the best for their clients. It was also clear that the relationship between the clinicians and management was not one of trust, with clinicians often being critical about the level of support they received from management. Team managers similarly were often critical of senior management who felt that they paid lip service to improving services but were not willing to put in the necessary resources.

Formulation and plan of action

It was clear that as is the case in many mental health services, history and tradition determined that the service was focused on providing care to individuals, and had not embraced a family-centred model of care. Following the assessment and various meetings, a plan of action was agreed to begin the progress of the overall goal of improving services to families, and taking account of the drivers and restraining forces listed above. It seemed as if there was sufficient motivation and commitment in the organisation to bring about change. The first agreed aim was to train the clinical staff in the skills needed to deliver evidence-based family approaches. It was clear that someone needed to be available in the organisation to coordinate this, and the Mental Health Services Manager did not have time to do this because of all of his other responsibilities. Fortuitously, some money became available from an underspend in a budget that enabled a half-time post to be backfilled. This enabled the creation of a half-time coordinator post for a year to facilitate getting the initiative underway. One of the nurses who had been running carer support groups applied for this post and was appointed. One-off funds were also made available to cover the cost of having external trainers provide some initial training, and to cover costs of training materials and catering on courses. Training facilities were available in-house and therefore did not incur any costs. This initial phase of the initiative took place over a 6-month period.

The intervention

Year 1: months 7–12. It was decided to train up a group of 30 clinicians initially to create a critical mass of trained therapists in order to give the initiative a kick-start. This first training course was delivered by three external trainers with three local clinicians, the systemic family therapist and the newly appointed coordinator, and the other staff member who had been delivering carer support groups acting as co-facilitators. The model of training used was that advocated through the Meriden West Midlands Family Programme which is a 5-day skills-based training with a 1:5 tutor to trainee ratio, a detailed training manual which acts as a guide for those trained, with training being followed by detailed ongoing supervision and ongoing training updates (Fadden and Birchwood, 2002). Following the training, it was anticipated that those trained would have the knowledge of the evidence base around family work and would have the skills to help families to increase their understanding of the disorder, and to help them to develop their communication and problem-solving skills.

The first issue that arose was how participants for the first course should be selected. The evidence is that team training or developing a critical mass of people trained in a particular area is more effective. In the trust described here, this would have meant training two or three teams to start off with. However, there were strong rivalries between the teams, and all of the team managers wanted some of their staff trained. All were reluctant to have their team wait for training, as they were concerned that their team would come out badly when the delivery of family work was audited again. Their argument was that it would look as if some teams had made progress and others had not. It was therefore agreed that two people would be trained from a large number of teams.

Knowing from follow-up of staff trained in the Thorn Programme (Brooker *et al.*, 2003) that two people trained from a team are unlikely to bring about major change, it was decided that three training courses with 30 staff on each would be held in the first 6 months in order to ensure that most teams would at least have a small number of staff trained making it more likely that a culture where family work was seen as the norm would begin to develop. This was an ambitious plan, but was achieved, and supervisory groups were put in place with each of the people who had been involved in training each supervising 15 clinicians.

Year 2: months 1–6. A review of progress was held at the end of the first year. This was attended by many of those who attended the initial workshop. Importantly, both the Chief Executive and Mental Health Services Manager stayed for the entire morning, thus giving a very clear message that they supported the initiative. Everyone was delighted that 90 people had already been trained in family work, and two people trained on the first course 6 months previously gave enthusiastic accounts of their experiences of engaging families, and the benefits that ensued both for the families and for them as clinicians.

It was agreed that the external trainers/supervisors would continue to be engaged for the following 6 months to ensure that the training was established and that supervisory structures were in place. It was then envisaged that a number of those who had been implementing family work successfully would do further training to become trainers and supervisors, and that the training and supervision would then take place in-house, with the family work consultant remaining in an advisory role until the end of year 2 to ensure that everything was going to plan and that family work was firmly embedded in the various services.

Training continued during this 6-month period, with two smaller courses of 20 people each being held. While those attending the first three courses were all qualified clinical staff, on the fourth and fifth courses there was more of a mix with some support workers and some people from voluntary agencies. The idea was that both of these groups could work alongside qualified staff.

Regular data on implementation were collected, and about two-thirds of those trained were either working with families or were attempting to engage families. This is often the case with the first groups of staff trained in that those who are most enthusiastic tend to volunteer for training first. Attendance at supervision was good – it had been emphasised throughout training that people should attend supervision even if they had not engaged a family in that they could learn from others and get support on methods of engagement that would be likely to be successful. One issue that was emerging at the end of this 6-month period however was that the supervision groups were now becoming too large with 130 people trained but only six supervisors.

Meetings between the family work consultant and the Mental Health Services Manager were held at regular intervals allowing problems to be ironed out quickly. Examples included funding for materials (workbooks), equipment (tape recorders, a video player) and refreshments, and advice on how to deal with a couple of team managers who were being particularly obstructive.

Year 2: months 7–12. During this 6-month period, it was decided that the focus should be on ensuring that implementation was taking place, and on developing robust supervision structures. Only one training course took place in this time slot, and this had to be rescheduled due to problems with the first dates that had been set. This was because on this particular course, the majority of the participants were inpatient staff along with a number of unqualified and support staff. Two days before the course was due to run, the inpatient ward managers said they could not release the staff for training due to staff shortages and crises on the ward. Obviously, this was very disruptive as venues had been booked and the trainers had set the time aside. In exploring the issues, it transpired that the ward managers had been raising this issue for some time and felt their concerns were not being heard by senior management. They realised that because of the emphasis being given to family work within the trust, and because external trainers and a consultant were being funded, that if they made an issue that affected the training, their concerns would then be listened to. A meeting was called with senior management to look at how these issues could be resolved.

A crisis that arose at the beginning of this period was that the funding for the half-time coordinator post that had been agreed for a year ran out, and this post was at risk of not being sustained. This person played a central role in terms of being a central link person for family work, organised training courses, coordinated supervision and along with the family work consultant played a key role in relation to monitoring implementation. Another unrelated issue that needed to be addressed was that it became clear that there were not adequate systems for recording family work as the recording systems were based on models of working with individuals. It was essential to address this.

Over this time the Mental Health Services Manager seemed more distracted, frequently interrupting meetings by taking calls on his mobile phone. He announced towards the end of the second year of the initiative that he was resigning and was taking a post in another Trust. This created a problem in that he was not replaced immediately, and there was therefore a gap in terms of having a senior link person. However, it also created an opportunity in that he had blocked all attempts up to now to establish a representative family work steering group stating that this was not necessary given that he was around and could sort out any difficulties.

Eight people attended a training course to train as family work trainers and supervisors at the end of this period. These included the three clinicians who had been assisting the external trainers, as well as five staff who had been working with families since completing training on the first two courses that were held. This meant that the trust would no longer have to purchase external trainers and supervisors. Perhaps because of this projected saving, concern over the fact that the Mental Health Services Manager was leaving, and the number of other issues that needed to be addressed, the Chief Executive, recognising that what had been achieved to date was threatened, found money to continue to support the half-time coordinator post.

Year 3: months 1–6. It felt that this year started with some uncertainties such as who would be the senior manager link person, and with a number of issues to be resolved. On the other hand, there were a number of positives in that the ongoing commitment from the Trust Board was clear, and the coordinator post was secure. The family work consultant saw it as priority to establish a Family Work Steering Group that would begin to take an overview of the whole process of family work implementation within the Trust. This group was established and began to meet monthly. Membership of the group consisted of the Head of Nursing until a new Mental Health Services Manager was appointed, a representative from social services, the family work consultant, the family work coordinator, three trainers/supervisors from different service areas in the Trust, two family members, a carer support worker and a service user.

The Steering Group began to identify some key issues that had to be addressed including the following:

- Numbers of staff trained in different service and geographical areas. It was clear that take-up of training varied, with some community teams and assertive outreach teams being overrepresented, while others such as home treatment/crisis teams and inpatient staff were underrepresented. The family members were concerned that the availability of family work varied from one area to another – if you were served by one team, you would receive help whereas in another area, nothing was available.
- *Recording systems for family work.* The existing paperwork and electronic systems did not pick up family work accurately. Because there were no actual categories for recording this type of intervention, staff were noting it down in a variety of ways as indirect contacts, or not recording it at all. Family members were also keen that there was some mechanism for recording in the inpatient notes whether the person admitted to hospital had a family, and also if they had been offered any information or support.
- *Implementation.* Although it was clear there was great enthusiasm among staff to receive training, the same energy was not being applied to implementation. There was a great deal of variation in terms of the extent to which those trained were delivering family work.
- *Supervision.* As more staff were trained, attendance at supervision which had been excellent initially began to fall off. This made it hard to monitor exactly what was happening and was of concern from the point of view of clinical governance.

Resolving the recording issues was a process that would take time, but a start was made with some of the group members agreeing to meet with those responsible for recording data within the Trust. The other priority focused on was supervision attendance. During this period, venues and timing of supervision were changed in response to requests from those who had been trained. Tighter record keeping of attendance was also introduced.

At the end of this period, a replacement Mental Health Services Manager was appointed who came from outside the Trust and therefore had to be brought up to speed with several areas of work, and did not see family work as a priority initially. It was quite hard to keep family work as a high priority on the Trust Board agenda without this senior point of contact.

Year 3: months 7–12. At the beginning of this period, the commissioners of the service began to express concerns that availability of services to families was still not widespread. This was reinforced by results of an audit of family work carried out by the Healthcare Commission showing that the delivery of family work in the service was patchy, with several areas where none was being delivered. Added to this were the continuing poor results in relation to the availability of carers' assessment as stipulated in the National Service Framework for Mental Health. The process research that was ongoing in this initiative confirmed the erratic nature of implementation. Because of the threat of some funding being withdrawn from the service, it was decided to bring forward the annual review meeting.

The new Mental Health Services Manager realised that he needed to become more closely involved in this issue. A number of key decisions were made at this meeting:

- The Mental Health Services Manager realised that he needed to give a renewed strong message on behalf of the Trust of the importance of this work. This would be communicated to staff and managers through a variety of media.
- The steering group was charged with drawing up a clear family work policy and associated implementation plan that would clearly delineate the responsibilities of staff at all levels in relation to the implementation of family work with clear time frames by which goals would be achieved.
- The geographical and team distribution of training was to be looked at more closely, with priority being given in the following year to areas where there were gaps, either on particular teams or in service areas, for example crisis and home treatment teams.
- It was agreed that the trainers/supervisors would between them arrange to meet all team managers individually to discuss with them whether there were any issues specific to their team in relation to implementation or freeing up staff to attend supervision.

- The system of supervision was to be looked at more closely with a view to ensuring that this was firmly in place either on a locality basis or by functional team group, whichever would be most effective in increasing the likelihood of attendance.
- Family members were to become more involved in training.
- Protected time to be agreed for the trainers/supervisors.
- A family link worker was to be identified on all teams.
- Audit data on implementation to be reviewed at three-monthly intervals.

This meeting was extremely constructive and resulted in everyone having renewed motivation to bring about change.

Year 4: months 1–6. The meetings with team managers helped to identify local issues that could then be resolved. It also helped to flush out those who had been passively opposing this initiative, and the strength of the message from the organisation made it clear that this was going to continue to be priority, and that managers needed to look seriously at progressing the targets that had been set, because they would not be changed. Some of the managers felt they had too many priorities to meet. The outcome of these meetings was an agreement on training for managers on their role in implementing family work, in addition to a meeting with senior management to look at how the various priorities could be accommodated.

It was agreed that team managers would be provided with more regular feedback on implementation figures and rates of attendance at supervision so that they could monitor more closely what was happening in their teams.

Many of the team managers felt that the psychiatrists in the organisation were not playing the role they could in relation to this, and that they could be much more influential if they emphasised the importance of family work more in their clinical meetings. This resulted in a meeting between the Medical Director, the Mental Health Services Director and the Family Work Consultant to discuss this. The outcome was a specific training session on this topic for psychiatrists as they had not attended many of the generic meetings or training events.

The steering group continued with its work on developing more effective recording systems, although it was a slow process to try to get the systems changed.

At the end of this 6-month period, it felt that there was a much clearer picture of what the issues were across the whole organisation, and what needed to be done to ensure widespread implementation.

Year 4: months 7–12. This 6-month period saw many developments in relation to driving implementation forward. Training was provided for team managers consisting of factual information about the family work evidence base, policy, and assisting them in reflecting on their role as culture carriers. This resulted in identifying practical ways in which they could improve implementation such as having family work as a standing item on the clinical team meeting agenda each week, asking clinicians whom they managed about clients' families and their needs when reviewing their caseloads with them, encouraging attendance at supervision by clinicians and rewarding staff who were engaging with families through praise, acknowledgement and encouragement.

Attendance at supervision overall improved, and because an additional group of trainers/supervisors had been trained, some of this could be delivered at team level, thus making it more accessible. The steering group continued to meet monthly during this crucial period. The family work policy and implementation plan, drawn up by the committee, was launched and communicated to all relevant managers and clinicians. The group was also successful in introducing other changes such as having family work written into the job descriptions of all new clinical staff joining the Trust. A system of monitoring and giving feedback directly to each team regarding the number of families in need of and receiving help was also introduced, which enabled problems to be identified and acted on quickly.

Attention in particular was paid to the training of the home treatment and crisis teams. The training programme was adapted to help them to identify how they could ensure they offered support to families during the short time frame during which they usually saw them. It proved difficult to keep this group of staff on track as they tended to have quite traditional views in terms of their role being primarily to meet the needs of the client. Their perception of family work often consisted of telling the family about changes in medication, or solving problems for the family rather than helping them to learn ways of dealing with crisis that did not involve dependency on the team. Team handovers frequently ran over using up some of the time that had been allocated for family work supervision. This area needed ongoing attention.

Year 5. By the fifth year, it felt as if most of the hard work had been done and that what remained was to ensure that robust structures were in place to sustain what had been achieved. The following is a summary of systems that were put in place:

- Performance management of the delivery of family work was linked in with clinical governance structures within the Trust.
- The half-time coordinator post was made substantive.
- It was agreed that two smaller training courses would be held each year to ensure that all staff including newly appointed staff would have access to training. The training department became involved so that this training would be seen as part of mainstream training. There was discussion about whether this training should be considered as mandatory, but a decision was made that it should be high priority rather than mandatory.
- A system of continuous monitoring of implementation and regular feedback to managers and teams was maintained.
- An agreement about a major annual review including review of the implementation plan was put in place. Presentations by families about the benefits to them of receiving this kind of help were to play a vital role in helping everyone to understand why this initiative was being supported.
- Regular meetings with the commissioners of the service were set in place so that any concerns could be identified early on, and could be addressed, rather than issues arising at the time when contracts and service level agreements were due for renewal.
- The role of family members was formally recognised with a family member being appointed along with the family work coordinator as the people who linked with the clinical governance committee.

Outcome and evaluation

The various outcomes of this initiative have been described above – in implementing family work the outcomes are multi-faceted. There are some simple numerical outcomes that can be described, such as numbers of therapists trained to deliver family work, numbers of those implementing the approach, number of families receiving help, attendance at supervision and audits of delivery of family work across geographical and service areas. There are then more detailed measures such as barriers to implementation and difficulties encountered by staff which have been used in many of the studies (Brooker *et al.*, 2003; Fadden, 1997). It is also possible to look at the perceptions and attitudes of staff (Bailey, Burbach and Lea, 2003) and levels of satisfaction in families receiving the approach (Stanbridge *et al.*, 2003). Measures of organisational change are also possible, though these are more common in industry than in health services. It is valuable to obtain measures of change, but as in the current example, those commissioning the work do not always see the value of this when they are eager to get a problem solved as quickly as possible, and are often unwilling to invest in the additional costs that this would give rise to.

Critical reflection

The service case study gives rise to a number of issues for readers to reflect on:

- The appointment of the part-time coordinator was crucial in terms of progressing family work. The person in this role can perform any number of tasks together with those who are charged with training and supervision. The range of tasks performed by people in these roles within the Meriden Programme is outlined in Appendix 2. Attention needs to be paid to how to ensure that they have protected time and a budget allocation if the role is to be established.
- The establishment of a critical mass of clinicians with family work skills is essential. This is probably best achieved through whole team training, but as the case study demonstrates, this is not always feasible initially.
- Involvement of carers/service users from the start and throughout is crucial for keeping the whole process on track.
- An interesting question is whether or not family work training should be mandatory? Some are of the view that if it is an essential part of the work of clinicians, then they should be obliged to receive training in it.
- Some budget allocation is necessary, whether this is small for venues, materials and equipment, or large, for example for coordinator post.
- A necessary condition for successful implementation is having a key link person in a senior management position.
- Implementation of family work is unlikely unless a system for the performance management of delivery of family work is established.
- Setting up a steering committee ensures representation of all key players, and ideally this should happen early on.
- A family work policy with a linked clear implementation plan gives status to initiatives such as this. The question of where to start – with a policy, with training or just encouraging people to get on and demonstrate early successes?

- Trusts often do not take into the equation the cost to the organisation of releasing staff for training when considering overall costs of training. Senior management need to be reminded of this outlay of money.
- The role of psychiatrists can be very supportive, but often can appear to be passive unless encouraged to play a more active role.
- Specific types of teams have specific needs, for example home treatment/ crisis teams who have short periods of contact with families, primary care liaison teams or community mental health teams who may not have out of hours systems in place, or inpatient staff who may be unsure about their roles.

Conclusions

Research has shown that clinicians can deliver family interventions, even after relatively brief training (Magliano *et al.*, 2006). However, the task of ensuring that family work becomes core business across an organisation is complex. It takes time and persistence, and should be seen as a process, not something that is achieved overnight. This is because you are dealing with a dynamic system, both in terms of those who deliver family work and the families who are the recipients. However, there is enough evidence now to show that it is possible.

In any organisation, there will always be some keen, enthusiastic people both at a clinical and managerial level who have experience, for example in relation to supervision that can be transferred to this area of work. Often, these members of staff are just waiting for an opportunity to develop their skills and to become involved in a challenging initiative such as that described. The trick is to tap into this resource.

When trying to bring about change, problems do not always arise at the beginning as there is often a honeymoon period, and it is after a couple of years that the real issues emerge. You need to be prepared for this, and not become despondent. Stand back, assess the situation and plan how to move forward again.

Inevitably, you get caught up in local politics. You know from the literature how things should best be done, but you do not always have control over this. You need to be pragmatic and think on your feet. Go with the best option you can manage, even though you know it is not ideal. There are always ups and downs, but you must not become despondent. You will usually find that after a setback, there are often positive consequences. The benefit of course is that you will never be bored and if you are a manager or clinician looking for a challenge, this is an ideal area in which to work!

References

Baguley, I., Butterworth, T., Fahy, K. *et al.* (2000) Bringing into clinical practice skills shown to be effective in research settings: a follow up of Thorn training in psychosocial interventions for psychosis, in *Psychosis: Psychological Approaches and Their Effectiveness* (eds B. Martindale, A. Bateman, M. Crowe and F. Margison), Gaskell, London, pp. 96–119.

Bailey, R., Burbach, F.R. and Lea, S. (2003) The ability of staff trained in family interventions to implement the approach in routing clinical practice. *Journal of Mental Health*, **12**, 131–41.

Brooker, C., Saul, C., Robinson, J. *et al.* (2003) Is training in psychosocial interventions worthwhile? Report of a psychosocial intervention trainee follow-up study. *International Journal of Nursing Studies*, **40**, 731–47.

Burbach, F. and Stanbridge, R. (2006) Somerset's family interventions in psychosis service: an update. *Journal of family Therapy*, **28**, 39–57.

Bustillo, J.R., Lauriello, J., Horan, W.P. and Keith, S.J. (2001) The psychological treatment of schizophrenia: an update. *American Journal of Psychiatry*, **158** (2), 163–75.

Cleary, M., Freeman, A. and Walter, G. (2006) Carer participation in mental health service delivery. *International Journal of Mental Health Nursing*, **15**, 189–94.

Corrigan, P.W., Steiner, L., McCracken, S.G. *et al.* (2001) Strategies for disseminating evidence-based practices to staff who treat people with serious mental illness. *Psychiatric Services*, **52**, 1598–606.

Department of Health (1999) *National Service Framework for Mental Health: Modern Standards and Service Models*, HMSO, London.

Department of Health (2004) Layers of Leadership: Hidden Influencers of Healthcare Improvement, Research into practice, Report No. 10, Department of Health, London.

Department of Health (2006) *Our Health, Our Care, Our Say: A New Direction for Community Health Services*, Department of Health, London.

Fadden, G. (1997) Implementation of family interventions in routine clinical practice: a major cause for concern. *Journal of Mental Health*, **6**, 599–612.

Fadden, G. (2006a) Training and disseminating family interventions for schizophrenia: developing family intervention skills with multi-disciplinary groups. *Journal of Family Therapy*, **28**, 23–38.

Fadden, G. (2006b) Family interventions, in *Enabling Recovery: The Principles and Practice of Rehabilitation Psychiatry* (eds G. Roberts, S. Davenport, F. Holloway and T. Tattan), Gaskell, London, pp. 158–69.

Fadden, G. (2007) Involving and training professionals in family work, in *Families as Partners in Care: A Guidebook for Implementing Family Work* (eds D. Froggatt, G. Fadden, D.L. Johnson *et al.*), World Fellowship for Schizophrenia and Allied Disorders, Toronto, pp. 38–49.

Fadden, G. and Birchwood, M. (2002) British models for expanding family psychoeducation in routine practice, in *Family Interventions in Mental Illness: International Perspectives* (eds H.P. Lefley and D.L. Johnson.), Praeger, Westport, CT.

Fadden, G., Shooter, M. and Holsgrove, G. (2005) Involving carers and service users in the training of psychiatrists. *Psychiatric Bulletin*, **29**, 270–4.

Froggatt, D., Fadden, G., Johnson, D.L. *et al.* (eds) (2007) *Families as Partners in Care: A Guidebook for Implementing Family Work*, World Fellowship for Schizophrenia and Allied Disorders, Toronto.

Georgiades, N.J. and Phillimore, L. (1975) The myth of the hero-innovator and alternative strategies for organisational change, in *Behaviour Modification in the Severely Retarded* (eds C.C. Kiernan and F.P. Woodford), Associated Science Press, Amsterdam.

Hemmelgarn, A.L., Glisson, C. and James, L.R. (2006) Organizational culture and climate: implications for services and interventions research. *Clinical Psychology: Science and Practice*, **13** (1), 73–89.

Hughes, I., Hailwood, R., Abbati-Yeoman, J. and Budd, R. (1996) Developing a family intervention service for serious mental illness: clinical observations and experiences. *Journal of Mental Health*, **5**, 145–59.

Iles, V. and Sutherland, K. (2001) *Organisational Change: A Review for Health Care Managers, Professionals and Researchers*, SDO, London.

James, C., Cushway, D. and Fadden, G. (2006) What works in engagement of families in behavioural family therapy? A positive model for the therapist perspective. *Journal of Mental Health*, **28**, 23–38.

Kanter, R.M., Stein, B. and Jick, T. (1992) *The Challenge of Organisational Change*, Free Press, London.

Kavanagh, D.J., Piatkowska, O., Clarke, D. *et al.* (1993) Application of cognitive-behavioural family intervention for schizophrenia in multi-disciplinary teams: what can the matter be? *Australian Psychologist*, **28**, 181–8.

Kelly, M. and Newstead, L. (2004) Family intervention in routine practice: it is possible! *Journal of Psychiatric and Mental Health Nursing*, **11**, 64–72.

Kotter, J. and Schlesinger, L. (1979) Choosing strategies for change. *Harvard Business Review*, **57** (2), 106–14.

Leggatt, M. (2007) Meeting the challenges, in *Families as Partners in Care: A Guidebook for Implementing Family Work* (eds D. Froggatt, G. Fadden, D.L. Johnson *et al.*), World Fellowship for Schizophrenia and Allied Disorders, Toronto, pp. 22–37.

Lewin, K. (1951) *Field Theory in Social Sciences*, Harper Row, New York.

Magliano, L., Fiorillo, A., Malangone, C. *et al.* (2006) Implementing psychoeducational interventions in Italy for patients with schizophrenia and their families. *Psychiatric Services*, **57**, 266–9.

McFarlane, W., McNary, S., Dixon, L. and Hornby, H. (2001) Predictors of dissemination of family psychoeducation in community mental health centres in Maine and Illinois. *Psychiatric Services*, **52**, 935–42.

National Institute of Clinical Excellence (2002) *Schizophrenia: Core Interventions in the Treatment and Management of Schizophrenia in Primary and Secondary Care*, National Collaborating Centre for Mental Health, London.

Palmer, C. and Fenner, J. (1999) *Getting the Message Across: Review of Research and Theory Disseminating Information within the NHS*, Gaskell, London.

Pfammatter, M., Junghan, U.M. and Brenner, H.D. (2006) Efficacy of psychological therapy in schizophrenia: conclusions from meta-analyses. *Schizophrenia Bulletin*, **32**, S64–80.

Pilling, S., Bebbington, P., Kuipers, E. *et al.* (2002) Psychological treatments in schizophrenia. I. Meta-analysis of family intervention and cognitive behaviour therapy. *Psychological Medicine*, **32**, 763–82.

Pitschel-Walz, G., Leucht, S., Bäuml, J. *et al.* (2001) The effect of family interventions on relapse and rehospitalisation in schizophrenia – a meta-analysis. *Schizophrenia Bulletin*, **27**, 73–92.

Repper, D. and Brooker, C. (2002) *Avoiding the Washout: Developing the Organisational Context to Increase the Uptake of Evidence-Based Practice for Psychosis*, Northern Centre for Mental Health Publication Series.

Rogers, E.M. (1976) New product adoption and diffusion. *Journal of Consumer Research*, **2**, 290–301.

Rogers, E.M. (1995) *Diffusion of Innovations*, 4th edn, Free Press, New York.

Smith, G., Gregory, K. and Higgs, A. (2007) *An Integrated Approach to Family Work for Psychosis: A Manual for Family Workers*, Jessica Kingsley, London.

Smith, G. and Velleman, R. (2002) Maintaining a family work service for psychosis service by recognising and addressing the barriers to implementation. *Journal of Mental Health*, **11**, 471–179.

Stanbridge, R.I. and Burbach, F.R. (2007) Developing family inclusive mainstream mental health services. *Journal of Family Therapy*, **29**, 21–43.

Stanbridge, R.I., Burbach, F.R., Lucas, A.S. and Carter, K. (2003) A study of families' satisfaction with a family interventions in psychosis service in Somerset. *Journal of Family Therapy*, **25**, 181–204.

Woodhams, P. (2007) Involving and training carers: Part 2, in *Families as Partners in Care: A Guidebook for Implementing Family Work* (eds D. Froggatt, G. Fadden, D.L. Johnson *et al.*), World Fellowship for Schizophrenia and Allied Disorders, Toronto, pp. 65–75.

Ywye, L. and McClenahan, T. (2000) *Getting Better with Evidence: Experience of Putting Evidence into Practice*, King's Fund, London.

Resources

Many of the articles in the reference list offer useful resources. Probably the best up to date single starting point to guide readers, and provide an overview of issues is the recent publication:

Froggatt, D., Fadden, G., Johnson, D.L. *et al.* (eds) (2007). *Families as Partners in Care: A Guidebook for Implementing Family Work*, World Fellowship for Schizophrenia and Allied Disorders, Toronto.

Copies of sample family work policies and implementation plans are available through the author, and the Somerset family service also have a range of policies and strategy documents, so making contact with those experiences in the area is useful.

Back copies of Meriden Newsletter available on the Meriden Programme web site, www.meridenfamilyprogramme.com also contain useful articles, for example on implementing family work in different service areas such as assertive outreach or on home treatment teams that readers will find helpful.

Further Reading

Fadden, G. (1998) 'Family Intervention', in *Serious Mental Health Problems in the Community* (eds C. Brooker and J. Repper), Balliere Tindall Limited, London.

Appendix 1: Assessment of the Position of Key Players in an Organisation

Identify the key people you manage who could support the implementation of family work, and tick where they are now in one colour, and where you would like them to be in another.

	Key players (name)	No commitment	Let it happen	Help it happen	Make it happen
1					
2					
3					
4					
5					
6					
7					
8					
9					
10					

Appendix 2: The Role of Trainer/Supervisor in the Meriden Programme

1. Running training courses in the Trust/Social Services area in collaboration with trainers from own area, or with trainers from other areas where they combine for training.
2. To provide supervision within the Trust for those attending training courses – preferably taking responsibility initially for those attending courses run by you.
3. To keep registers of those who attend supervision, and to follow-up actively those who fail to attend supervision. Problem-solve issues with them.
4. To coordinate supervision sessions provided by the Meriden team in the trust groupings (usually 4). This involves the following:
   - Arranging venue and refreshments.
   - Sending details of the date/venue to all those in the supervision group and to the relevant Meriden supervisor 2–4 weeks prior to the event.
   - Agree on someone to coordinate the meeting – being there when people arrive and so on.
5. Attend regional update days on the programme.
6. Disseminate information from the programme staff, evaluator or administrator to all trainees in the Trust regarding the programme.
7. To liaise with management in Trust/Social services area to ensure that the programme retains a high profile within Trusts, and to promote the approach.
8. To conduct audits of those trained in terms of who is practicing, who is not, what difficulties they encounter, what teams/areas people have been trained in and so on.
9. To assist with data collection for the evaluation.
10. To plan with the other trainers and with management how this approach will be maintained and embedded as 'core business' in mental health services.
11. To act as a referral point for families.
12. To liaise with the relevant training departments.
13. To liaise with health or social services departments as appropriate.
14. To run refresher days for existing trainees.

15. To arrange that there is a coordinator for the group of trainers.
16. To promote the programme where possible with GPs, voluntary agencies, families, the public and so on.
17. To assist and be supportive of other Trusts/Social Services Departments in the region who may be experiencing difficulties, and to be helpful where possible in sharing ideas and expertise in relation to the programme.
18. To help to recruit other trainers/supervisors onto the programme.
19. To take responsibility for one of the target areas outlined in the business plan, either alone or shared with another trainer.

VII

Relatives' Supporting Each Other

15

The COOL Approach

Claudia Benzies, Gwen Butcher and Tom Linton

Introduction

This chapter differs from most others in the book because it shows how one woman's vision and philanthropy made a significant impact on the well-being of mental health carers and service users in a rural area of Britain. It tells how her intervention brought about a support network for carers that is wholly independent of statutory services and yet retains its ability to work with them. The chapter describes how carers can, with help, do much to contribute towards their own recovery and thereby towards the recovery of those they care for. To illustrate what is being achieved the chapter uses a series of personal accounts.

The network was set up towards the end of the millennium when our benefactor, who prefers to remain anonymous, felt that she was being deprived of information about her son's diagnosis of schizophrenia. She decided to do something about it. Even though the medical professionals treating her son were sympathetic, she felt that they kept her in the dark about details of his illness. To her mind there seemed almost to be a conspiracy of silence. She realised that other carers were similarly troubled by lack of information and that this added to their anxiety at an extremely stressful time in their lives. In 1999, she set up an organisation that offered support to families affected by mental health issues. The organisation, Carers' one-to-one Link, or COOL for short, is now known as Cool Recovery to take account of its wider aims.

A Casebook of Family Interventions for Psychosis   Edited by Fiona Lobban and Christine Barrowclough
© 2009 John Wiley & Sons, Ltd

About COOL

COOL made a stuttering start but before long it achieved a strong following and eventually fledged into something much bigger than a mere information exchange. The anonymous mother's initiative is an example of family intervention making a difference – in this case a huge difference over a fairly wide geographical area where public transport is generally inadequate. This determined woman provided considerable funding so that a national mental health charity could set up a support network for families and friends affected by severe mental illness. She stipulated that the money should be spent locally rather than nationally. Initially, the main aim was to supply information useful to carers and to help them to communicate easily with the statutory services and other sources of support. In 1999, there were no other local services for carers, let alone carer-led ones. After 5 years, COOL left the security of the much larger national charity and became an independent charitable organisation in its own right providing a range of services for carers and their families in south United Kingdom.

In the recent past, if carers wanted to gain access to supportive services it was a hit-and-miss affair. That was probably because the main avenue for information was through the hospitals. But hospital psychiatry is an extremely demanding occupation that seldom permits its practitioners time to minister to the needs of the carer as well as of the patient. Carers usually had to struggle alone enveloped by an overwhelming bubble of guilt, misery and helplessness. There were organisations that they could turn to, but they had to know about them in the first place. Lack of knowledge was common among carers. COOL's approach was to track down carers and to offer them support. A former psychiatric nurse was appointed as coordinator to set the ball rolling. Initially, identifying carers was like trying to find a needle in a haystack, but lots of detective work eventually brought results. She found that there were hundreds of desolate carers unaware that there could be some resolution of their distress. For the first 3 months, COOL's representative felt that she was not earning her corn; then, all of her efforts to meet and talk to people had a cumulative effect. Carers responded in droves.

At a COOL seminar in 2000, the first of a series called 'Beating the Boundaries', 45 relatives and friends met and were astonished to find so many others sharing the experience of caring for someone with a severe mental health problem. At subsequent seminars, the numbers attending increased and on one occasion exceeded a hundred. Members of the caring professions and local authority providers of services were invited to attend, and many did so. It was immediately obvious that both sides had a lot to say to each other and that barriers were being dismantled at a satisfying rate, something that had not been expected to happen so quickly or easily. As a result, several carers received a sympathetic ear from professionals and, better still, some of their problems were given due attention. The seminars were held quarterly but, as with many successful ideas, they gradually outlived their usefulness as the state began to provide more information. The meetings were the visible face of COOL but few realised that a huge amount of unsung activity was taking place in the background to help carers and their dependants (of which more later). It was felt that COOL needed to evolve by meeting fresh challenges rather than by duplicating much of what was at last being provided by statute. In 2005, it decided to relinquish its ties with the national charity and it became instead an independent organisation with charitable status. And that is how Cool Recovery came into being. Even before the change of name, relatives and friends, strengthened by the knowledge that they were no longer alone, came together under COOL's auspices to advance the notion that 'recovery is possible for everyone'.

COOL's members believed, and still do, that when services become involved in a case they ought to listen and respond to the concerns of relatives and friends and include them in planning and treatment. That had not always happened. Families and friends usually know the patient best, having lived, loved, worked and had fun with them, maybe for their entire lives. COOL believes that these often forgotten carers, many of them worn down and in poor health themselves, must be helped to consider their own needs which, after all, are often close to their dependants' needs. They also expect transparency from the services.

To press home its message, COOL sometimes arranges to visit and talk to services or agencies that they believe need to raise awareness of carers' needs and mental health issues. The intention is to provide information and to improve communication. This work includes visiting general medical practices by arrangement, community mental health teams and inpatient staff to show how carers can help them to provide an improved and more enlightened service. COOL has been invited to talk to student nurses and social workers, care home staff, pharmacists, Women's Institutes, carers groups and other organisations concerned with mental health and carers' issues. It has reached the stage where COOL is invited to sit on panels recruiting staff for mental health services and also to participate in staff induction and nurse and social worker training.

COOL has also spoken by invitation at a number of conferences throughout Britain and uses television, radio and the press to promote the message of recovery and to raise awareness while at the same time aiming to reduce the fear and ignorance surrounding mental health issues.

Recovery – More Than a Notion

The notion that recovery was possible had for some time played a central role in the thinking of some carers and, increasingly, service users. They began to meet to seek ways of achieving this. The meetings were structured. In all, there were 18 Beating the Boundaries seminars. They had various themes covering such subjects as carers, primary care, nutrition (Eating the Boundaries), spirituality, recovery, advocacy, home sweet home, psychiatry, law as applied to mental health, housing and mental health workers. The half-day seminars took place at a country pub. The interaction between those attending was so vigorous that usually the 'networking' continued over lunch and well into the afternoon. Questionnaires were handed out asking people what they found useful, what they wanted to know, who they would like to hear speak, what services they needed information about, and so on. As a consequence, open workshops, discussion groups and training sessions were organised. Topics included anger management, solution-focused approach, mental health awareness, spirituality, optimum nutrition, the Mental Health Bill, presentation skills and interview techniques. These sessions were often led by relatives and people with mental health problems who had the expertise and personality to reach their audiences.

COOL's *raison d'être* was simple: to help carers to cope. No special equipment or training was needed – just the friendship and kindness of people, and a lot of effort on the part of coordinator and founder members. It helped that key people within the organisation had professional qualifications. Even so, this unstructured system worked. COOL had a one-to-one telephone link for those who needed to talk, and one-to-one contacts with the coordinator to discuss more serious problems. It organised regular carers' support groups in different localities, Sunday breakfast and lunch gatherings, walks, 'musicool' and poetry evenings, creative writing and laughter workshops, befriending, dog-and-cat-sitting, picnics and barbecues, car boot sales, cream teas, a patchwork group and an art group. It also had publicity stands outside supermarkets, at county shows, health fairs and rural health centres.

COOL Puts Down Roots

In 2005, after much research among carers and service users – mainly through meetings, questionnaires and *ad hoc* conversations – COOL's bene-factor purchased a former guest house in a local town centre. It was to be used as a base for carers and their dependants. A development manager was appointed to work with the organisation's coordinator, who had been responsible for its development and growth from the beginning, and COOL became an independent charity known as Cool Recovery Ltd. The wistful dream of a number of relatives, friends and people with mental health concerns was fully realised on 1 November, 2005 with the opening in the partly refurbished building of the Cool House. It is now a warm and wel-coming house that is comfortable and pleasantly decorated. It is open to all (no referral is sought). Cool House is a place of relaxation, recuperation and recovery, with an attractive café serving nutritious, home-made food. Cool volunteers, including cooks, cleaners, complementary therapists, counsel-lors, builders, decorators, craftsmen, a poet and others, see to the daily running and offer regular workshops and activities. In effect, the users of Cool House determine what happens there.

Is It Working and Has It Been Worth It?

Having spent what to most people is a considerable sum to fund COOL and later Cool Recovery, the benefactor must have asked herself if it had been worth it. The answer lies in the fact that she has offered the Cool House building to the charity at a peppercorn rent of a penny a year for 10 years. In the meantime – a period of 7 years at the time of writing – she has funded the salary of the coordinator, paid for the quarterly Beating the Boundaries seminars for nearly 5 years, funded an office with telephones and defrayed the costs of extensive travelling. She has also set up the Cool House, guaranteed its existence for a year until alternative funding can be found and paid the salaries of its manager and the coordinator for a year.

Has it all been plain sailing? Few things run smoothly all of the time, but the enthusiasm shown by the manager, the coordinator and a host of very eager volunteers has kept the ship watertight and in good trim. Within a year, funding amounting to £250 000 was found, including a substantial grant from the National Lottey. Fund-raising has an essential role in Cool Recovery's activities (for brevity, we shall from now on refer to Cool Recovery as Cool).

To guard its independence, Cool has a board of trustees with wide experience of mental health issues and also of running businesses and organisations. It is entirely voluntary and, as far as we know, unique. What began as a carer-led intervention, commissioned and funded by a carer, has succeeded well beyond everyone's expectations (including the parent charity and local mental health services) in helping carers and their families. It worked because the funder gave Cool the freedom to let the money be used as carers wanted. It was not based on any model or preconception. Furthermore, there was a lack of formality. It is sobering to realise that COOL had existed for 6 years without a committee. It would seem that to emulate Cool one would need to find a rich benefactor who is content to keep a low profile, to guide rather than to impose and to allow 'grass roots' needs and endeavours to shape the course of events. Without such a person Cool would never have existed and could not have survived.

The following case histories show how Cool's members have intervened, often against the odds, to make a difference. To preserve their anonymity they are identified by pseudonyms.

Alice's story

Alice was unhappy about the treatment her daughter was receiving under the National Health Service and so she took on the local health authority in an unrelenting three-year struggle that was eventually resolved in her favour. This case shows how, with persistence, carers can make a real difference to the way mental health services are developed.

In the spring of 2005, a scheme was initiated in the South West of England to recognise the dedicated work and steadfast efforts of a number of carers who aimed to bring about beneficial changes in a variety of care fields. Alice

Woods, one of those carers, received the first award it gave to a mental health carer.

For 4 years, Alice's daughter had suffered from increasingly frequent psychotic episodes. She spent several spells in hospital but, over time, her response to prescribed medication diminished and ultimately became ineffective. When another drug was tried the side effects were severe, extensive and near fatal. The physical nature of these side effects required the immediate attention of a physician and a dermatologist but there was no provision for such emergency interventions in the psychiatric unit. As a result, Alice's daughter was taken, belatedly, to the accident and emergency department to pass through the triage system required for admission to a medical ward. When, 4 days after the appearance of the first symptoms, she was finally examined by a consultant dermatologist it was determined that she needed specialist care in a burns unit. In spite of her emergency status, a 10-hour wait ensued while the technicalities of moving a 'sectioned' mental health patient were sorted out. The transfer was finally achieved by ambulance to the regional general hospital nearly 40 miles away.

This unhappy series of events which came close to a tragic conclusion led Alice to an unwavering determination that this should never happen to anyone again. She argued persistently and cogently with hospital and trust directors over a 3-year period until there was a closer meeting of minds. As a result of her work, there is now a policy in place that allows for mental health patients detained under the Mental Health Act to be transferred as needed without delay to appropriate medical services. Furthermore, a protocol has been established whereby medical staff and specialists are required to visit patients in the psychiatric unit as needed, thereby removing the necessity for triage in medical emergencies.

Alice's interventions have encouraged and empowered other carers to bring about important changes.

Helen's story

Helen turned the distress caused by her daughter's severe illness into positive action that helped to mitigate her negative thoughts and benefited many others in the process.

I was devastated by my daughter's illness – by not recognising at first that it was an illness and later by being shut out of her life by the intrusion of 'confidentiality' issues imposed by mental health service professionals. My caring, which had nurtured her for 30 years, counted for nothing. Her own paranoid assessment of her illness and my part in causing it became the accepted view of how things were. For me, 'devastated' meant a constant state of worried anxiety. Day and night there was extreme unease and sometimes conflict when she was in the house, and even greater distress when I did not know she had gone or where she was.

We both suffered for several years, she bravely denying her illness, before the 'voices', the withdrawal, the delusions and chaotic lifestyle finally led to a compulsory spell in hospital. The first of several as it turned out, but of course I did not know that at the time – I was relieved that professional care was now in place and this precious eldest child would be restored to health and her former rich and creative life. Disillusionment quickly followed. I found staff willing to talk with me only on a mundane level of platitudes, barely acknowledging my existence and never coming even close to any explanation as to what was happening or what we might expect. Exclusion and disempowerment prevailed and almost overnight a 'glass wall' separated me from this beloved daughter. Grief, disbelief and outrage were added to anxiety and distress. We were only three in the family and we two who were not ill focused all our energies and intelligence towards helping our loved one, but it was a lonely path to follow. In the mid-1990s, support for mental health carers was not adequate to the task – our need was neither understood nor addressed. It was no one's job to include the carer.

My own recovery began when I made the conscious decision that we should not all be unwell that I must make an effort and take steps to discover sense and order and reason for myself and my family.

One fact was very much to my advantage, I did not need to breach the barrier of the hospital itself since, as the mother of a patient, I was already on the inside! Through a small carers' group I became familiar with various specialists – the mental health pharmacist, the head of nursing, the mental health legal adviser and others. I joined a committee which was redesigning the psychiatric unit and another which was reviewing services. In due course I was able to use all these contacts as informants and I talked to as many carers as possible wherever they could be found. I became familiar with jargon and acronyms, the most common 'sections', medication categories and side effects, the staffing hierarchy, hospital protocols and practices, benefits and carers' rights. Armed with such basics, I could cast a wider net and compiled a dedicated directory and booklist, until a reliable body of facts was ready to be assembled into an information pack for carers.

Just as I had finished writing it, the Carers One-to-One Link (COOL) was established in September 1999 and, at about the same time, the UK government's National Service Framework (NSF) for Mental Health was published. I was sustained by the former and vindicated by the latter. I sought no payment for my work but it was recognised as a ready-made tool which conformed to the NSF Standard 6 Guidelines for Carers Services and, so, the local Social Services funded publication of 3000 copies. We launched the Carers Information pack on World Mental Health Day, 10 October, 2000. It has since been updated annually, revamped for two other administrative areas, served as a prototype for an 'over 65s' version and can now be downloaded from the National Institute for Mental Health England (NIMHE) web site.

This has proved to be an intervention that has eased the way for many carers, informed many families and now has many imitators. For me, producing the carers' pack was a catharsis of sorts.

Henry's story

Henry's parents fought to keep their semi-vagrant son within the system of health care and were rewarded after many years by seeing him return to a more regular and much happier existence.

Henry was a bright, outgoing young man studying for an honours degree in applied physics when his mental condition deteriorated. He was extremely fit and used to run half-marathons, take part in orienteering events, play golf to a decent standard, parachute at weekends and practise karate. His parents first noticed that something was wrong with his behaviour during regular telephone conversations to keep in touch with him while he was at university 200 miles away. They became so alarmed that they decided to visit him. His disorientated condition convinced them that he should come home immediately to see his GP (general practitioner). The GP suggested that he was suffering from schizophrenia, but it later turned out that he was suffering from bipolar disorder (manic depression).

His condition worsened and he was eventually admitted under section to a mental hospital. He was put on chlorpromazine and lithium carbonate but the chlorpromazine inhibited him to such a marked extent that he frequently stopped taking the medication. This usually resulted in him becoming intensely 'high' before reverting to his previous depressed state.

When high, he believed that he had incredible powers to do anything he set his mind to. From time to time, he ran up serious debts. He sometimes came to the notice of the police and on one occasion, when he was thought to be suicidal, a search with dogs and a helicopter was made for him. He would often disappear from home and began to lead a vagrant's life. As a result, he was no longer within the 'system' and receiving care.

He was admitted to hospital on three other occasions, once under section. During a period of 5 weeks, he telephoned his parents three times from different parts of Britain with requests to collect him because he was tired and hungry and had not eaten for several days. Once, he had to be picked up from a city more than 300 miles away, after he had telephoned home at 2.30 a.m. Police at a nearby port had intercepted him after he tried to board a ferry with an out-of-date passport. All of these events over many years and his apparent suicidal behaviour put enormous strain on his parents who stuck by him through thick and thin. Perhaps as a result, his mother, now in her mid-70s, is in poor health. For several years, his father felt overwhelmed by the constant worry.

About 6 years ago, things changed for the better. Henry was put on Risperidone and was admitted to a house run by a charity for people with mental health problems. This was achieved through the intervention of a perceptive social worker who fought resolutely on his behalf for settled accommodation away from the family home. The combination of the newer medication and a more settled regime brought about a huge change in his condition. He is now on Olanzapine and has moved into another housing unit run by the same charity where he has freedom to live a more regular life, even though he is unemployed. There is little doubt that, without the steadfast efforts of his parents over 20 years to keep tabs on him while he was frequently out of the 'system' and to fight bureaucracy on occasions, the outcome for Henry could have been much different. As it is, he is fitting well into society and now has a regular girlfriend.

Mary's story

Mary realised that her son's illness was making her ill too. She determined to climb out of her depression and stay well by taking command of her life.

I believe that when mental illness strikes it embraces the whole family. Everyone within the family somehow manages to keep the pot boiling, even though they may be unaware that that is what they are doing. The carer is supposed to halt the illness, to make it get better or to get someone else to make it better, to clear up the inevitable messes, to take the blame, to believe that it is really their fault, to be the strong one and do things for the 'ill' person they could do for themselves, to be on a full-time rescue operation, even to cover it up.

In the midst of this chaos you lose sight of what is really going on – also of who you are. In my opinion, the only way to recover is to STOP. And this I have found out is not easy. Things have been so bad that I have needed the support of fellow recoverers, a belief and faith in God and trust in the resilience of the human spirit to recover. I truly believe recovery is an option.

Thus, recovery is the priority in my life. I believe that as I change and grow, the family patterns must also change. I cannot make my son recover, but I can get my own life on an even keel which, in the long run, should benefit him. I went through a grieving process that took more than 2 years before I could accept the reality of what had happened. I could not believe it at first. I was so shocked and devastated. Then I became angry about everything. Eventually, I started to bargain. I thought that if I did family therapy maybe he would get better. So I did, and it was incredibly painful but ultimately healing. I did one-to-one therapy and I still go to Al-Anon's 12 Step meetings twice a week. At first I did it for him; now I do it for me.

I made a wellness recovery action plan (WRAP), a positive response to mental illness which is rapidly gaining credence. It helped me through frequent bouts of depression and despair. I kept it simple – ate three meals a day, got some fresh air, did some exercise, called a friend, and went to bed early. I also kept a journal and cried and cried and cried. One step at a time, I forced myself to do things just for me – things I liked to do instead of having to do. I am learning to care about myself as well as for other people, learning to set boundaries and not to tolerate so much abuse. This is my recovery from co-dependence. I am learning about healthy nutrition, how to listen to my body and to give it what it needs, whether it be exercise, rest, massage, relaxation, fun. It is hard to change a pattern of a lifetime (putting everyone else first) and it takes time, commitment and patience. I am willing to do whatever it takes. It has become my spiritual journey. Most days I accept the situation. I care about my son, but not for him. I trust him to find his own path. It may sound uncaring, but I am letting him take responsibility for his behaviour and trying not to react – trying to mind my own business in other words. I believe he will find recovery when he is ready – maybe he already has. And, in the meantime, I get on with my own recovery. It is no good both of us being unwell.

Al-Anon
Wellness Recovery Action Planning (WRAP) Mary-Ellen Copeland
http://www.mentalhealthrecovery.com/

Hugh's story

> Hugh initially found it hard to adjust to his adult son being ill. But, with time and the tolerance it often engenders, he turned the situation into a positive experience so that he grew much closer to the son who had disturbed the contented life he and his wife enjoyed.

I think that all my initial, instinctive reactions to learning that my son was mentally ill were unhelpful. I was concerned about what this would do to us, his parents. He was in his early 30s. We were in our 60s. I was retired. We were having a good life. He had been working abroad. We were not used to having someone else living with us. If his illness had been cancer, I would not have thought first about how that might affect my life, yet that was how I reacted to being told that he was suffering from schizophrenia.

I worried about what might happen. I was afraid. That was an entirely rational response to the situation of living with an angry, unpredictable person who said that he hated me and believed me to be in league with his enemies. I wanted to help. In any difficult situation I need to do something. I am not easily passive and so I tried to help by making suggestions, trying to persuade him to do things that would make him better. I can see now how wrong I was and how near we all came to disaster.

I think it must be very difficult for anyone who is alone in this situation. My wife and I could talk. My wife would notice things that I did not see. It does help to talk but talking to neighbours, friends and relations about this situation is not easy and probably not wise. So we keep it to ourselves and the benefit of being able to talk together about it is immense. I do not think either of us could have got through alone and probably not if there had been strains in our relationship or in our circumstances, but we did get through. We were lucky in all sorts of ways but, most importantly, we came to recognise eventually how unhelpful all of those instant, initial responses had been and we deliberately changed course and, from that moment, things began to get better.

He was a sufferer, not us. We use our brains to solve problems and make choices. It must be dreadful to have a fault there because then nothing can be trusted. It must be very frightening. In that situation, the last thing you want is pressure from someone who is arguing with you, criticising you, telling you to do this or that. What you need is space. Instead of taking decision making away from the sufferer he should be allowed to decide for himself because that means using the brain and accepting consequences.

It is difficult to live with someone who has mental illness and to be relaxed, but that is what the illness requires. If people are pumping out more anxiety and fear into the atmosphere, the sufferer will get worse. It was a great help to me that I have no fear of death. It will come and when it comes I shall be finished and nothing more will concern me. My death will affect other people, including of course my son, but it will be nothing to me so that is not an issue for me. I can therefore take the view that what will be will be. I cannot change things. I think that accepting the situation is helpful to the sufferer because he has to accept it too. As I got to this point, I realised that the less we talked with him about his illness the better it would be for all of us. What the sufferer needs is normality and normality is simply what we accept as normal.

When things got very bad indeed, we realised that we were going through with this whatever the outcome. That colours everything. It is the other side of the decision to let things happen. We are not trying to control events but also we are not going to quit. Parentage does not have a get-out clause. We made it clear that he can live with us for as long as he likes and go away whenever he wants. What he does when he is living with us is up to him. We do not talk about his illness or about what might happen in the future. We cannot know and it is so important not to create anxieties.

There was a moment when we realised what we had to do. We found ourselves doing it, doing what he wanted us to do and leaving him alone when he wanted to be alone, putting no pressure on him but leaving him in no doubt that we were here for the duration.

It does not help me to think of myself as a carer. He has to care for himself. All that I am is a father. He is not on one side of a line that means he has to be cared for while others are on the other side of that line and can therefore care for themselves. I do not feel that there is a clear line between mental illness and mental health. I think that we all have to cope as best we can with what we have got.

I know that people do not get better but I think it is best to believe that people get better. It is not necessary to say that, but what we believe appears in the way we act and I think it has been really important for me and my son that I have believed that he will get better. In fact, he has been getting better from the moment that we began to behave appropriately. We all live together now very reasonably. He is helpful and considerate. He has a job at fractionally above the minimum wage. He works 9 hours a day taking breaks if and when there is an opportunity. He has a full social life. If anyone came to live with us, I doubt if they would detect anything abnormal about our household unless it was that we are all rather surprisingly considerate and careful. Conversation tends to be superficial. We do not talk about it but we know where we have been and we hope that we are not going back there. But, if we do, we will all know that we will come through again.

I think that the loneliness of mental illness must be very hard to bear. Living with people who are not worrying about themselves, not pressurising but just getting on with their own lives in an ordinary friendly way because they know that it will all get better must be what the sufferer needs in order to feel that he is not alone.

It is easy to think that mental illness is all in the mind but it is also physical; and something that has obviously been very important in our case has been food. Regular, well-cooked meals, home-grown vegetable and fruit and very little in the way of processed food has been a factor. The current incidence of mental illness may be connected with chemicals in food. And, of course, it is good to eat together. We have eaten meals in almost total silence but without embarrassment. But now we talk and, of course, there is a lot of conversation around food and he always makes the coffee and usually washes up.

When I learnt that my son was suffering from schizophrenia, I could not imagine that anything good could come out of it and I feared what it would do to us. But now I feel that is it one of the better things that I have done. I would not wish it on anyone but we do spend quite a lot of our lives not doing very much, and doing something that is difficult, even dangerous, but which really helps another person and knowing the difference it has made, has turned this experience into something that I now feel good about. I only wish that in the darkest time I had known that to be possible.

Conclusion

Many of these case histories show how people living with illness, either directly or vicariously, can take charge of their lives through acting positively and trying to alleviate their circumstances. It is not always easy; it seldom is. Usually it takes time for people to learn from experience, especially when they are ill and not prepared to accept circumstances as they are. Families sometimes help, sometimes they hinder. But when a family really pulls out all the stops it makes an immense difference. Therefore, it is vital that families are supported rather than excluded by mental health services. The story of Alice's intervention, which she insisted should be told modestly rather than at length in its harrowing detail, is a fine example of this happening. She changed official thinking and attitudes. What is more, she is now in a position to police those changes.

What it also shows is that people who seek to recover their lives can very often succeed in doing so to a greater extent than they initially thought possible. There are many examples of this among Cool's members. The attitude at Cool is that recovery is possible. When like-minded people meet and act positively the effects are often contagious. And, although Cool is careful not to make extravagant claims of success, there is little doubt that, if you believe you can improve, improvement follows. Whether or not it is sustained, only time will tell. Our belief is that it can be.

Resources

Cool Recovery Ltd
The Cool House
17 Morgan Avenue
Torquay
TQ2 5RP
01803 299511
info@coolrecovery.org.uk (accessed 5 January 2009).
Authors: Claudia Benzies, Gwen Butcher and Tom Linton, c/o the above address.
Publications:
Recovery for Carers (pamphlet)
Cool News (monthly newsletter)
National Service Framework for Mental Health: http://www.dh.gov.uk/assetRoot/
04/01/26/60/04012660.pdf (accessed 5 January 2009).

Rethink: http://www.rethink.org (accessed 5 January 2009).

National Institute for Mental Health in England: http://nimhe.csip.org.uk (accessed 5 January 2009).

http://www.mind.org.uk/Information/Factsheets/Carers/ (accessed 5 January 2009).

Wellness Recovery Action Planning (WRAP) Mary-Ellen Copeland: http://www.mentalhealthrecovery.com (accessed 5 January 2009).

Al-Anon: http://www.al-anonuk.org.uk/ (accessed 5 January 2009).

COMPASS Pack (Carers' Own Mental Health Pathways and Stepping Stones). This is a carers' guide to local mental health services and resources with a comprehensive glossary written in plain English by a carer.

VIII

Conclusion

16

Summary and Conclusions – Where Are We up to and Where Are We Going?

Fiona Lobban and Christine Barrowclough

The Importance of Working with Families

There are strong and compelling reasons why mental health services should offer high quality interventions to families of people with psychosis. Firstly, families are of central importance to recovery from psychosis. Many people will return to live with family following their first episode of psychosis and relatives often acquire increased importance since wider social networks can diminish as a consequence of mental health problems. Therefore, families play a key role in providing the environment in which the process of recovery can take place. Research shows that the emotional climate in which people live is a good predictor of whether or not they will go on to experience further episodes of psychosis (Butzlaff and Hooley, 1998). Understandably, the impact of psychosis on family members can be severe in both emotional and practical terms, and there can be high levels of depression and anxiety associated with the experience of psychosis in other family members (e.g. Scazufca and Kuipers, 1996). Secondly, we know that clinical interventions with families can be effective in improving outcome for the person with psychosis (Pfammatter, Junghan and Brenner, 2006; Pharoah *et al.*, 2006; Pilling *et al.*, 2002). Although the exact mechanism for this is unclear, families are well placed to provide social and practical support in low-stress environments and to learn to pick up early warning signs of relapse so that future relapses can be prevented. Thirdly, because of the evidence for the effectiveness of family interventions, many clinical guidelines explicitly state that family interventions should be offered to all families where there are

A Casebook of Family Interventions for Psychosis   Edited by Fiona Lobban and Christine Barrowclough
© 2009 John Wiley & Sons, Ltd

persistent difficulties or risk of relapse (Newcastle Early Psychosis declaration, 2002; National Service Framework, Department of Health, UK, 1999; NICE Guidelines, 2003). Finally, assisting families can be very rewarding for clinicians who work in mental health services. Family members can be extremely valuable partners in caring for someone experiencing psychosis. They often bring a wealth of expertise and experience and successfully combining this with the clinical expertise of the mental health practitioner is likely to provide the most effective interventions to minimise the negative impact of psychosis and maximise opportunities for recovery.

What Is Currently Being Offered to Families?

The cases described in these chapters give a rich insight into the wide range of interventions offered to support families in which someone has experienced psychosis. Strong common themes emerge around the presenting needs of families: their search for understanding about psychosis; the need to tell their story and feel listened to; the importance of receiving accurate and timely information. At the same time, the chapters reflect important differences in the needs of families at various stages in their journey of recovery and also differences in how family interventions are delivered. These differences include a variety of theoretical models used by clinicians as well as variation in format and duration of interventions and in the service settings in which these interventions are offered. What conclusions can we draw from these accounts that will help guide clinicians in supporting families they work with?

Firstly, many of the authors in this book have identified the importance of understanding the wider system in which family work is offered. In some instances, family intervention services are a key part of a fully integrated service such as the Calgary Early Psychosis Programme (Chapter 3) and the EPPIC service in Melbourne (Chapter 4). This has the advantage that families are offered some level of support as a matter of course. A range of options is often open to them to suit their particular needs. Family work is seen as the norm and therefore does not increase anxiety in family members or make them feel they are being targeted as the cause of any problems. In addition, the ethos of family work is inherent throughout the system and communication is likely to be less problematic. Such organisations may be the ideal, but it is rarely the norm for many clinicians working in local services. Attracting funding for training, supervision or the additional time needed to spend with families can be difficult. Genuine support for family work at all levels of the organisation is needed for long-term maintenance of high-quality services. Burbach and Stanbridge (Chapter 13) and Fadden (Chapter 14) describe how they succeeded in gaining this support. Their methods might be used by others to achieve the necessary conditions for progress if they are able to harness sufficient motivation within other organisations. A critical mass of people to form a steering committee consisting of people with a vested interest and the power to make it happen would seem a good place to start.

Assuming there is a genuine commitment from the service to work with families – What is the best way to structure the service? The meta-analytic review of controlled trials of family intervention for schizophrenia of Pilling et al. (2002) indicates that there has been a diminishing effect over time in terms of service user gains. It has been suggested that the enthusiasm and charisma of early proponents of family intervention was not maintained in later studies (Mari and Streiner, 1994) and Pilling et al. (2002) suggest this points to a requirement for 'robust implementation of these interventions, if they are to be used'. They also draw attention to the many unknown factors regarding optimum formats and components of interventions. For example, the research indicates group interventions do not seem to produce such favourable service user outcomes, but Pilling et al. suggest that group work may have benefits for relatives that were not measured in the studies including reducing isolation and perceived stigma. This would certainly fit our personal experiences and those of contributors who describe group interventions in this book. Other unanswered questions from research to date include the following: Is it important to include service users in the intervention? What is the optimum duration and frequency? What people and families benefit most? More research is needed that addresses all of these issues and also focuses on translational studies which can test the effectiveness of interventions in real-world clinical services.

Given these many 'unknowns' it is hardly surprising that the cases presented in this book demonstrate how clinicians are employing a wide range of options including: single therapists working with single families; two therapists working with single families; multiple family groups; interventions in which the person with psychosis is present and those in which they are not; young siblings present or not and a variety of lengths from short interventions of less than 10 sessions, to interventions lasting many months or even occurring over several years. In the absence of clear guidance from the literature the variation is likely to be influenced by the theoretical model on which the intervention is based; the training background of the clinicians involved; the specific aims for each family and the availability of resources within the service. Some of the cases described were identified as being part of a research trial which may attract additional resources; dedicated and highly motivated therapists and more substantial interventions. Further, important gaps in our knowledge highlighted in these chapters include how best to support siblings (Chapter 9), how to work with challenging problems like substance abuse (Chapters 5 and 6) and how to empower relatives to share their expertise and support each other in partnership with mental health services (Chapter 15).

The focus of this book is on clinical case examples, rather than describing theoretical models. However, the authors have each briefly outlined the model or framework that informs the approach they have used and have provided references for those who wish to explore these in further detail. What is clear is that a wide range of therapeutic models are influencing family work including: behavioural family therapy; cognitive behaviour therapy; systemic family therapy; motivational interviewing and stages of change model; compassionate mind therapy; relapse prevention and early signs monitoring. This array of therapy models may at first seem daunting but many clinicians will already have familiarity with some of these models in the work they do with their individual clients. These skills can be built on to develop support to families, rather than clinicians having to adopt a whole new framework to work within. In addition, many common elements exist across all of the interventions. These are summarised in Table 16.1.

These common elements are essential to build a platform on which more complex interventions can be offered. Examples of additional interventions described in this book include the following: challenging unhelpful attributions that may be linked to high levels of distress or expressed emotion (Chapters 5, 6, 7 and 11); problem-solving skills training (Chapters 1, 2, 7, 9 and 12); communication training (Chapters 7, 9 and 12); motivational approaches (Chapters 5 and 6); grief work (Chapter 8); early warning signs recognition and relapse prevention (Chapter 3). The timing of these interventions may be very important. For example, family members currently experiencing complex emotional reactions including grief and loss responses may not be ready to recognise the importance of working to prevent relapse or looking at problem-solving approaches. Some families may require long periods of engagement work to allow them to become

Table 16.1 Common Elements of Family Interventions

Common elements	Aim and rationale
Offer support early	Relatives are likely to be highly motivated and good support early on can prevent the development of unhelpful beliefs and coping strategies
Clear rationale for family work	Family members often question whether they are to blame for psychosis. Offering to support the family may inadvertently reinforce this belief. An explicit statement is needed to state that there is no evidence to suggest families can cause psychosis but families can play an important role in helping the person to recover, and relatives often need support to help them deal with what can be a very challenging life event
Allowing family members to tell their story	Unless family members feel that they have been listened to and understood they are unlikely to develop the trust to work with clinicians on any other tasks. Without listening to the stories, clinicians will be unable to understand the challenges facing the family. The process of telling the story is important to help family members to understand what has happened. Many people value the opportunity to do this with an empathic listener since it is often difficult to do this with members of the wider family or with friends
Acknowledging and validating the impact of psychosis on the family	Experiencing a loved one suffering with psychosis can be devastating. Helping relatives to acknowledge this impact and recognise it as a common experience can be empowering
Providing information	Just providing information does not change beliefs. It is important that clinicians understand the model of psychosis that the relative holds and are able to provide information in targeted ways that can challenge inaccurate or unhelpful beliefs. This is likely to involve cognitive behavioural techniques including behavioural experiments
Identifying clear and realistic goals for family work	All families have problems. Many of these are not linked to psychosis and may not be suitable targets for the intervention. It is necessary to work with relatives to identify clear and realistic goals that build on their existing strengths

(*Continued*)

Table 16.1 (*Continued*)

Common elements	Aim and rationale
A pragmatic approach	All families are different. Services need to be flexible in how they offer support for the variety of presenting problems. This may include flexibility in structure, timing and content of family interventions
Supervision and service support	Working with families is demanding of clinicians' time, skills and emotional commitment. Support for clinicians at all levels of the service is crucial to long-term maintenance of a family service

sufficiently confident in the intentions and abilities of staff before they feel ready to commit themselves to more formal interventions.

These complexities of family work may sound rather daunting and, given the barriers that can occur at every stage, it is not hard to see why many families do not receive the support they need. For many clinicians, feeling insufficiently skilled and thus fearful of getting it wrong prevents them engaging with families. However, the common elements listed in the table above require basic skills that most clinicians do possess and use on an everyday basis with their individual clients. Some will also have additional training in the more structured approaches such as cognitive behavioural therapy or motivational interviewing. It is inevitable that in facing the challenge of using these skills in a new context of working with families, problems will arise. The chapters in this book show how all clinicians – no matter how well trained or experienced – encounter difficulties and attempt to overcome them. We hope these narratives will provide people with the confidence to persevere. Throughout the book, useful resources are listed to offer further guidance. Working with families requires embarking with them on their journey of recovery in which everyone will make mistakes as they learn new ways to understand and adapt to the impact that psychosis has on the family. This journey is beautifully described by Hugh's story in Chapter 15. The alternative is that families are excluded and disempowered. The more we can do to ensure that families of people experiencing psychosis can be offered effective interventions, the less likely it is that other family members will have to experience the 'grief, disbelief and outrage' that Helen's story describes as a result of poor clinical services (Chapter 15).

Future Directions in Working with Families

Research into family interventions in psychosis has a relatively short history. The first studies demonstrating that working with families could have major benefits for people with psychosis only appeared in the 1980s. These were hugely influential and shaped our thinking about psychosis: people began to look beyond medication alone to provide the conditions necessary for people to make successful recoveries. The chapters in this book are testament to how those early studies provided the impetus for service planners and clinicians across the world to take forward this work. However, despite the subsequent two or three decades of research and clinical effort around family environments of people with psychosis, all those active in these endeavours agree that there is still much to learn about how best to help relatives.

A continued legacy of family work in psychosis is that the emphasis has traditionally been placed on reducing stress in families in order to improve service user outcomes – family member outcomes such as reducing distress and burden were seen as important but were not the prime target. While many of the chapters attest to efforts of clinicians to try and alleviate relatives' distress, research findings are not very helpful in outlining how best to do this. Szmukler *et al.* (2003) identify three randomised controlled trials aimed specifically at improving relatives' well-being. These studies showed some gains in knowledge and attitudes, but not distress and burden (although the use of different measures makes comparisons between studies assessing relative outcomes problematic). A recent trial with a longer duration of intervention which did focus primarily on improving relative outcomes did not produce encouraging results (Szmukler *et al.*, 2003) and these authors conclude that there is still uncertainty about the most effective interventions for relatives of people with psychotic disorders.

It has long been thought that relatives' understanding of psychosis is an important aspect of family work, and hence the importance of including information giving or 'psychoeducation' in family sessions. A number of studies have now demonstrated that relatives' appraisals of mental health problems – how they perceive and understand different aspects of the psychosis – are important mediators of the relationship between the psychosis and relatives' responses. Most work in this area has focused on the kind of explanations or causal attributions that relatives make about problematic behaviours associated with schizophrenia (see Barrowclough and Hooley,

2003 for a review). Relatives who are more critical of service users tend to have attributions that are different from those who are less distressed by the behaviour of service users. More specifically, relatives who are critical consistently attribute more control to patients for their symptoms and problems than do relatives low in criticism, that is they are more likely to hold them responsible for their difficulties. In contrast, relatives who find it difficult not to sacrifice their own well-being in trying to get the service user well, tend to make sense of the psychosis in terms of factors outside the person's control and see the person as an unfortunate victim of a severe illness. It seems to be quite hard to get a balanced view that prevents both these extremes – ascribing some control to service users that will help promote their autonomy and independence, without getting frustrated and feeling that they could do more to help themselves.

Other work has focused on a wider range of relatives' cognitions about mental health problems as a means of understanding variability in how people respond to close relatives with psychosis. In the area of physical health, it is widely accepted that cognitive processes mediate people's adaptation to their own health problems, and the most notable theoretical framework adopted in this work is the self-regulation model of Leventhal and colleagues (Leventhal, Nerenz and Steele, 1984). It has been demonstrated that patients' illness representations or models of illness are based around distinct components – identity (what the problem is), cause (why it has happened), timeline (how long it will last for) and illness consequences (the likely impact), as well as controllability (what can be done to manage or cure it). These representations have been shown to carry emotional, behavioural and coping implications and are related to health outcomes. It has been suggested that illness representations may also have important implications for people's responses to individuals with mental health problems (Lobban, Barrowclough and Jones, 2003). Studies (Barrowclough *et al.*, 2001; Lobban, Barrowclough and Jones, 2006) have supported the utility of this model in the context of relatives of people with a schizophrenia diagnosis. It is clear that relatives do hold 'lay models' of schizophrenia and dimensions of these models are related to important family outcomes including distress and burden. Since we know that service users also have their own models of the psychosis (Lobban, Barrowclough and Jones, 2004) there is clearly the potential for discrepancies between the service user and their relatives in how they see important aspects of the mental health problems. Evidence suggests that such discrepancies may be associated with relationship difficulties (Lobban, Barrowclough and Jones, 2006).

The findings concerning the importance of different dimensions of relatives' and service users' beliefs have considerable potential clinical implications for helping families to accommodate to mental health problems. Research would suggest that approaches that simply communicate new knowledge and attempt to teach new interaction skills are unlikely to be successful if they ignore the underlying complex belief systems that exist within the family. Thus, interventions based on the simple provision of information to relatives of people with psychosis are unlikely to work since relatives already have their own models which will be used to actively process information provided leading to rejection and accommodation of incongruent facts. There is support for this contention in a recent review of family intervention studies which found that short education or counselling programmes do not affect relapse rates: 'a few lessons on schizophrenia . . . was simply not sufficient to substantially influence the relapse rate' (Pitschel-Waltz *et al.*, 2001, p. 84). Cognitive behavioural techniques as used in the treatment of emotional disorders are more likely to be effective in guiding discussion of evidence supporting beliefs and introduction of counter information using Socratic dialogue, and behavioural experiments designed to challenge old beliefs (see for example, Wells, 1997, for a description of techniques). However, bringing about meaningful change in the beliefs of families regarding psychosis is likely to be complex. Beliefs are functional, and people are reluctant to let go of longstanding ideas without confidence that new beliefs are going to be helpful in directing how they manage the family problems. Belief changes may be particularly difficult to accomplish in relationships characterised by longstanding difficulties or where there are high levels of distress, and family members will find it difficult to take on board new ideas. Efforts to bring about belief change need to be conducted in a slow and measured way and in a manner that is respectful of the relatives' perspectives. Clinicians need to be aware that their own models of psychosis and of family dynamics are likely to be strongly influenced by their own life history. Many clinicians reading this book are likely to be working within a system that proposes a Western biopsychosocial model of psychosis which highlights a stress–vulnerability diathesis based on that originally proposed by Zubin and Spring (1977). Information that is provided to relatives is generally consistent with this model. However, some of the users of family intervention services from different ethnic or cultural origins may understand psychosis within a very different framework and disagree with the underlying assumptions of this model (see Chapter 10). It is important that the time is taken to understand the families' own beliefs rather than trying to impose alternative frameworks. Finding common ground and acknowledging areas of disagreement in an open, respectful and non-judgemental way can be helpful in allowing families to accommodate the additional information they are being provided with in a way that makes sense and enables them to move forward.

Concluding Remarks – Learning from the Relatives

Much of the research effort around families and psychosis has focused on identifying factors that exacerbate psychosis and are associated with relapse. Whilst this research has provided a key impetus to developing family interventions, it may also have served to perpetuate the myth that families play a causative role in psychosis. Sadly, there has been very little research as regards what family members do well in facilitating the recovery of people with psychosis. Clearly, more knowledge about the positive aspects of family environments would greatly assist the development of valid and meaningful family interventions that are precisely focused on key protective factors for service users and build on the enormous strengths of families. A handful of studies in Europe (Bertrando, Beltz and Bressi, 1992; Ivanovic, Vuletic and Bebbington, 1994) and the United States (Lopez *et al.*, 2004) have indicated that where family members show positive emotions and warmth towards the person with psychosis, then relapse is less likely. Many of the chapters in this book give evidence of the tremendous strengths and resources of relatives and we hope that future researchers' efforts may be more focused on understanding the positive aspects of family environments.

References

Barrowclough, C., Lobban, F., Hatton, C. and Quinn, J. (2001) An investigation of models of illness in carers of schizophrenia patients using the Illness Perception Questionnaire. *British Journal of Clinical Psychology*, **40**, 371–85.

Barrowclough, C. and Hooley, J.M. (2003) Attributions and expressed emotion: a review. *Clinical Psychology Review*, **23**, 849–80.

Bertrando, P., Beltz, J., Bressi, C. *et al.* (1992) Expressed emotion and schizophrenia in Italy – a study of an urban-population. *British Journal of Psychiatry*, **161**, 223–9.

Butzlaff, R.L. and Hooley, J.M. (1998) Expressed emotion and psychiatric relapse – a meta-analysis. *Archives of General Psychiatry,* **55** (6), 547–52.

Ivanovic, M., Vuletic, Z. and Bebbington, P. (1994) Expressed emotion in the families of patients with schizophrenia and its influence on the course of illness. *Social Psychiatry and Psychiatric Epidemiology,* **29** (2), 61–5.

Leventhal, H., Nerenz, D.R. and Steele, D.F. (1984) Illness representations and coping with health threats, in *A Handbook of Psychology and Health* (eds A. Baum and J. Singer), Erlbaum, Hillsdale, NJ, pp. 219–52.

Lobban, F., Barrowclough, C. and Jones, S. (2003) A review of the role of illness models in severe mental health problems. *Clinical Psychology Review,* **23,** 171–96.

Lobban, F., Barrowclough, C. and Jones, S. (2004) The impact of beliefs about mental health problems and coping on outcome in schizophrenia. *Psychological Medicine,* **34,** 1165–76.

Lobban, F., Barrowclough, C. and Jones, S. (2006) Does expressed emotion need to be understood within a more systemic framework? An examination of discrepancies in appraisals between patients diagnosed with schizophrenia and their relatives. *Social Psychiatry and Psychiatric Epidemiology,* **41** (1), 50–5.

Lopez, S.R., Hipke, K.N., Polo, A.J. *et al.* (2004) Ethnicity, expressed emotion, attributions, and course of schizophrenia: family warmth matters. *Journal of Abnormal Psychology,* **113** (3), 428–39.

Mari, J.J. and Streiner, D.L. (1994) An overview of family interventions and relapse in schizophrenia: meta-analysis of research findings. *Psychological Medicine,* **24,** 565–78.

National Institute for Clinical Excellence (NICE) Guidelines for Schizophrenia (2003) *Schizophrenia: Core Interventions in the Treatment and Management of Schizophrenia in Primary and Secondary Care,* Clinical Guideline 1, National Institute for Clinical Excellence, London, http://www.nice.org.uk/nicemedia/pdf/CG1NICEguideline.pdf (accessed 11 November 2008).

National Service Framework, Department of Health (1999) *National Service Framework for Mental Health: Modern Standards and Service Models,* Department of Health, London, http://www.dh.gov.uk/en/Publicationsandstatistics/Publications/PublicationsPolicyAndGuidance/DH4009598 (accessed 11 November 2008).

Pfammatter, M., Junghan, U.M. and Brenner, H.D. (2006) Efficacy of psychological therapy in schizophrenia: conclusions from meta-analyses. *Schizophrenia Bulletin,* **32** (S1), S64–80.

Pharoah, F., Mari, J., Rathbone, J. and Wong, W. (2006) Family intervention for schizophrenia. *Cochrane Database of Systematic Reviews* (4). Art. No.: CD000088. DOI: 10.1002/14651858.CD000088.pub2.

Pilling, S., Bebbington, P., Kuipers, E. *et al.* (2002) Psychological treatments in schizophrenia: I. Meta-analysis of family intervention and cognitive behaviour therapy. *Psychological Medicine,* **32,** 763–82.

Pitschel-Waltz, G., Leucht, S., Bauml, J. *et al.* (2001) The effect of family interventions on relapse and rehospitalisation in schizophrenia – a meta-analysis.
Schizophrenia Bulletin, **27**, 73–92.

Scazufca, M. and Kuipers, E. (1996) Links between expressed emotion and burden
of care in relatives of patients with schizophrenia. *British Journal of Psychiatry*,
68, 580–7.

Szmukler, G., Kuipers, E., Joyce, J. *et al.* (2003) An exploratory randomised controlled trial of a support programme for carers of patients with a psychosis.
Soc Psychiatry Psychiatric Epidemiology, **38**, 411–8.

UK Newcastle Early Psychosis Declaration (2002) http://www.rethink.org/about_
mental_illness/early_intervention/support_for_family_and_carers/the_early.
html (accessed 11 November 2008).

Wells, A. (1997) *Cognitive Therapy of Anxiety Disorders – A Practice Manual and
Conceptual Guide.* John Wiley & Sons, Ltd, Chichester.

Zubin, J. and Spring, B. (1977) Vulnerability: a new view of schizophrenia. *Journal
of Abnormal Psychology*, **86**, 103–26.

Index

Note: Page numbers in *italics* denote figures and tables. The abbreviation FI is used for family intervention.

A Casebook of Family Interventions for Psychosis Edited by Fiona Lobban and Christine Barrowclough
© 2009 John Wiley & Sons, Ltd